Shojo Beat

ANONYMOUS NOISE

Ryoko Fukuyama

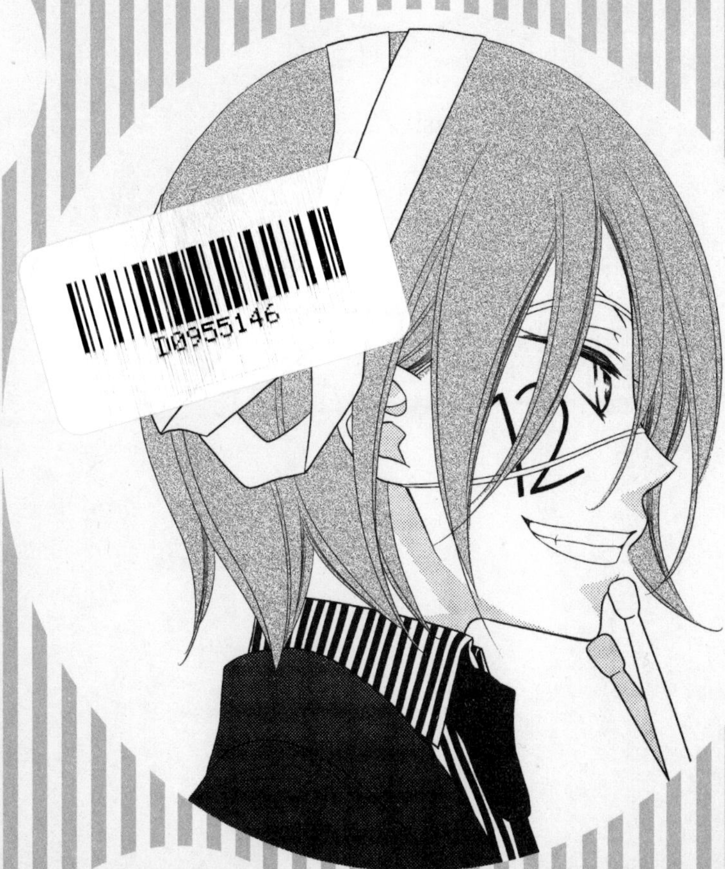

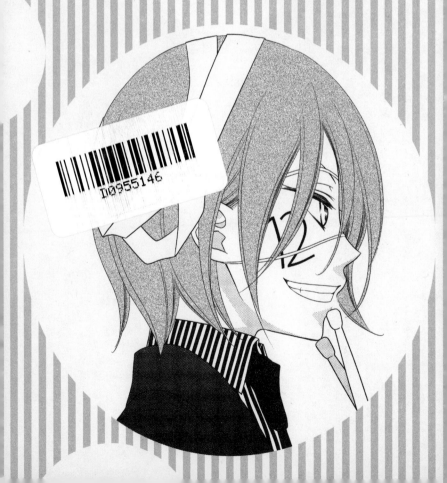

Anonymous Noise

Volume 12

CONTENTS

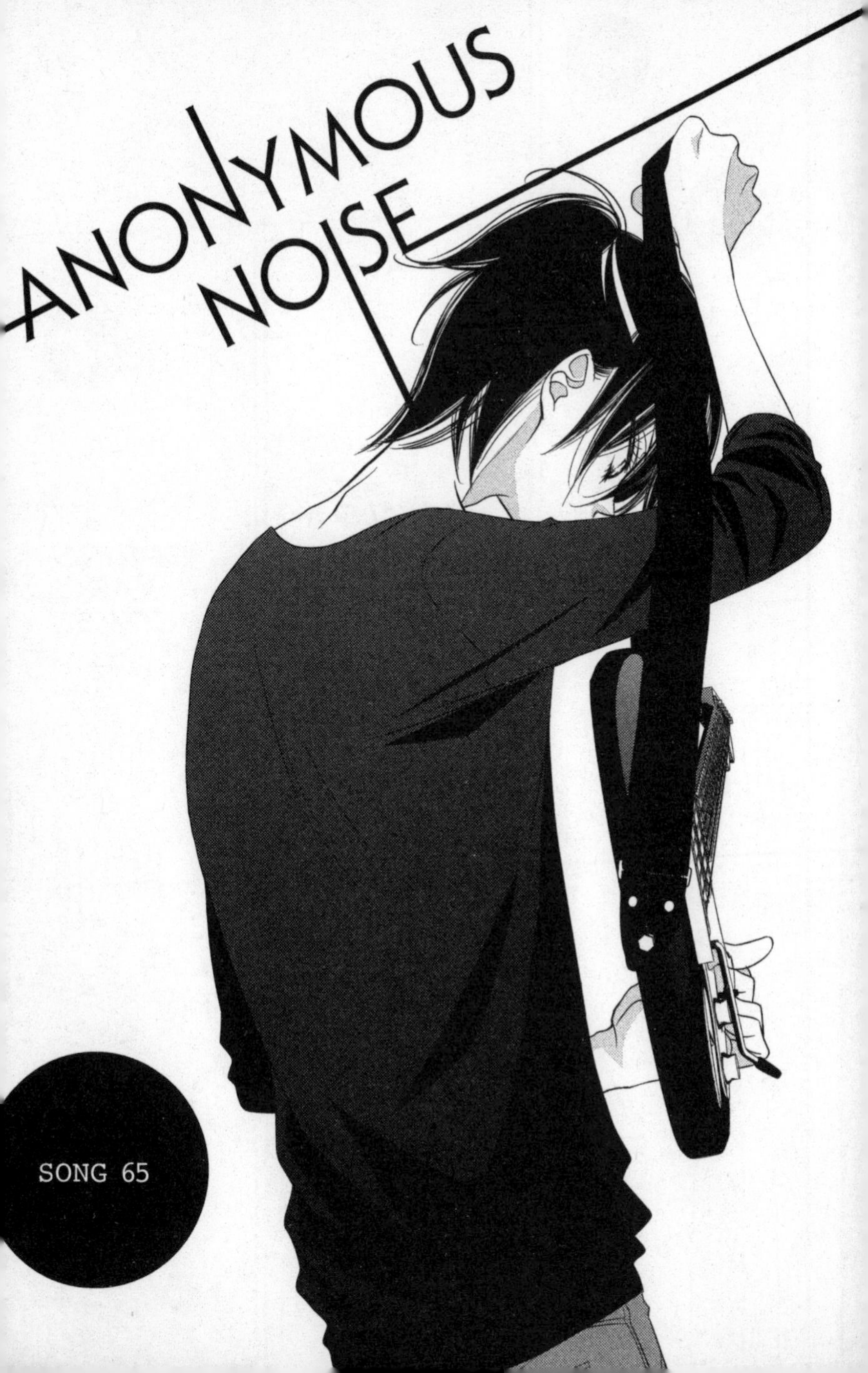
ANONYMOUS
NOISE
SONG 65

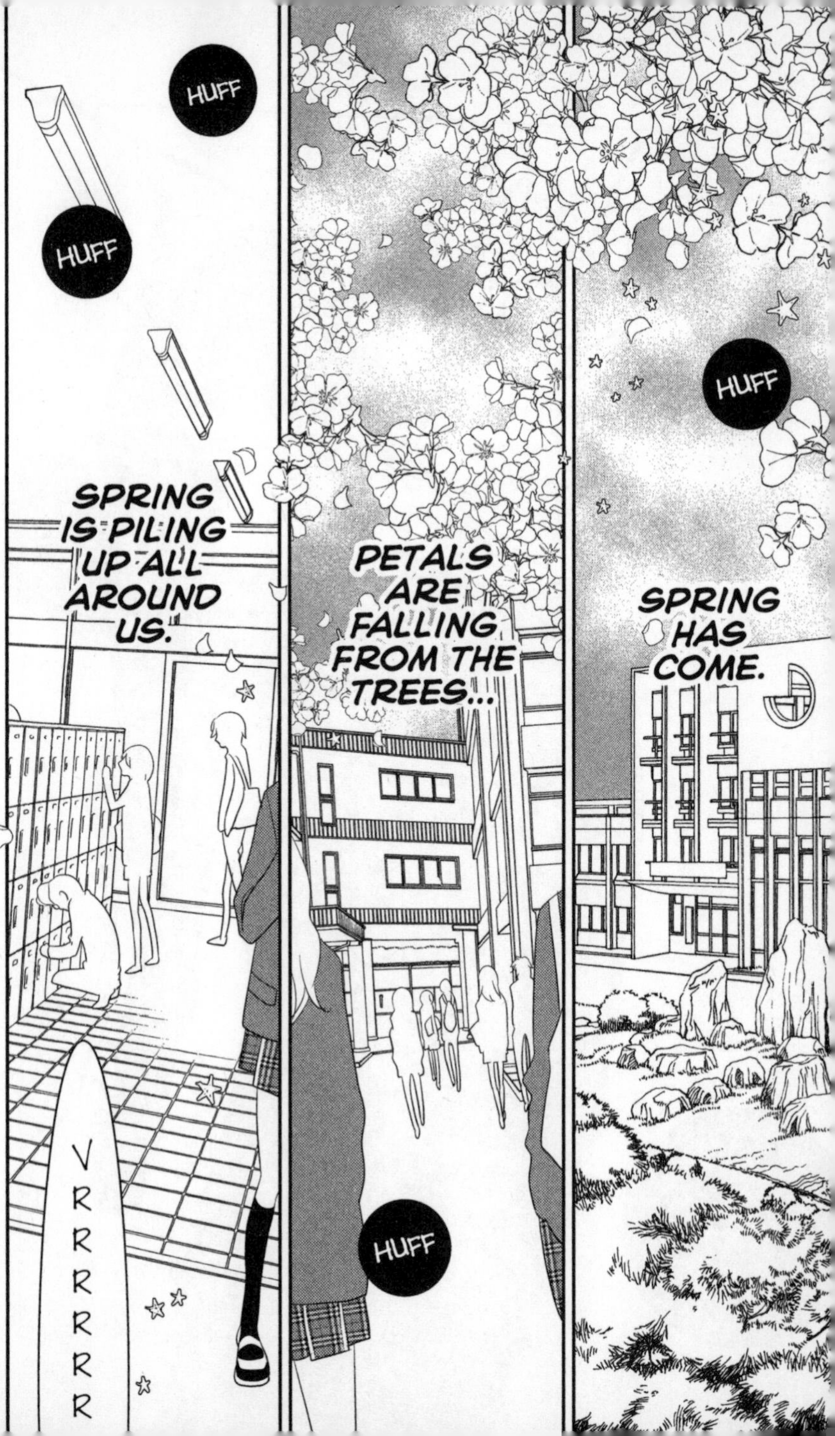
HUFF
SPRING HAS COME.
PETALS ARE FALLING FROM THE TREES...
HUFF
HUFF
HUFF
SPRING IS PILING UP ALL AROUND US.
VRRRRRR

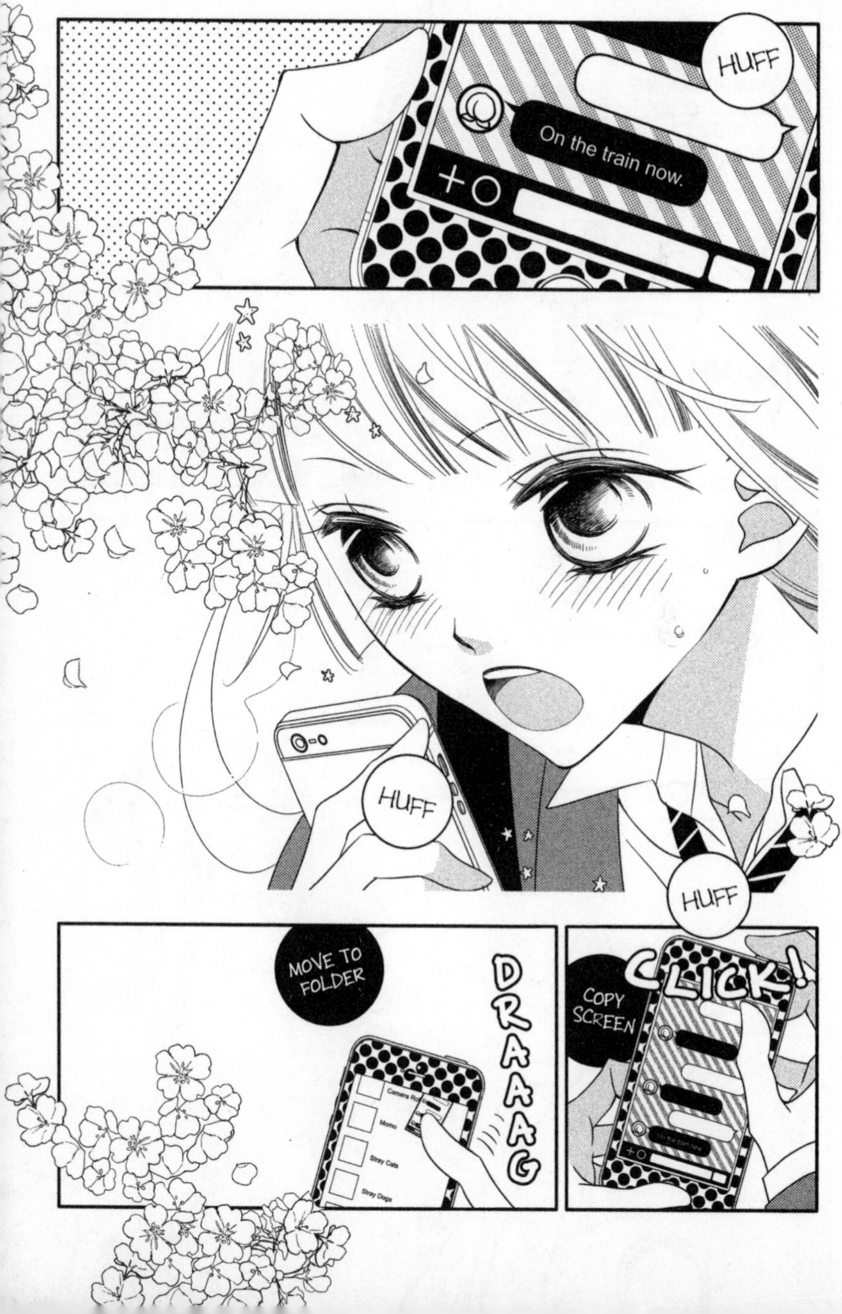
HUFF
On the train now.
HUFF
HUFF
CLICK!
COPY SCREEN
DRAAAG
MOVE TO FOLDER
Momo
Stray Cats
Stray Dogs

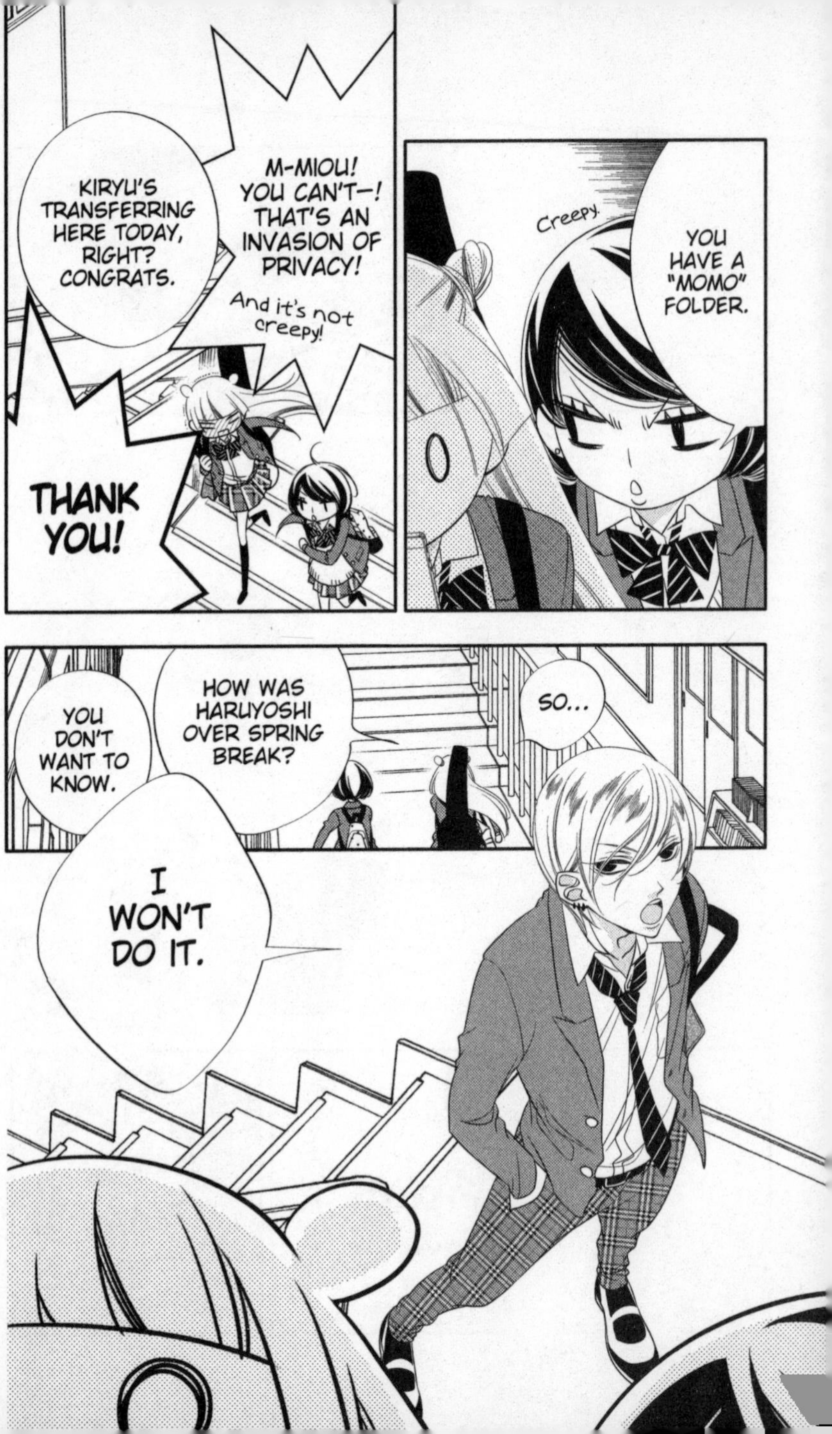
Creepy.
YOU HAVE A "MOMO" FOLDER.
M-MIOU! YOU CAN'T—! THAT'S AN INVASION OF PRIVACY!
And it's not creepy!
KIRYU'S TRANSFERRING HERE TODAY, RIGHT? CONGRATS.
THANK YOU!
SO...
HOW WAS HARUYOSHI OVER SPRING BREAK?
YOU DON'T WANT TO KNOW.
I WON'T DO IT.

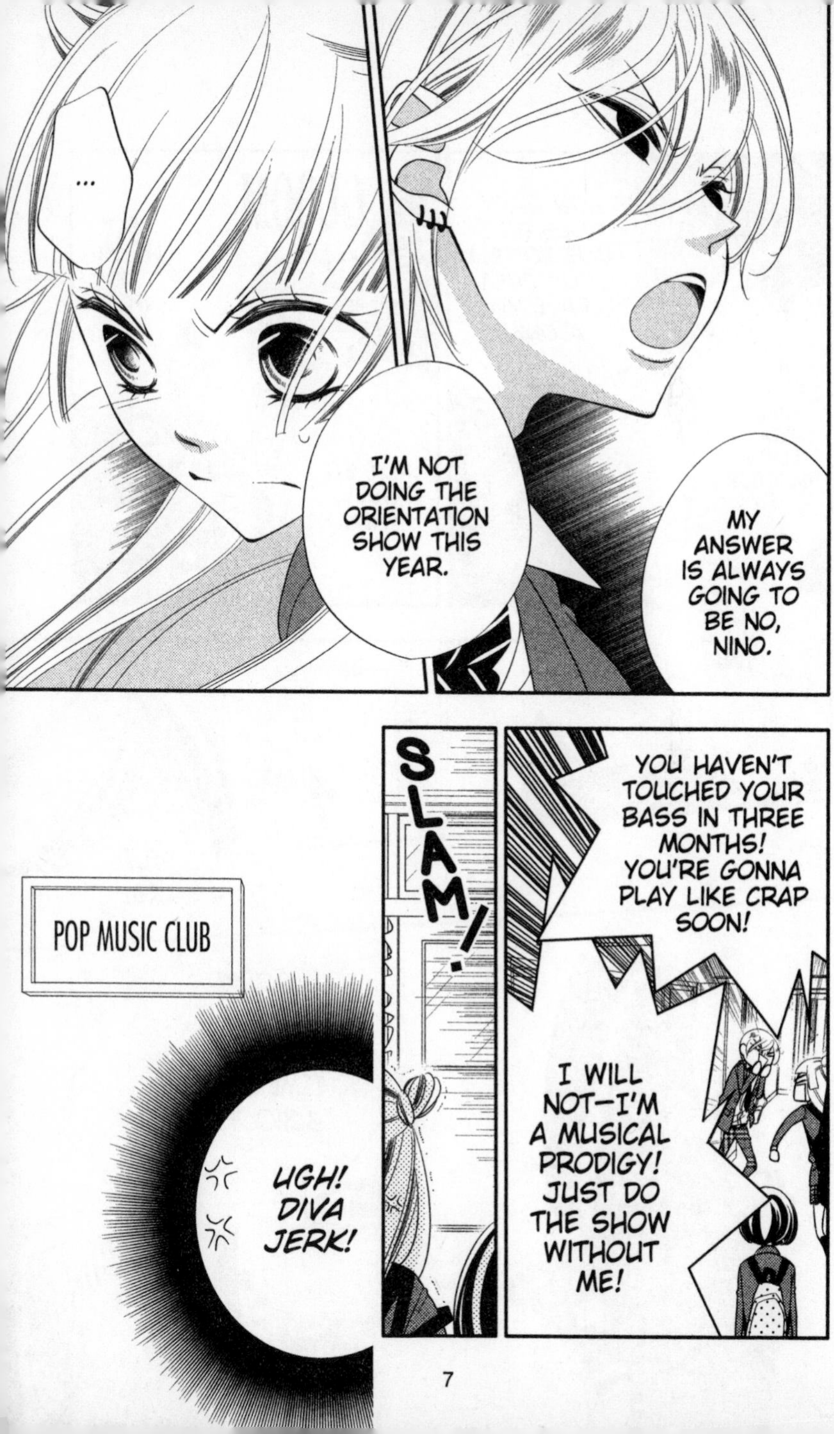
I'M NOT DOING THE ORIENTATION SHOW THIS YEAR.
MY ANSWER IS ALWAYS GOING TO BE NO, NINO.
...
YOU HAVEN'T TOUCHED YOUR BASS IN THREE MONTHS! YOU'RE GONNA PLAY LIKE CRAP SOON!
I WILL NOT—I'M A MUSICAL PRODIGY! JUST DO THE SHOW WITHOUT ME!
SLAM!
POP MUSIC CLUB
UGH! DIVA JERK!

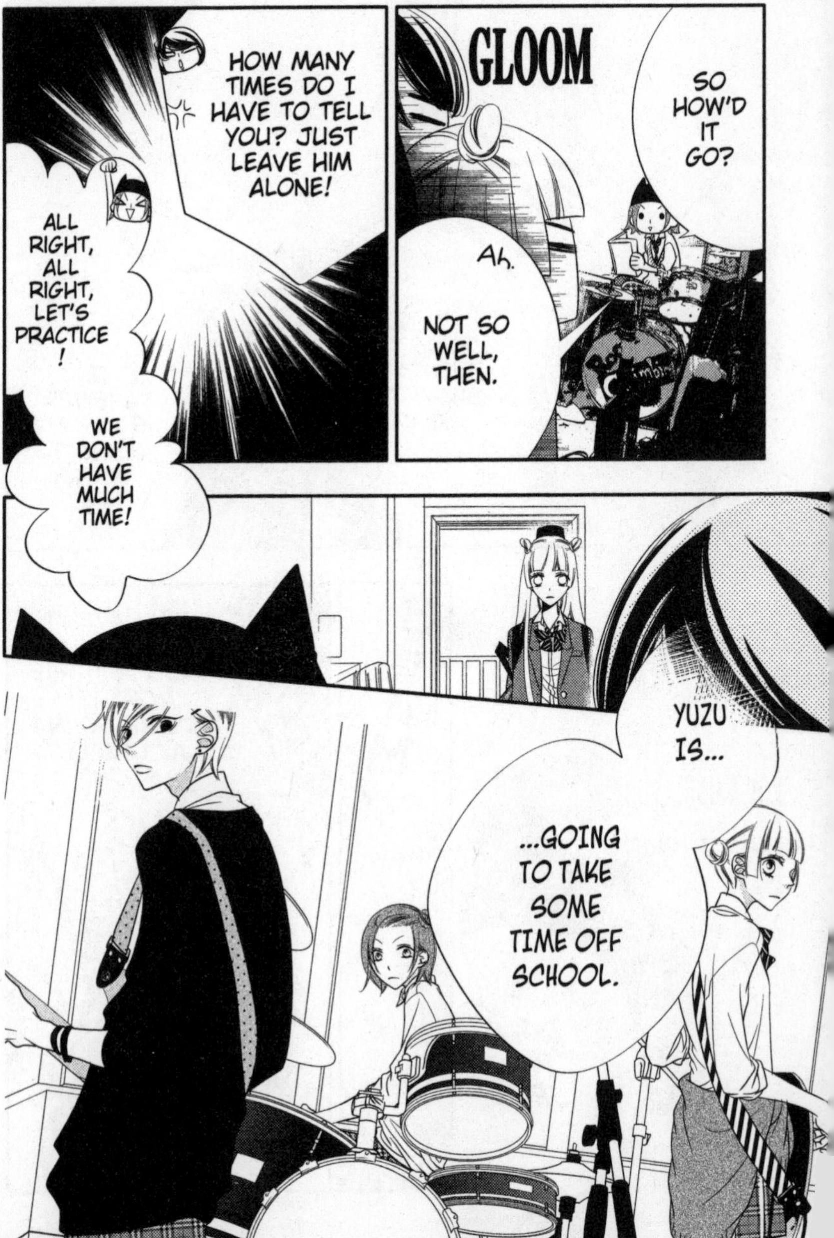
GLOOM
SO HOW'D IT GO?
Ah.
NOT SO WELL, THEN.
HOW MANY TIMES DO I HAVE TO TELL YOU? JUST LEAVE HIM ALONE!
ALL RIGHT, ALL RIGHT, LET'S PRACTICE!
WE DON'T HAVE MUCH TIME!
YUZU IS...
...GOING TO TAKE SOME TIME OFF SCHOOL.

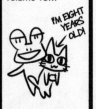

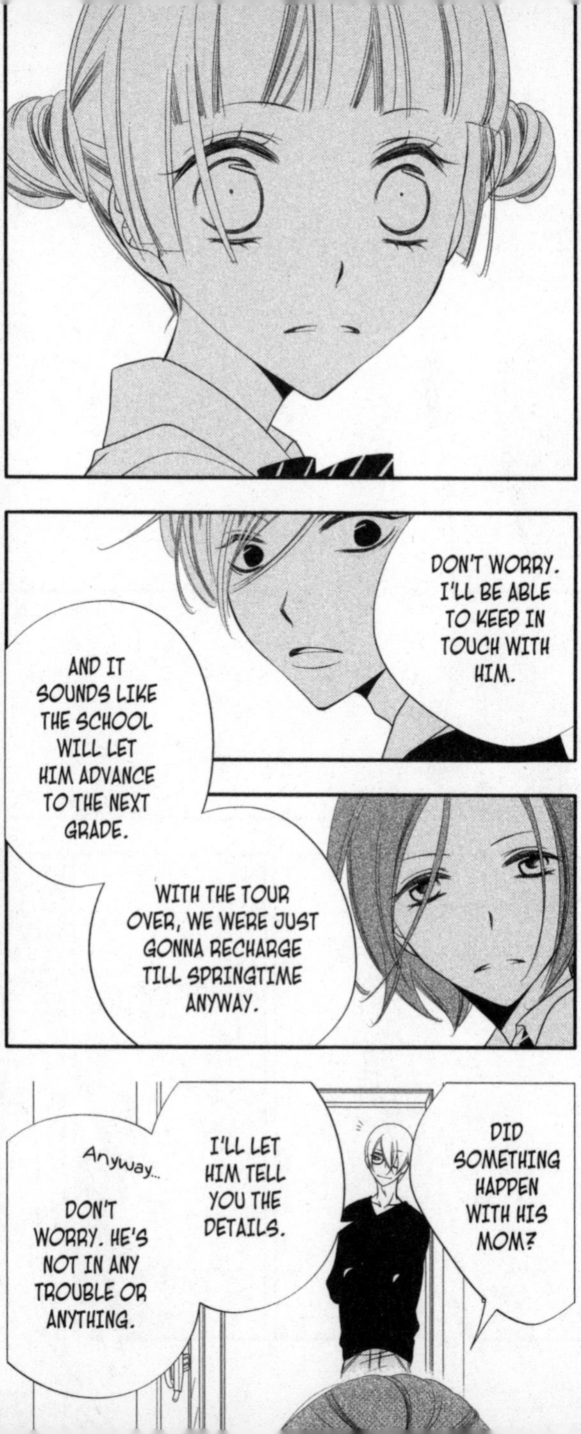
DON'T WORRY. I'LL BE ABLE TO KEEP IN TOUCH WITH HIM.
AND IT SOUNDS LIKE THE SCHOOL WILL LET HIM ADVANCE TO THE NEXT GRADE.
WITH THE TOUR OVER, WE WERE JUST GONNA RECHARGE TILL SPRINGTIME ANYWAY.
DID SOMETHING HAPPEN WITH HIS MOM?
I'LL LET HIM TELL YOU THE DETAILS.
Anyway...
DON'T WORRY. HE'S NOT IN ANY TROUBLE OR ANYTHING.

1

It's good to see you! I'm Ryoko Fukuyama. Thank you so much for picking up volume 12 of *Anonymous Noise*! For the first time since volume 10, I'm typing my columns instead of writing them out. Sorry about that! In volume 10, I used a handwriting-style font, and all anyone could talk about was how much better my penmanship had become. (It's amazing how real those hand-writing fonts look!) But this time I'll come clean and use a typed font instead. Anyway, it's volume 12, which means it's Kuro's turn to be on the cover. With that, I've done each character twice. Now I don't know what I'm going to do for volume 13...

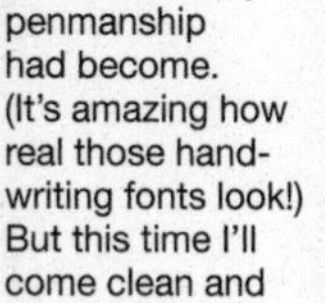
I'M EIGHT YEARS OLD!

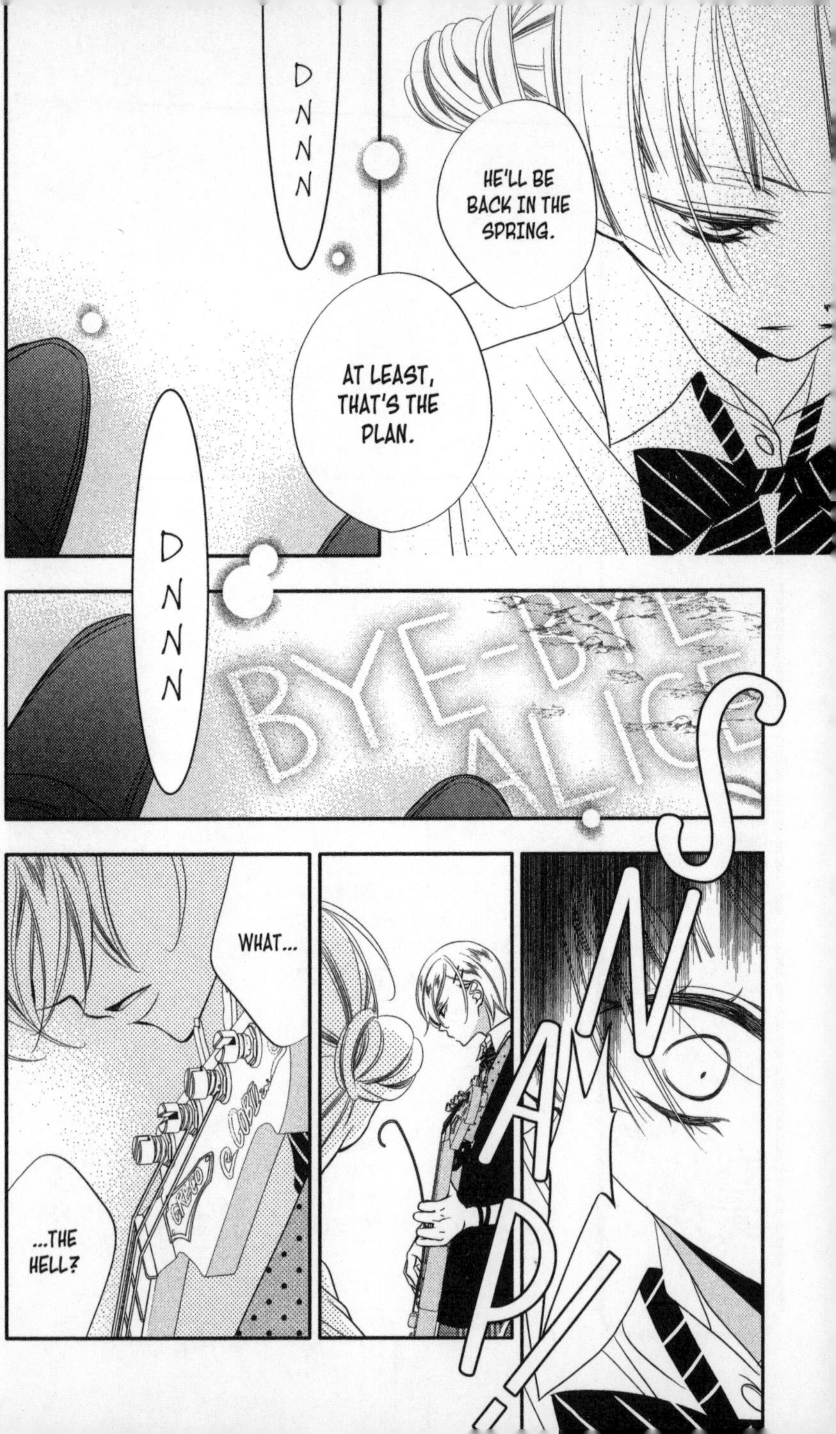
HE'LL BE BACK IN THE SPRING.
AT LEAST, THAT'S THE PLAN.
DNNN
DNNN
BYE-BYE ALICE
SNAP!
WHAT...
...THE HELL?

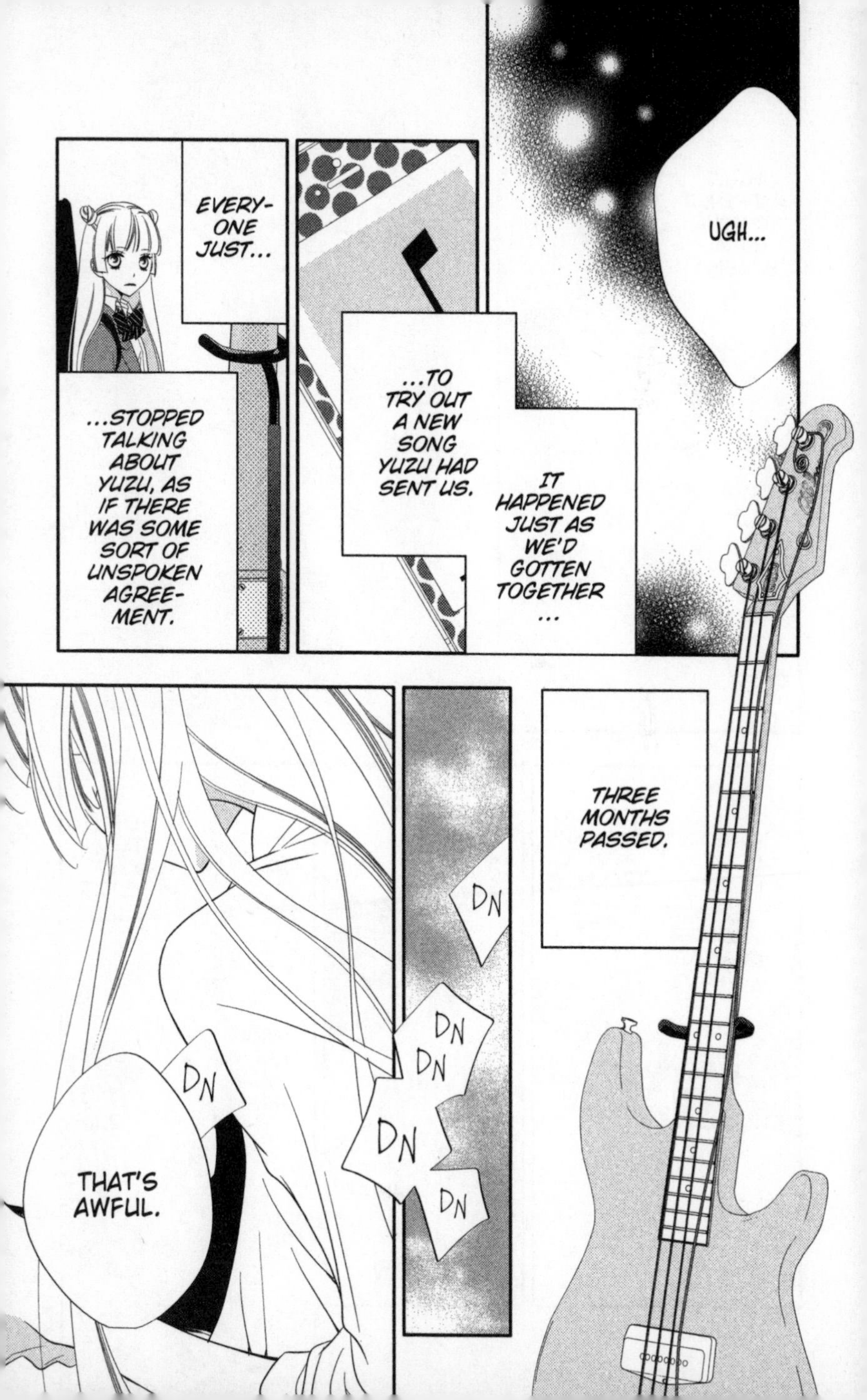
UGH...
IT HAPPENED JUST AS WE'D GOTTEN TOGETHER...
...TO TRY OUT A NEW SONG YUZU HAD SENT US.
EVERY-ONE JUST...
...STOPPED TALKING ABOUT YUZU, AS IF THERE WAS SOME SORT OF UNSPOKEN AGREE-MENT.
THREE MONTHS PASSED.
DN
DN
DN
DN
DN
DN
THAT'S AWFUL.

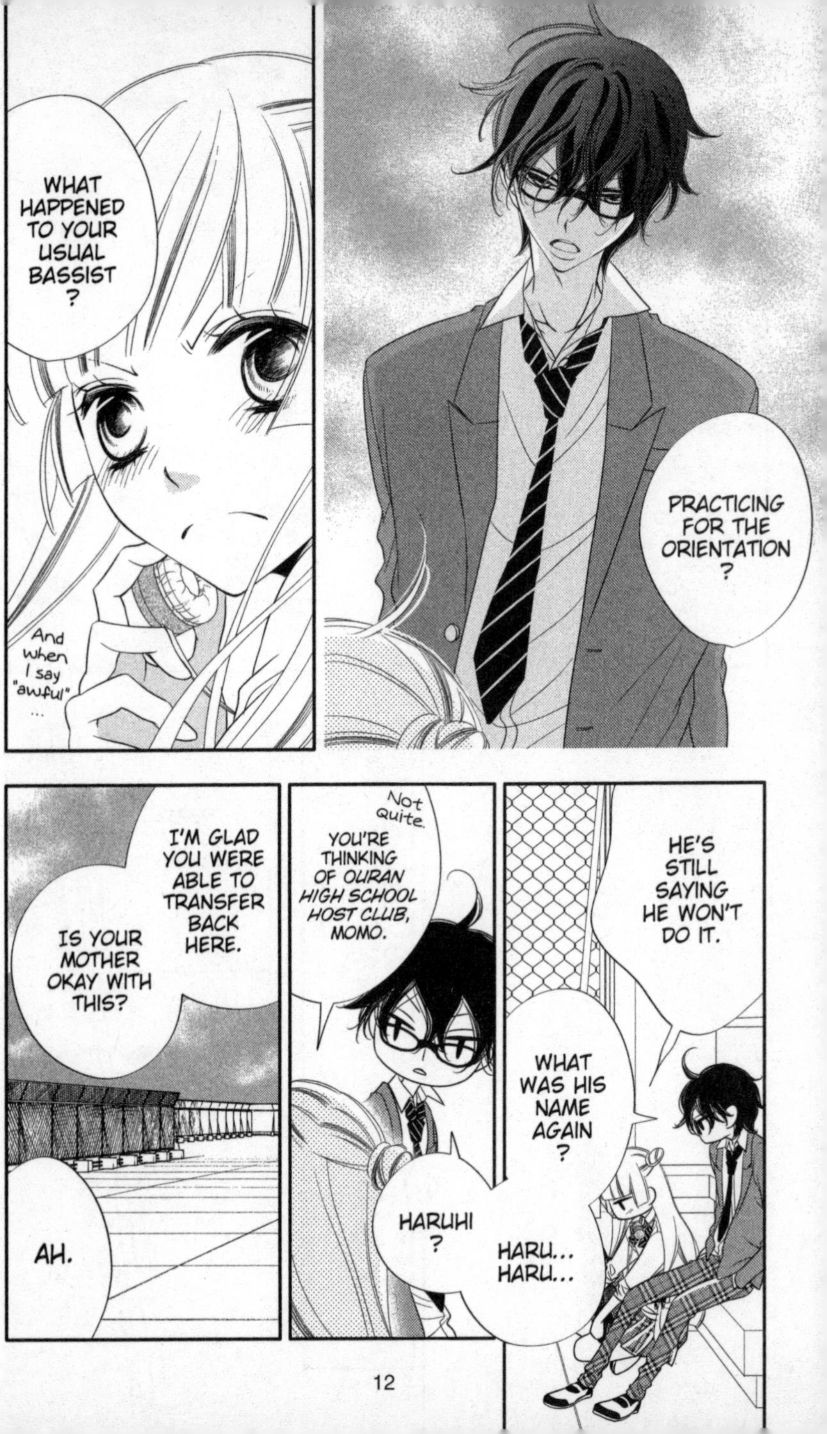
PRACTICING FOR THE ORIENTATION?
WHAT HAPPENED TO YOUR USUAL BASSIST?
And when I say "awful"...
HE'S STILL SAYING HE WON'T DO IT.
WHAT WAS HIS NAME AGAIN?
HARU... HARU...
HARUHI?
YOU'RE THINKING OF *OURAN HIGH SCHOOL HOST CLUB*, MOMO.
Not quite.
I'M GLAD YOU WERE ABLE TO TRANSFER BACK HERE.
IS YOUR MOTHER OKAY WITH THIS?
AH.

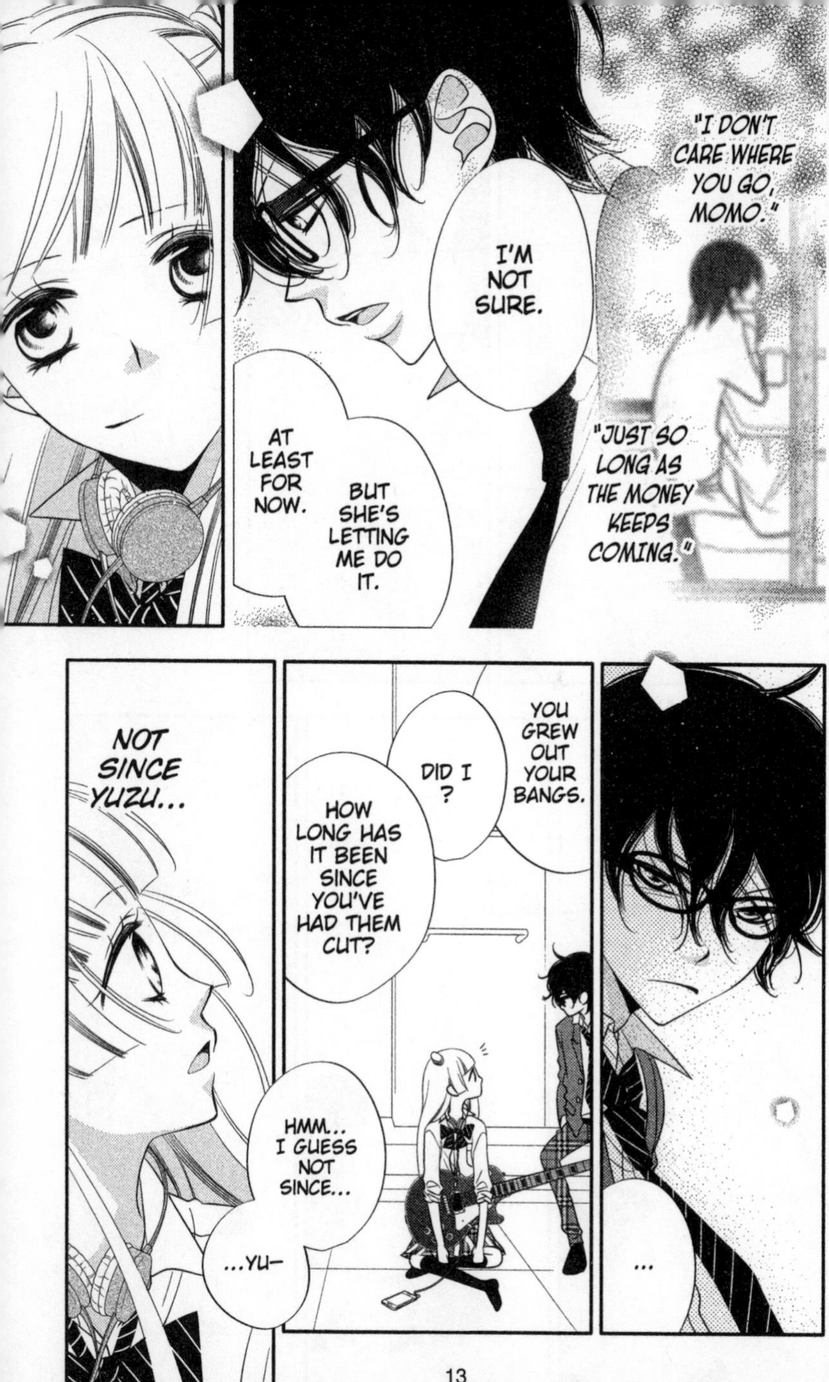
"I DON'T CARE WHERE YOU GO, MOMO."
I'M NOT SURE.
"JUST SO LONG AS THE MONEY KEEPS COMING."
BUT SHE'S LETTING ME DO IT.
AT LEAST FOR NOW.
...
YOU GREW OUT YOUR BANGS.
DID I ?
HOW LONG HAS IT BEEN SINCE YOU'VE HAD THEM CUT?
HMM.. I GUESS NOT SINCE...
...YU–
NOT SINCE YUZU...

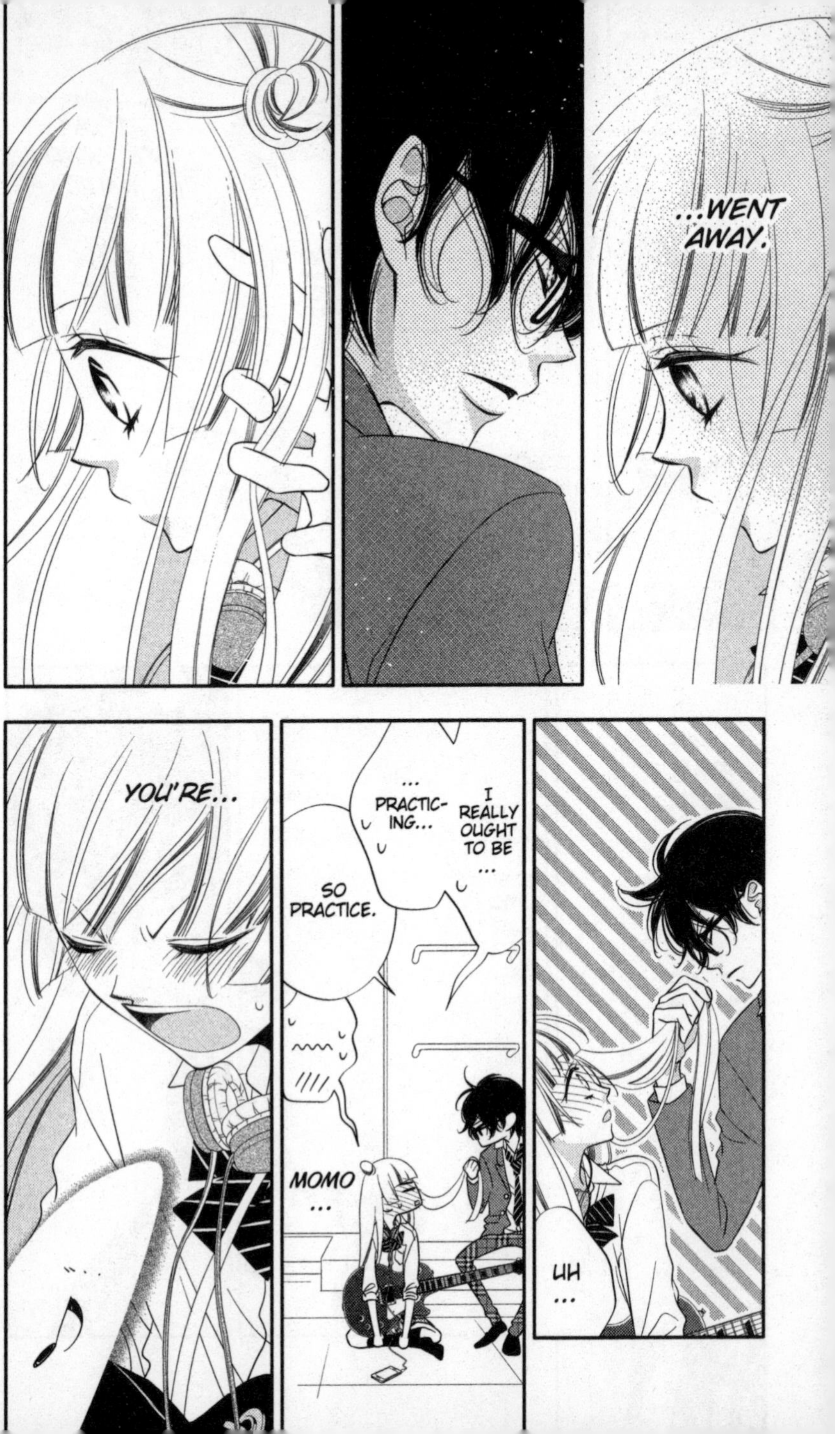
...WENT AWAY.
UH ...
I REALLY OUGHT TO BE ...
... PRACTIC-ING...
SO PRACTICE.
MOMO ...
YOU'RE...

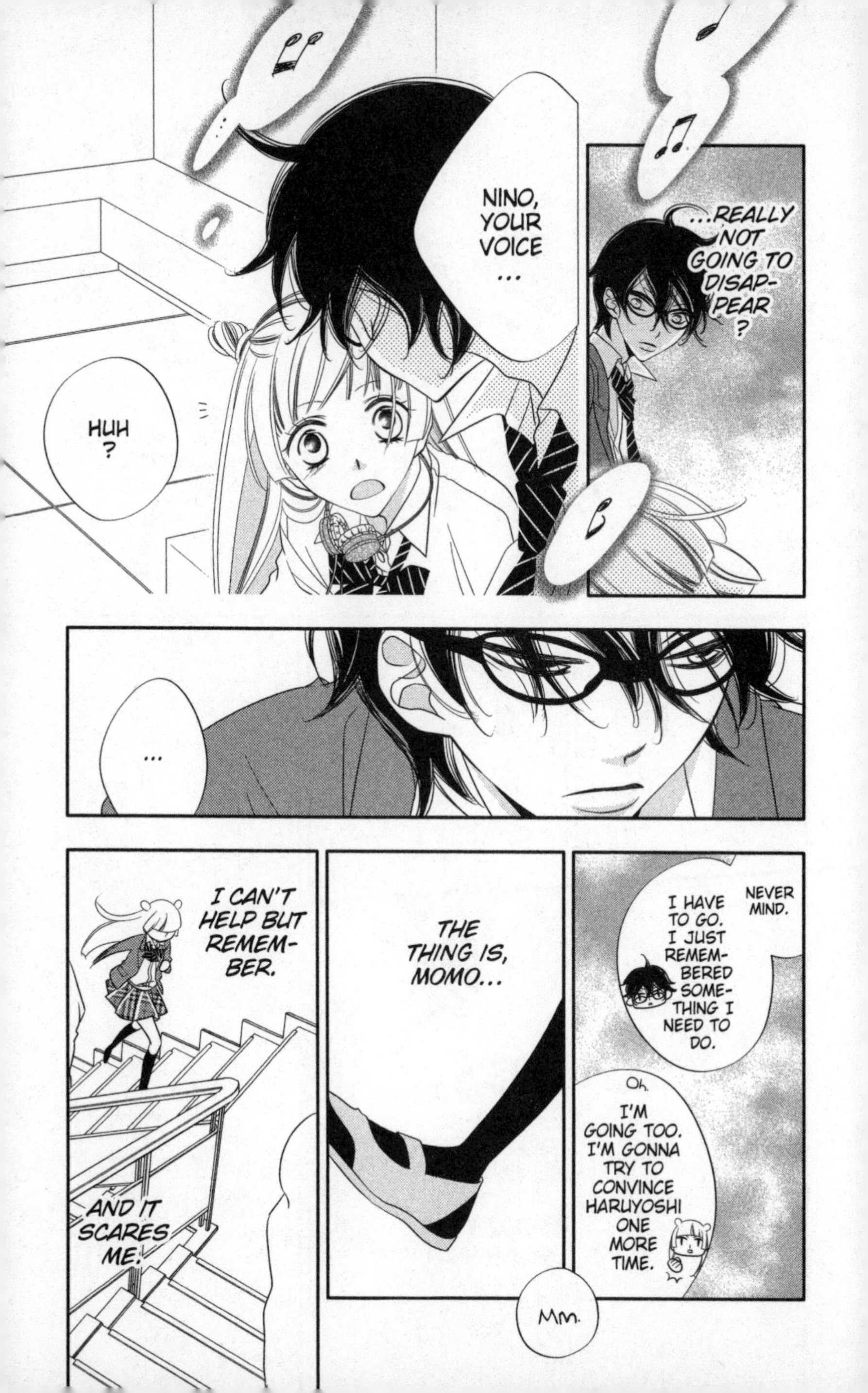
...REALLY NOT GOING TO DISAPPEAR?
NINO, YOUR VOICE...
HUH?
...
NEVER MIND.
I HAVE TO GO. I JUST REMEMBERED SOMETHING I NEED TO DO.
Oh.
I'M GOING TOO. I'M GONNA TRY TO CONVINCE HARUYOSHI ONE MORE TIME.
Mm.
THE THING IS, MOMO...
I CAN'T HELP BUT REMEMBER.
AND IT SCARES ME.

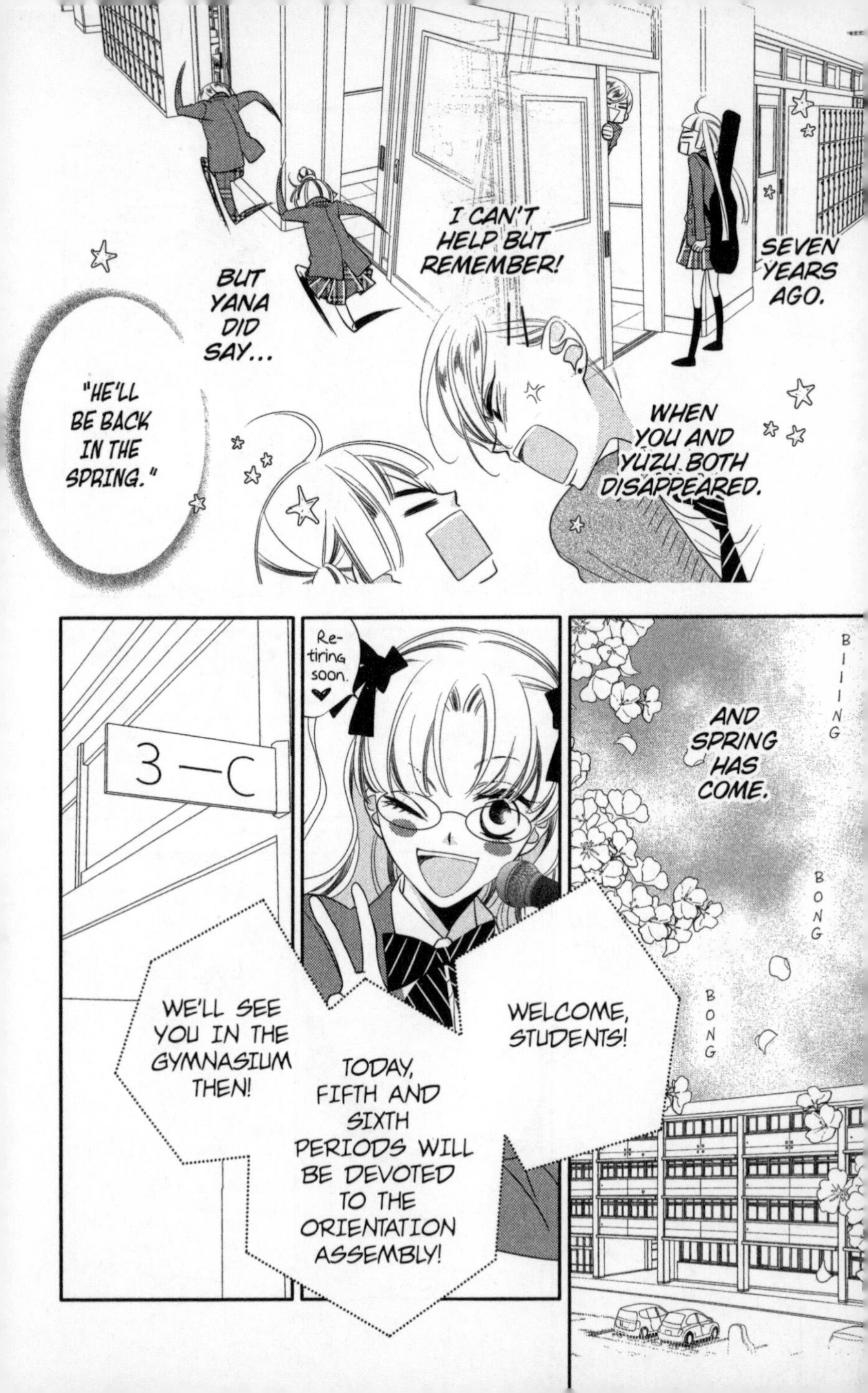
SEVEN YEARS AGO.
I CAN'T HELP BUT REMEMBER!
WHEN YOU AND YUZU BOTH DISAPPEARED.
BUT YANA DID SAY...
"HE'LL BE BACK IN THE SPRING."
BIIING
AND SPRING HAS COME.
BONG
BONG
Re-tiring soon.
WELCOME, STUDENTS!
TODAY, FIFTH AND SIXTH PERIODS WILL BE DEVOTED TO THE ORIENTATION ASSEMBLY!
WE'LL SEE YOU IN THE GYMNASIUM THEN!
3—C

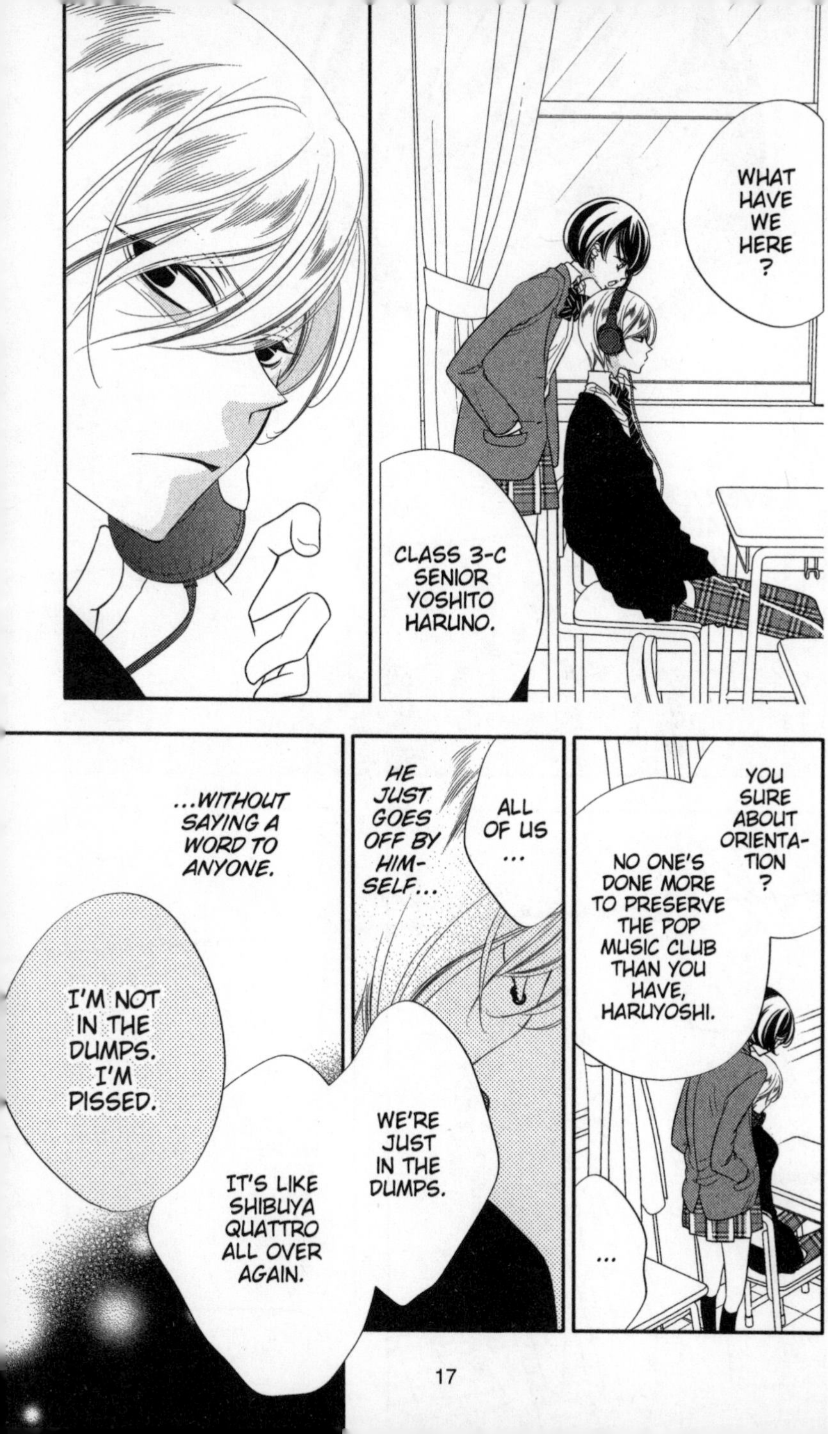
WHAT HAVE WE HERE?
CLASS 3-C SENIOR YOSHITO HARUNO.
YOU SURE ABOUT ORIENTATION?
NO ONE'S DONE MORE TO PRESERVE THE POP MUSIC CLUB THAN YOU HAVE, HARUYOSHI.
...
ALL OF US...
HE JUST GOES OFF BY HIMSELF...
...WITHOUT SAYING A WORD TO ANYONE.
WE'RE JUST IN THE DUMPS.
IT'S LIKE SHIBUYA QUATTRO ALL OVER AGAIN.
I'M NOT IN THE DUMPS. I'M PISSED.

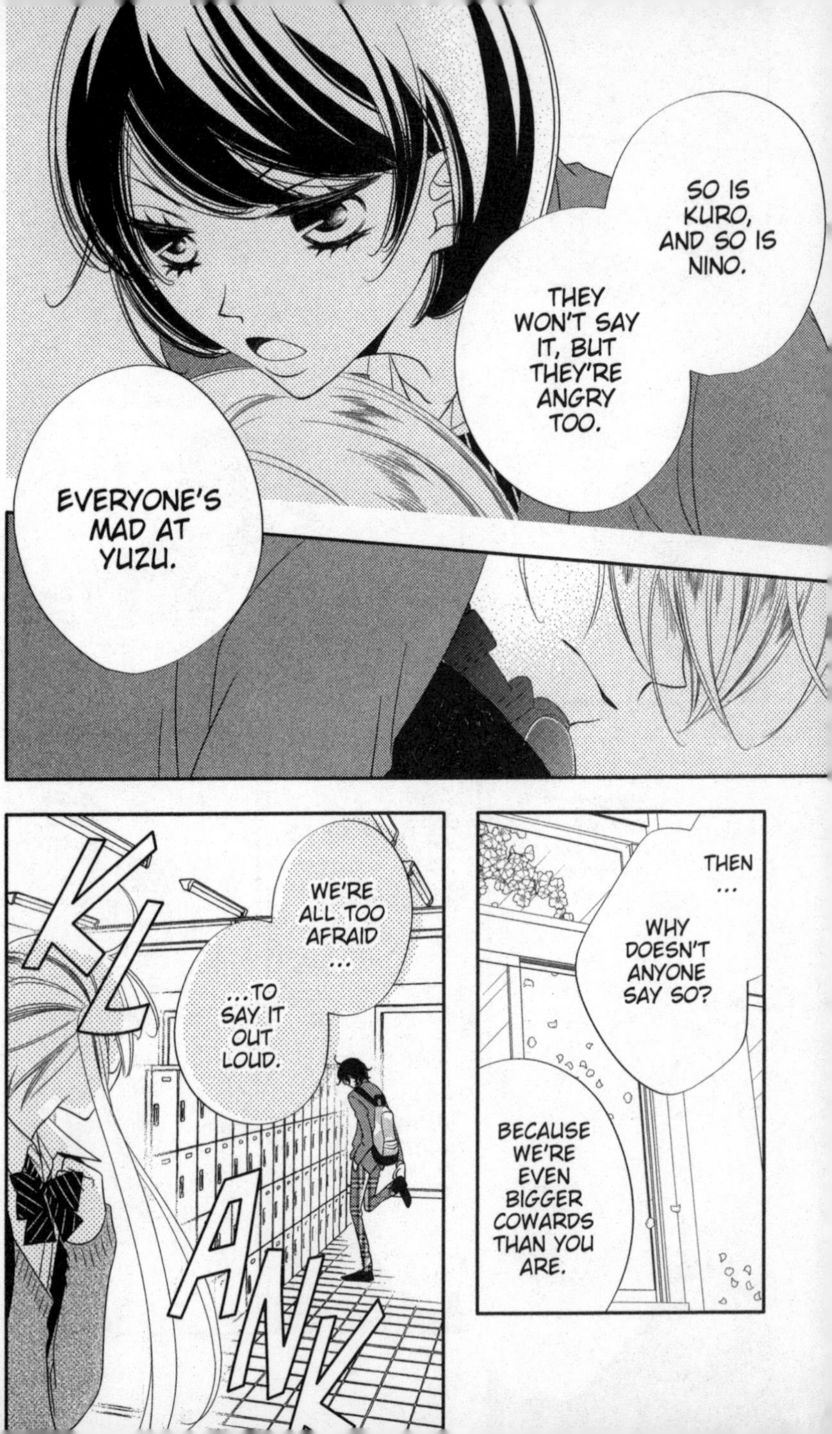
SO IS KURO, AND SO IS NINO.
THEY WON'T SAY IT, BUT THEY'RE ANGRY TOO.
EVERYONE'S MAD AT YUZU.
THEN ...
WHY DOESN'T ANYONE SAY SO?
BECAUSE WE'RE EVEN BIGGER COWARDS THAN YOU ARE.
WE'RE ALL TOO AFRAID ...
...TO SAY IT OUT LOUD.
KLANK

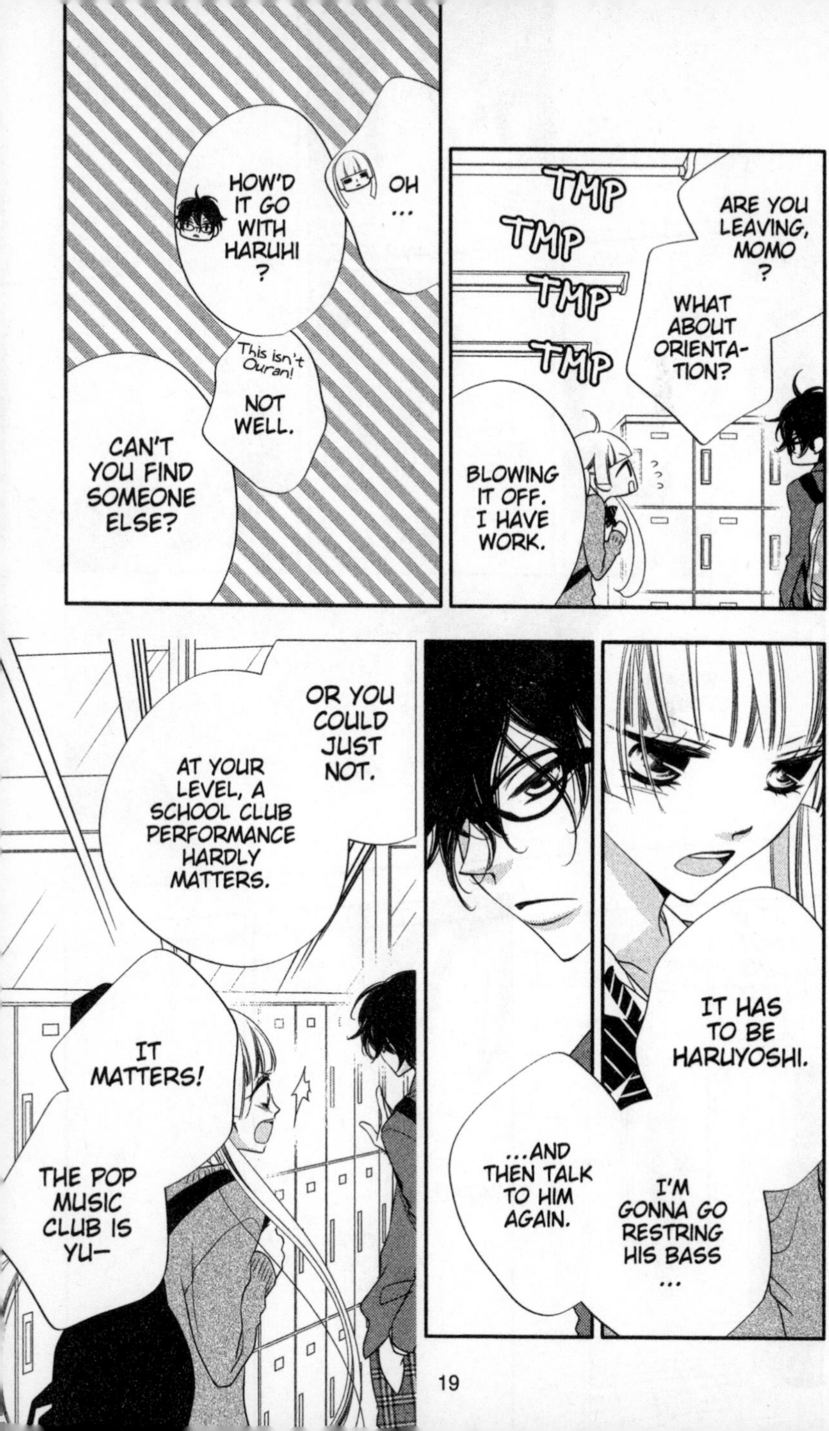
TMP
TMP
TMP
TMP
ARE YOU LEAVING, MOMO?
WHAT ABOUT ORIENTATION?
BLOWING IT OFF. I HAVE WORK.
OH...
HOW'D IT GO WITH HARUHI?
NOT WELL.
This isn't Ouran!
CAN'T YOU FIND SOMEONE ELSE?
IT HAS TO BE HARUYOSHI.
I'M GONNA GO RESTRING HIS BASS...
...AND THEN TALK TO HIM AGAIN.
OR YOU COULD JUST NOT.
AT YOUR LEVEL, A SCHOOL CLUB PERFORMANCE HARDLY MATTERS.
IT MATTERS!
THE POP MUSIC CLUB IS YU—

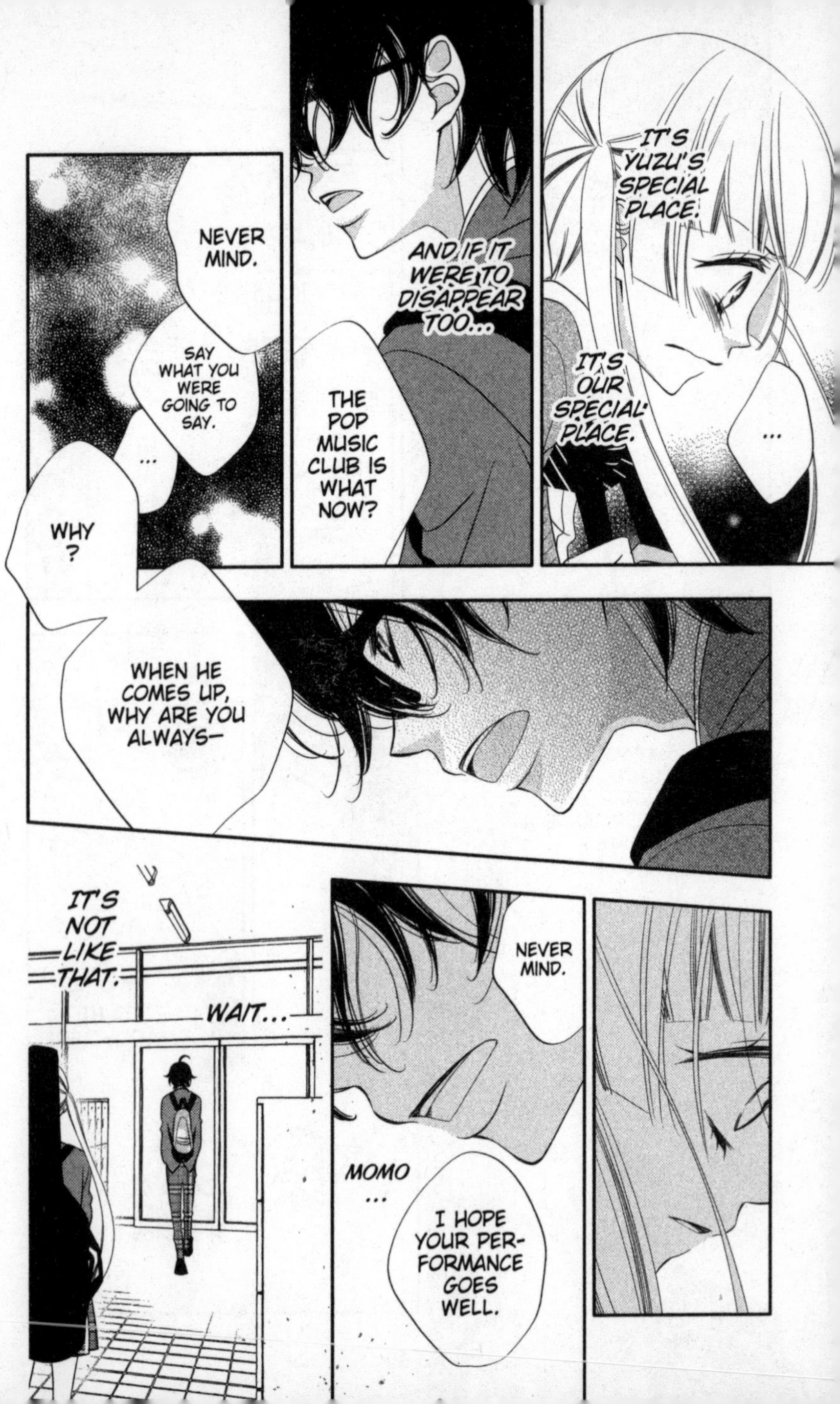

IT'S YUZU'S SPECIAL PLACE.
IT'S OUR SPECIAL PLACE.
...
AND IF IT WERE TO DISAPPEAR TOO...
THE POP MUSIC CLUB IS WHAT NOW?
NEVER MIND.
SAY WHAT YOU WERE GOING TO SAY.
...
WHY?
WHEN HE COMES UP, WHY ARE YOU ALWAYS—
NEVER MIND.
MOMO...
I HOPE YOUR PER-FORMANCE GOES WELL.
IT'S NOT LIKE THAT.
WAIT...

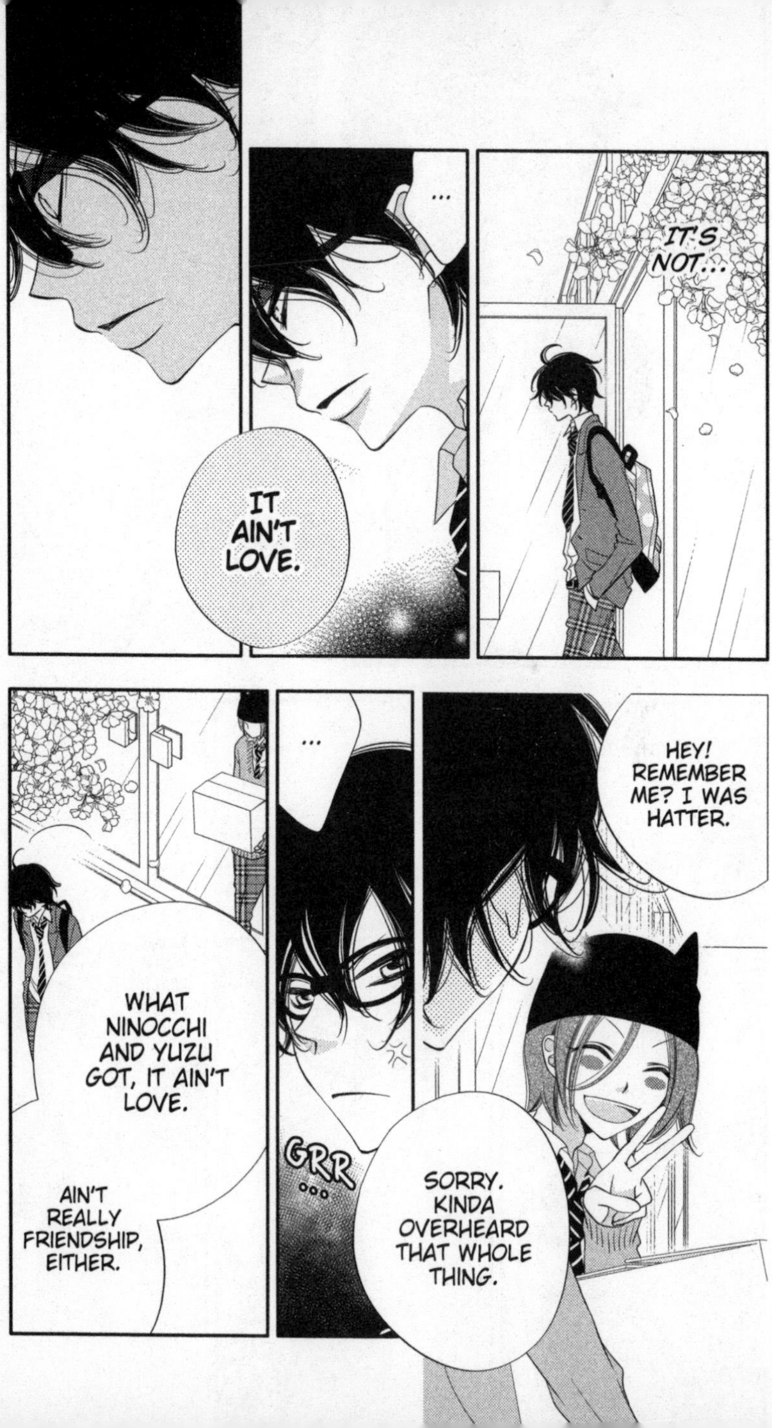
IT'S NOT...
...
IT AIN'T LOVE.
HEY! REMEMBER ME? I WAS HATTER.
SORRY. KINDA OVERHEARD THAT WHOLE THING.
...
GRR...
WHAT NINOCCHI AND YUZU GOT, IT AIN'T LOVE.
AIN'T REALLY FRIENDSHIP, EITHER.

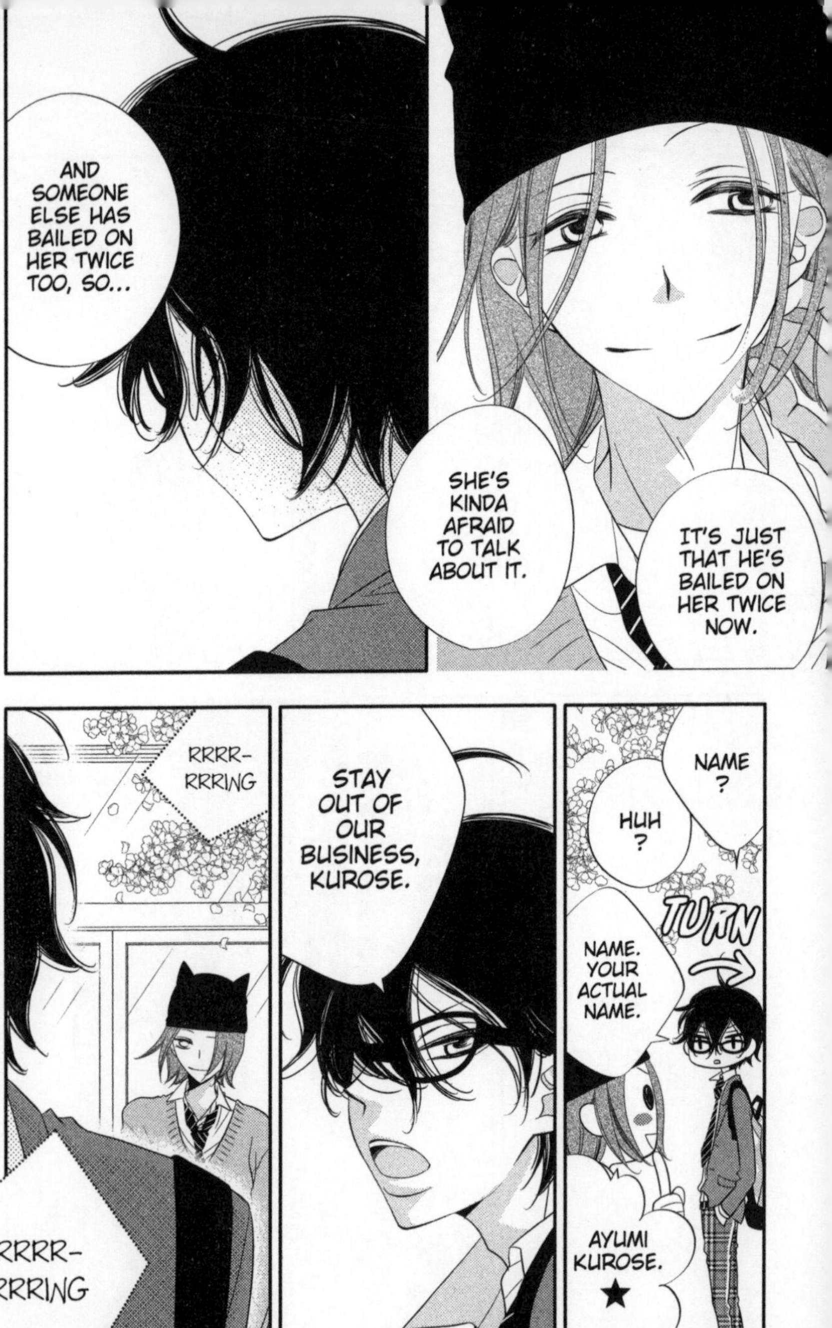
IT'S JUST THAT HE'S BAILED ON HER TWICE NOW.
SHE'S KINDA AFRAID TO TALK ABOUT IT.
AND SOMEONE ELSE HAS BAILED ON HER TWICE TOO, SO...
NAME?
HUH?
TURN
NAME. YOUR ACTUAL NAME.
AYUMI KUROSE. ★
STAY OUT OF OUR BUSINESS, KUROSE.
RRRR-RRRING
RRRR-RRRING

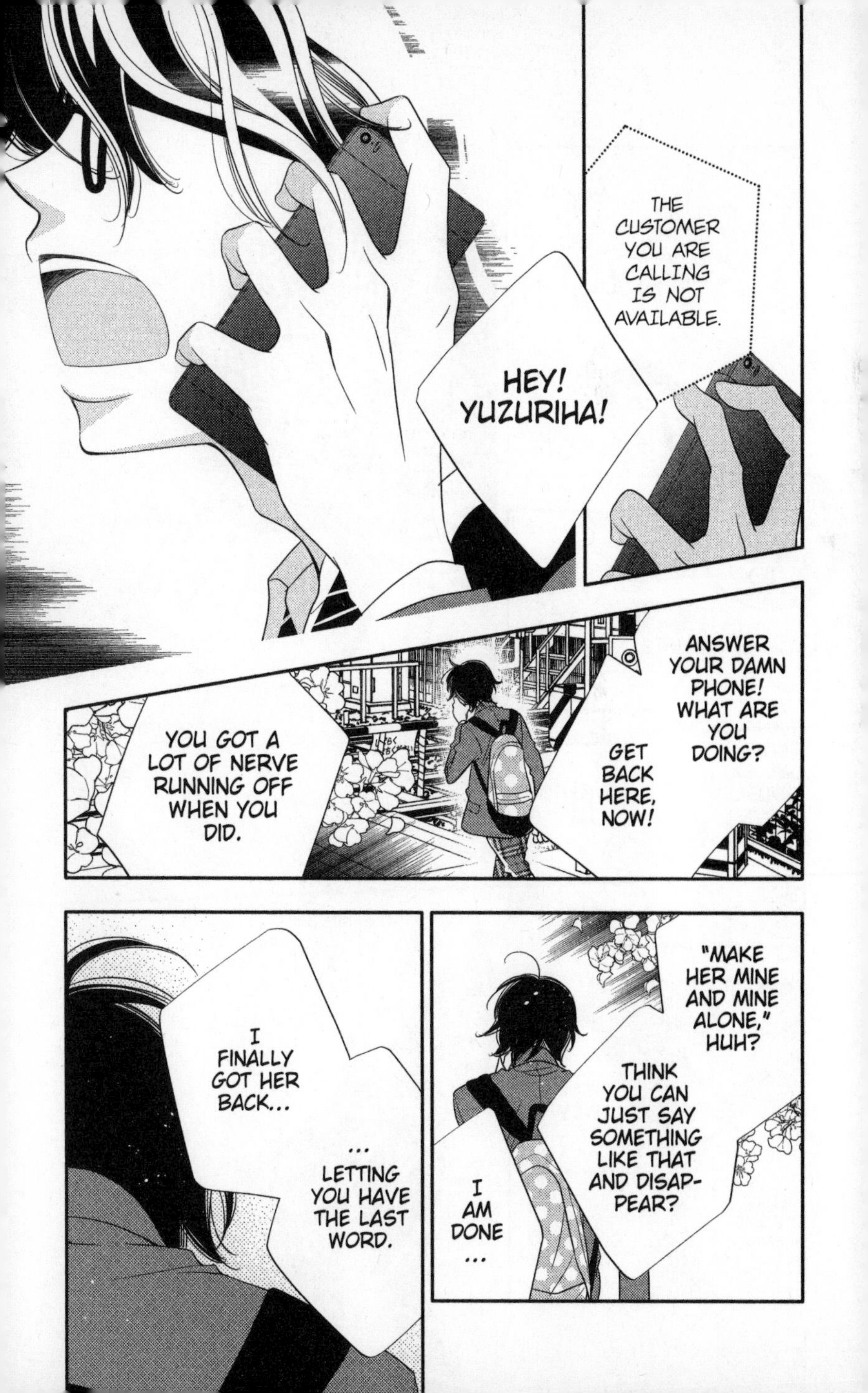
THE CUSTOMER YOU ARE CALLING IS NOT AVAILABLE.
HEY! YUZURIHA!
ANSWER YOUR DAMN PHONE! WHAT ARE YOU DOING?
GET BACK HERE, NOW!
YOU GOT A LOT OF NERVE RUNNING OFF WHEN YOU DID.
"MAKE HER MINE AND MINE ALONE," HUH?
THINK YOU CAN JUST SAY SOMETHING LIKE THAT AND DISAP-PEAR?
I AM DONE...
I FINALLY GOT HER BACK...
...LETTING YOU HAVE THE LAST WORD.

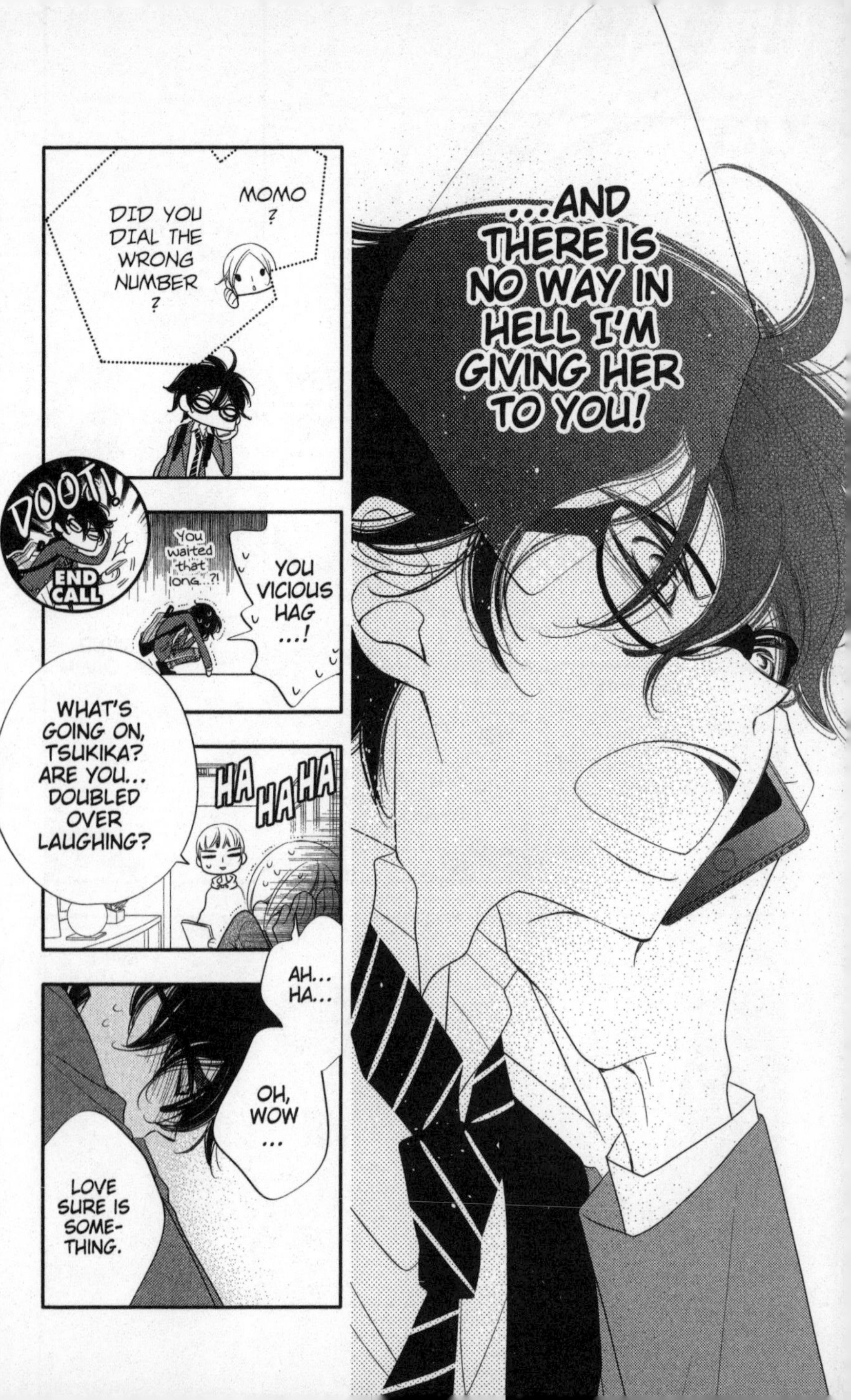
...AND THERE IS NO WAY IN HELL I'M GIVING HER TO YOU!
MOMO?
DID YOU DIAL THE WRONG NUMBER?
YOU VICIOUS HAG...!
You waited that long...?!
DOOT!
END CALL
HAHAHA
WHAT'S GOING ON, TSUKIKA? ARE YOU... DOUBLED OVER LAUGHING?
AH... HA...
OH, WOW...
LOVE SURE IS SOME-THING.

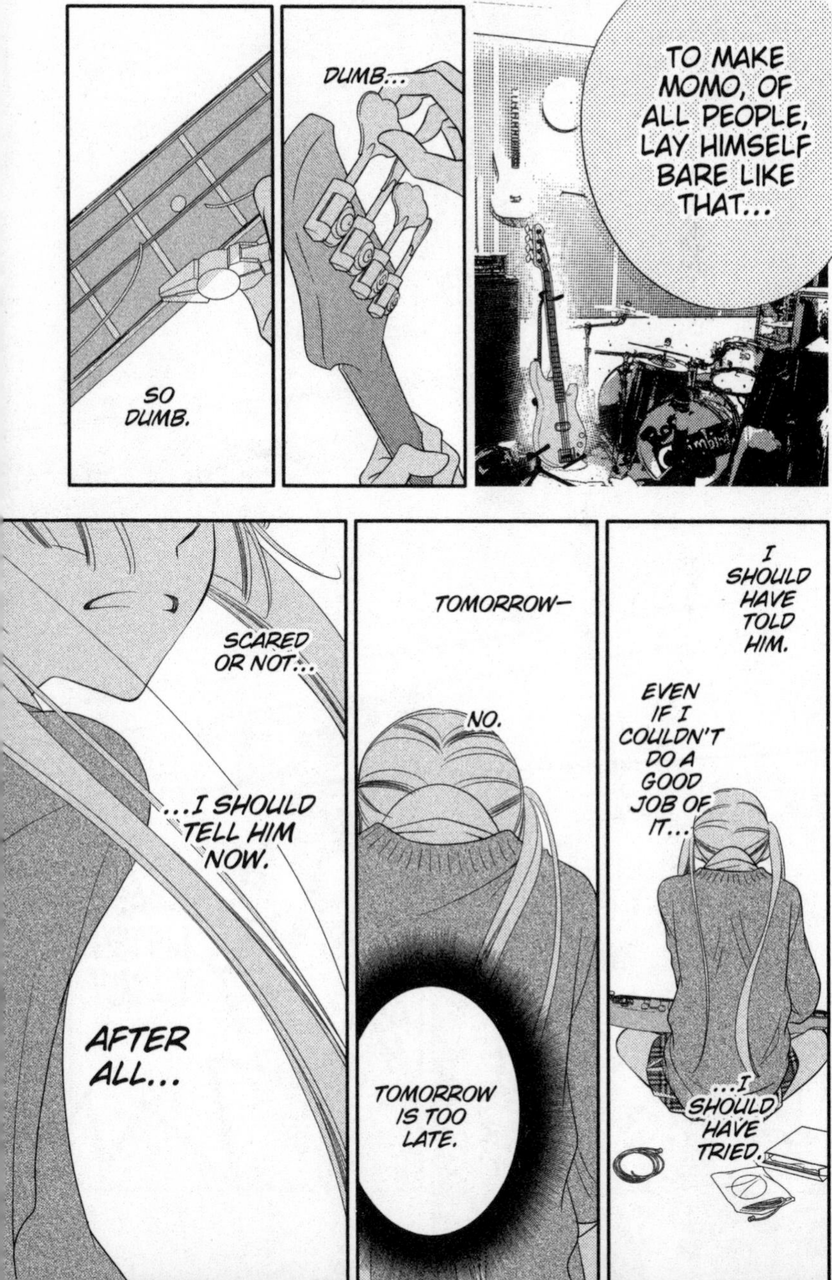
TO MAKE MOMO, OF ALL PEOPLE, LAY HIMSELF BARE LIKE THAT...
DUMB...
SO DUMB.
I SHOULD HAVE TOLD HIM.
EVEN IF I COULDN'T DO A GOOD JOB OF IT...
...I SHOULD HAVE TRIED.
TOMORROW—
NO.
TOMORROW IS TOO LATE.
SCARED OR NOT...
...I SHOULD TELL HIM NOW.
AFTER ALL...

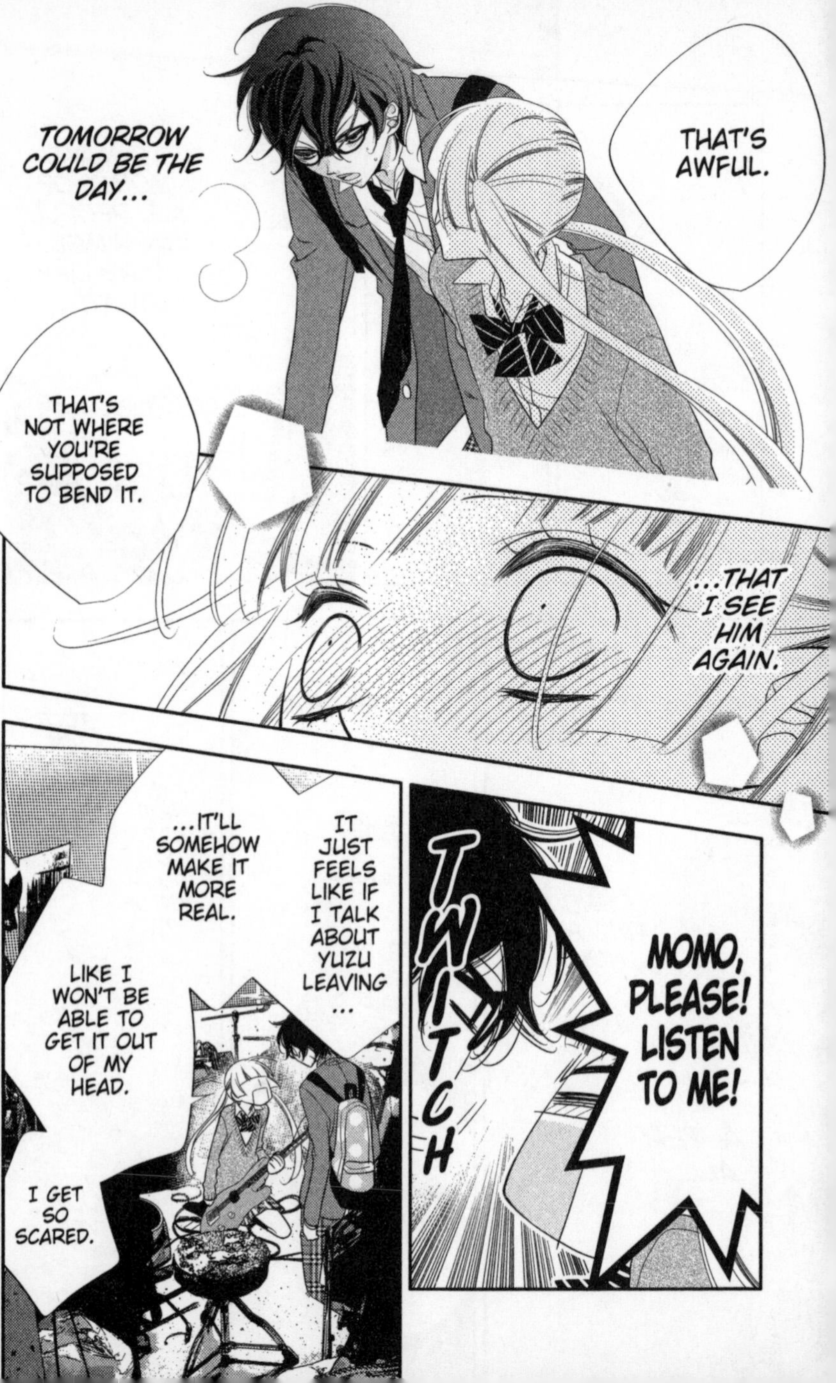
THAT'S AWFUL.
TOMORROW COULD BE THE DAY...
THAT'S NOT WHERE YOU'RE SUPPOSED TO BEND IT.
...THAT I SEE HIM AGAIN.
TWITCH
MOMO, PLEASE! LISTEN TO ME!
IT JUST FEELS LIKE IF I TALK ABOUT YUZU LEAVING...
...IT'LL SOMEHOW MAKE IT MORE REAL.
LIKE I WON'T BE ABLE TO GET IT OUT OF MY HEAD.
I GET SO SCARED.

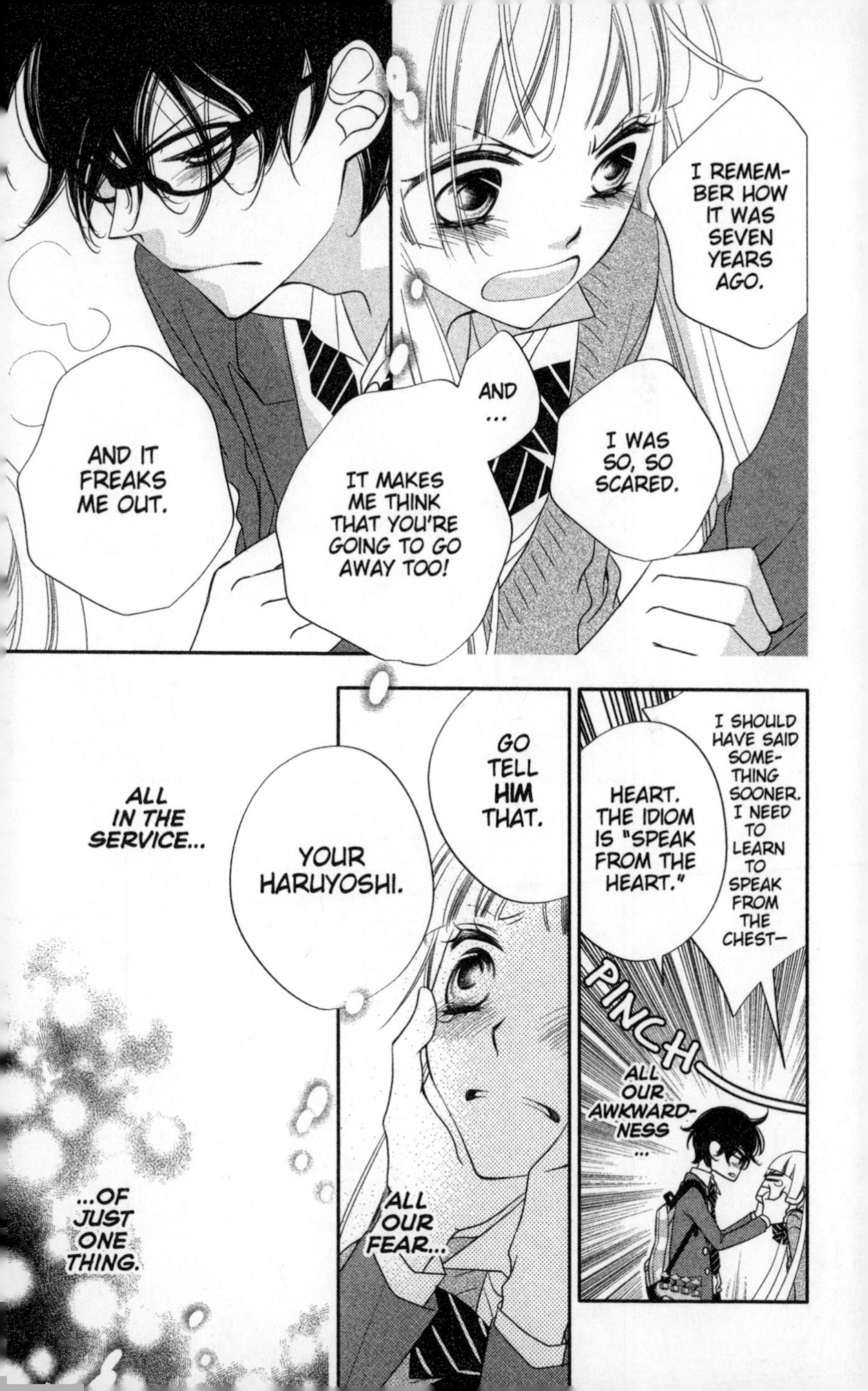
I REMEMBER HOW IT WAS SEVEN YEARS AGO.
I WAS SO, SO SCARED.
AND ...
IT MAKES ME THINK THAT YOU'RE GOING TO GO AWAY TOO!
AND IT FREAKS ME OUT.
I SHOULD HAVE SAID SOMETHING SOONER. I NEED TO LEARN TO SPEAK FROM THE CHEST—
HEART. THE IDIOM IS "SPEAK FROM THE HEART."
PINCH
ALL OUR AWKWARDNESS ...
GO TELL HIM THAT.
YOUR HARUYOSHI.
ALL OUR FEAR...
ALL IN THE SERVICE...
...OF JUST ONE THING.

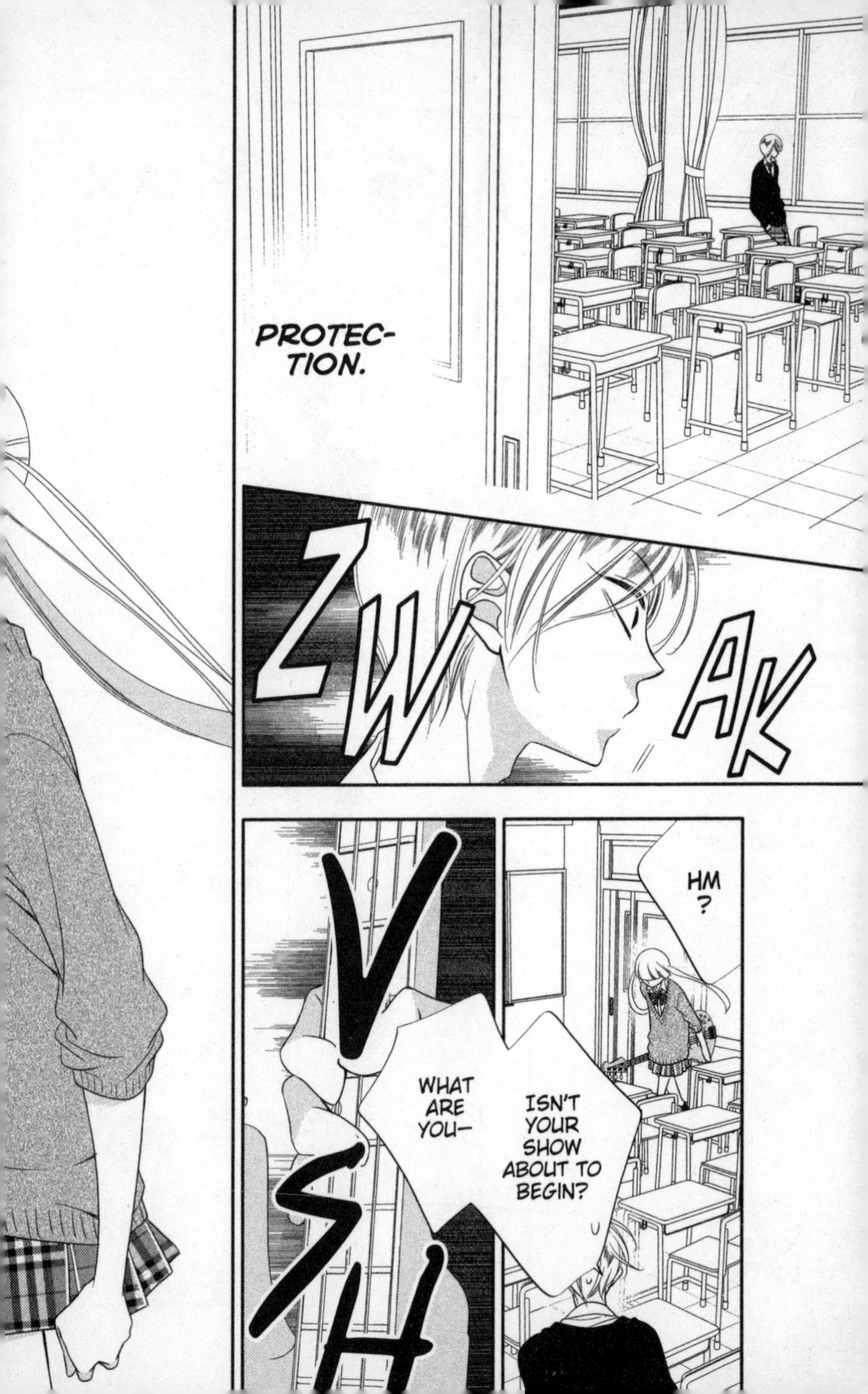
PROTEC-
TION.
ZWAK
HM
?
ISN'T YOUR SHOW ABOUT TO BEGIN?
WHAT ARE YOU—
VSSH

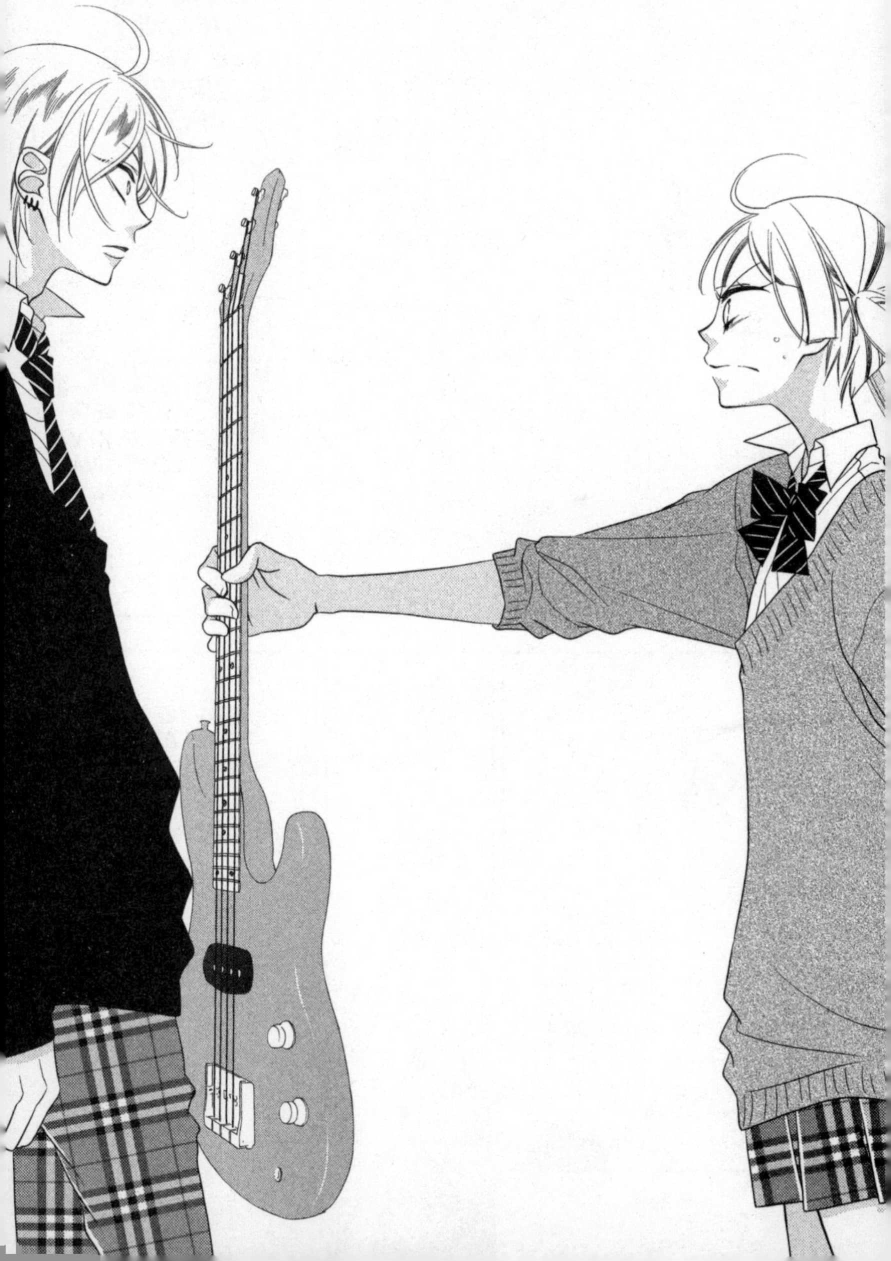

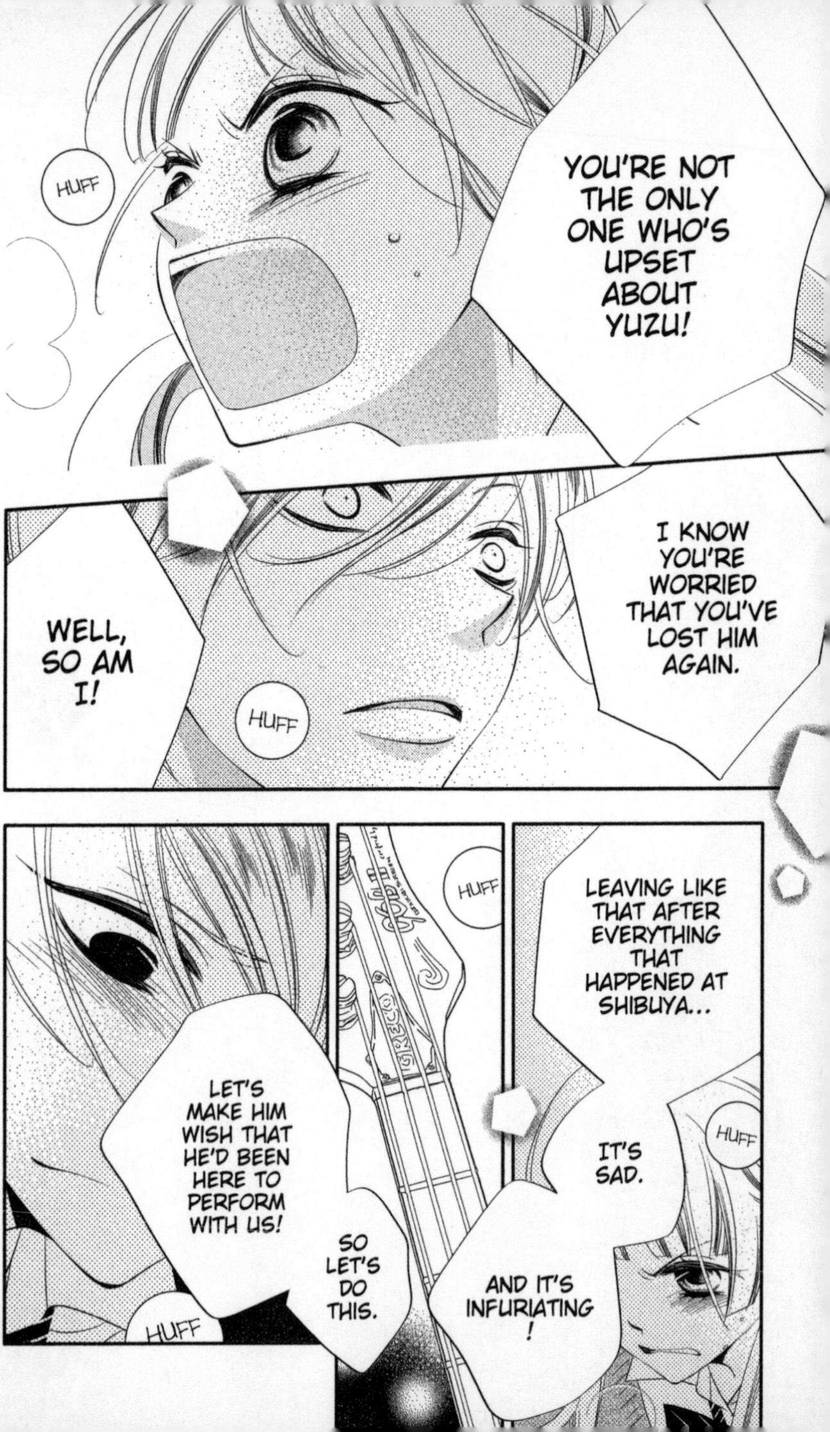
YOU'RE NOT THE ONLY ONE WHO'S UPSET ABOUT YUZU!
HUFF
I KNOW YOU'RE WORRIED THAT YOU'VE LOST HIM AGAIN.
HUFF
WELL, SO AM I!
LEAVING LIKE THAT AFTER EVERYTHING THAT HAPPENED AT SHIBUYA...
HUFF
IT'S SAD.
AND IT'S INFURIATING!
HUFF
SO LET'S DO THIS.
LET'S MAKE HIM WISH THAT HE'D BEEN HERE TO PERFORM WITH US!
HUFF

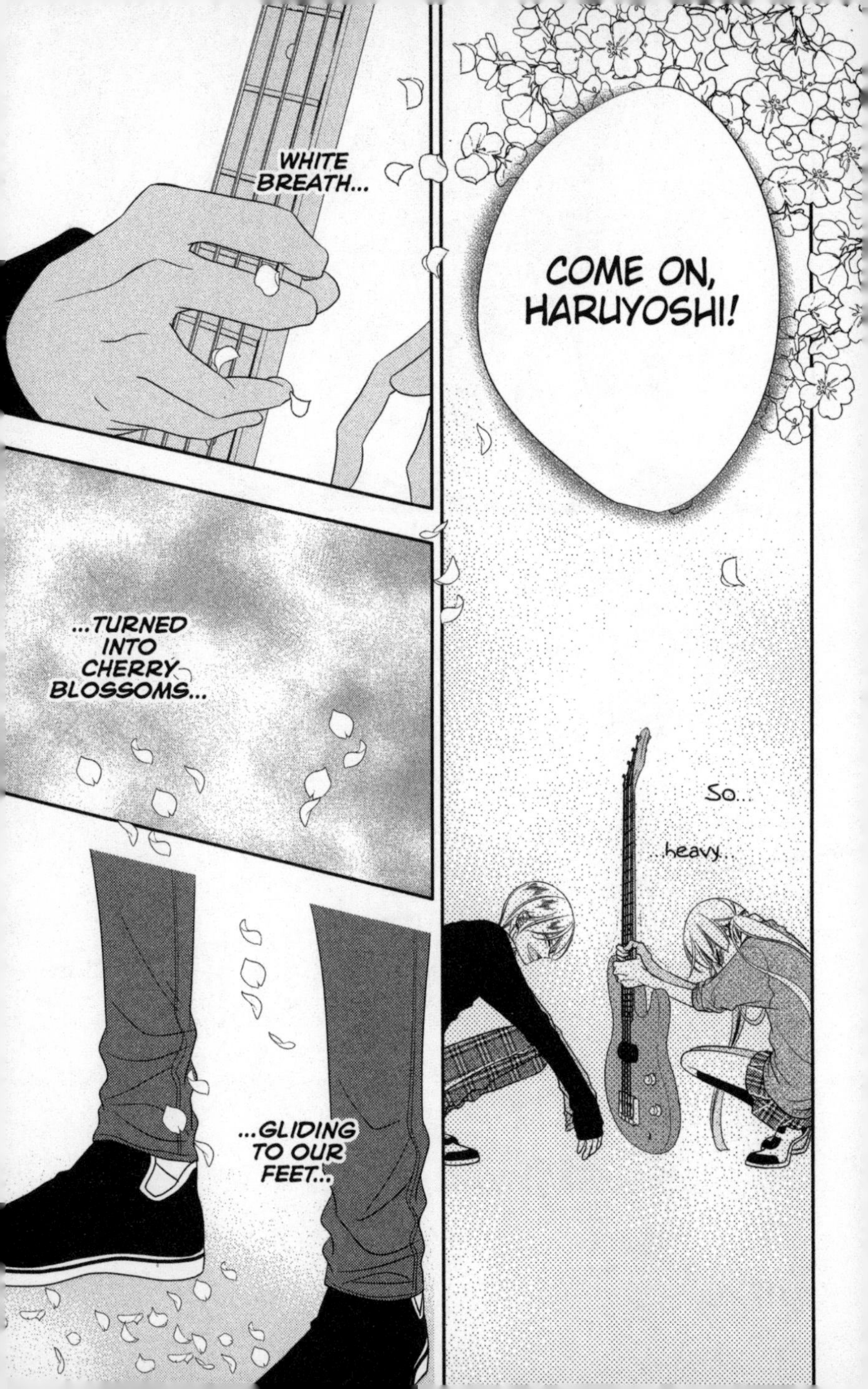
COME ON, HARUYOSHI!
So...
...heavy...
WHITE BREATH...
...TURNED INTO CHERRY BLOSSOMS...
...GLIDING TO OUR FEET...

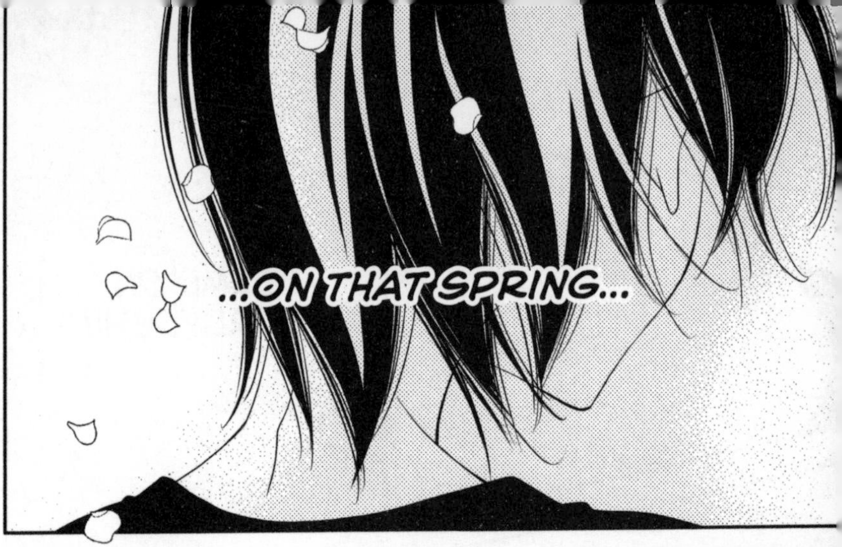
...ON THAT SPRING...
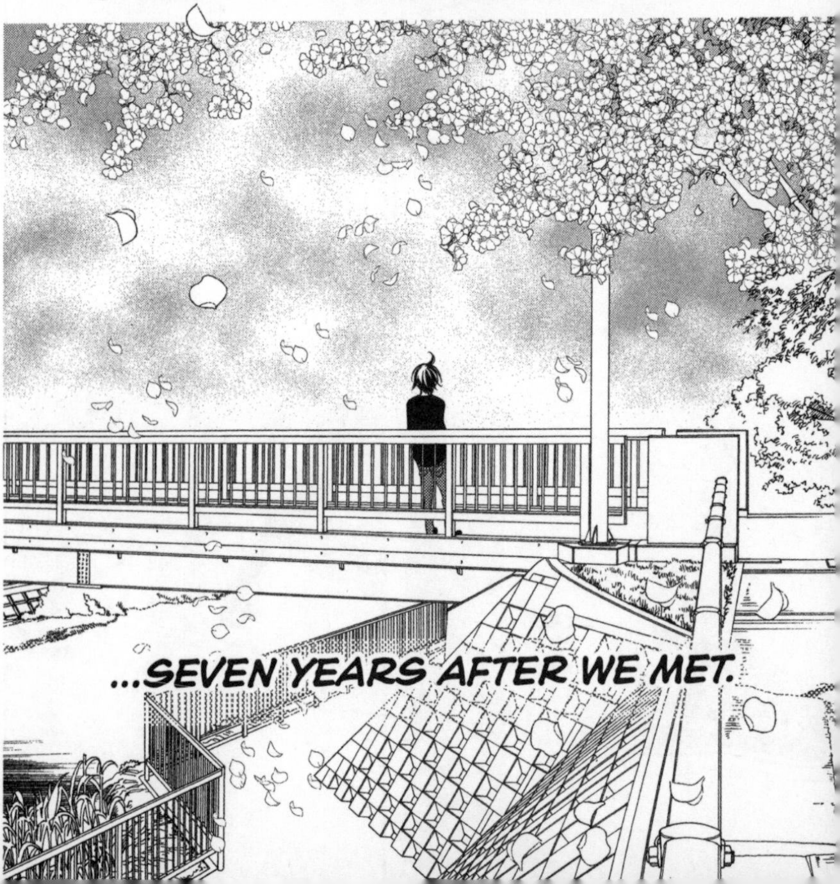
...SEVEN YEARS AFTER WE MET.

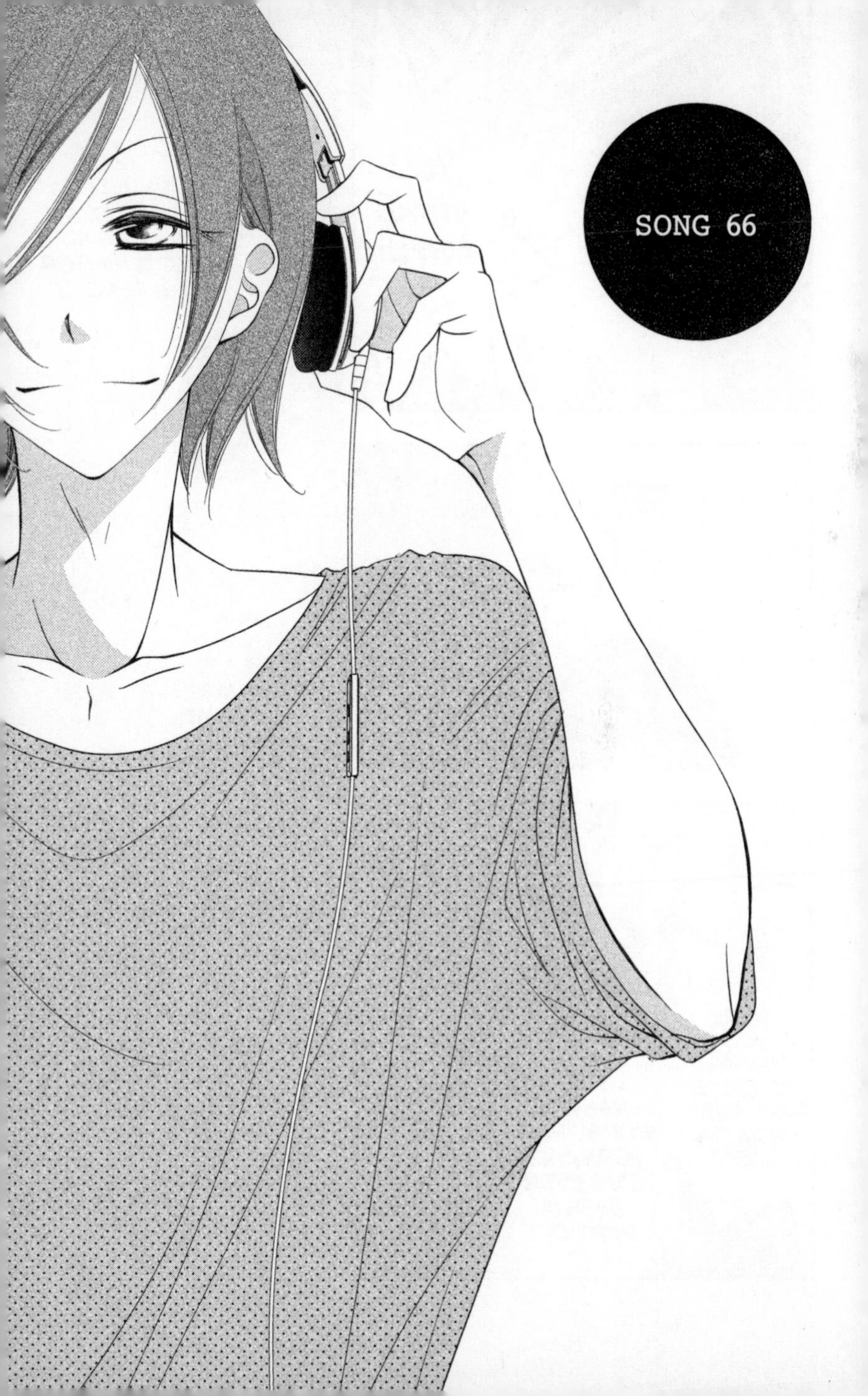
SONG 66

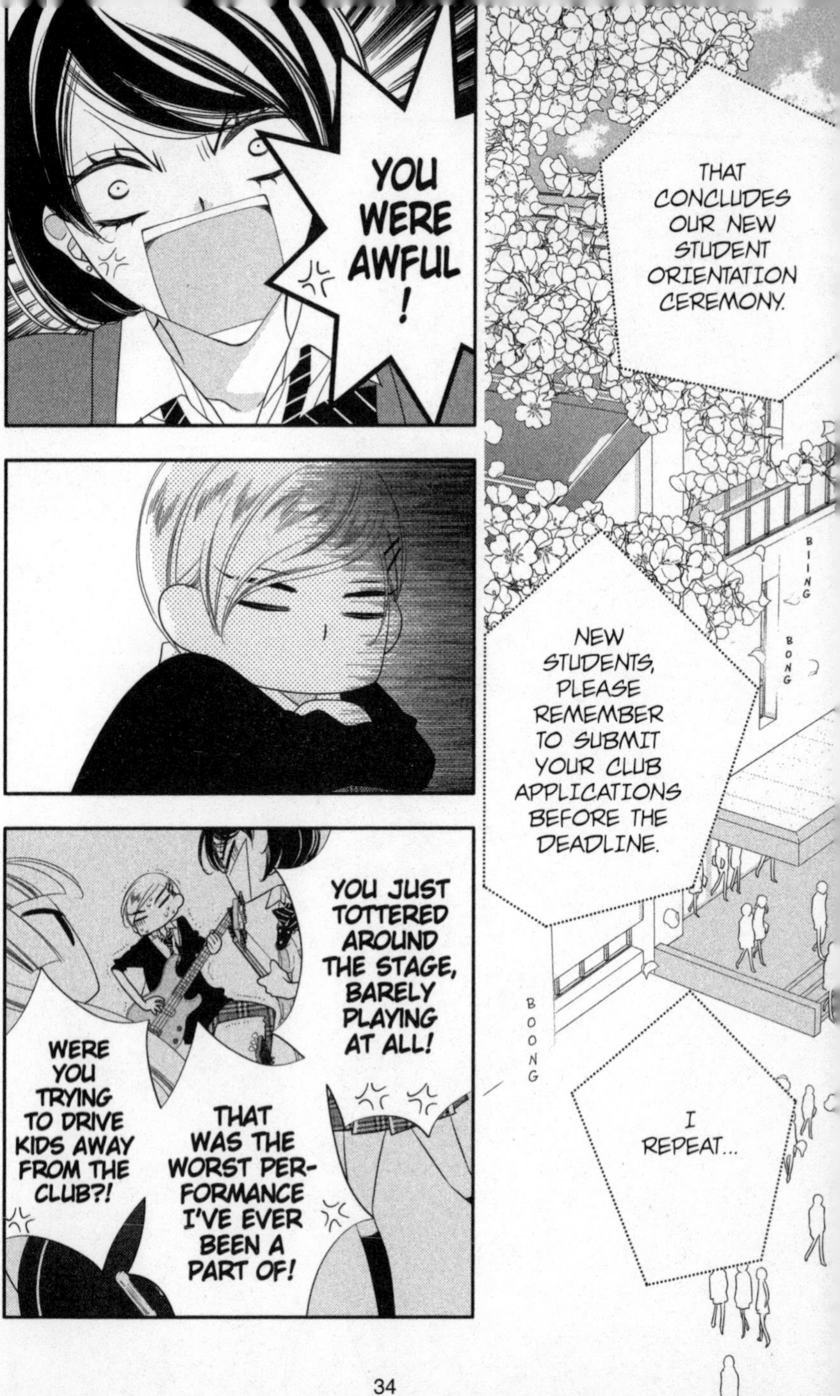
THAT CONCLUDES OUR NEW STUDENT ORIENTATION CEREMONY.
BIING
BONG
NEW STUDENTS, PLEASE REMEMBER TO SUBMIT YOUR CLUB APPLICATIONS BEFORE THE DEADLINE.
BOONG
I REPEAT...
YOU WERE AWFUL!
YOU JUST TOTTERED AROUND THE STAGE, BARELY PLAYING AT ALL!
THAT WAS THE WORST PERFORMANCE I'VE EVER BEEN A PART OF!
WERE YOU TRYING TO DRIVE KIDS AWAY FROM THE CLUB?!

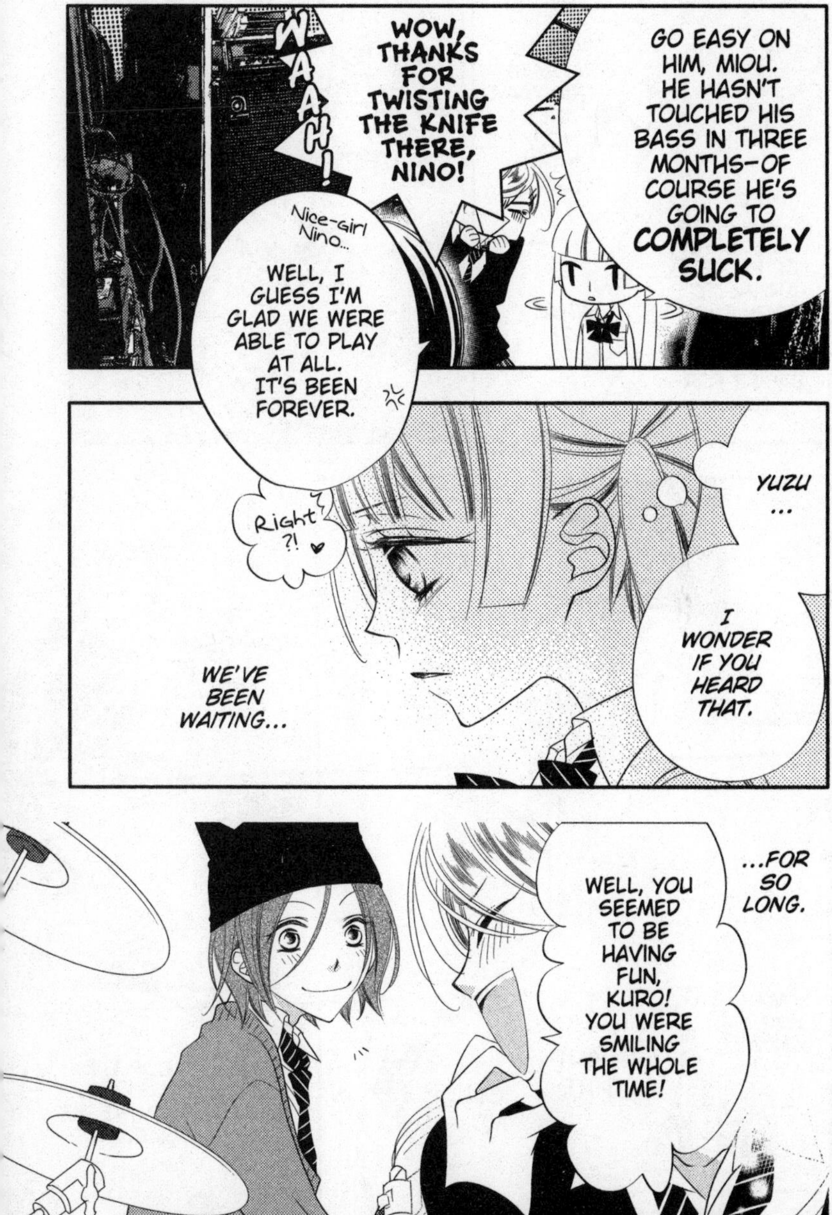
GO EASY ON HIM, MIOU. HE HASN'T TOUCHED HIS BASS IN THREE MONTHS—OF COURSE HE'S GOING TO **COMPLETELY SUCK.**
WOW, THANKS FOR TWISTING THE KNIFE THERE, NINO!
WAAH!
Nice-girl Nino...
WELL, I GUESS I'M GLAD WE WERE ABLE TO PLAY AT ALL. IT'S BEEN FOREVER.
YUZU...
I WONDER IF YOU HEARD THAT.
Right?!
WE'VE BEEN WAITING...
...FOR SO LONG.
WELL, YOU SEEMED TO BE HAVING FUN, KURO! YOU WERE SMILING THE WHOLE TIME!

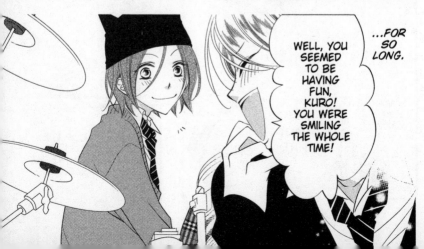

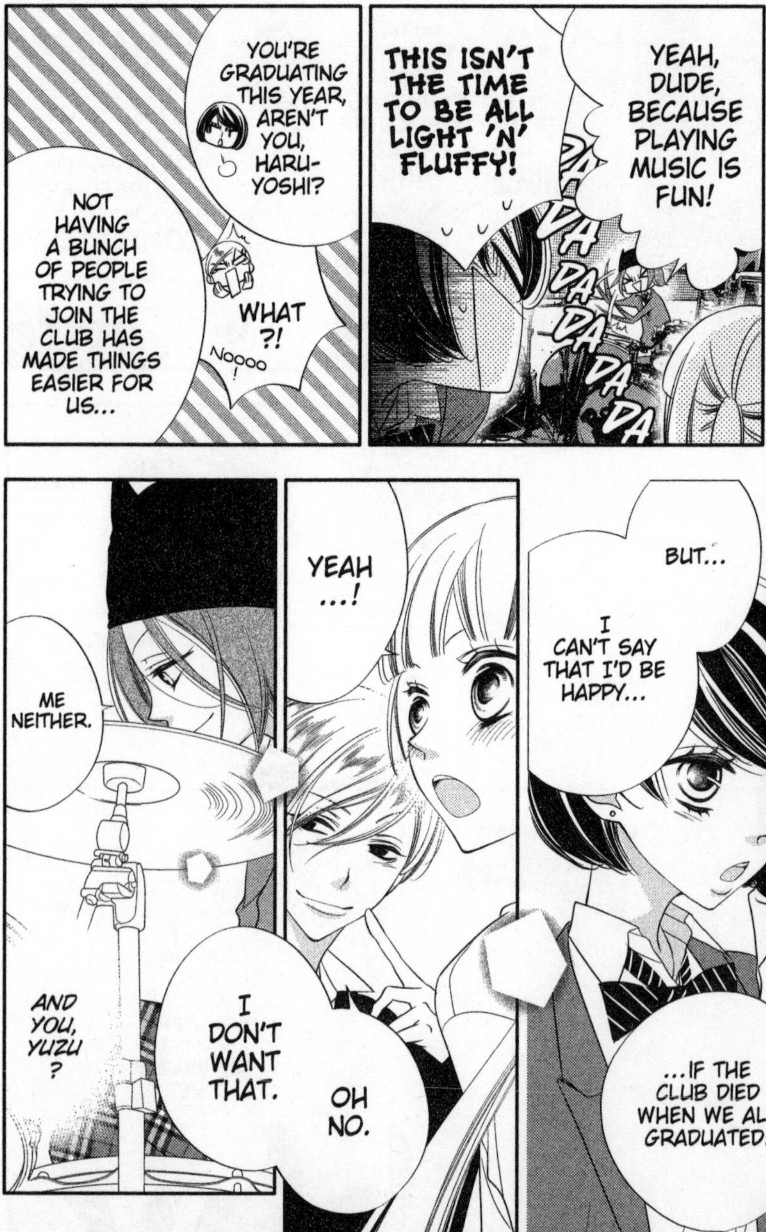
YEAH, DUDE, BECAUSE PLAYING MUSIC IS FUN!
THIS ISN'T THE TIME TO BE ALL LIGHT 'N' FLUFFY!
VA DA DA DA DA
YOU'RE GRADUATING THIS YEAR, AREN'T YOU, HARU-YOSHI?
WHAT?!
Noooo!
NOT HAVING A BUNCH OF PEOPLE TRYING TO JOIN THE CLUB HAS MADE THINGS EASIER FOR US...
BUT...
I CAN'T SAY THAT I'D BE HAPPY...
...IF THE CLUB DIED WHEN WE ALL GRADUATED.
YEAH...!
I DON'T WANT THAT.
OH NO.
ME NEITHER.
AND YOU, YUZU?

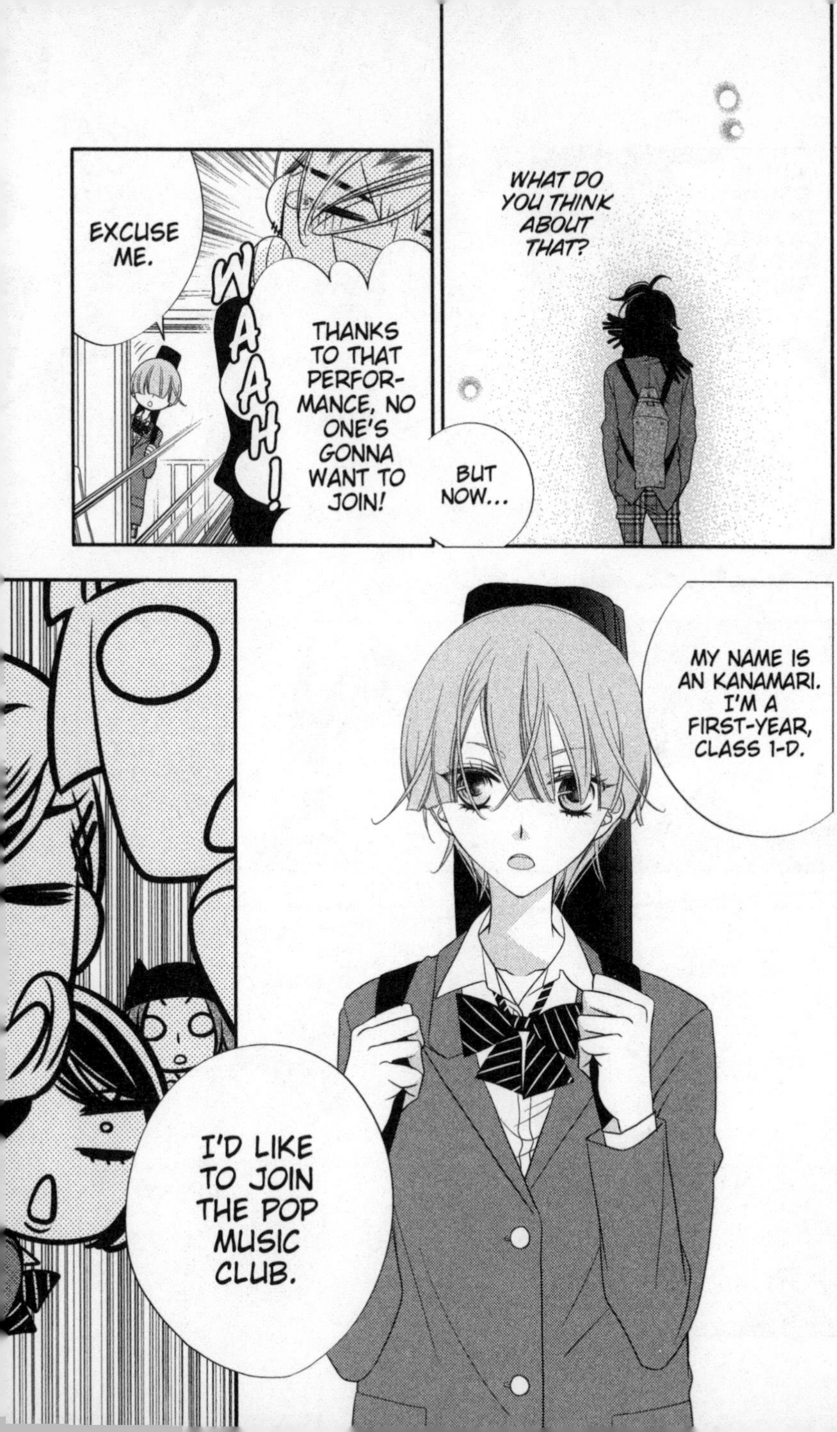
WHAT DO YOU THINK ABOUT THAT?
BUT NOW...
THANKS TO THAT PERFORMANCE, NO ONE'S GONNA WANT TO JOIN!
WAAH!
EXCUSE ME.
MY NAME IS AN KANAMARI. I'M A FIRST-YEAR, CLASS 1-D.
I'D LIKE TO JOIN THE POP MUSIC CLUB.

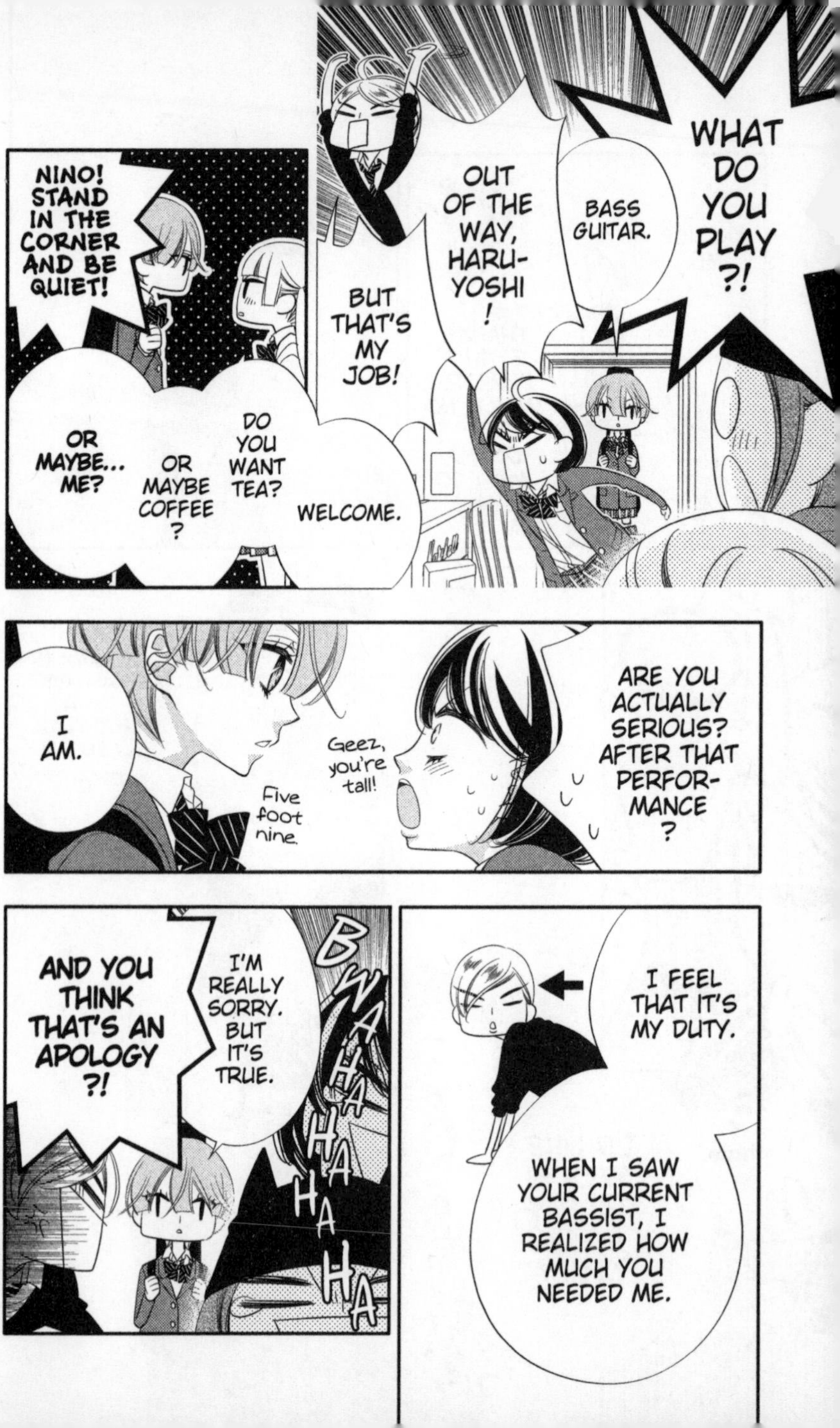
WHAT DO YOU PLAY?!
BASS GUITAR.
OUT OF THE WAY, HARUYOSHI!
BUT THAT'S MY JOB!
NINO! STAND IN THE CORNER AND BE QUIET!
WELCOME.
DO YOU WANT TEA?
OR MAYBE COFFEE?
OR MAYBE... ME?
ARE YOU ACTUALLY SERIOUS? AFTER THAT PERFORMANCE?
Geez, you're tall!
Five foot nine.
I AM.
I FEEL THAT IT'S MY DUTY.
WHEN I SAW YOUR CURRENT BASSIST, I REALIZED HOW MUCH YOU NEEDED ME.
BWAHAHAHAHAHA
I'M REALLY SORRY. BUT IT'S TRUE.
AND YOU THINK THAT'S AN APOLOGY?!

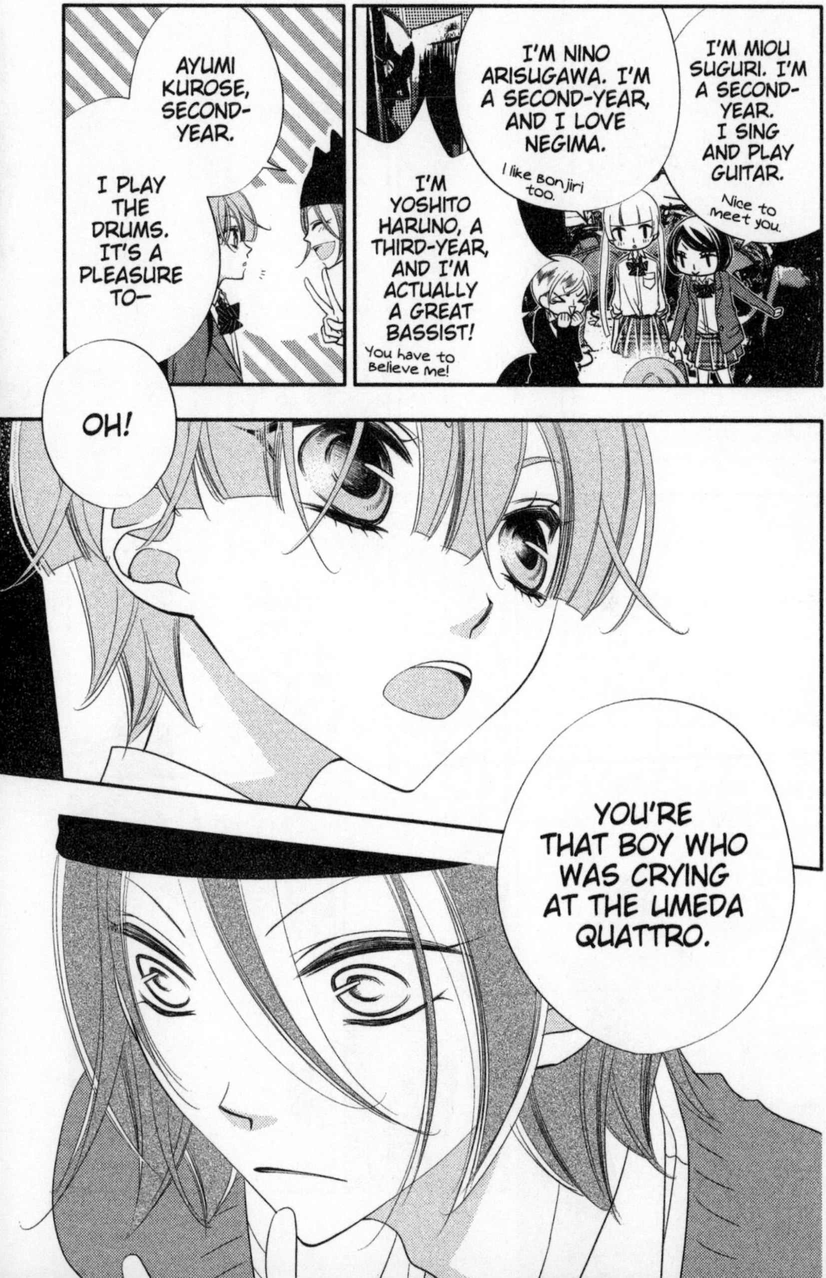
I'M MIOU SUGURI. I'M A SECOND-YEAR. I SING AND PLAY GUITAR.
Nice to meet you.
I'M NINO ARISUGAWA. I'M A SECOND-YEAR, AND I LOVE NEGIMA.
I like Bonjiri too.
I'M YOSHITO HARUNO, A THIRD-YEAR, AND I'M ACTUALLY A GREAT BASSIST!
You have to Believe me!
AYUMI KUROSE, SECOND-YEAR.
I PLAY THE DRUMS. IT'S A PLEASURE TO—
OH!
YOU'RE THAT BOY WHO WAS CRYING AT THE UMEDA QUATTRO.

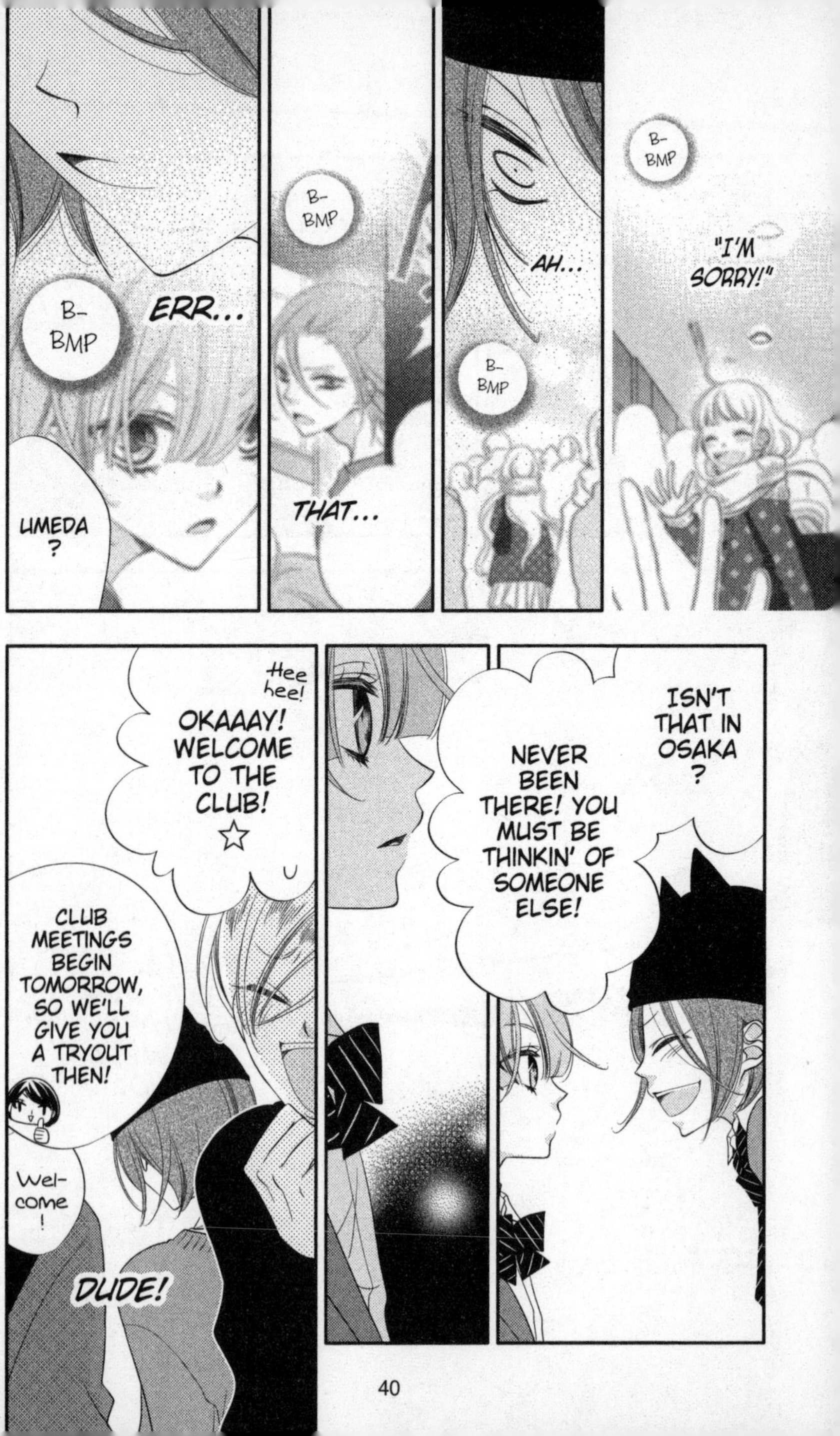
B-BMP
"I'M SORRY!"
AH...
B-BMP
B-BMP
THAT...
ERR...
B-BMP
UMEDA?
ISN'T THAT IN OSAKA?
NEVER BEEN THERE! YOU MUST BE THINKIN' OF SOMEONE ELSE!
Hee hee!
OKAAAY! WELCOME TO THE CLUB! ☆
CLUB MEETINGS BEGIN TOMORROW, SO WE'LL GIVE YOU A TRYOUT THEN!
Wel-come!
DUDE!

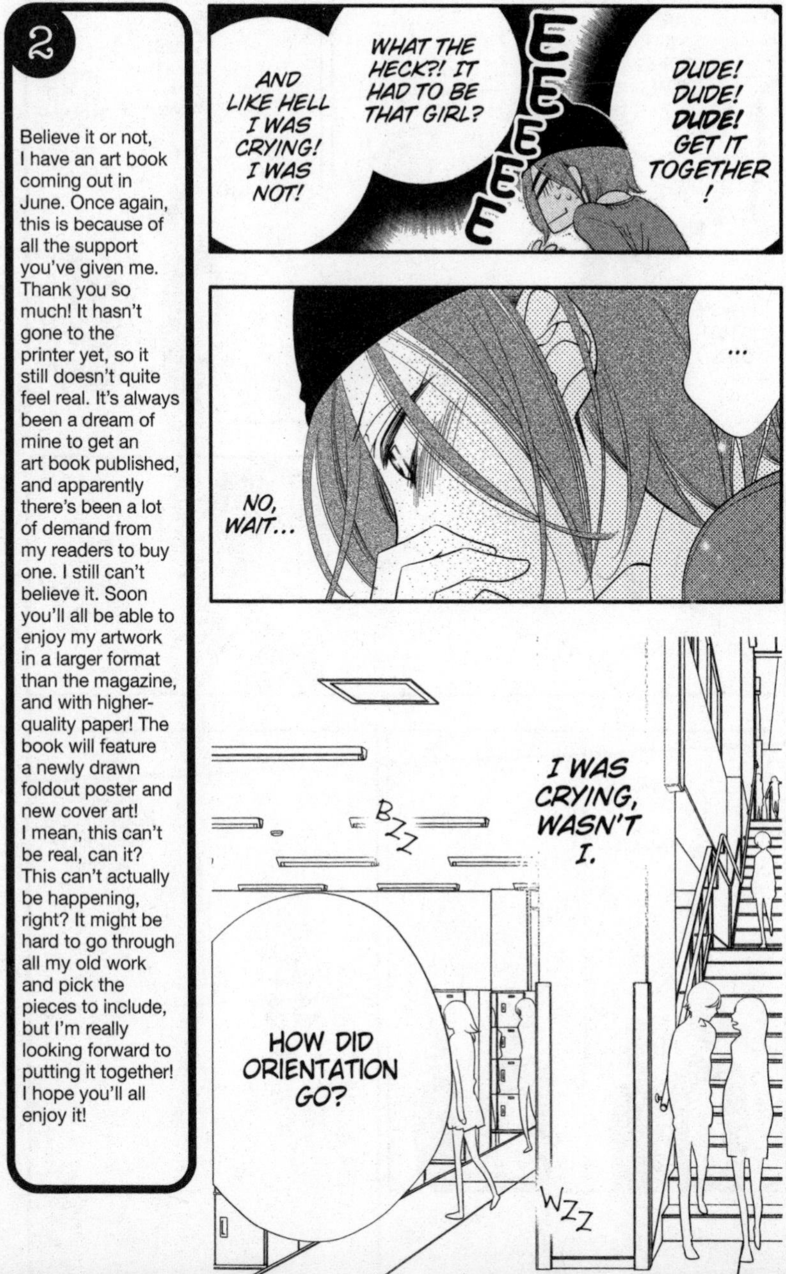
DUDE! DUDE! DUDE! GET IT TOGETHER!
EEEEEE
WHAT THE HECK?! IT HAD TO BE THAT GIRL?
AND LIKE HELL I WAS CRYING! I WAS NOT!
...
NO, WAIT...
I WAS CRYING, WASN'T I.
BZZ
HOW DID ORIENTATION GO?
WZZ

2

Believe it or not, I have an art book coming out in June. Once again, this is because of all the support you've given me. Thank you so much! It hasn't gone to the printer yet, so it still doesn't quite feel real. It's always been a dream of mine to get an art book published, and apparently there's been a lot of demand from my readers to buy one. I still can't believe it. Soon you'll all be able to enjoy my artwork in a larger format than the magazine, and with higher-quality paper! The book will feature a newly drawn foldout poster and new cover art! I mean, this can't be real, can it? This can't actually be happening, right? It might be hard to go through all my old work and pick the pieces to include, but I'm really looking forward to putting it together! I hope you'll all enjoy it!

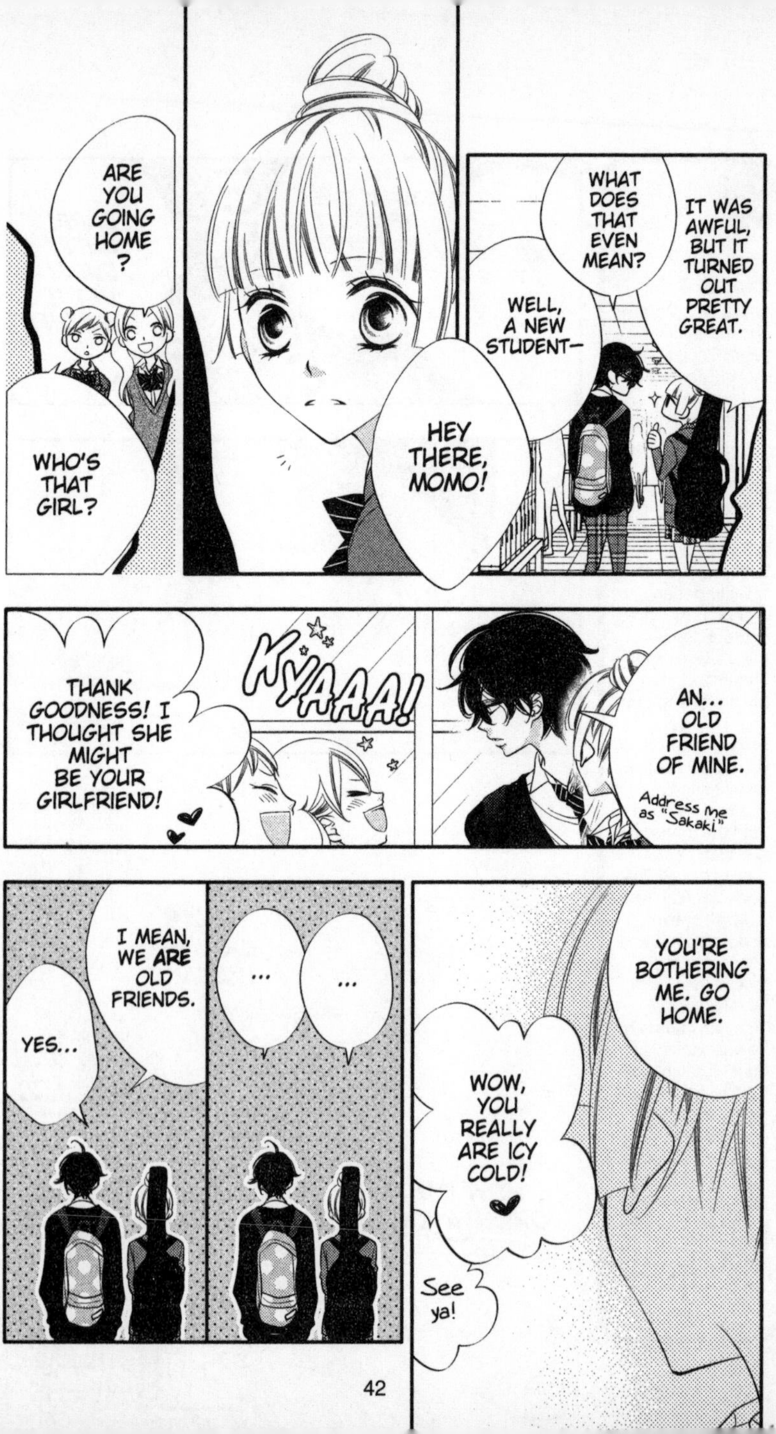
IT WAS AWFUL, BUT IT TURNED OUT PRETTY GREAT.
WHAT DOES THAT EVEN MEAN?
WELL, A NEW STUDENT—
HEY THERE, MOMO!
ARE YOU GOING HOME?
WHO'S THAT GIRL?
AN... OLD FRIEND OF MINE.
Address me as "Sakaki."
KYAAA!
THANK GOODNESS! I THOUGHT SHE MIGHT BE YOUR GIRLFRIEND!
YOU'RE BOTHERING ME. GO HOME.
WOW, YOU REALLY ARE ICY COLD!
See ya!
...
...
I MEAN, WE ARE OLD FRIENDS.
YES...

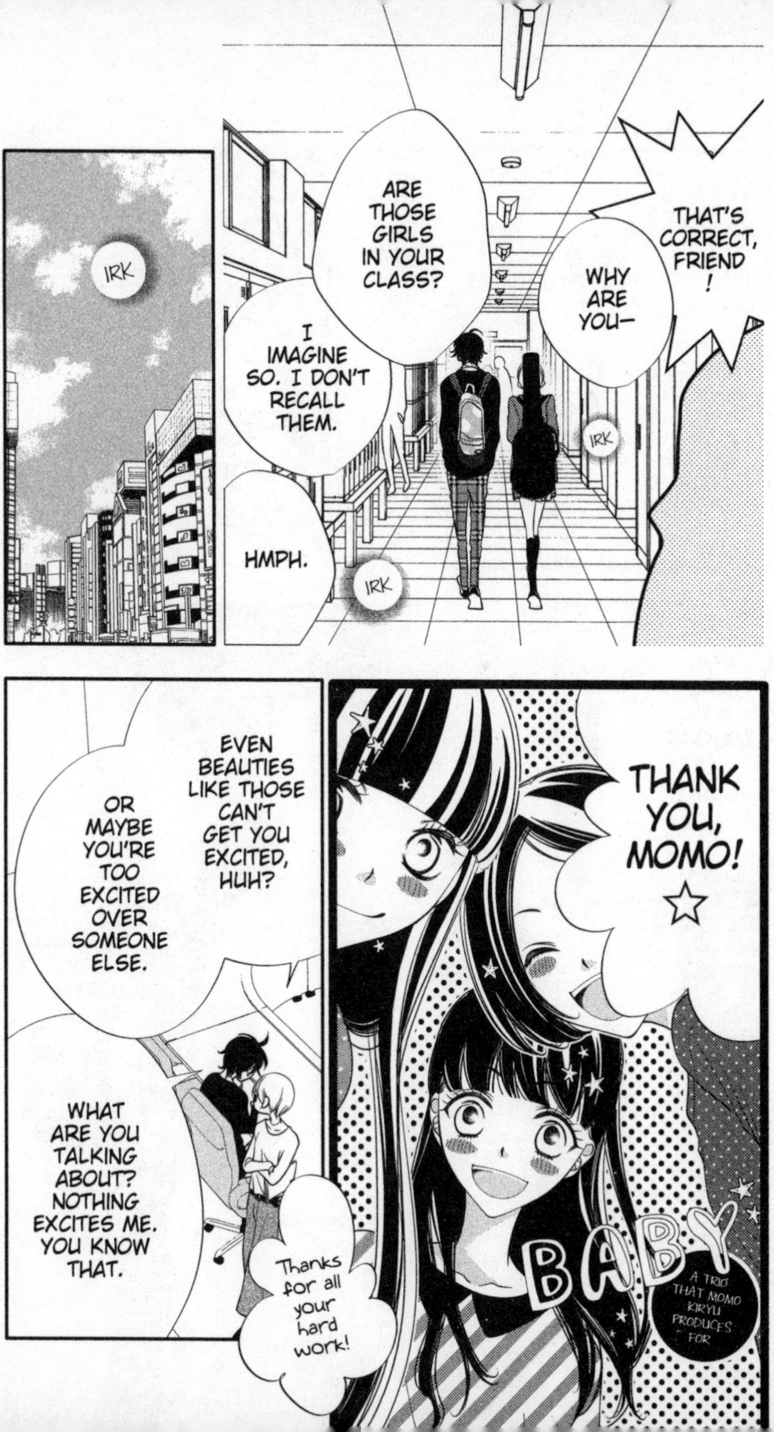
THAT'S CORRECT, FRIEND!
WHY ARE YOU—
ARE THOSE GIRLS IN YOUR CLASS?
IRK
I IMAGINE SO. I DON'T RECALL THEM.
HMPH.
IRK
IRK
THANK YOU, MOMO! ☆
BABY
A TRIO THAT MOMO KIRYU PRODUCES FOR
EVEN BEAUTIES LIKE THOSE CAN'T GET YOU EXCITED, HUH?
OR MAYBE YOU'RE TOO EXCITED OVER SOMEONE ELSE.
WHAT ARE YOU TALKING ABOUT? NOTHING EXCITES ME. YOU KNOW THAT.
Thanks for all your hard work!

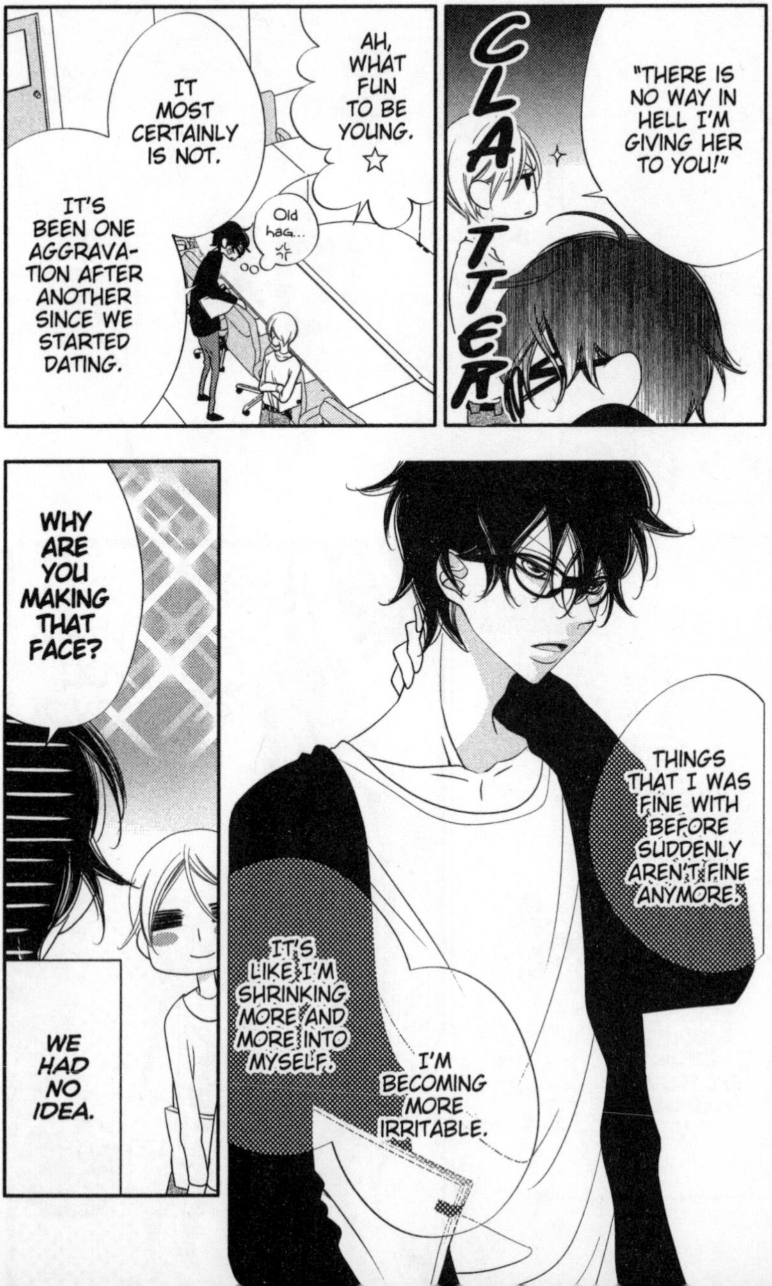
CLATTER
"THERE IS NO WAY IN HELL I'M GIVING HER TO YOU!"
AH, WHAT FUN TO BE YOUNG. ☆
IT MOST CERTAINLY IS NOT.
Old hag...
IT'S BEEN ONE AGGRAVATION AFTER ANOTHER SINCE WE STARTED DATING.
THINGS THAT I WAS FINE WITH BEFORE SUDDENLY AREN'T FINE ANYMORE.
IT'S LIKE I'M SHRINKING MORE AND MORE INTO MYSELF.
I'M BECOMING MORE IRRITABLE.
WHY ARE YOU MAKING THAT FACE?
WE HAD NO IDEA.

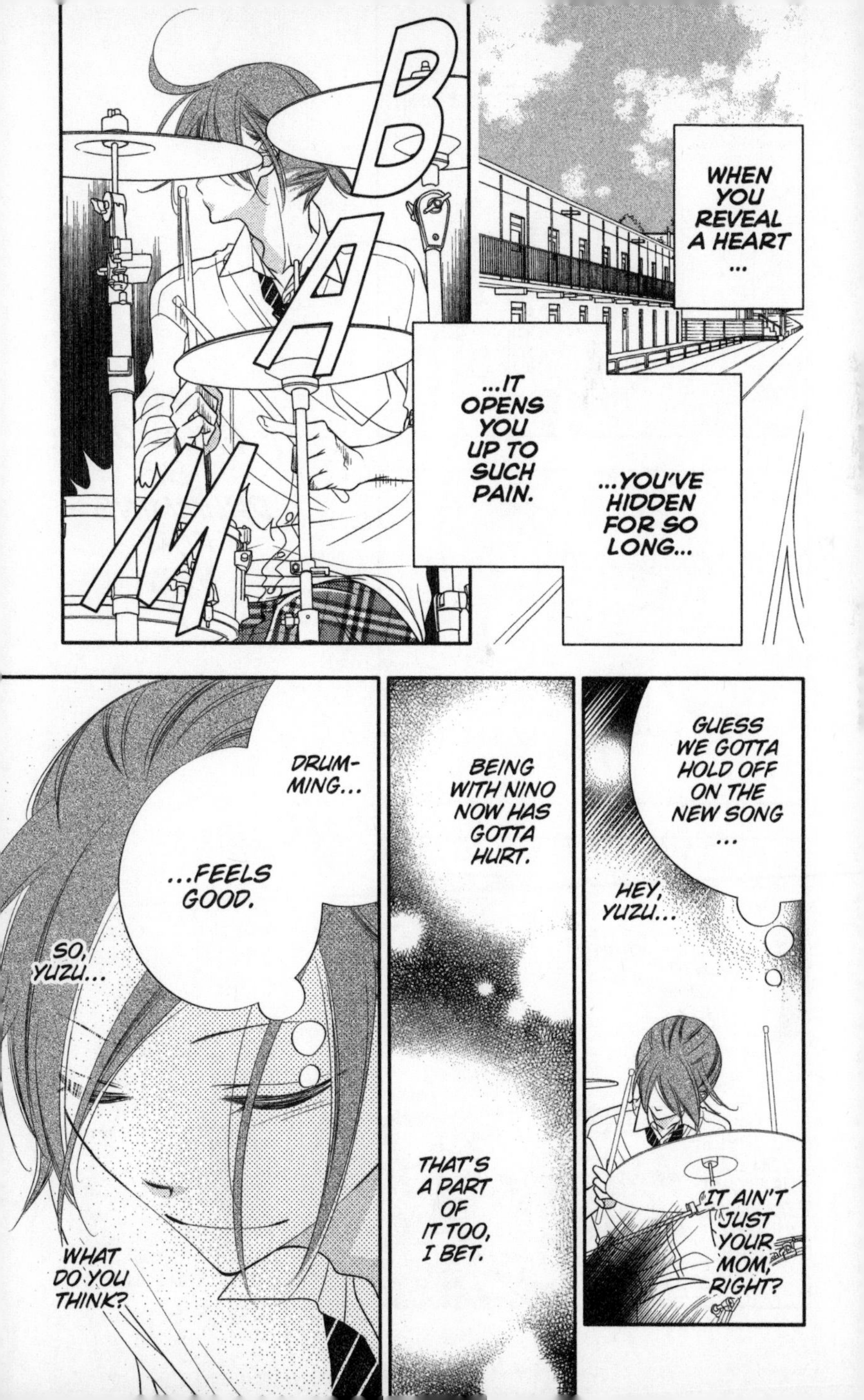
WHEN YOU REVEAL A HEART...
...YOU'VE HIDDEN FOR SO LONG...
...IT OPENS YOU UP TO SUCH PAIN.
BAM
GUESS WE GOTTA HOLD OFF ON THE NEW SONG...
HEY, YUZU...
IT AIN'T JUST YOUR MOM, RIGHT?
BEING WITH NINO NOW HAS GOTTA HURT.
THAT'S A PART OF IT TOO, I BET.
DRUM-MING...
...FEELS GOOD.
SO, YUZU...
WHAT DO YOU THINK?

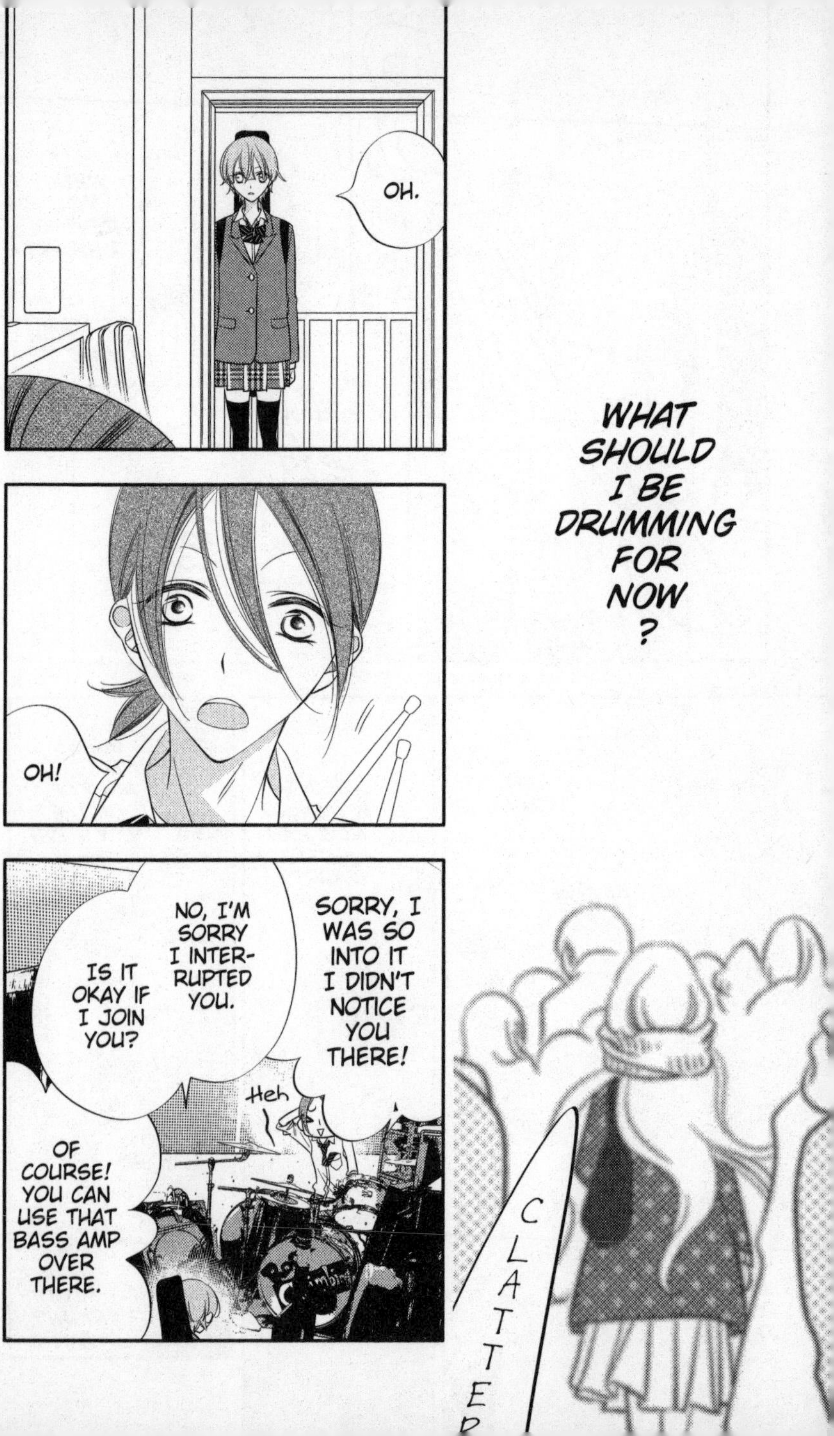
WHAT SHOULD I BE DRUMMING FOR NOW ?
CLATTER
OH.
OH!
SORRY, I WAS SO INTO IT I DIDN'T NOTICE YOU THERE!
NO, I'M SORRY I INTER-RUPTED YOU.
IS IT OKAY IF I JOIN YOU?
Heh
OF COURSE! YOU CAN USE THAT BASS AMP OVER THERE.

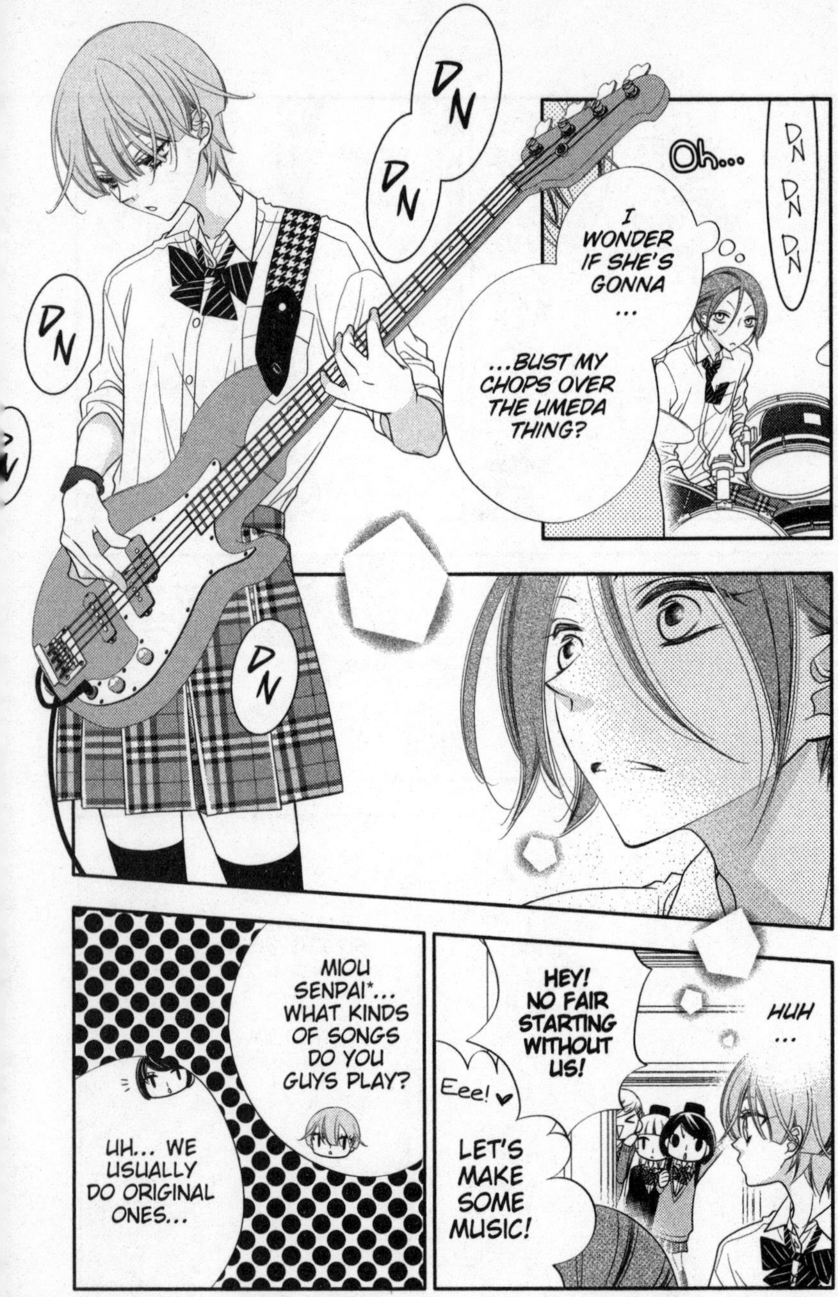
DN DN DN DN
Oh...
I WONDER IF SHE'S GONNA ...
...BUST MY CHOPS OVER THE UMEDA THING?
DN DN
DN
DN
HUH ...
HEY! NO FAIR STARTING WITHOUT US!
Eee! ♥
LET'S MAKE SOME MUSIC!
MIOU SENPAI*... WHAT KINDS OF SONGS DO YOU GUYS PLAY?
UH... WE USUALLY DO ORIGINAL ONES...

*Senpai is an honorific used for upperclassmen.

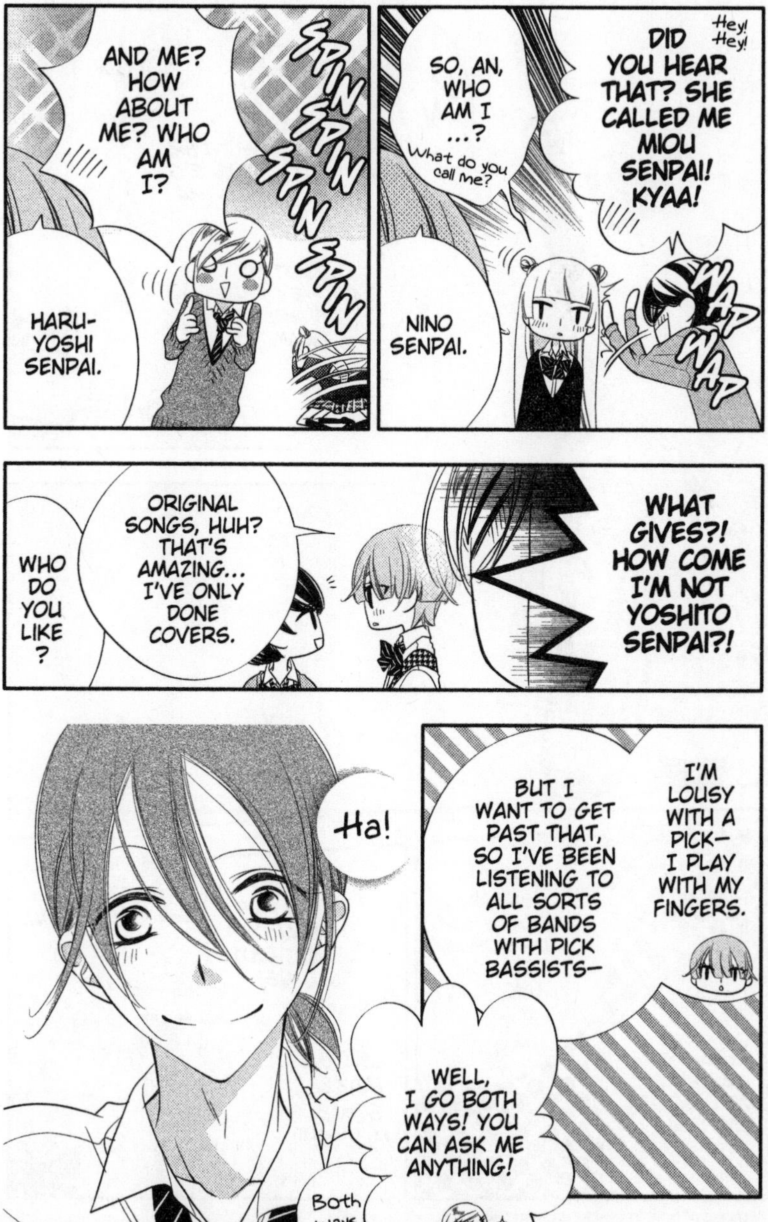
Hey! Hey!
DID YOU HEAR THAT? SHE CALLED ME MIOU SENPAI! KYAA!
SO, AN, WHO AM I ...?
What do you call me?
NINO SENPAI.
WAP WAP
AND ME? HOW ABOUT ME? WHO AM I?
SPIN SPIN SPIN SPIN
HARU-YOSHI SENPAI.
WHAT GIVES?! HOW COME I'M NOT YOSHITO SENPAI?!
ORIGINAL SONGS, HUH? THAT'S AMAZING... I'VE ONLY DONE COVERS.
WHO DO YOU LIKE?
I'M LOUSY WITH A PICK— I PLAY WITH MY FINGERS.
BUT I WANT TO GET PAST THAT, SO I'VE BEEN LISTENING TO ALL SORTS OF BANDS WITH PICK BASSISTS—
Ha!
WELL, I GO BOTH WAYS! YOU CAN ASK ME ANYTHING!
Both ways, huh?

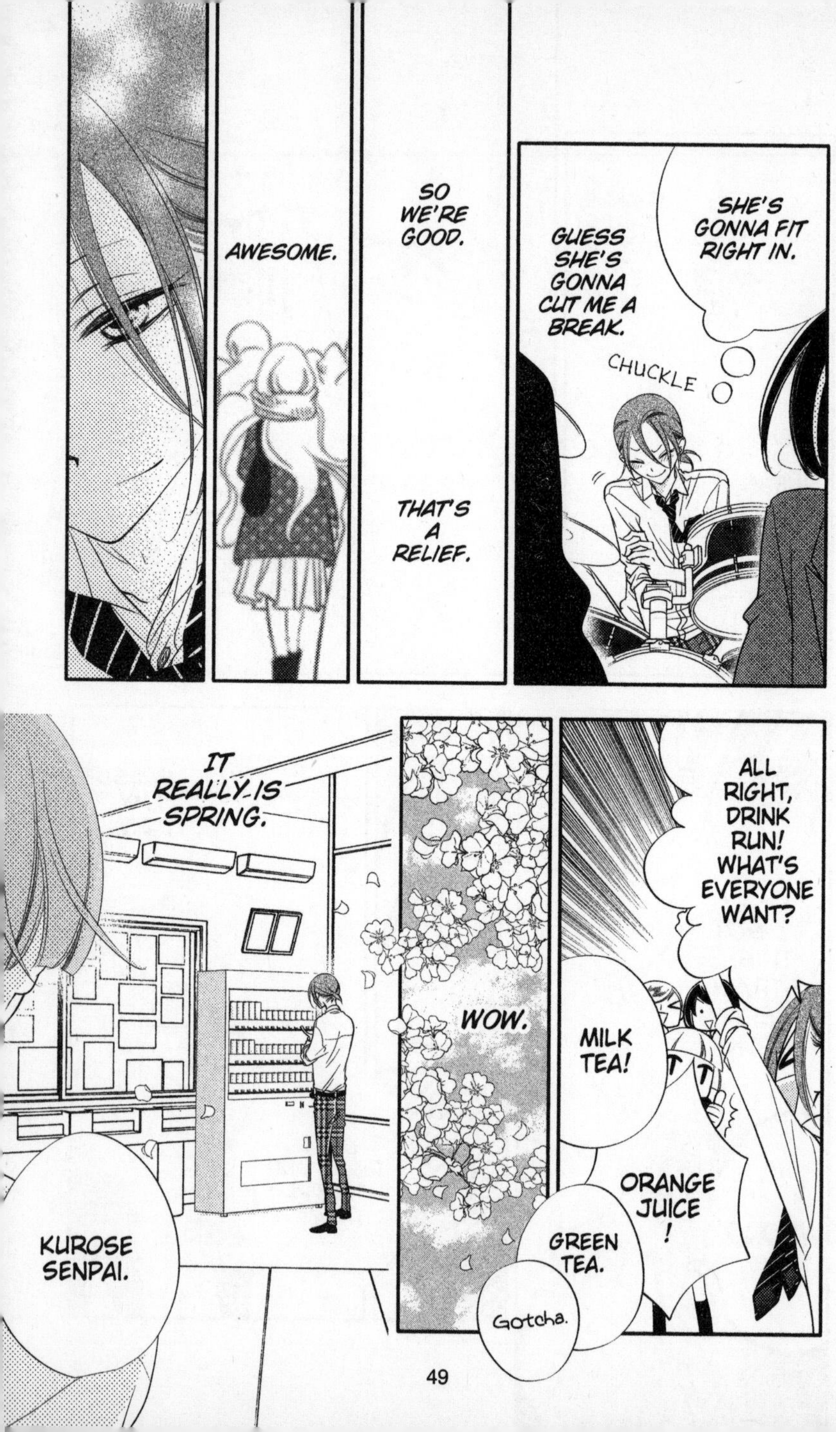

SHE'S GONNA FIT RIGHT IN.
GUESS SHE'S GONNA CUT ME A BREAK.
CHUCKLE
SO WE'RE GOOD.
THAT'S A RELIEF.
AWESOME.
ALL RIGHT, DRINK RUN! WHAT'S EVERYONE WANT?
MILK TEA!
ORANGE JUICE!
GREEN TEA.
Gotcha.
WOW.
IT REALLY IS SPRING.
KUROSE SENPAI.

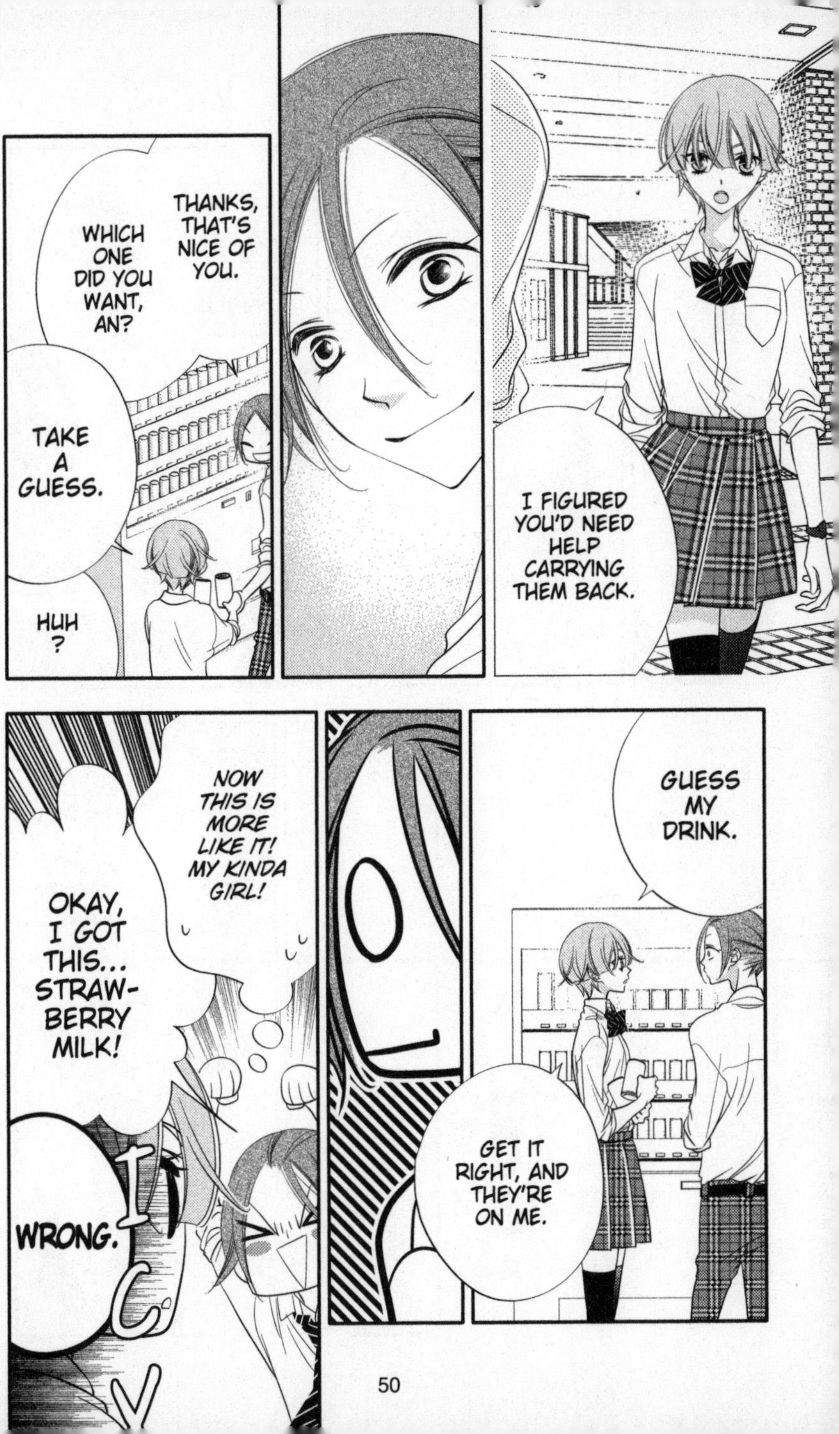
I FIGURED YOU'D NEED HELP CARRYING THEM BACK.
THANKS, THAT'S NICE OF YOU.
WHICH ONE DID YOU WANT, AN?
TAKE A GUESS.
HUH?
GUESS MY DRINK.
GET IT RIGHT, AND THEY'RE ON ME.
NOW THIS IS MORE LIKE IT! MY KINDA GIRL!
OKAY, I GOT THIS... STRAWBERRY MILK!
WRONG.

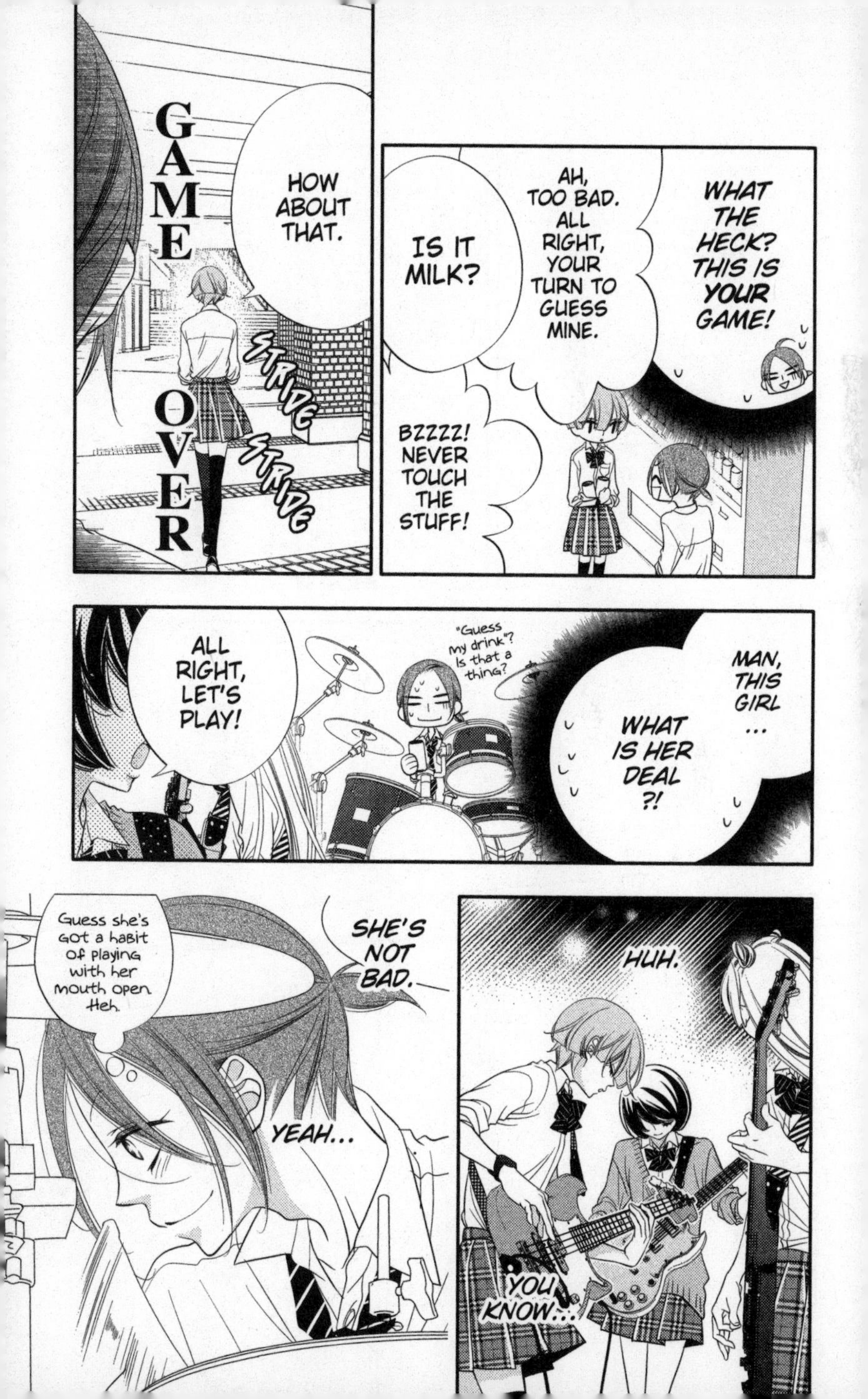

WHAT THE HECK? THIS IS YOUR GAME!
AH, TOO BAD. ALL RIGHT, YOUR TURN TO GUESS MINE.
IS IT MILK?
BZZZZ! NEVER TOUCH THE STUFF!
HOW ABOUT THAT.
GAME OVER
STRIDE STRIDE
MAN, THIS GIRL...
WHAT IS HER DEAL?!
"Guess my drink"? Is that a thing?
ALL RIGHT, LET'S PLAY!
HUH.
YOU KNOW...
SHE'S NOT BAD.
Guess she's got a habit of playing with her mouth open. Heh.
YEAH...

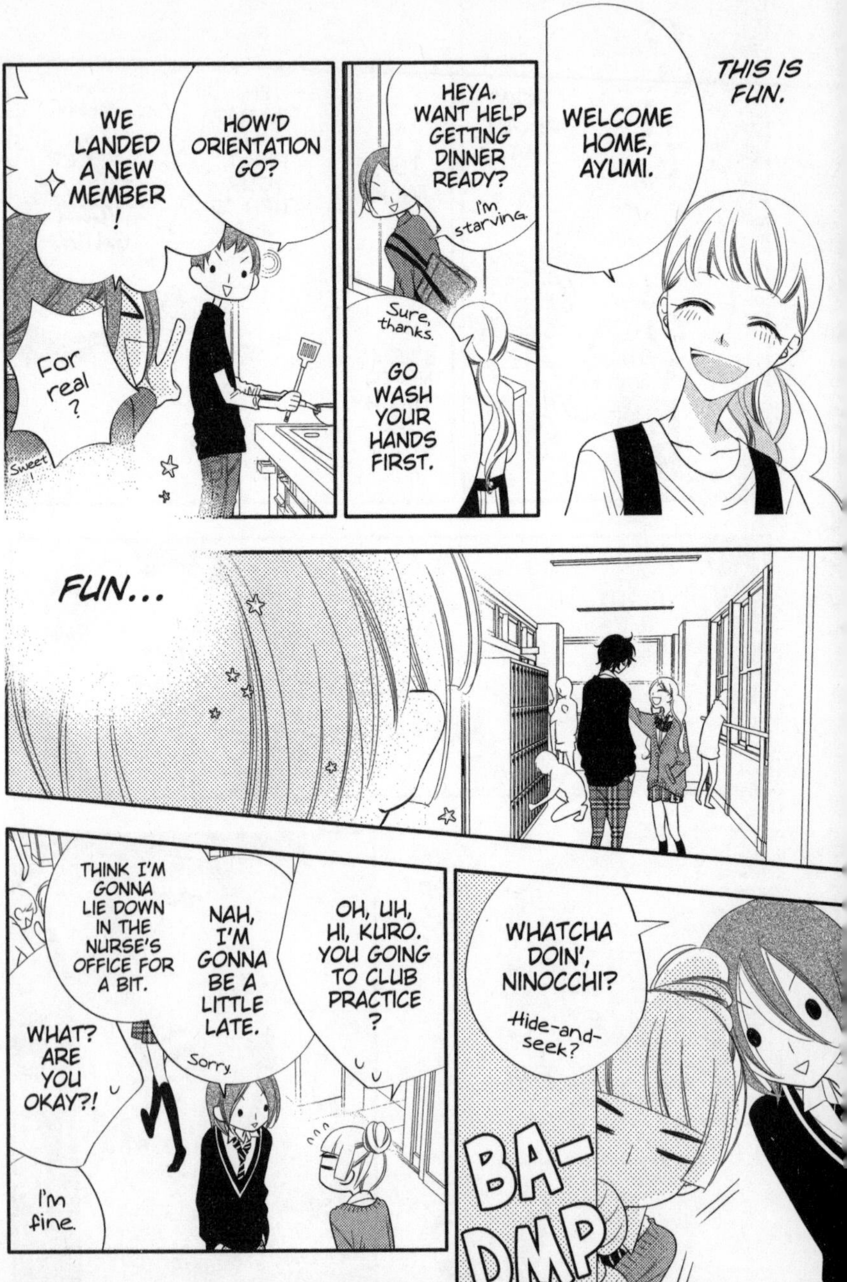
THIS IS FUN.
WELCOME HOME, AYUMI.
HEYA. WANT HELP GETTING DINNER READY?
I'm starving.
Sure, thanks.
GO WASH YOUR HANDS FIRST.
HOW'D ORIENTATION GO?
WE LANDED A NEW MEMBER!
For real?
Sweet!
FUN...
WHATCHA DOIN', NINOCCHI?
Hide-and-seek?
BA-DMP
OH, UH, HI, KURO. YOU GOING TO CLUB PRACTICE?
NAH, I'M GONNA BE A LITTLE LATE.
Sorry.
THINK I'M GONNA LIE DOWN IN THE NURSE'S OFFICE FOR A BIT.
WHAT? ARE YOU OKAY?!
I'm fine.

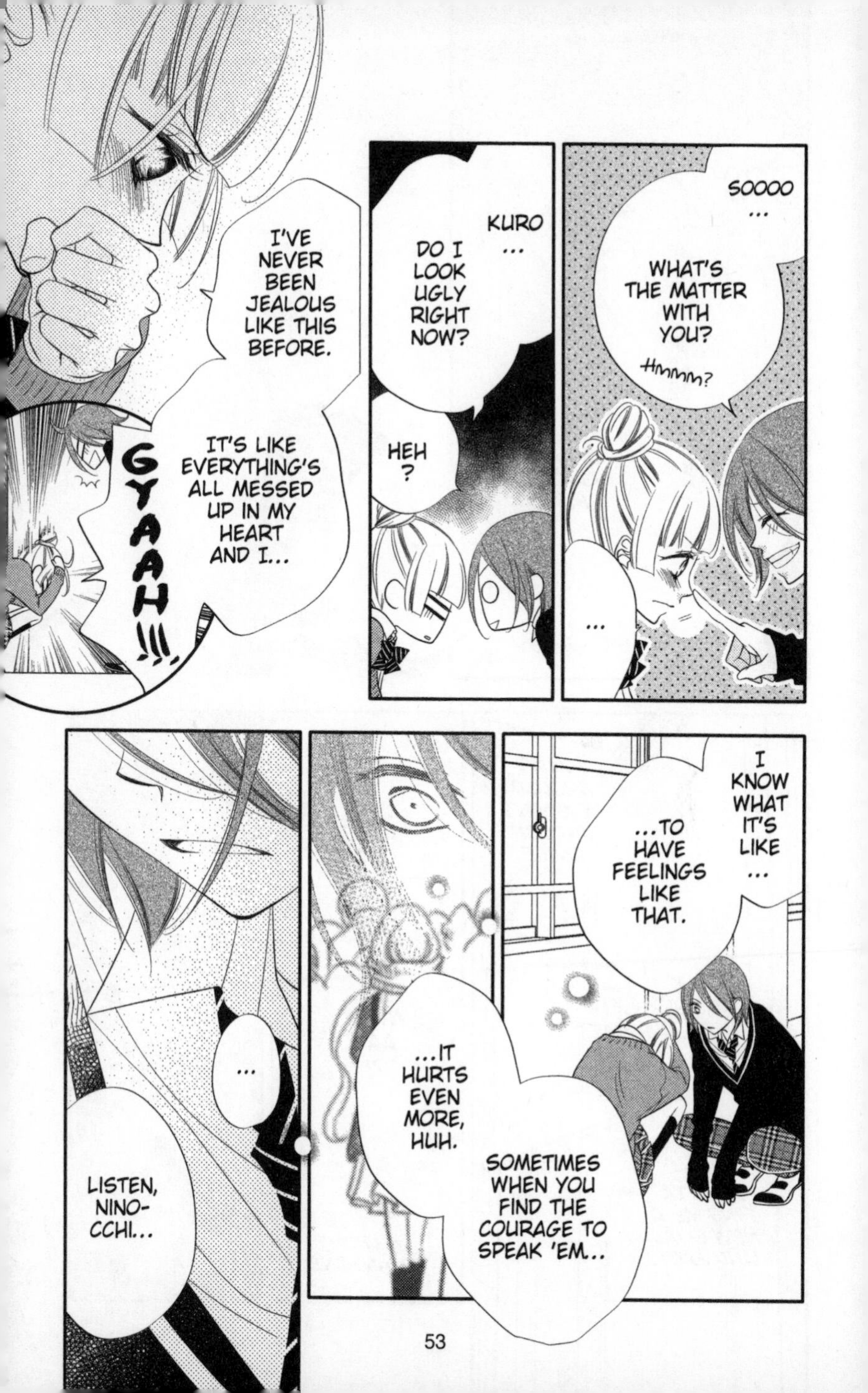
SOOOO...
WHAT'S THE MATTER WITH YOU?
Hmmm?
...
KURO...
DO I LOOK UGLY RIGHT NOW?
HEH?
I'VE NEVER BEEN JEALOUS LIKE THIS BEFORE.
IT'S LIKE EVERYTHING'S ALL MESSED UP IN MY HEART AND I...
GYAAH!!!
I KNOW WHAT IT'S LIKE...
...TO HAVE FEELINGS LIKE THAT.
SOMETIMES WHEN YOU FIND THE COURAGE TO SPEAK 'EM...
...IT HURTS EVEN MORE, HUH.
...
LISTEN, NINO-CCHI...

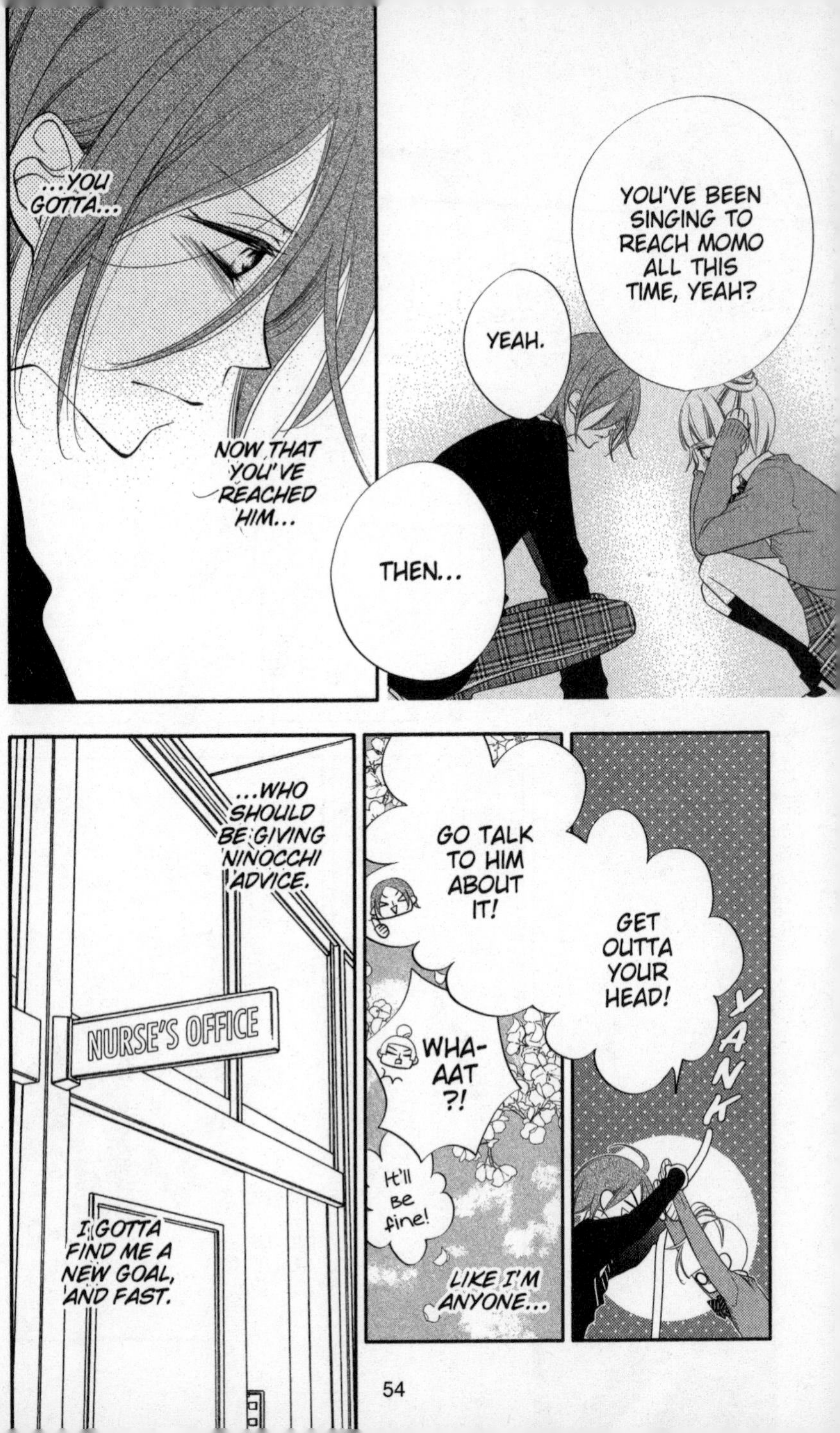
YOU'VE BEEN SINGING TO REACH MOMO ALL THIS TIME, YEAH?
YEAH.
THEN...
...YOU GOTTA...
NOW THAT YOU'VE REACHED HIM...
GET OUTTA YOUR HEAD!
YANK
GO TALK TO HIM ABOUT IT!
WHA-AAT?!
It'll be fine!
LIKE I'M ANYONE...
...WHO SHOULD BE GIVING NINOCCHI ADVICE.
NURSE'S OFFICE
I GOTTA FIND ME A NEW GOAL, AND FAST.

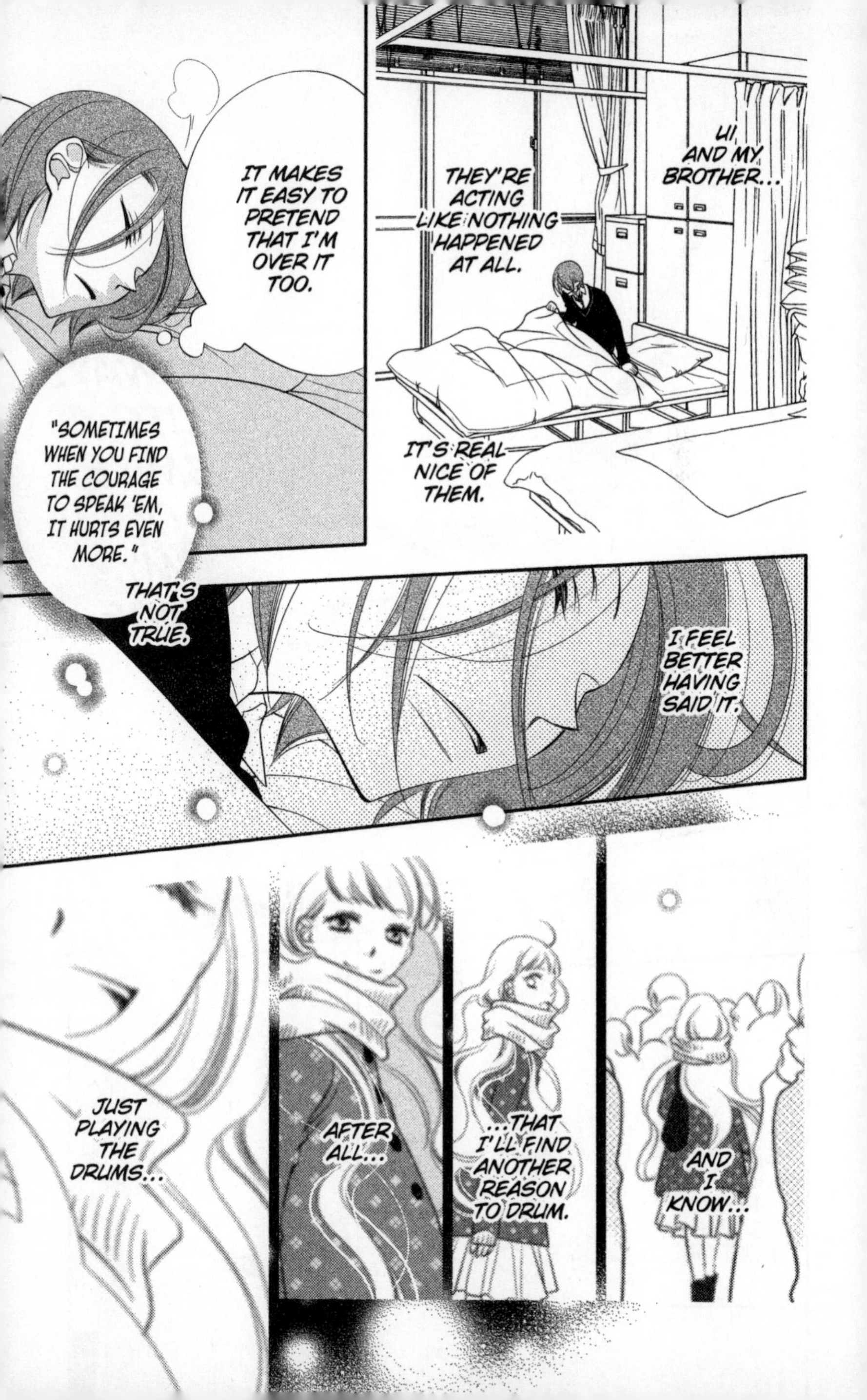
UI, AND MY BROTHER...
THEY'RE ACTING LIKE NOTHING HAPPENED AT ALL.
IT'S REAL NICE OF THEM.
IT MAKES IT EASY TO PRETEND THAT I'M OVER IT TOO.
"SOMETIMES WHEN YOU FIND THE COURAGE TO SPEAK 'EM, IT HURTS EVEN MORE."
THAT'S NOT TRUE.
I FEEL BETTER HAVING SAID IT.
AND I KNOW...
...THAT I'LL FIND ANOTHER REASON TO DRUM.
AFTER ALL...
JUST PLAYING THE DRUMS...

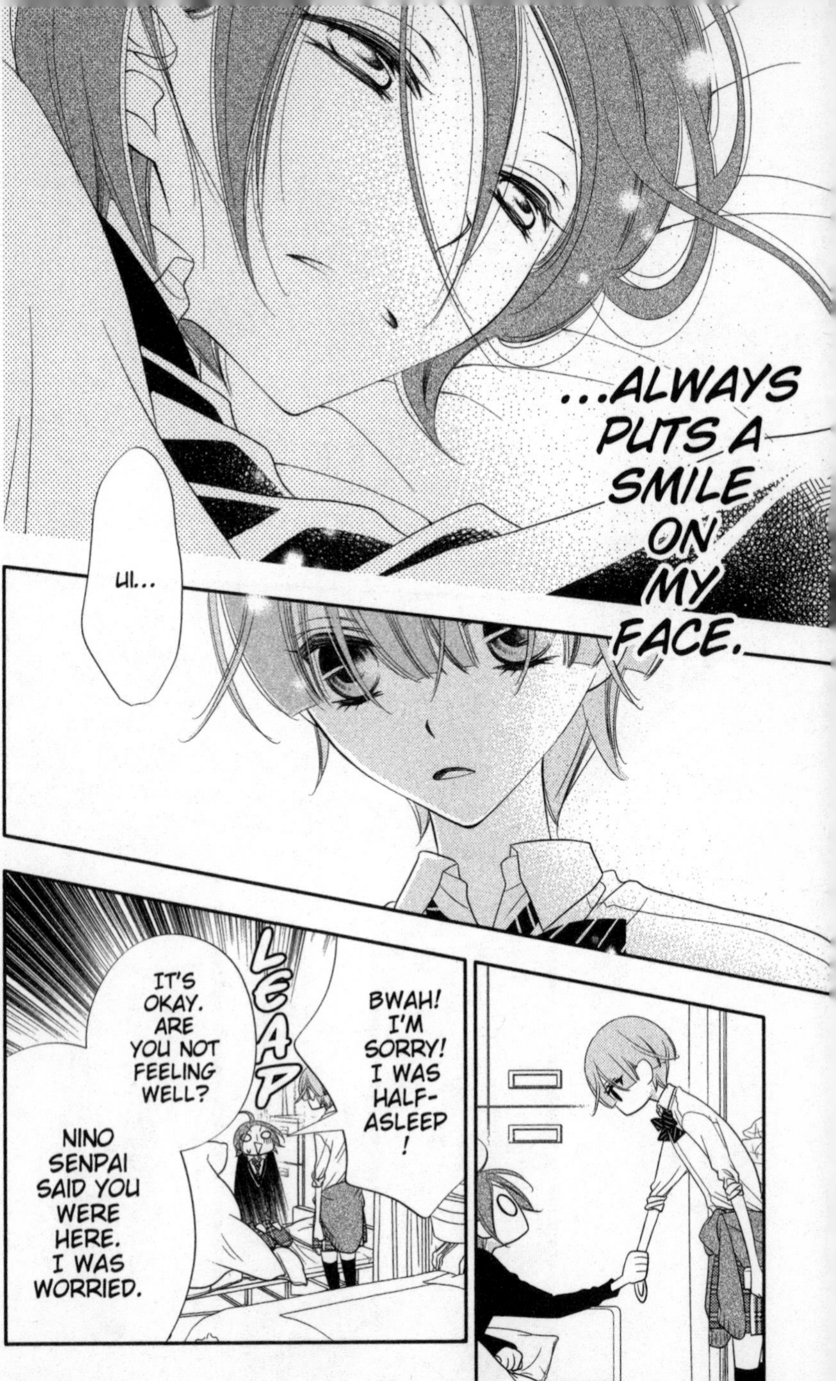
...ALWAYS PUTS A SMILE ON MY FACE.
UI...
BWAH! I'M SORRY! I WAS HALF-ASLEEP!
LEAP
IT'S OKAY. ARE YOU NOT FEELING WELL?
NINO SENPAI SAID YOU WERE HERE. I WAS WORRIED.

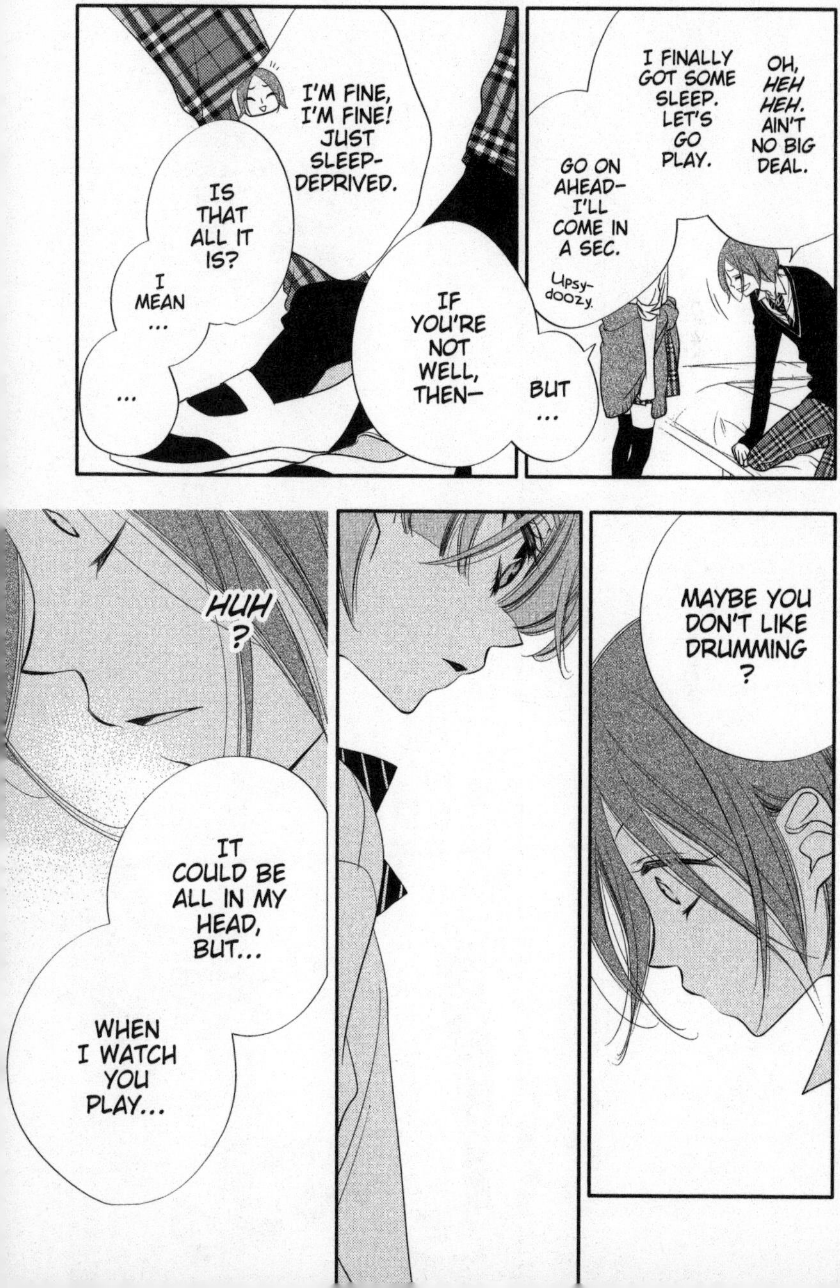
OH, *HEH HEH.* AIN'T NO BIG DEAL.
I FINALLY GOT SOME SLEEP. LET'S GO PLAY.
GO ON AHEAD— I'LL COME IN A SEC.
Upsy-doozy.
I'M FINE, I'M FINE! JUST SLEEP-DEPRIVED.
IF YOU'RE NOT WELL, THEN—
BUT ...
IS THAT ALL IT IS?
I MEAN ...
...
MAYBE YOU DON'T LIKE DRUMMING?
HUH?
IT COULD BE ALL IN MY HEAD, BUT...
WHEN I WATCH YOU PLAY...

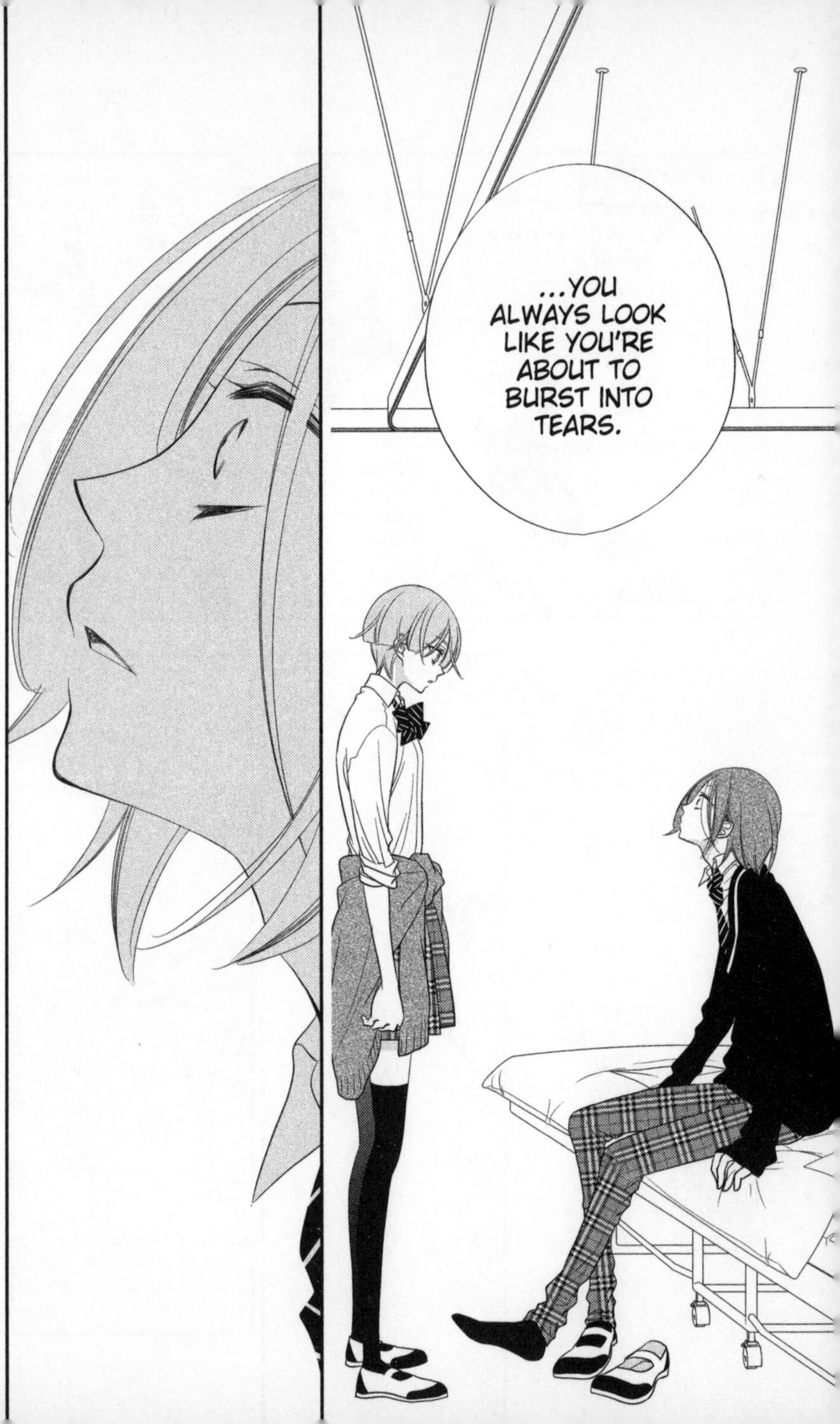
...YOU ALWAYS LOOK LIKE YOU'RE ABOUT TO BURST INTO TEARS.

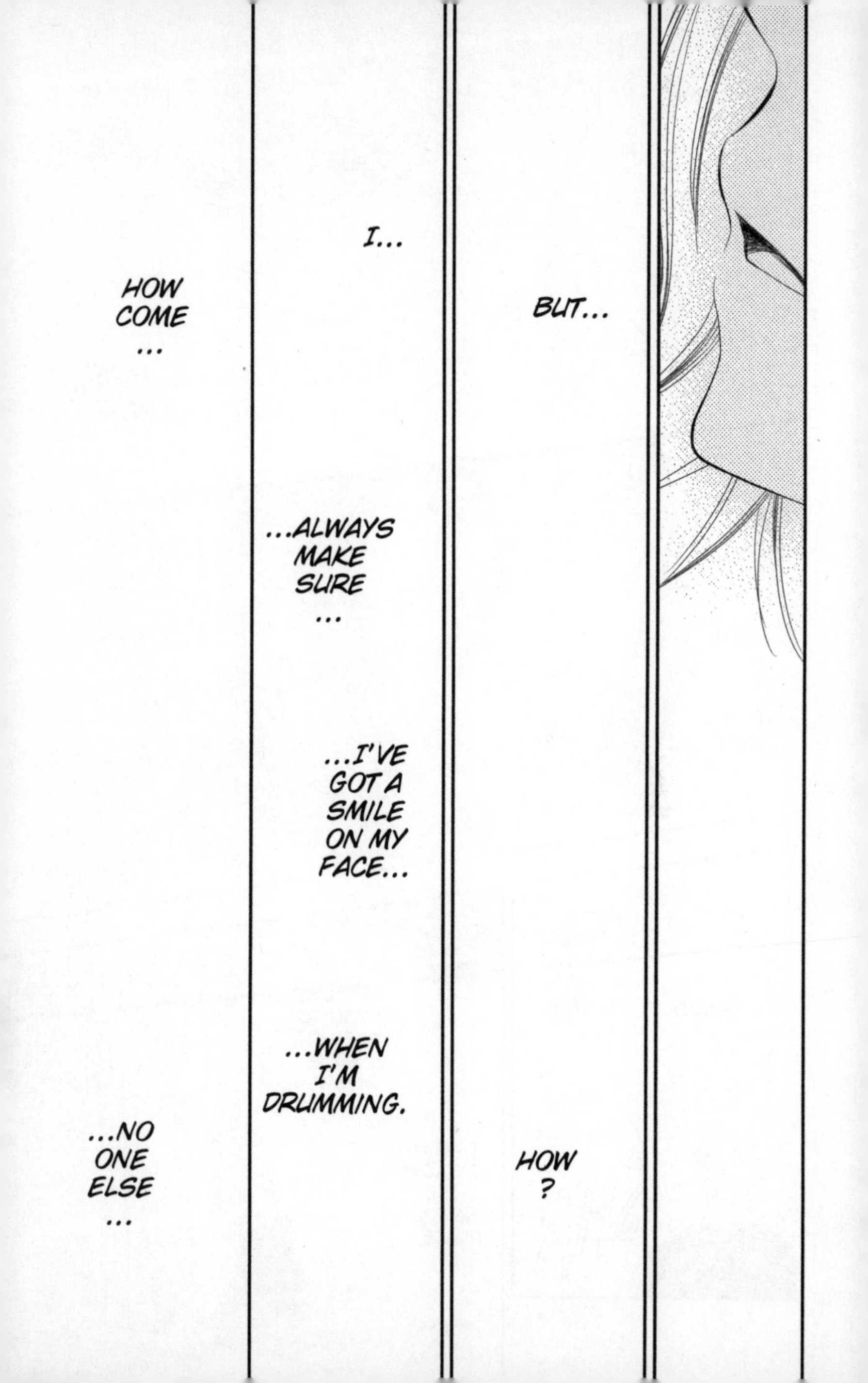
BUT...
HOW?
I...
...ALWAYS MAKE SURE...
...I'VE GOT A SMILE ON MY FACE...
...WHEN I'M DRUMMING.
HOW COME...
...NO ONE ELSE...

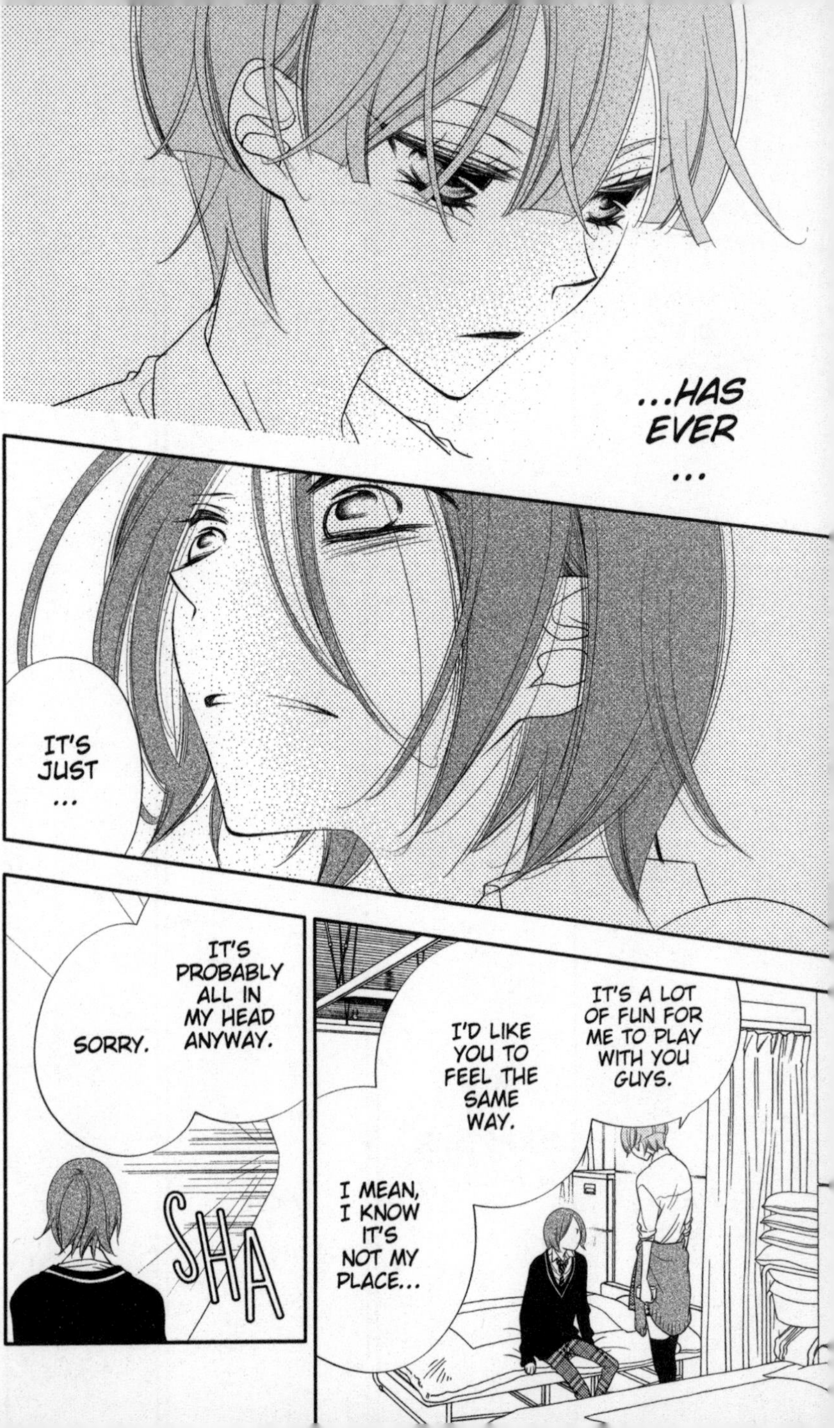
...HAS EVER ...
IT'S JUST ...
IT'S A LOT OF FUN FOR ME TO PLAY WITH YOU GUYS.
I'D LIKE YOU TO FEEL THE SAME WAY.
I MEAN, I KNOW IT'S NOT MY PLACE...
IT'S PROBABLY ALL IN MY HEAD ANYWAY.
SORRY.
SHA

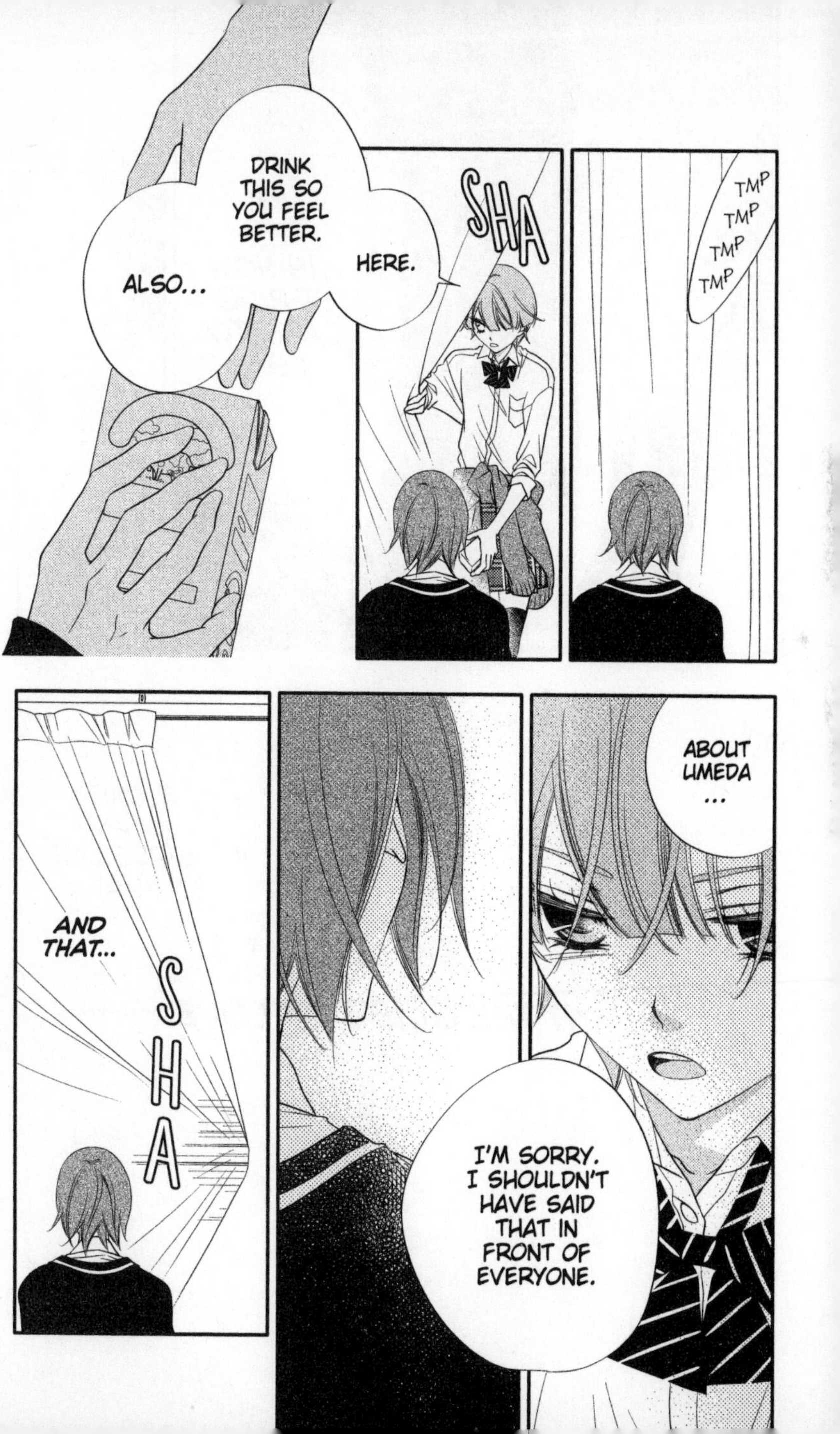
TMP TMP TMP TMP
SHA
HERE.
DRINK THIS SO YOU FEEL BETTER.
ALSO...
ABOUT UMEDA...
I'M SORRY. I SHOULDN'T HAVE SAID THAT IN FRONT OF EVERYONE.
AND THAT...
SHA

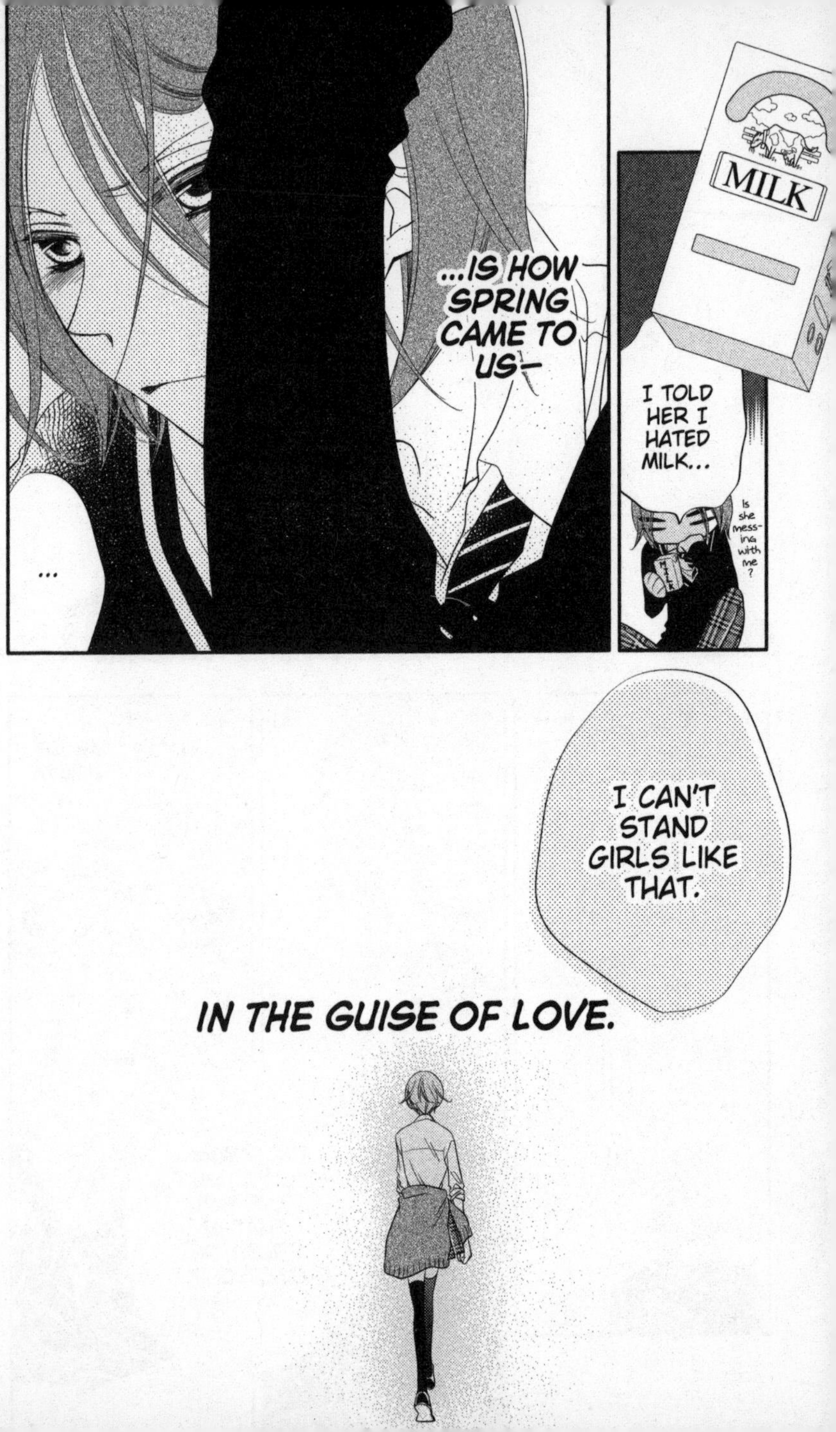

MILK
I TOLD HER I HATED MILK...
Is she messing with me?
...IS HOW SPRING CAME TO US—
...
I CAN'T STAND GIRLS LIKE THAT.
IN THE GUISE OF LOVE.

in NO
hurry
to shout;

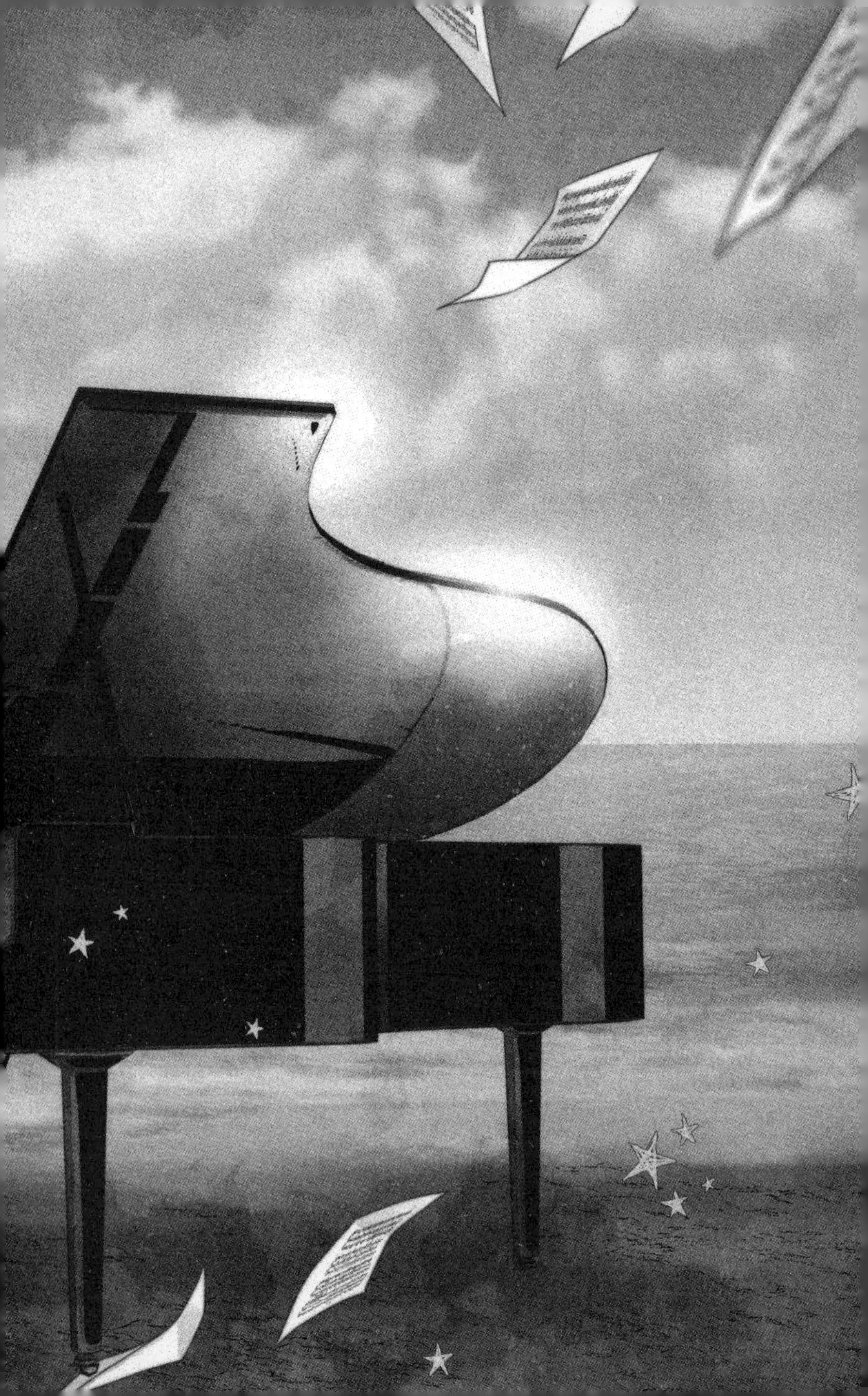

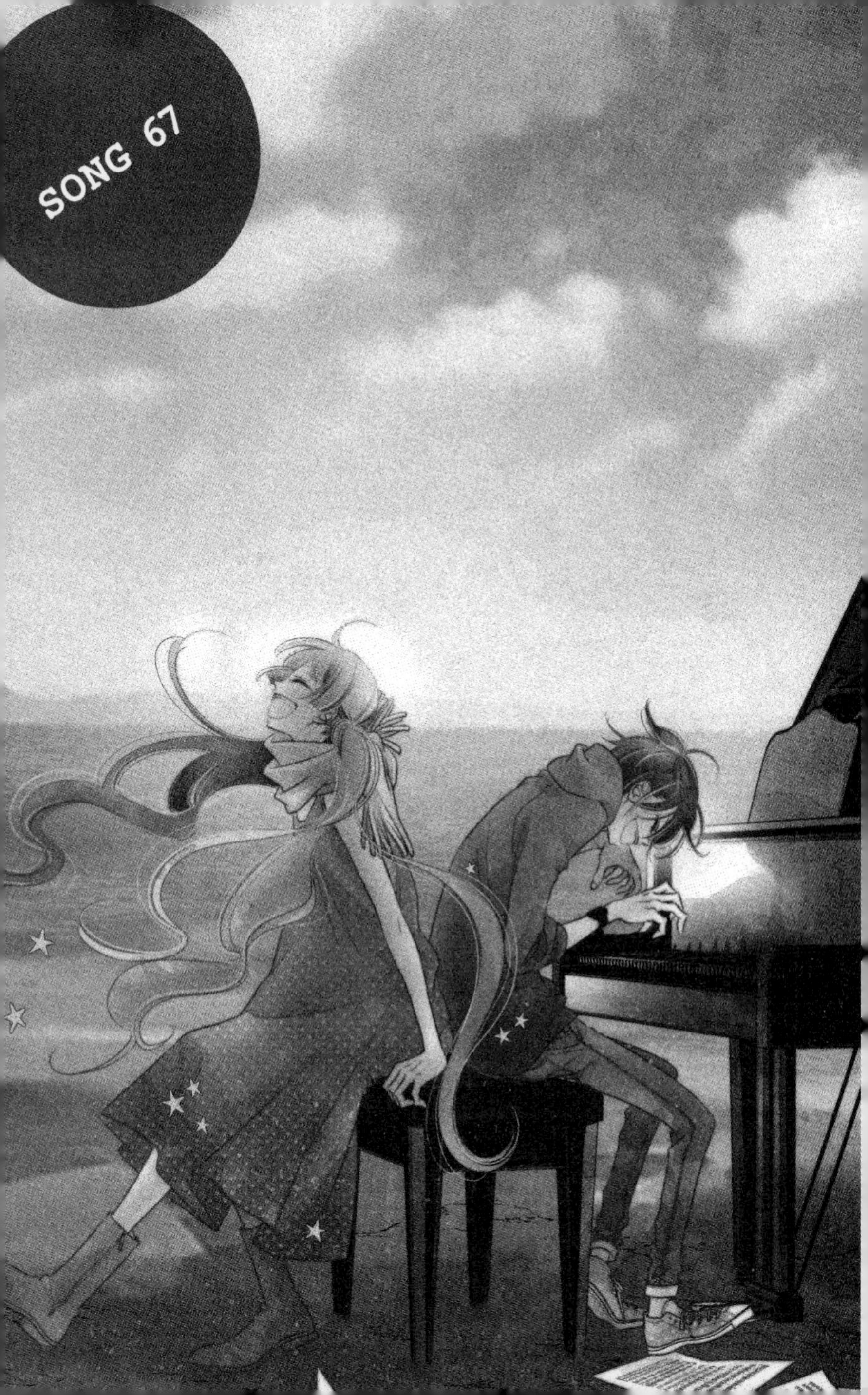
SONG 67

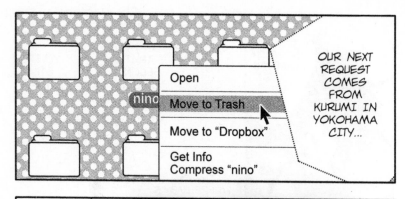

OUR NEXT REQUEST COMES FROM KURUMI IN YOKOHAMA CITY...

Open
Move to Trash
Move to "Dropbox"
Get Info
Compress "nino"

nino

KURUMI SAYS, "I STILL CAN'T GET THEIR TOUR OUT OF MY HEAD, AND THAT'S WHY I WANT YOU TO PLAY..."

...

DOOM

RRINNG

CLATTER

SIIIGH

nino
Move
Move
Get I
Com

"...'NOISE' BY IN NO HURRY TO SHOUT!"

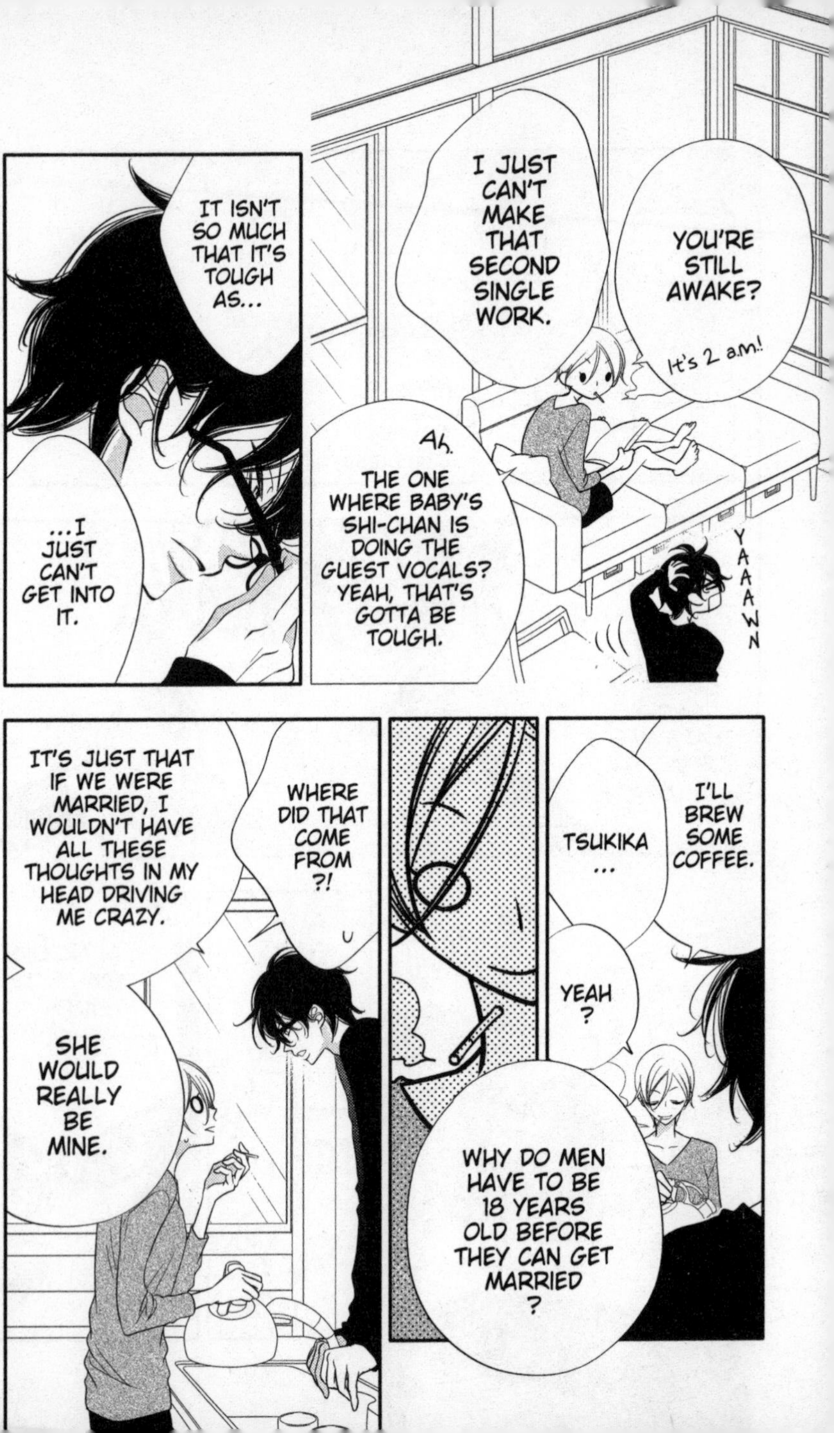
YOU'RE STILL AWAKE?
It's 2 a.m.!
I JUST CAN'T MAKE THAT SECOND SINGLE WORK.
Ah.
THE ONE WHERE BABY'S SHI-CHAN IS DOING THE GUEST VOCALS? YEAH, THAT'S GOTTA BE TOUGH.
YAAAAWN
IT ISN'T SO MUCH THAT IT'S TOUGH AS...
...I JUST CAN'T GET INTO IT.
I'LL BREW SOME COFFEE.
TSUKIKA...
YEAH?
WHY DO MEN HAVE TO BE 18 YEARS OLD BEFORE THEY CAN GET MARRIED?
WHERE DID THAT COME FROM?!
IT'S JUST THAT IF WE WERE MARRIED, I WOULDN'T HAVE ALL THESE THOUGHTS IN MY HEAD DRIVING ME CRAZY.
SHE WOULD REALLY BE MINE.

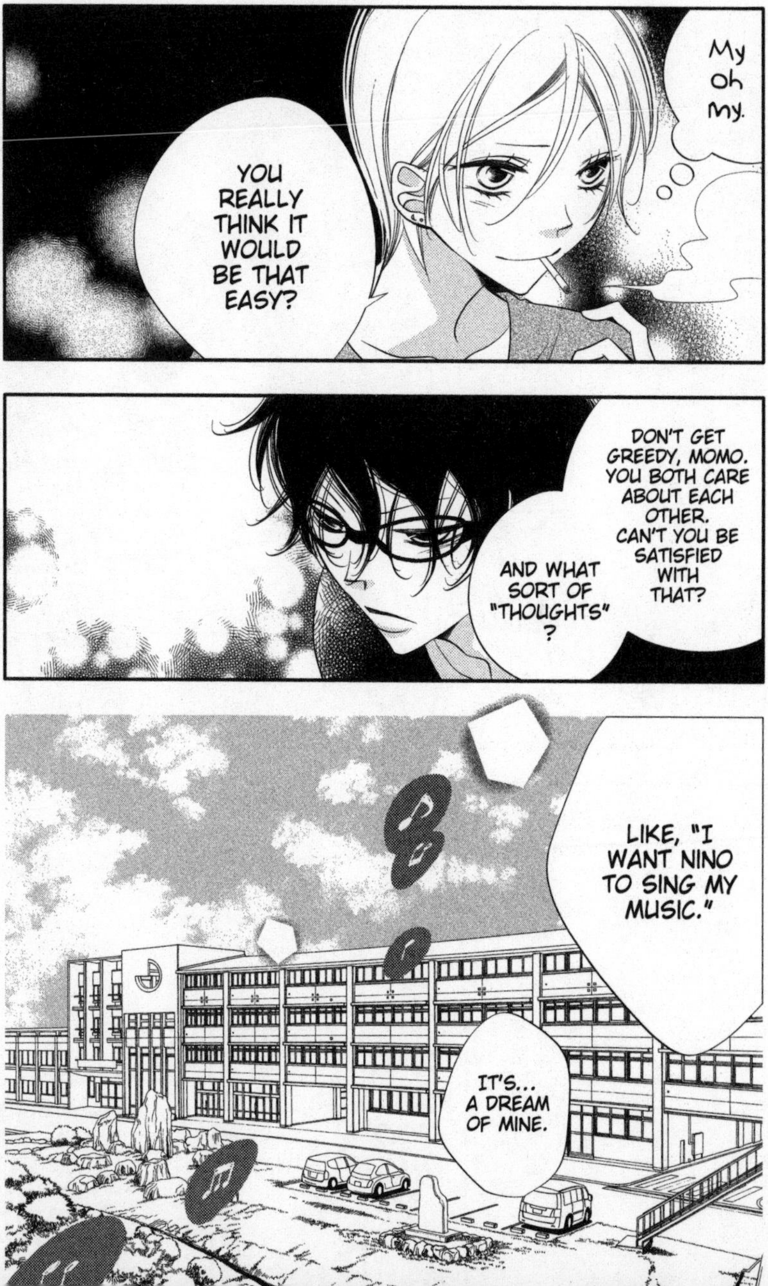
My oh my.
YOU REALLY THINK IT WOULD BE THAT EASY?
DON'T GET GREEDY, MOMO. YOU BOTH CARE ABOUT EACH OTHER. CAN'T YOU BE SATISFIED WITH THAT?
AND WHAT SORT OF "THOUGHTS"?
LIKE, "I WANT NINO TO SING MY MUSIC."
IT'S... A DREAM OF MINE.

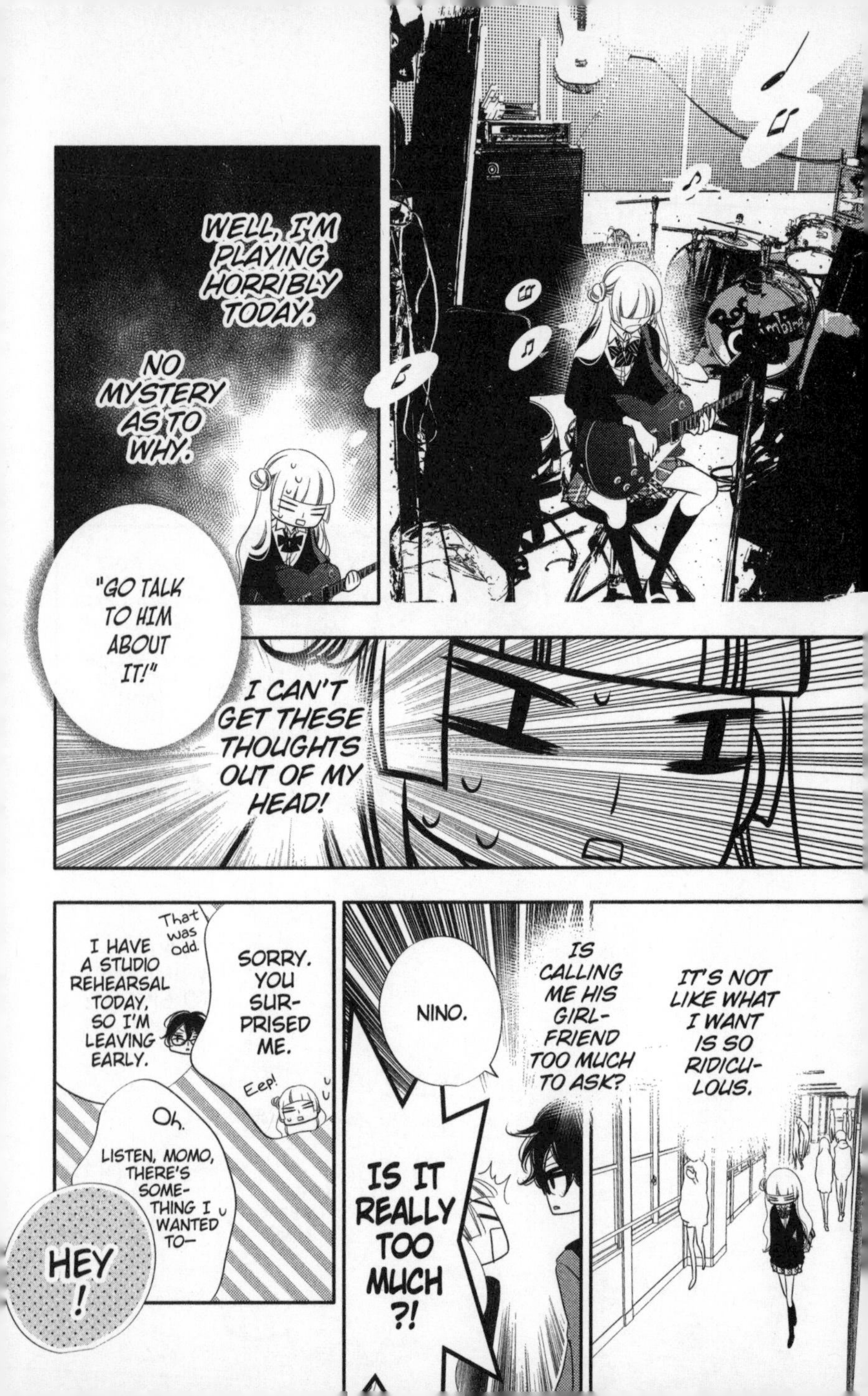
WELL, I'M PLAYING HORRIBLY TODAY.
NO MYSTERY AS TO WHY.
"GO TALK TO HIM ABOUT IT!"
I CAN'T GET THESE THOUGHTS OUT OF MY HEAD!
IT'S NOT LIKE WHAT I WANT IS SO RIDICULOUS.
IS CALLING ME HIS GIRLFRIEND TOO MUCH TO ASK?
NINO.
IS IT REALLY TOO MUCH?!
HEY!
Eep!
SORRY. YOU SURPRISED ME.
Oh.
LISTEN, MOMO, THERE'S SOMETHING I WANTED TO—
I HAVE A STUDIO REHEARSAL TODAY, SO I'M LEAVING EARLY.
That was odd.

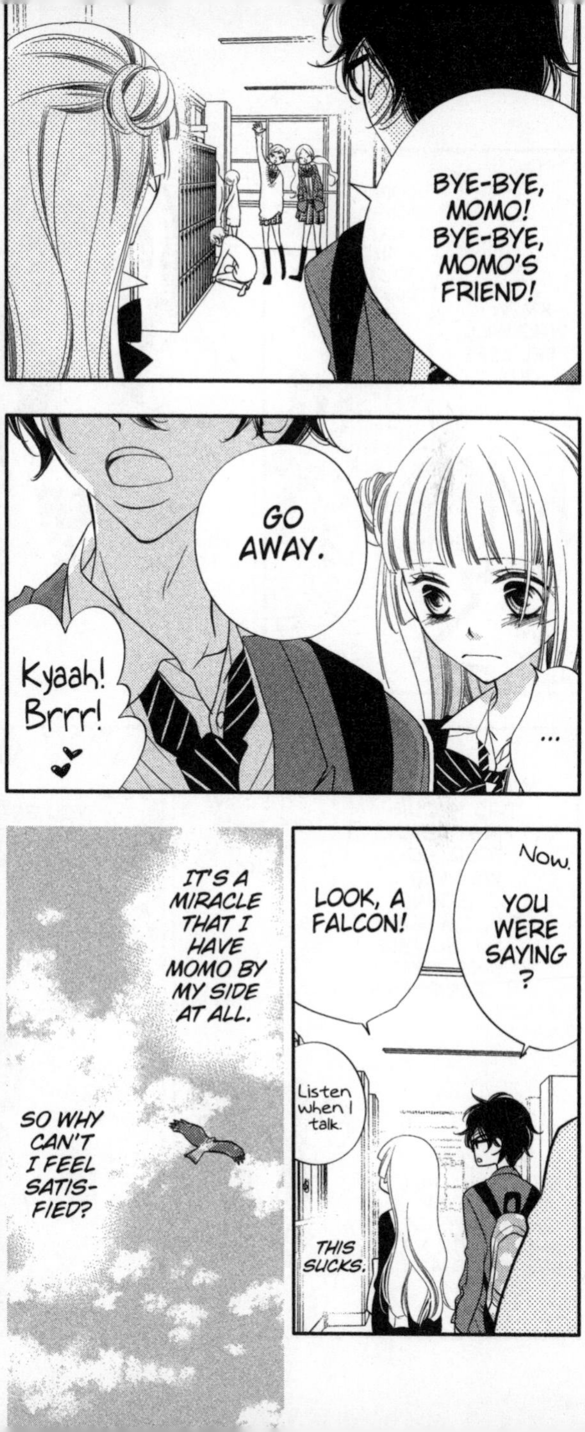
BYE-BYE, MOMO! BYE-BYE, MOMO'S FRIEND!
...
GO AWAY.
Kyaah! Brrr!
Now.
YOU WERE SAYING?
LOOK, A FALCON!
Listen when I talk.
THIS SUCKS.
IT'S A MIRACLE THAT I HAVE MOMO BY MY SIDE AT ALL.
SO WHY CAN'T I FEEL SATISFIED?

3

Chapter 66 features the debut of a new character, An Kanamari! I went through a lot of trial and error on her design back when she briefly appeared in volume 11. Back at the naming stage, I had pictured her with loosely permed long hair, but there were too many long-haired characters in the series already, so I made it short and boyish instead. I'd used up a wide variety of heights already, so I figured what the heck, I'll make her really tall! I'd never actually drawn a woman of that size before, so that was kind of fresh and fun for me. I can't believe how easy it is for her to move around! (Although it's a lot harder for every-one around her! *Ha ha*.) I've been toying with the idea of adding another new character (a boy) to the circuit arc that I'm working on now... Hmmm...

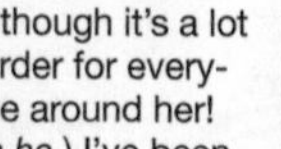

FROG AND CAT FOR NO PARTICULAR REASON

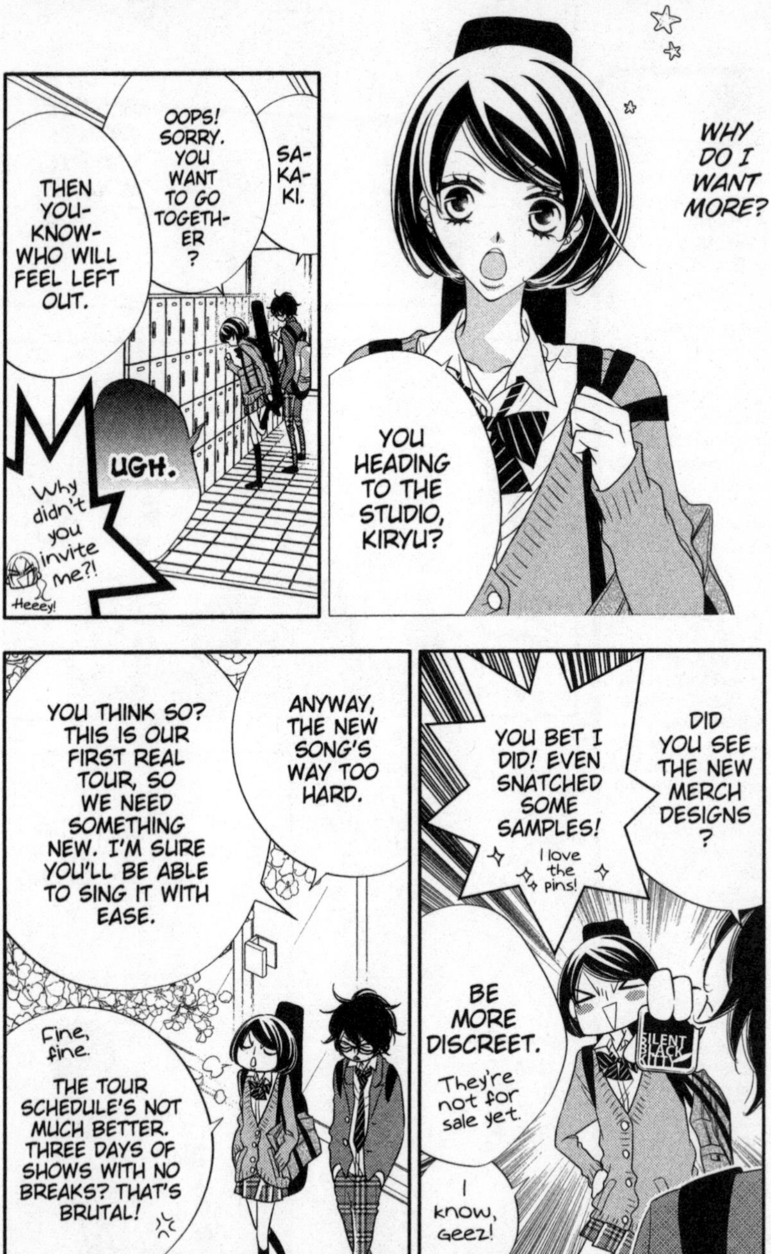
WHY DO I WANT MORE?
YOU HEADING TO THE STUDIO, KIRYU?
SA-KA-KI.
OOPS! SORRY. YOU WANT TO GO TOGETH-ER?
THEN YOU-KNOW-WHO WILL FEEL LEFT OUT.
UGH.
Why didn't you invite me?!
Heeey!
DID YOU SEE THE NEW MERCH DESIGNS?
YOU BET I DID! EVEN SNATCHED SOME SAMPLES!
I love the pins!
BE MORE DISCREET.
They're not for sale yet.
SILENT BLACK KITTY
I know, Geez!
ANYWAY, THE NEW SONG'S WAY TOO HARD.
YOU THINK SO? THIS IS OUR FIRST REAL TOUR, SO WE NEED SOMETHING NEW. I'M SURE YOU'LL BE ABLE TO SING IT WITH EASE.
Fine, fine.
THE TOUR SCHEDULE'S NOT MUCH BETTER. THREE DAYS OF SHOWS WITH NO BREAKS? THAT'S BRUTAL!

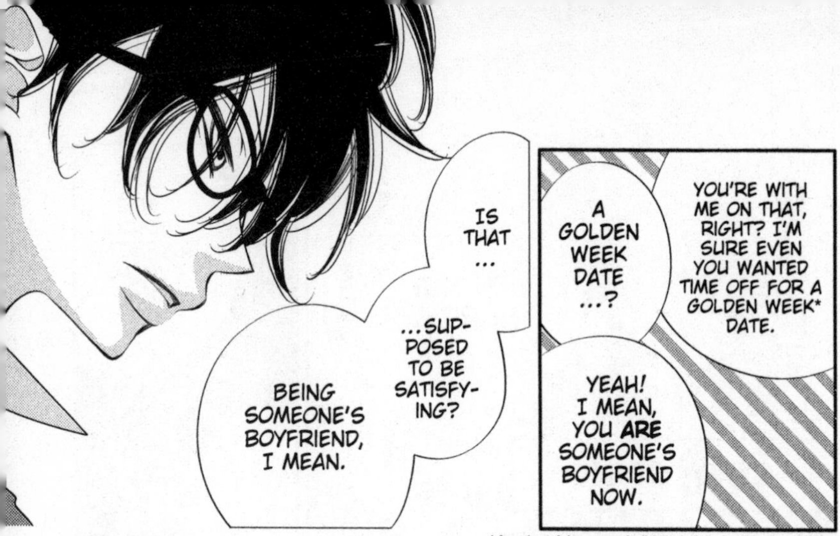
YOU'RE WITH ME ON THAT, RIGHT? I'M SURE EVEN YOU WANTED TIME OFF FOR A GOLDEN WEEK* DATE.
A GOLDEN WEEK DATE ...?
YEAH! I MEAN, YOU **ARE** SOMEONE'S BOYFRIEND NOW.
IS THAT ...
...SUP-POSED TO BE SATISFY-ING?
BEING SOMEONE'S BOYFRIEND, I MEAN.

*A series of Japanese holidays in late April and early May

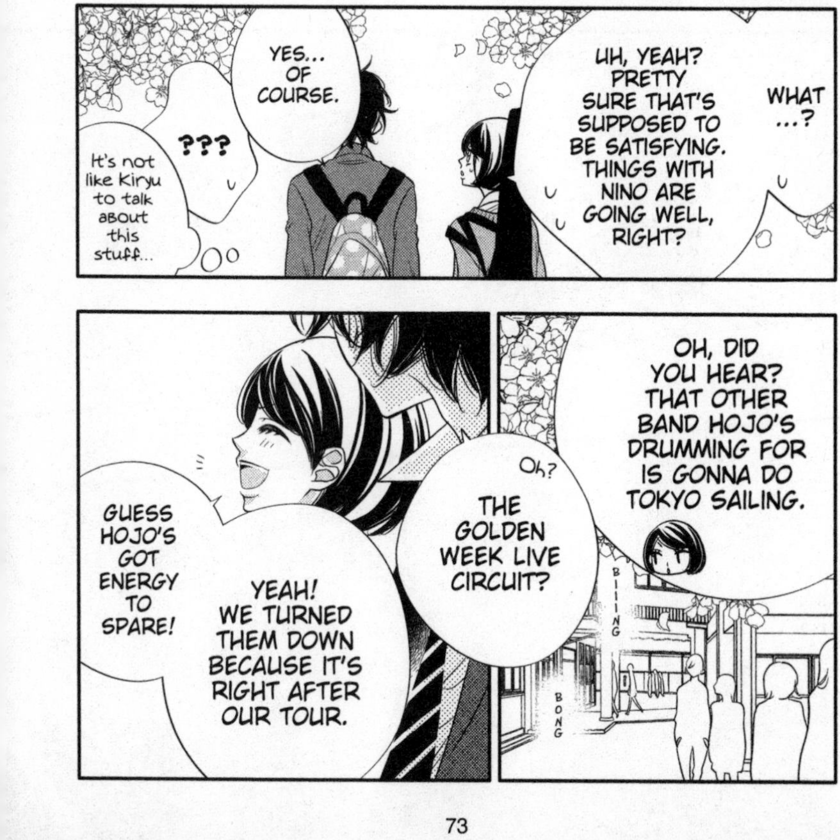
WHAT ...?
UH, YEAH? PRETTY SURE THAT'S SUPPOSED TO BE SATISFYING. THINGS WITH NINO ARE GOING WELL, RIGHT?
YES... OF COURSE.
???
It's not like Kiryu to talk about this stuff...
OH, DID YOU HEAR? THAT OTHER BAND HOJO'S DRUMMING FOR IS GONNA DO TOKYO SAILING.
BIING
BONG
Oh?
THE GOLDEN WEEK LIVE CIRCUIT?
YEAH! WE TURNED THEM DOWN BECAUSE IT'S RIGHT AFTER OUR TOUR.
GUESS HOJO'S GOT ENERGY TO SPARE!

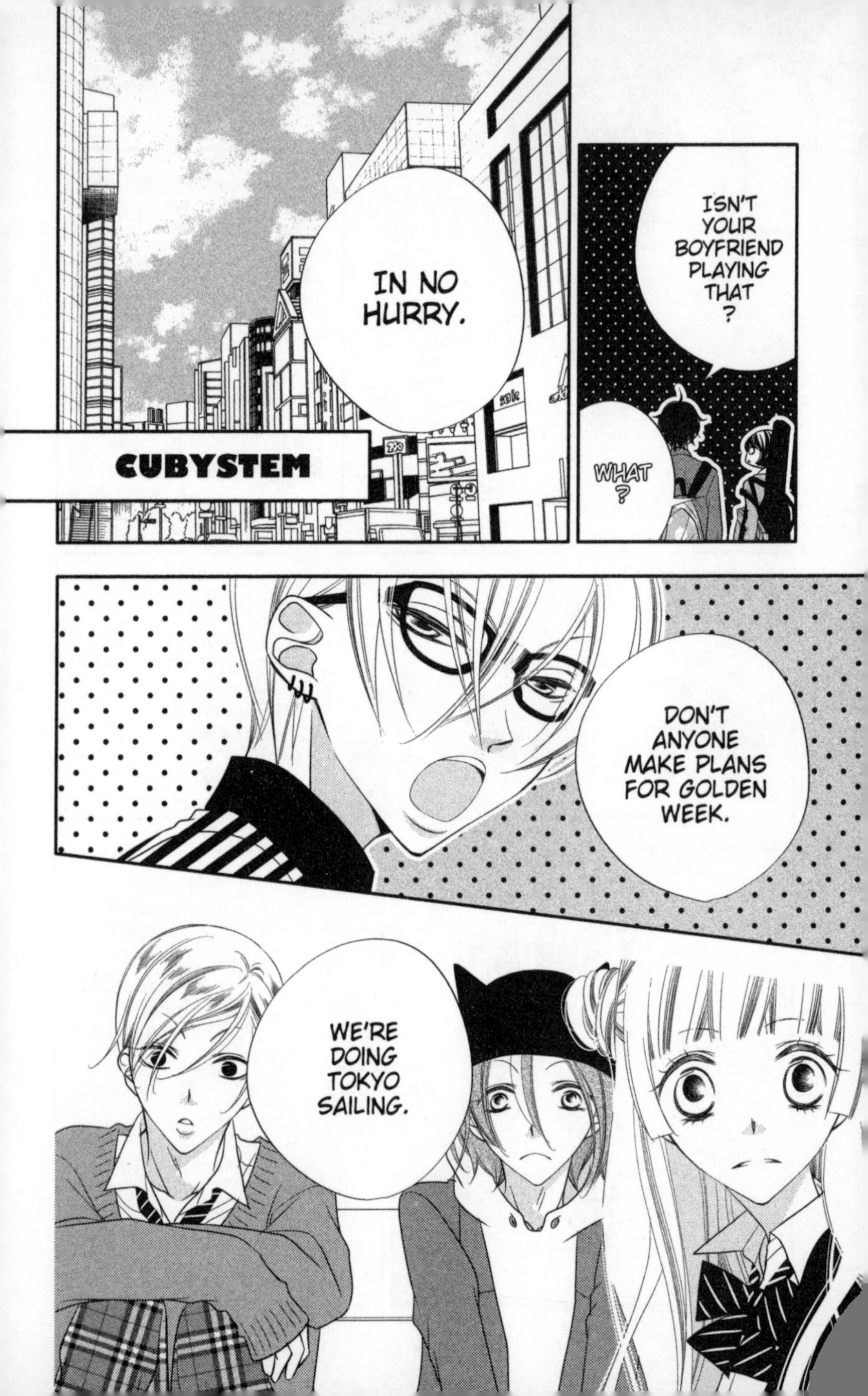
ISN'T YOUR BOYFRIEND PLAYING THAT?
WHAT?
IN NO HURRY.
CUBYSTEM
DON'T ANYONE MAKE PLANS FOR GOLDEN WEEK.
WE'RE DOING TOKYO SAILING.

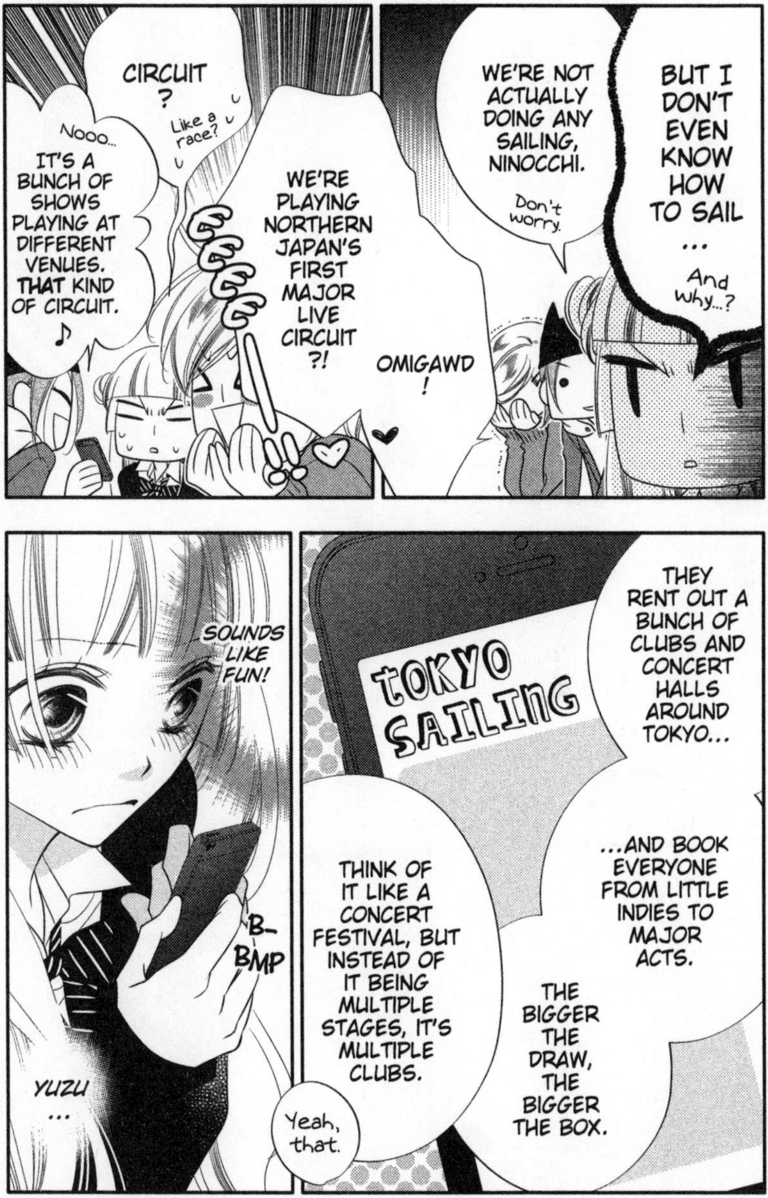
BUT I DON'T EVEN KNOW HOW TO SAIL...
And why...?
WE'RE NOT ACTUALLY DOING ANY SAILING, NINOCCHI.
Don't worry.
WE'RE PLAYING NORTHERN JAPAN'S FIRST MAJOR LIVE CIRCUIT?!
OMIGAWD!
CIRCUIT?
Like a race?
Nooo...
IT'S A BUNCH OF SHOWS PLAYING AT DIFFERENT VENUES. THAT KIND OF CIRCUIT. ♪
TOKYO SAILING
THEY RENT OUT A BUNCH OF CLUBS AND CONCERT HALLS AROUND TOKYO...
...AND BOOK EVERYONE FROM LITTLE INDIES TO MAJOR ACTS.
THE BIGGER THE DRAW, THE BIGGER THE BOX.
THINK OF IT LIKE A CONCERT FESTIVAL, BUT INSTEAD OF IT BEING MULTIPLE STAGES, IT'S MULTIPLE CLUBS.
Yeah, that.
SOUNDS LIKE FUN!
B-BMP
YUZU...

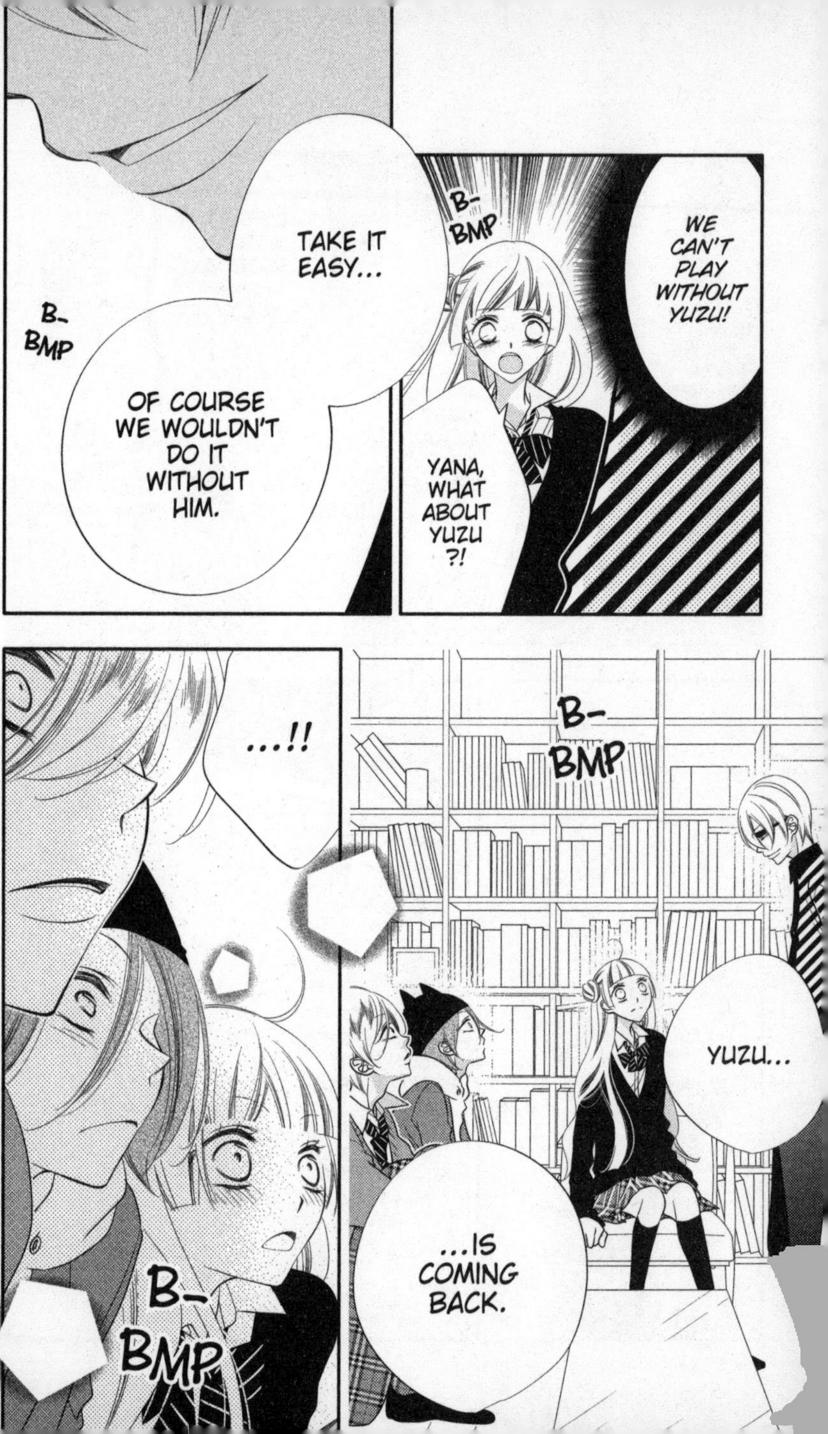
WE CAN'T PLAY WITHOUT YUZU!
B-BMP
YANA, WHAT ABOUT YUZU?!
TAKE IT EASY...
B-BMP
OF COURSE WE WOULDN'T DO IT WITHOUT HIM.
B-BMP
YUZU...
...IS COMING BACK.
...!!
B-BMP

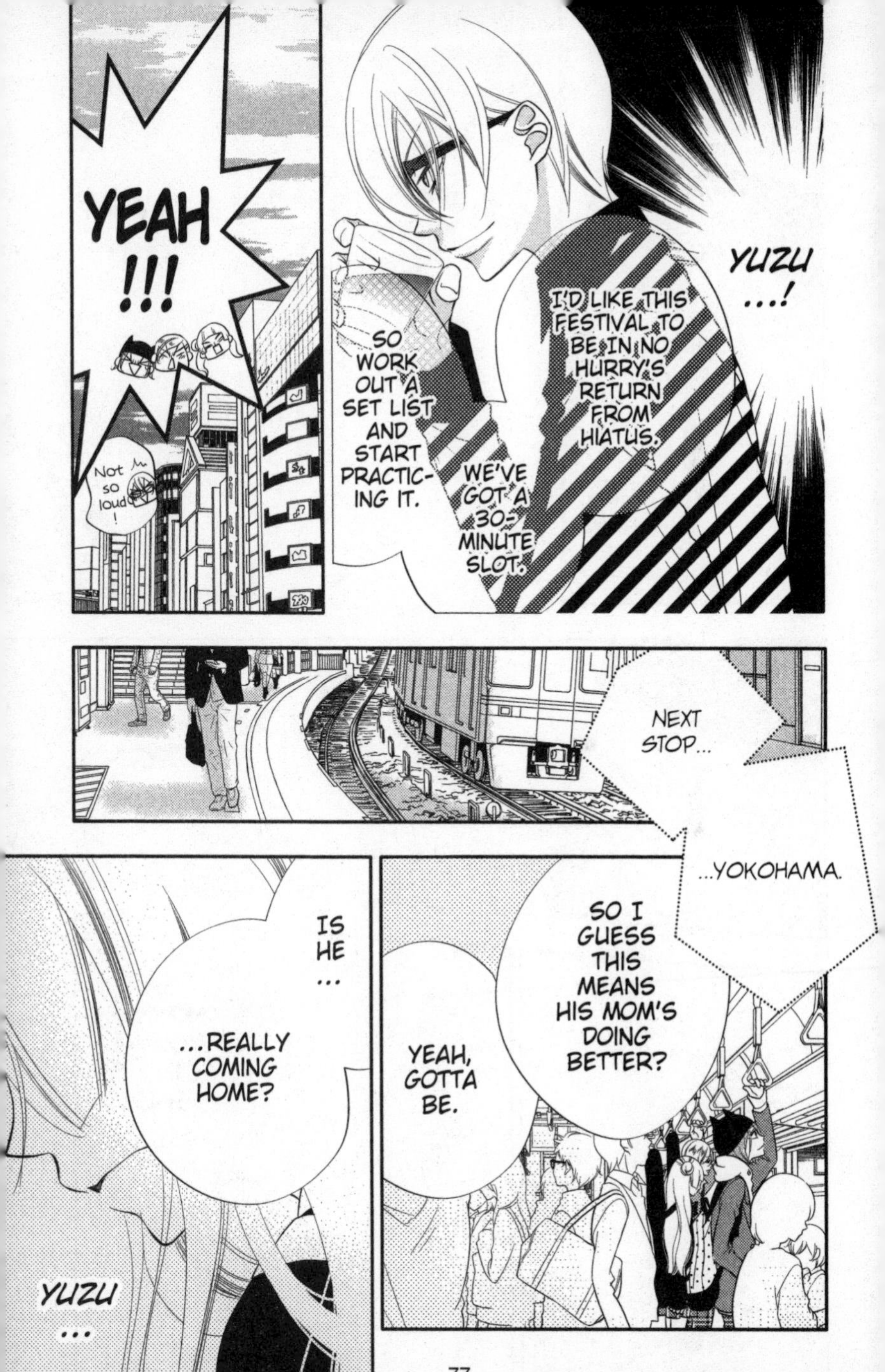
YUZU ...!
I'D LIKE THIS FESTIVAL TO BE IN NO HURRY'S RETURN FROM HIATUS.
WE'VE GOT A 30-MINUTE SLOT.
SO WORK OUT A SET LIST AND START PRACTICING IT.
YEAH !!!
Not so loud!
NEXT STOP...
...YOKOHAMA.
SO I GUESS THIS MEANS HIS MOM'S DOING BETTER?
YEAH, GOTTA BE.
IS HE ...
...REALLY COMING HOME?
YUZU ...

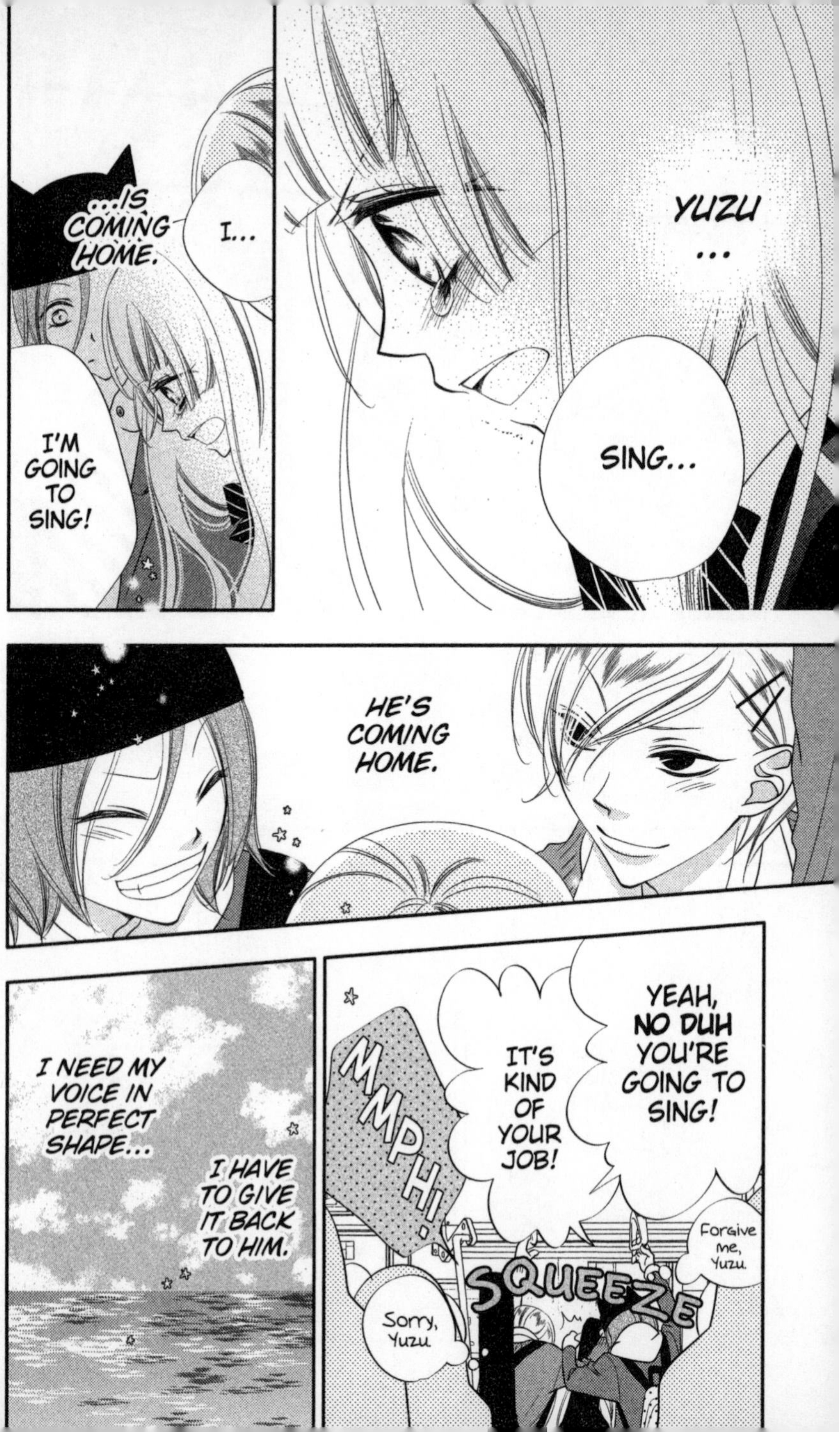
YUZU...
SING...
I...
...IS COMING HOME.
I'M GOING TO SING!
HE'S COMING HOME.
YEAH, NO DUH YOU'RE GOING TO SING!
IT'S KIND OF YOUR JOB!
MMPH!
Forgive me, Yuzu.
SQUEEZE
Sorry, Yuzu
I NEED MY VOICE IN PERFECT SHAPE...
I HAVE TO GIVE IT BACK TO HIM.

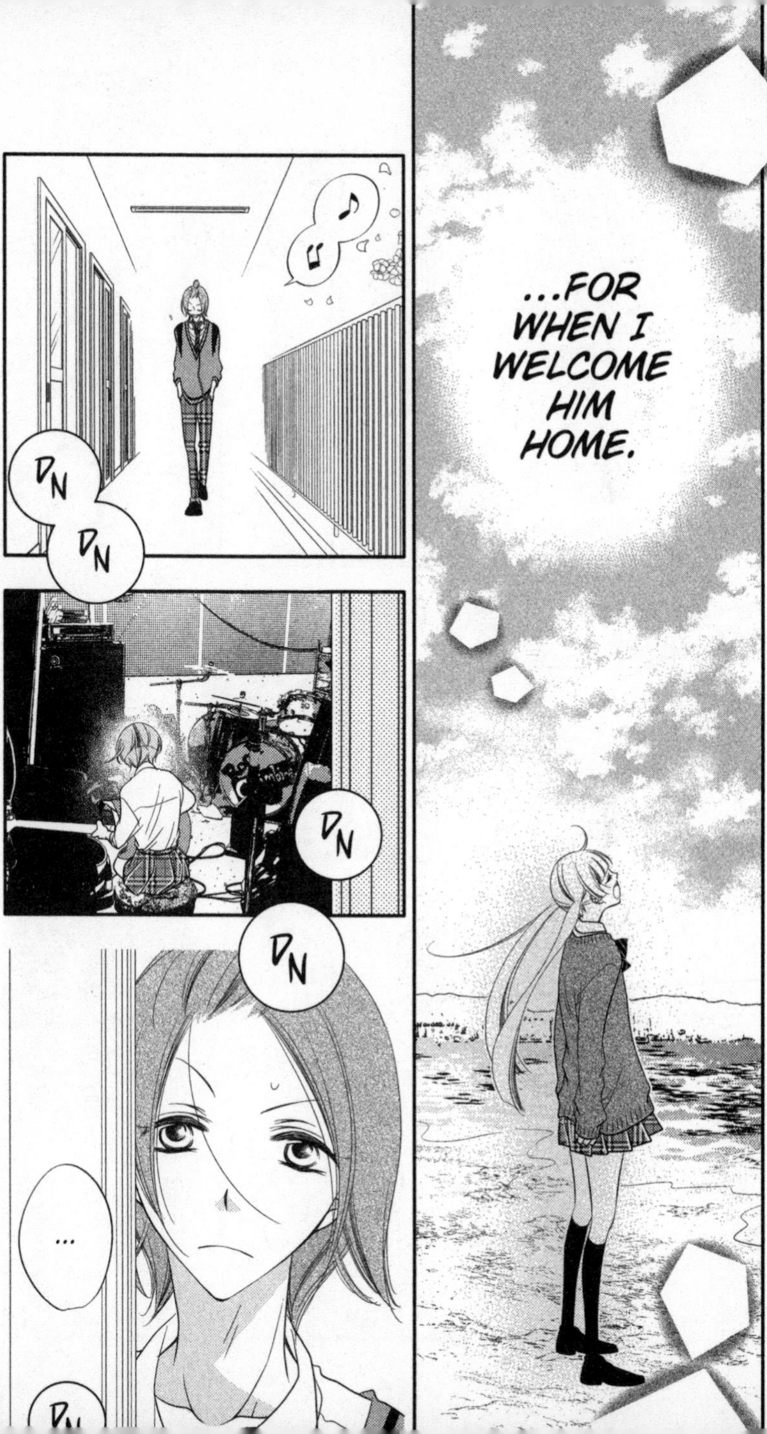
...FOR WHEN I WELCOME HIM HOME.
DN
DN
DN
DN
...

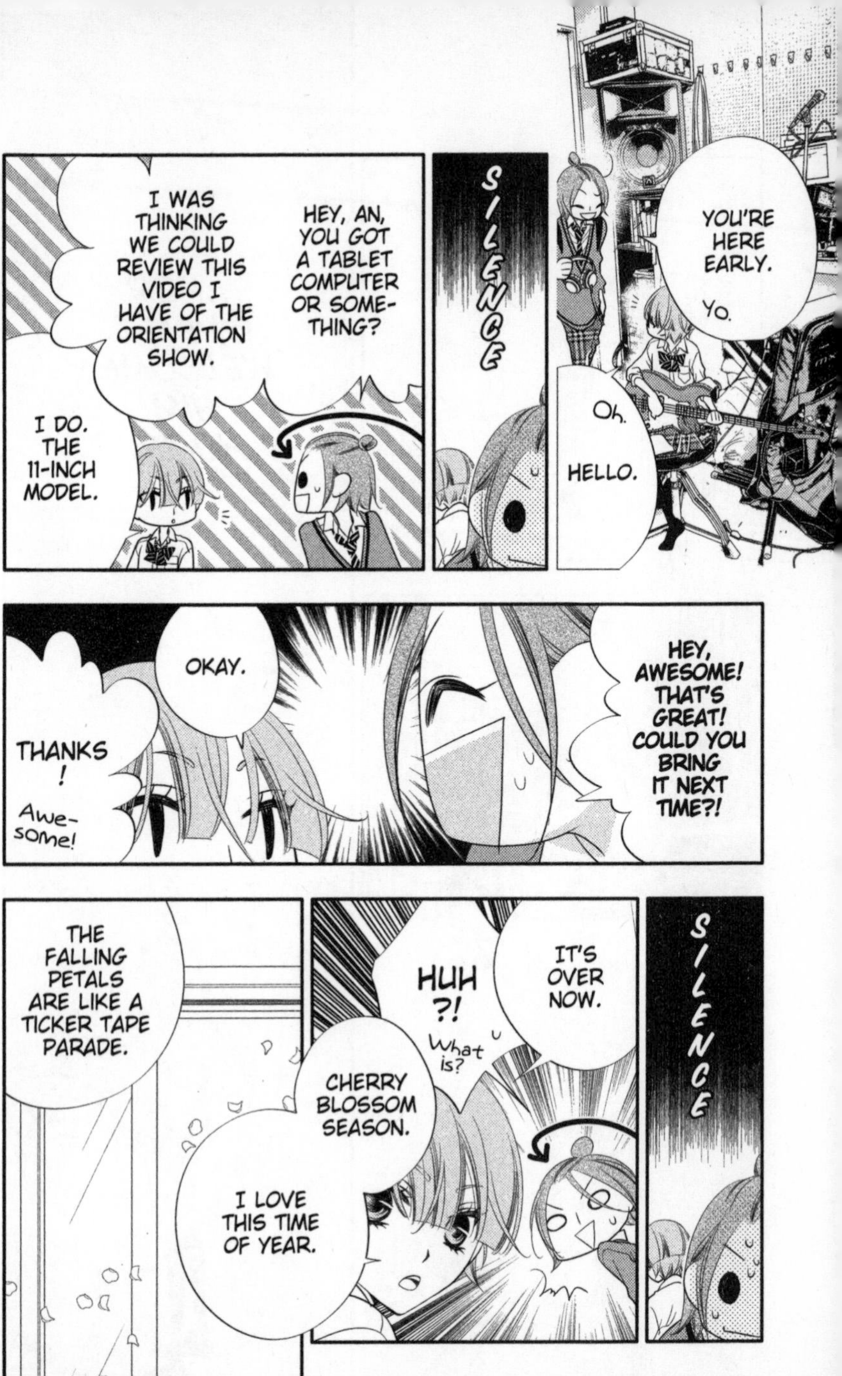

YOU'RE HERE EARLY.
Yo.
Oh.
HELLO.
SILENCE
HEY, AN, YOU GOT A TABLET COMPUTER OR SOME-THING?
I WAS THINKING WE COULD REVIEW THIS VIDEO I HAVE OF THE ORIENTATION SHOW.
I DO. THE 11-INCH MODEL.
HEY, AWESOME! THAT'S GREAT! COULD YOU BRING IT NEXT TIME?!
OKAY.
THANKS!
Awe-some!
SILENCE
IT'S OVER NOW.
HUH?!
What is?
CHERRY BLOSSOM SEASON.
I LOVE THIS TIME OF YEAR.
THE FALLING PETALS ARE LIKE A TICKER TAPE PARADE.

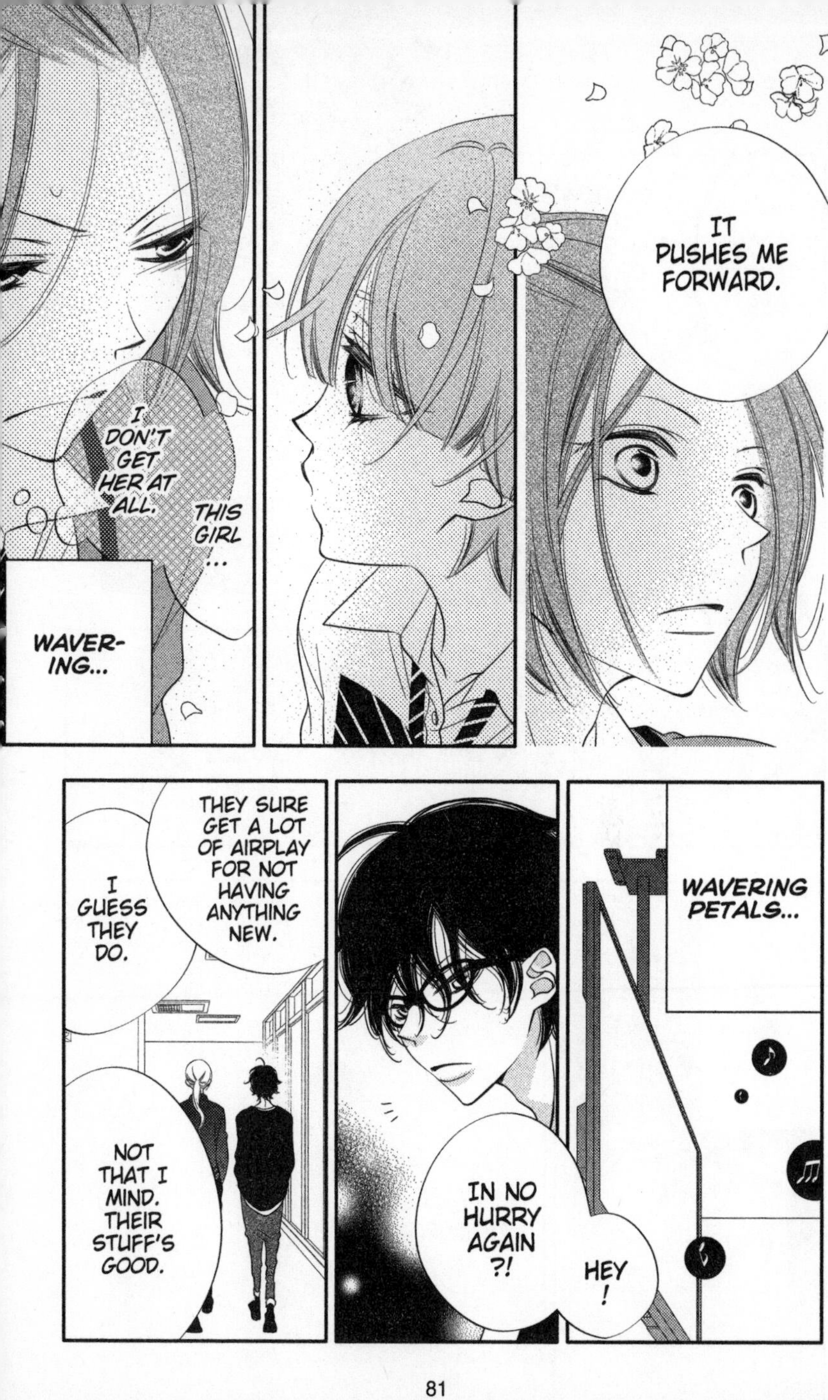
IT PUSHES ME FORWARD.
THIS GIRL...
I DON'T GET HER AT ALL.
WAVER-ING...
WAVERING PETALS...
HEY!
IN NO HURRY AGAIN?!
THEY SURE GET A LOT OF AIRPLAY FOR NOT HAVING ANYTHING NEW.
I GUESS THEY DO.
NOT THAT I MIND. THEIR STUFF'S GOOD.

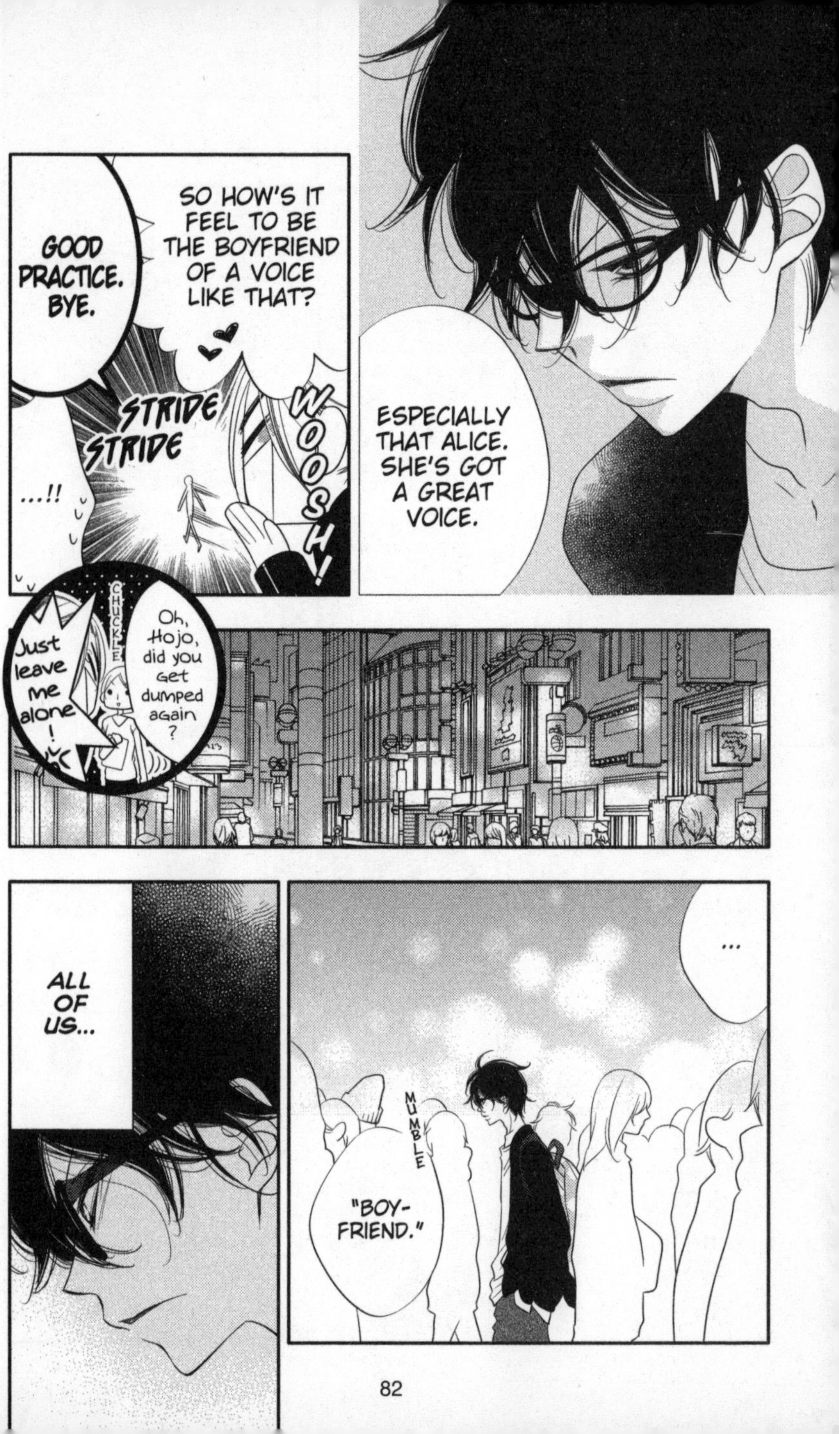
ESPECIALLY THAT ALICE. SHE'S GOT A GREAT VOICE.
SO HOW'S IT FEEL TO BE THE BOYFRIEND OF A VOICE LIKE THAT?
WOOSH!
GOOD PRACTICE. BYE.
STRIDE STRIDE
...!!
CHUCKLE
Oh, Hojo, did you get dumped again?
Just leave me alone!
...
MUMBLE
"BOY-FRIEND."
ALL OF US...

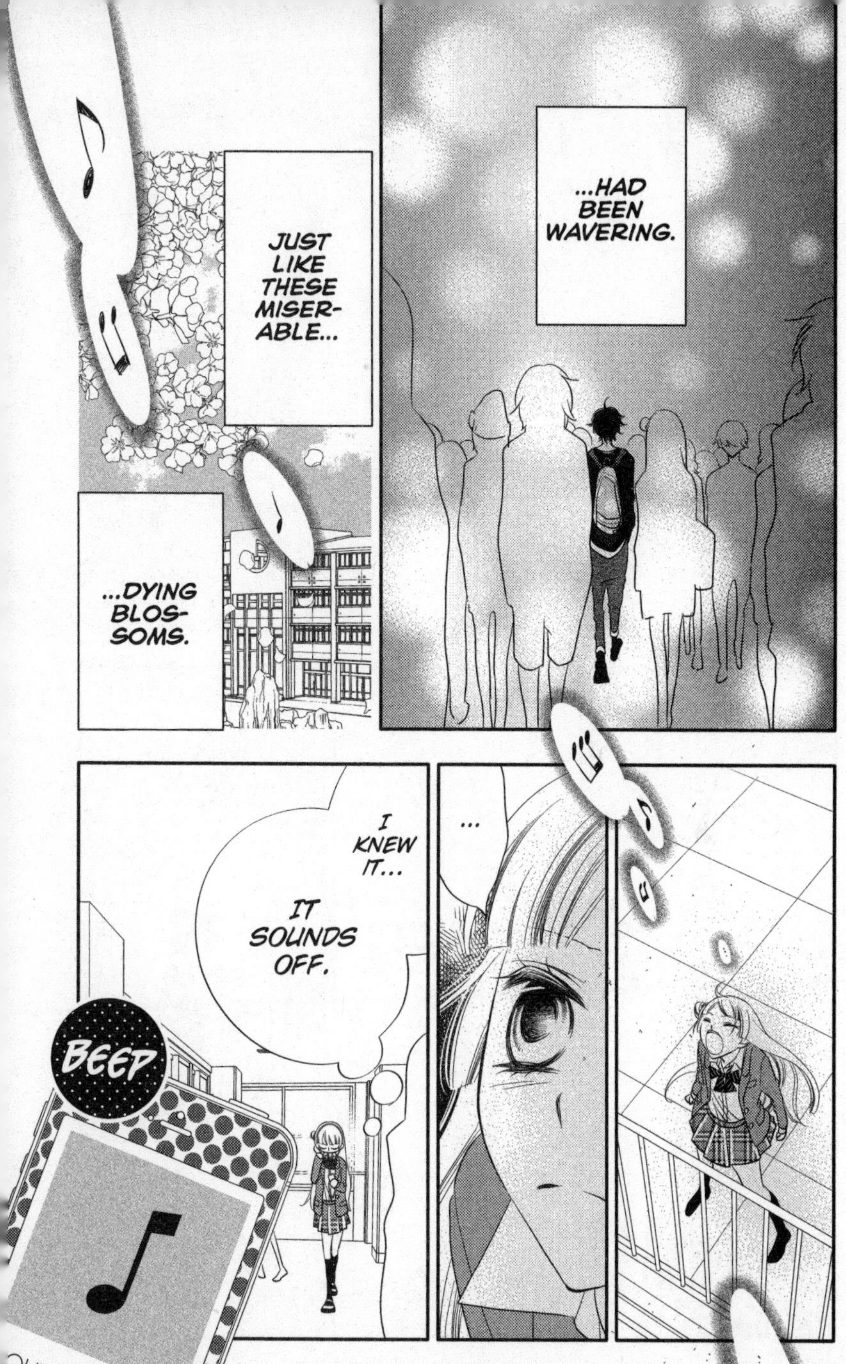
...HAD BEEN WAVERING.
JUST LIKE THESE MISERABLE...
...DYING BLOSSOMS.
...
I KNEW IT...
IT SOUNDS OFF.
BEEP

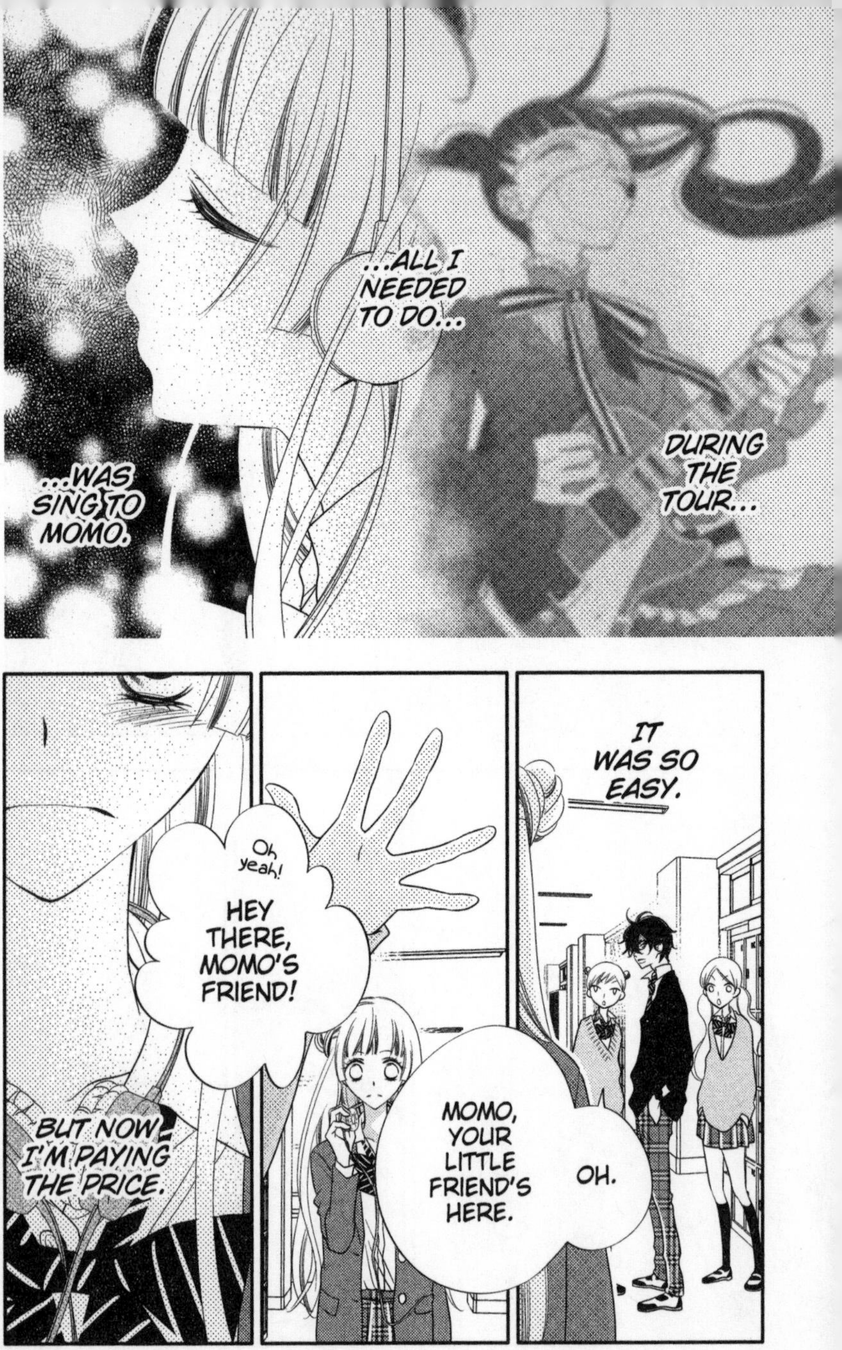
DURING THE TOUR...
...ALL I NEEDED TO DO...
...WAS SING TO MOMO.
IT WAS SO EASY.
OH.
MOMO, YOUR LITTLE FRIEND'S HERE.
Oh yeah!
HEY THERE, MOMO'S FRIEND!
BUT NOW I'M PAYING THE PRICE.

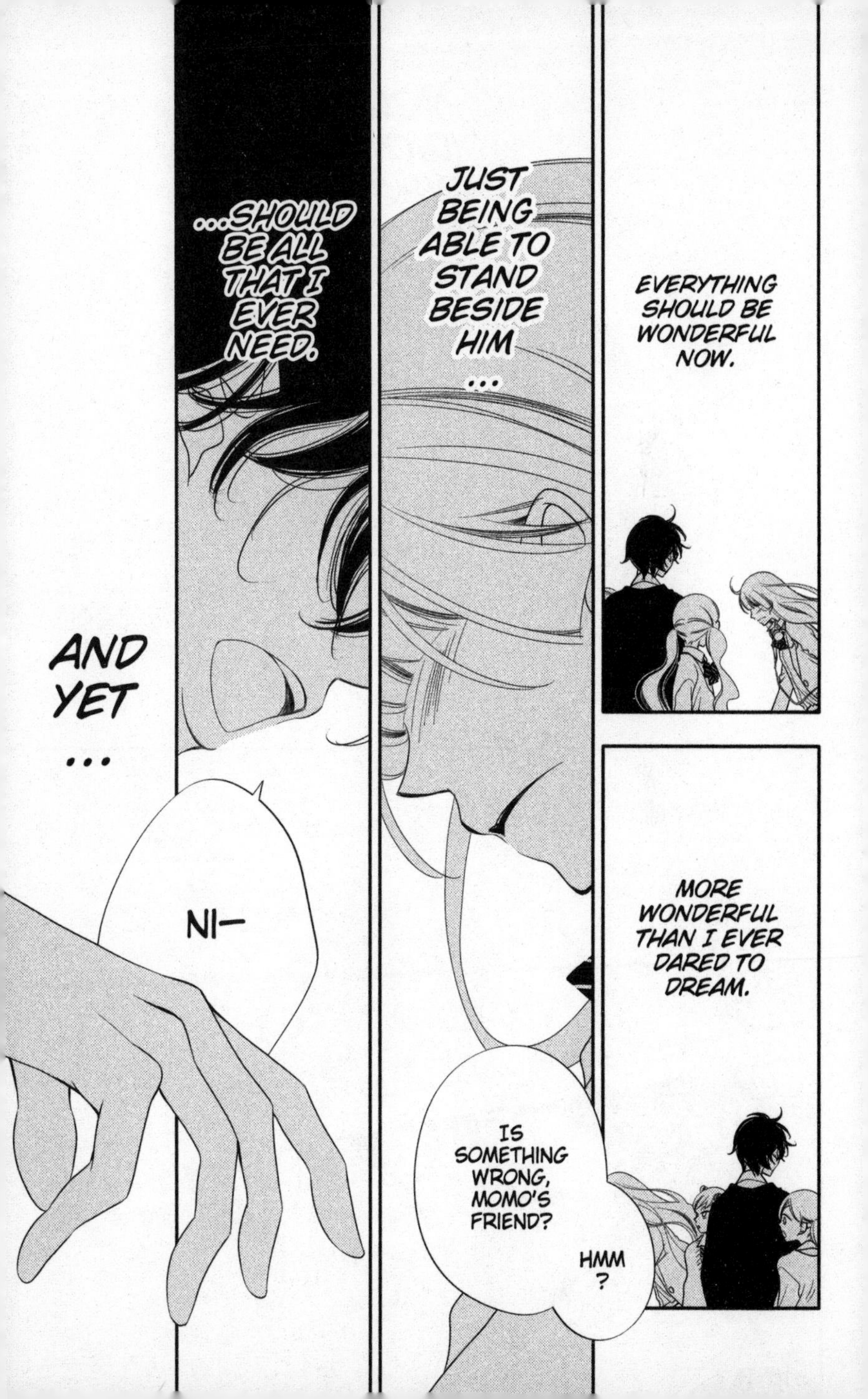
EVERYTHING SHOULD BE WONDERFUL NOW.
MORE WONDERFUL THAN I EVER DARED TO DREAM.
IS SOMETHING WRONG, MOMO'S FRIEND?
HMM?
JUST BEING ABLE TO STAND BESIDE HIM...
...SHOULD BE ALL THAT I EVER NEED.
AND YET...
NI—

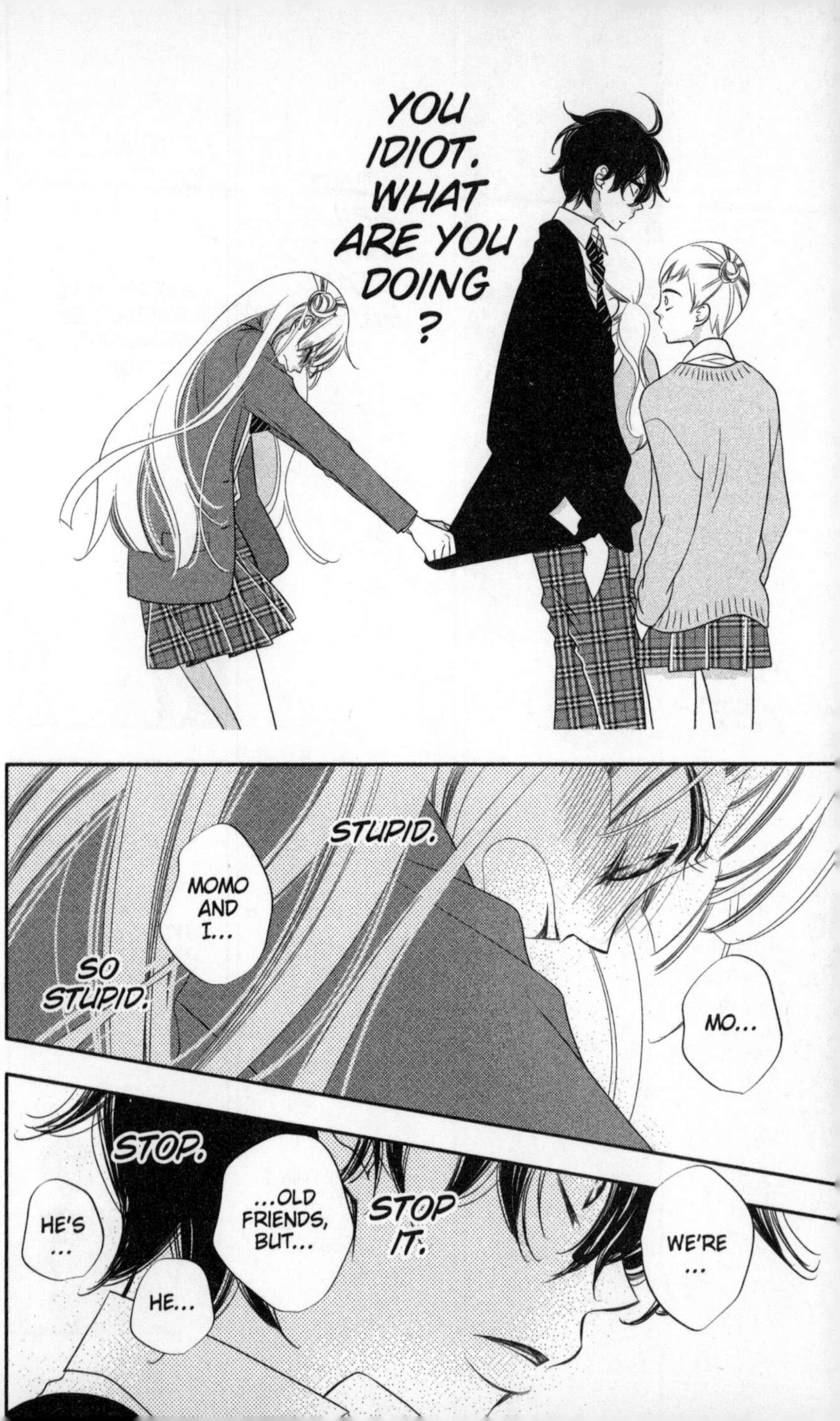
YOU IDIOT. WHAT ARE YOU DOING?
MO...
STUPID.
MOMO AND I...
SO STUPID.
WE'RE...
STOP IT.
...OLD FRIENDS, BUT...
STOP.
HE'S...
HE...

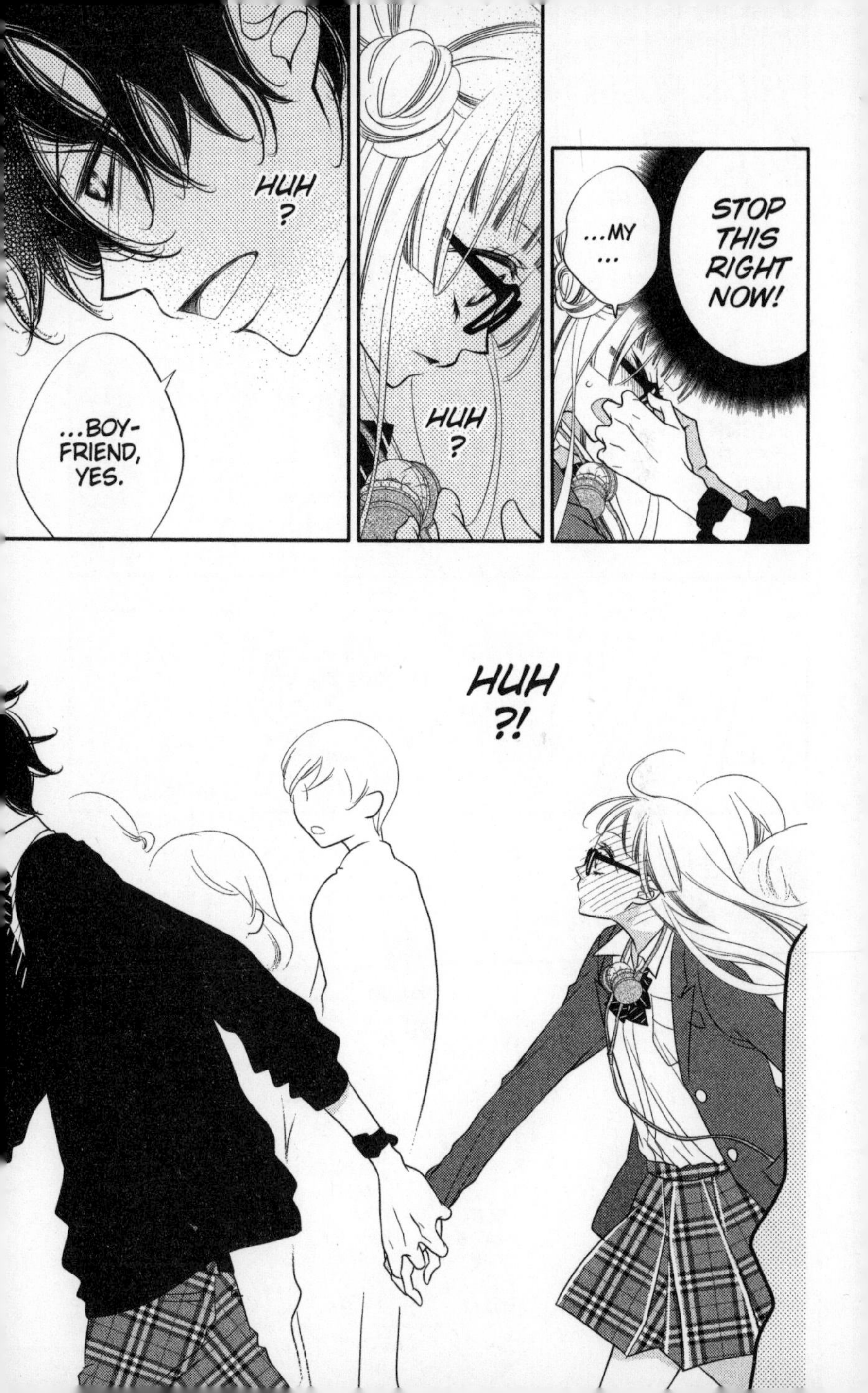
STOP THIS RIGHT NOW!
...MY ...
HUH ?
HUH ?
...BOY-FRIEND, YES.
HUH ?!

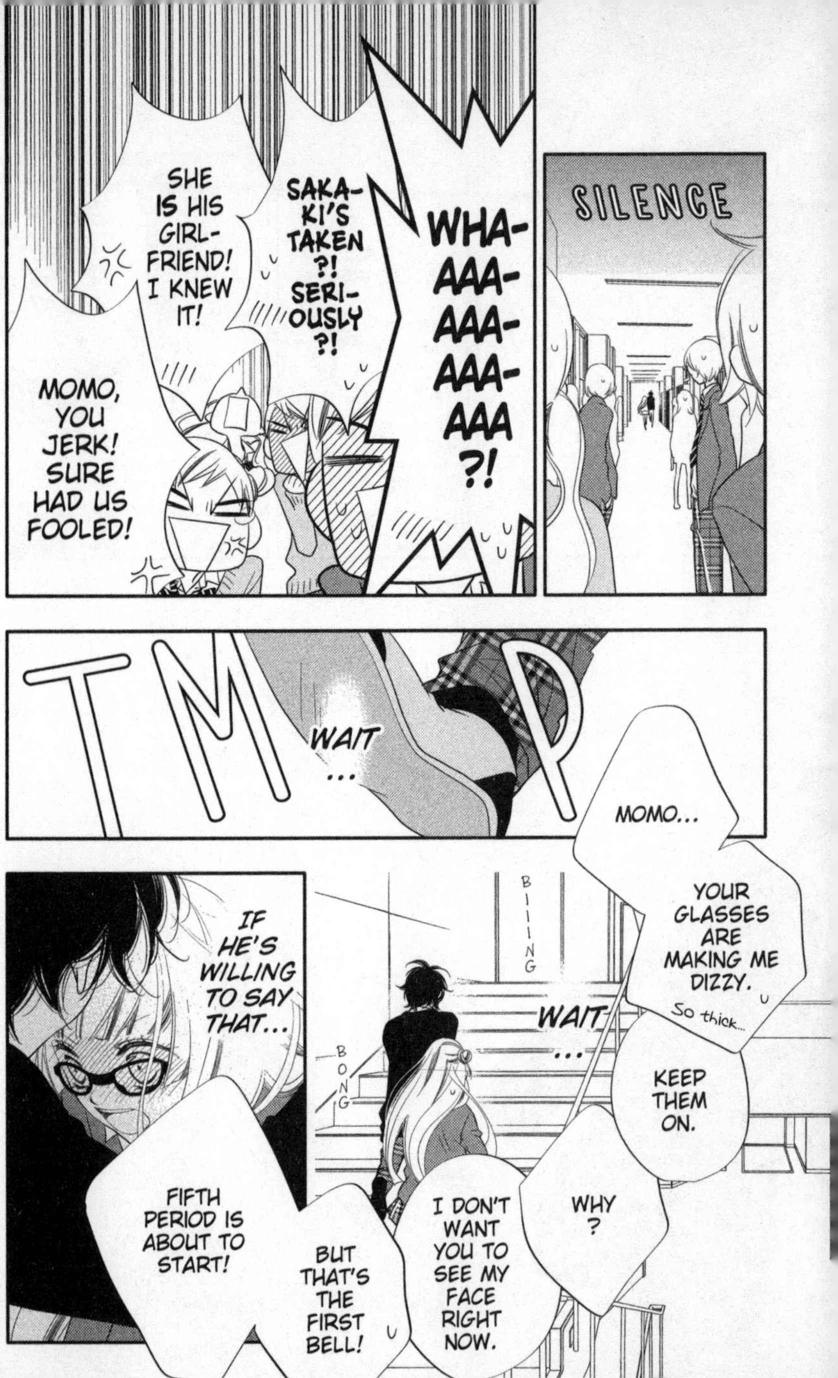
SILENCE
WHA-AAA-AAA-AAA-AAA?!
SAKA-KI'S TAKEN?! SERI-OUSLY?!
SHE IS HIS GIRL-FRIEND! I KNEW IT!
MOMO, YOU JERK! SURE HAD US FOOLED!
TMP
WAIT...
MOMO...
YOUR GLASSES ARE MAKING ME DIZZY.
So thick...
KEEP THEM ON.
WAIT...
BIIING
WHY?
I DON'T WANT YOU TO SEE MY FACE RIGHT NOW.
BONG
BUT THAT'S THE FIRST BELL!
FIFTH PERIOD IS ABOUT TO START!
IF HE'S WILLING TO SAY THAT...

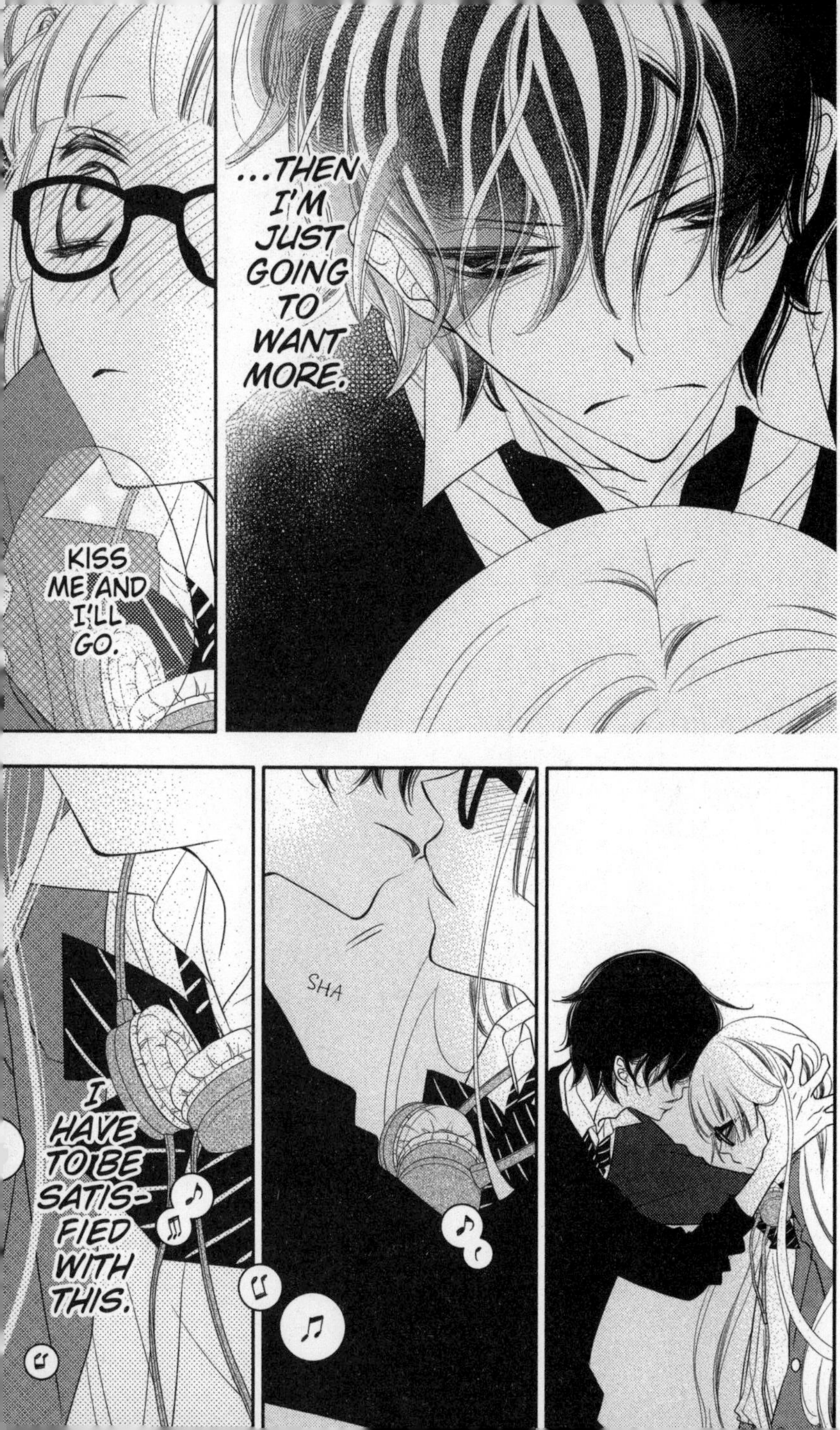
...THEN I'M JUST GOING TO WANT MORE.
KISS ME AND I'LL GO.
SHA
I HAVE TO BE SATIS-FIED WITH THIS.

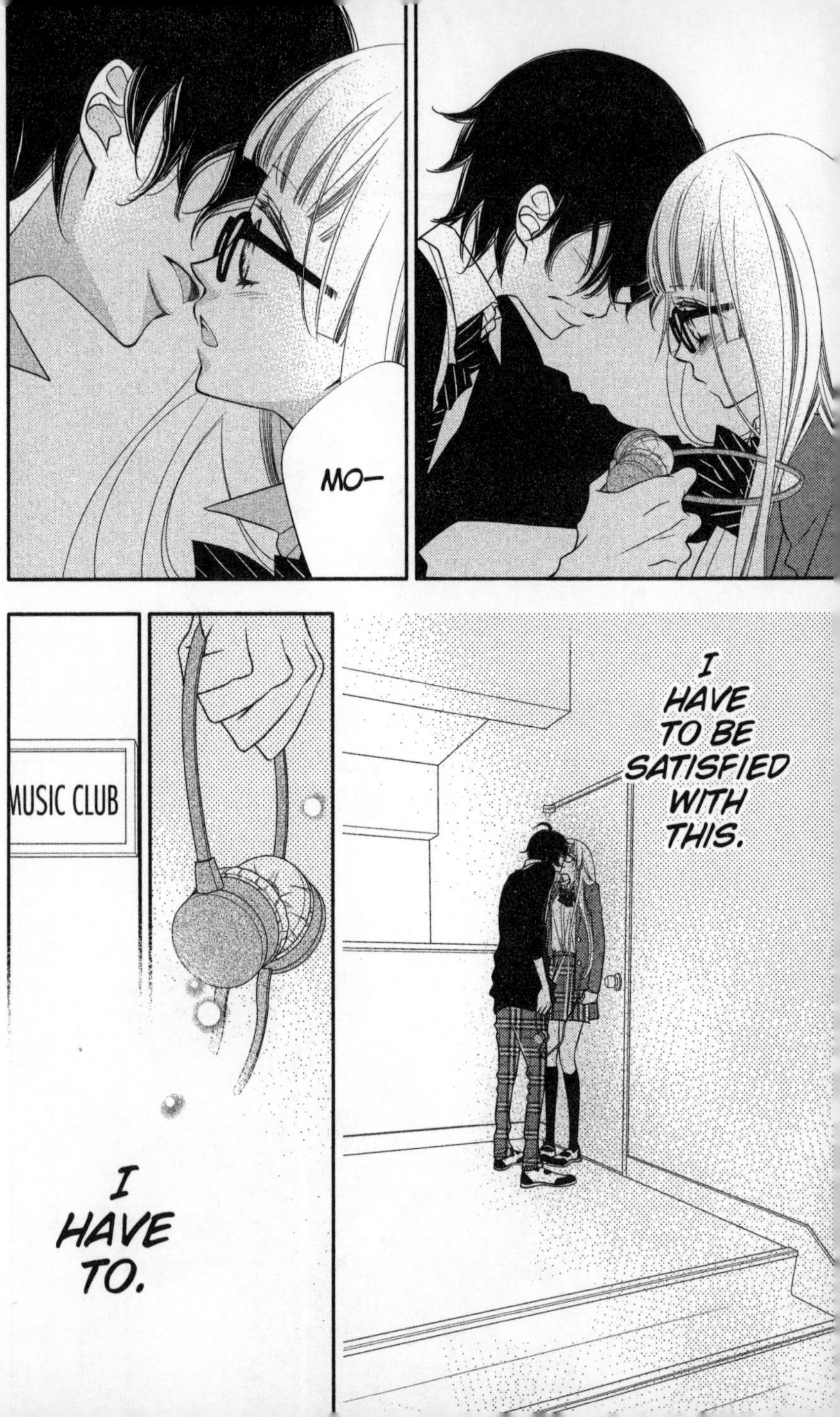
MO—
I HAVE TO BE SATISFIED WITH THIS.
MUSIC CLUB
I HAVE TO.

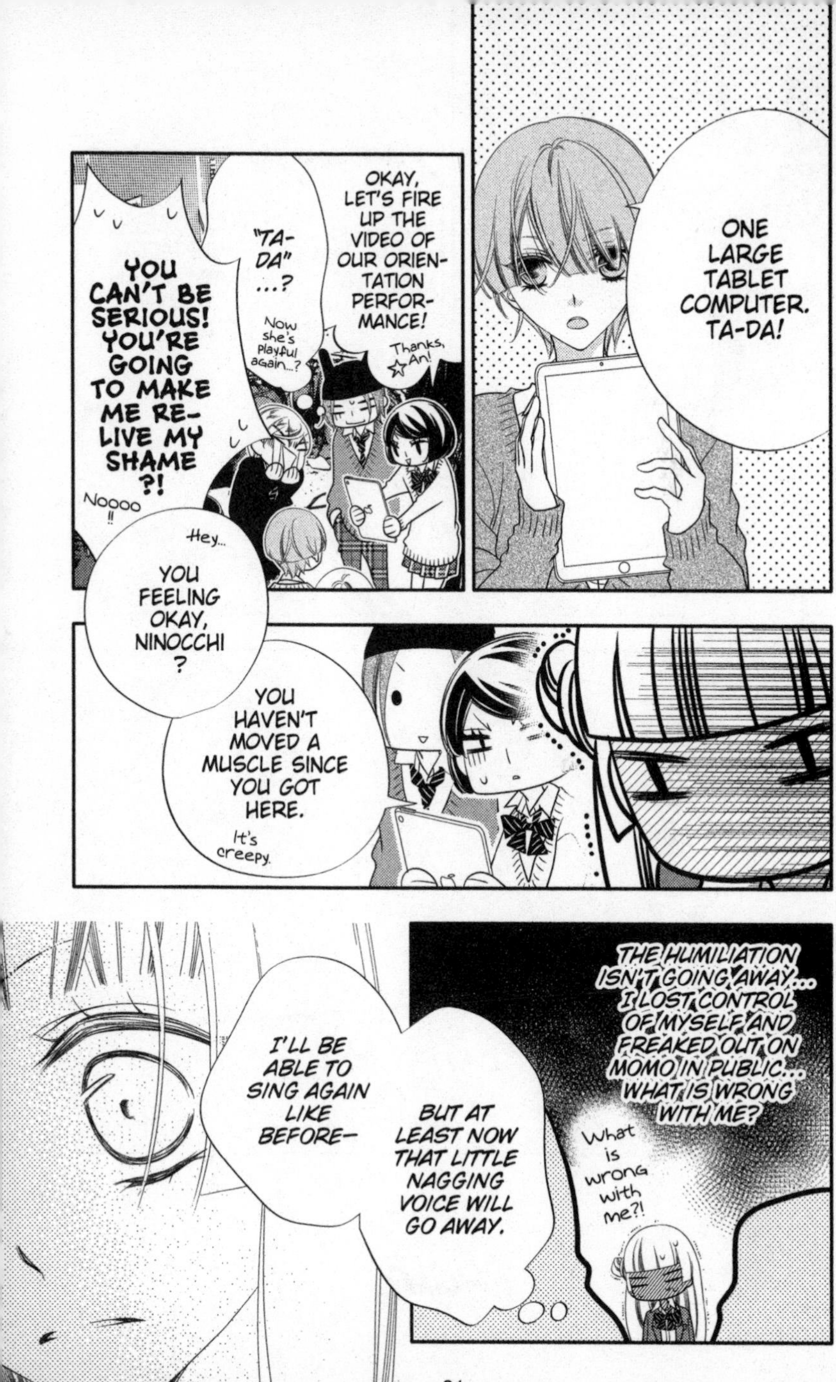
ONE LARGE TABLET COMPUTER. TA-DA!
OKAY, LET'S FIRE UP THE VIDEO OF OUR ORIENTATION PERFORMANCE!
Thanks, An!
"TA-DA" ...?
Now she's playful again...?
YOU CAN'T BE SERIOUS! YOU'RE GOING TO MAKE ME RELIVE MY SHAME?!
Noooo!!
Hey...
YOU FEELING OKAY, NINOCCHI?
YOU HAVEN'T MOVED A MUSCLE SINCE YOU GOT HERE.
It's creepy.
THE HUMILIATION ISN'T GOING AWAY... I LOST CONTROL OF MYSELF AND FREAKED OUT ON MOMO IN PUBLIC... WHAT IS WRONG WITH ME?
What is wrong with me?!
I'LL BE ABLE TO SING AGAIN LIKE BEFORE—
BUT AT LEAST NOW THAT LITTLE NAGGING VOICE WILL GO AWAY.

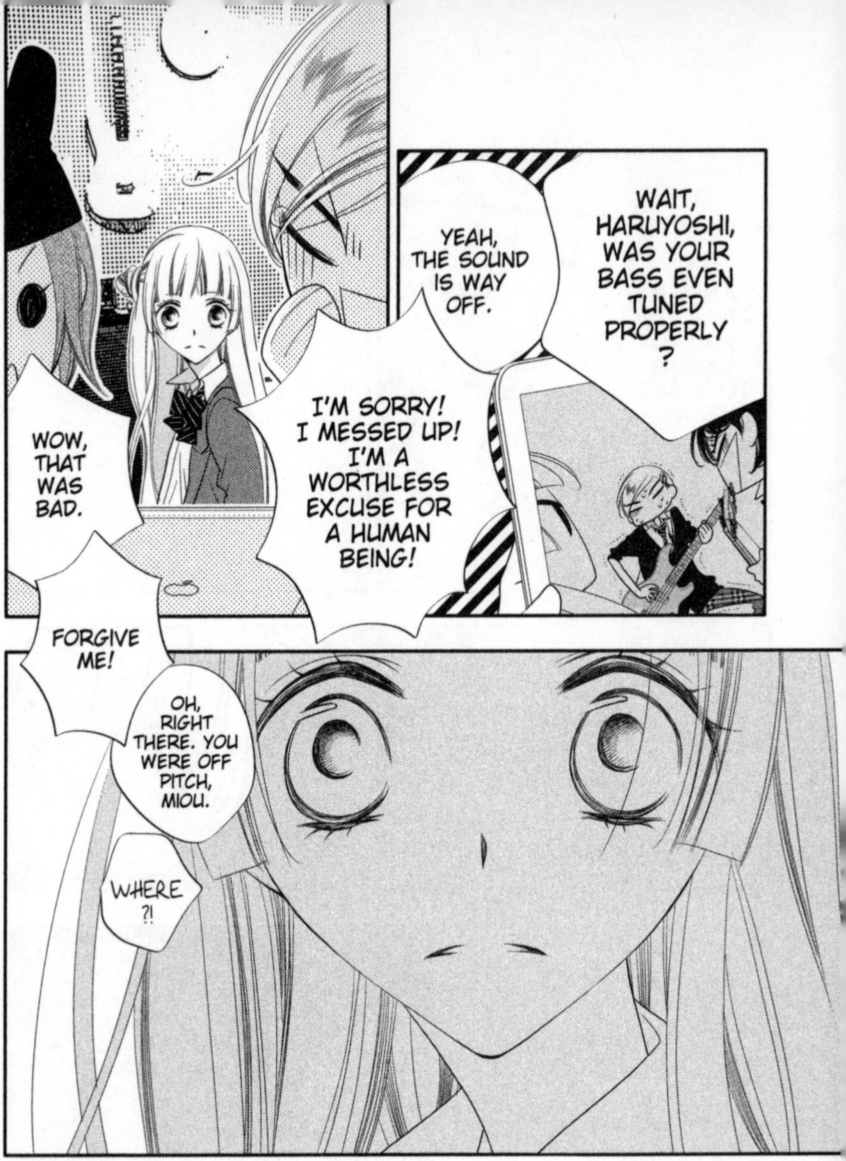
WAIT, HARUYOSHI, WAS YOUR BASS EVEN TUNED PROPERLY?
YEAH, THE SOUND IS WAY OFF.
I'M SORRY! I MESSED UP! I'M A WORTHLESS EXCUSE FOR A HUMAN BEING!
WOW, THAT WAS BAD.
FORGIVE ME!
OH, RIGHT THERE. YOU WERE OFF PITCH, MIOU.
WHERE ?!
HUH?

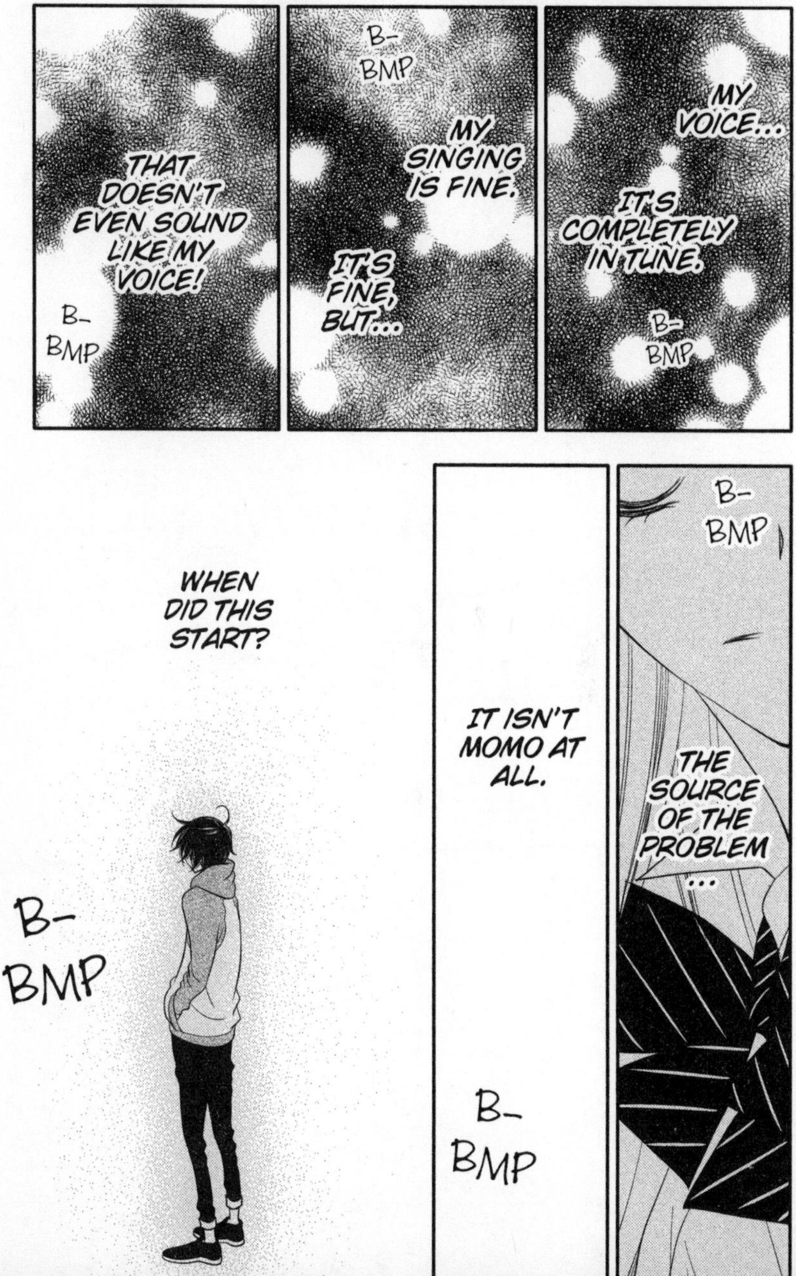
MY VOICE...
IT'S COMPLETELY IN TUNE.
B-BMP
B-BMP
MY SINGING IS FINE.
IT'S FINE, BUT...
THAT DOESN'T EVEN SOUND LIKE MY VOICE!
B-BMP
B-BMP
THE SOURCE OF THE PROBLEM...
IT ISN'T MOMO AT ALL.
B-BMP
WHEN DID THIS START?
B-BMP

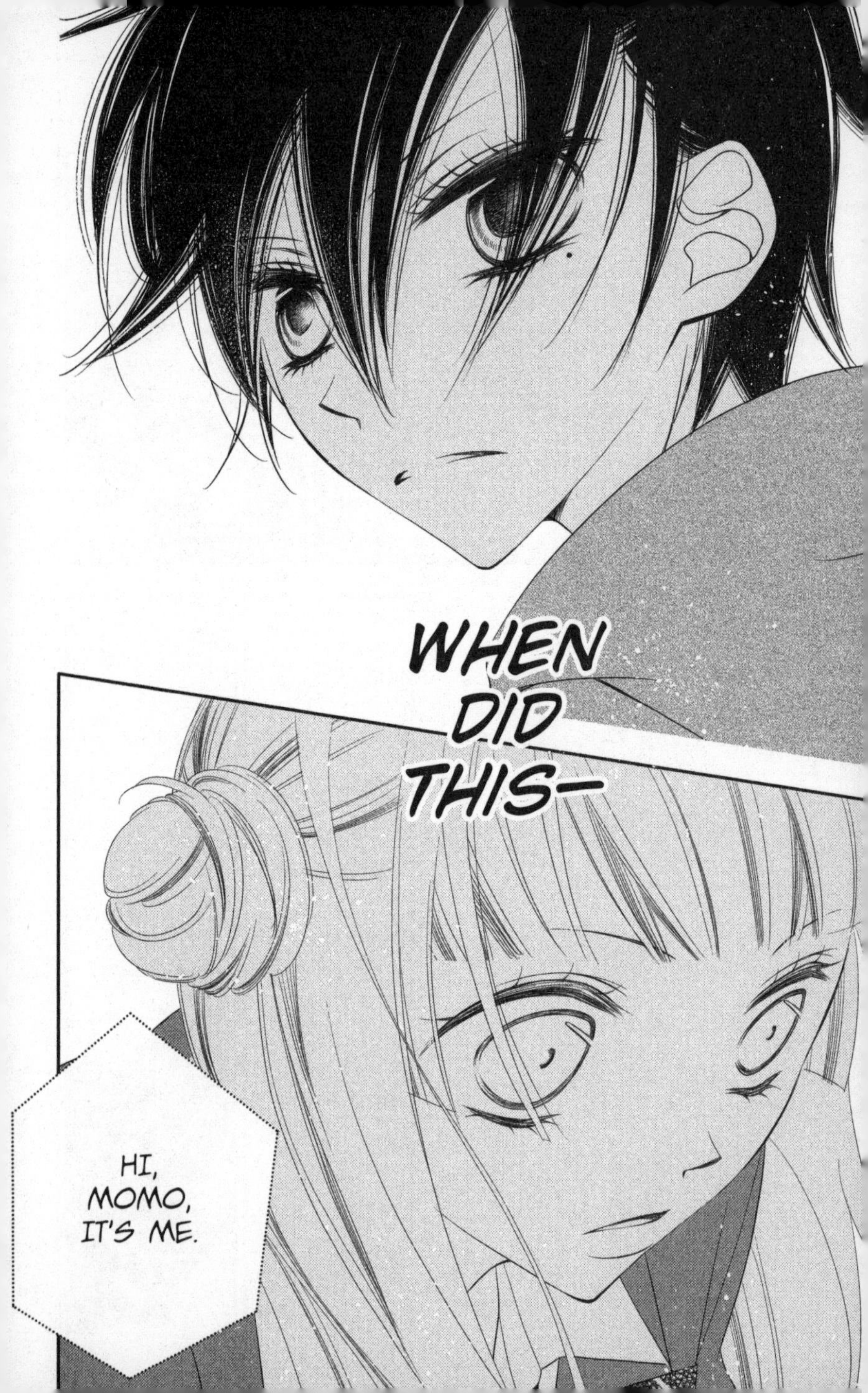
WHEN DID THIS—
HI, MOMO, IT'S ME.

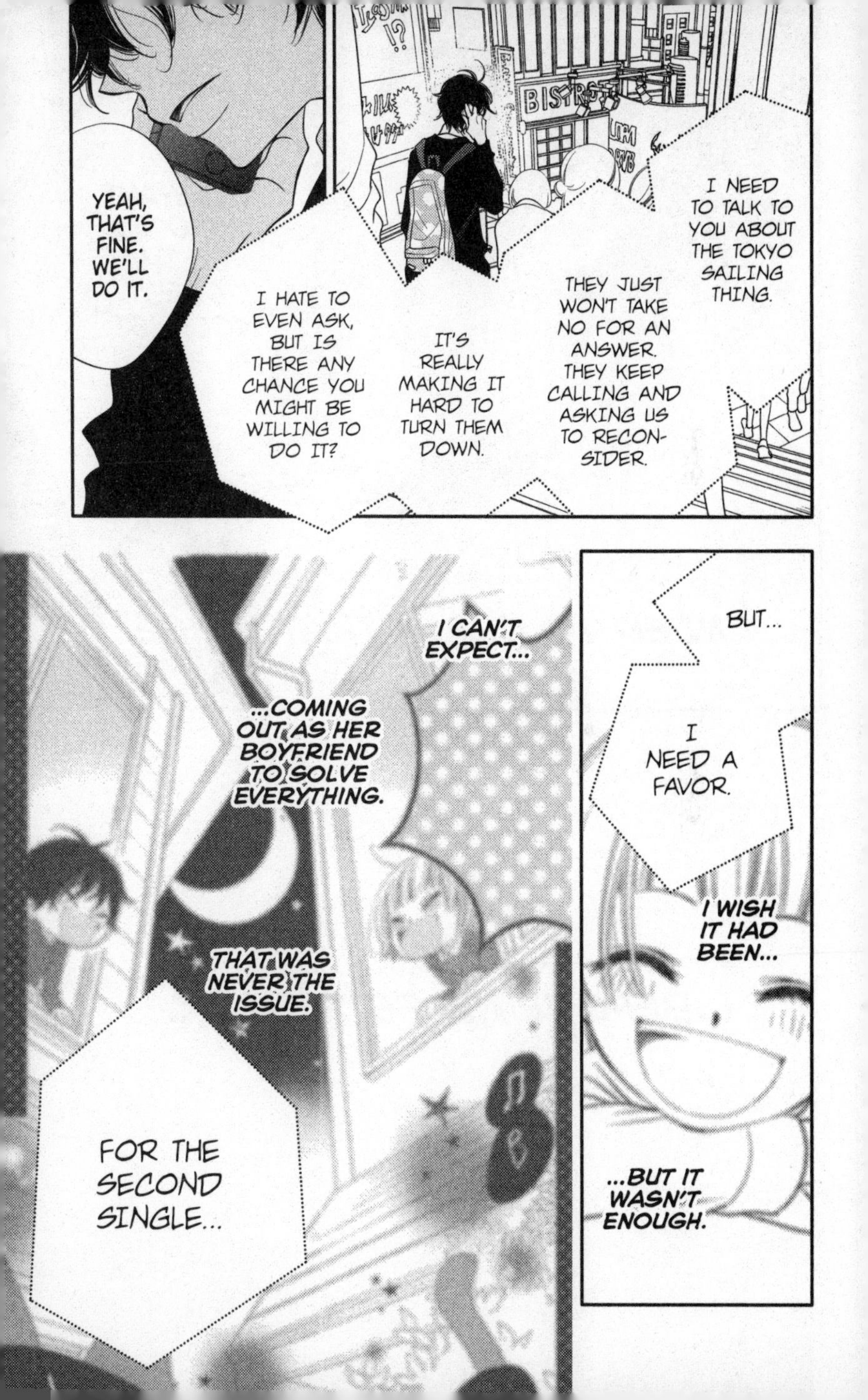
I NEED TO TALK TO YOU ABOUT THE TOKYO SAILING THING.
THEY JUST WON'T TAKE NO FOR AN ANSWER. THEY KEEP CALLING AND ASKING US TO RECONSIDER.
IT'S REALLY MAKING IT HARD TO TURN THEM DOWN.
I HATE TO EVEN ASK, BUT IS THERE ANY CHANCE YOU MIGHT BE WILLING TO DO IT?
YEAH, THAT'S FINE. WE'LL DO IT.
BUT...
I NEED A FAVOR.
I WISH IT HAD BEEN...
...BUT IT WASN'T ENOUGH.
I CAN'T EXPECT...
...COMING OUT AS HER BOYFRIEND TO SOLVE EVERYTHING.
THAT WAS NEVER THE ISSUE.
FOR THE SECOND SINGLE...

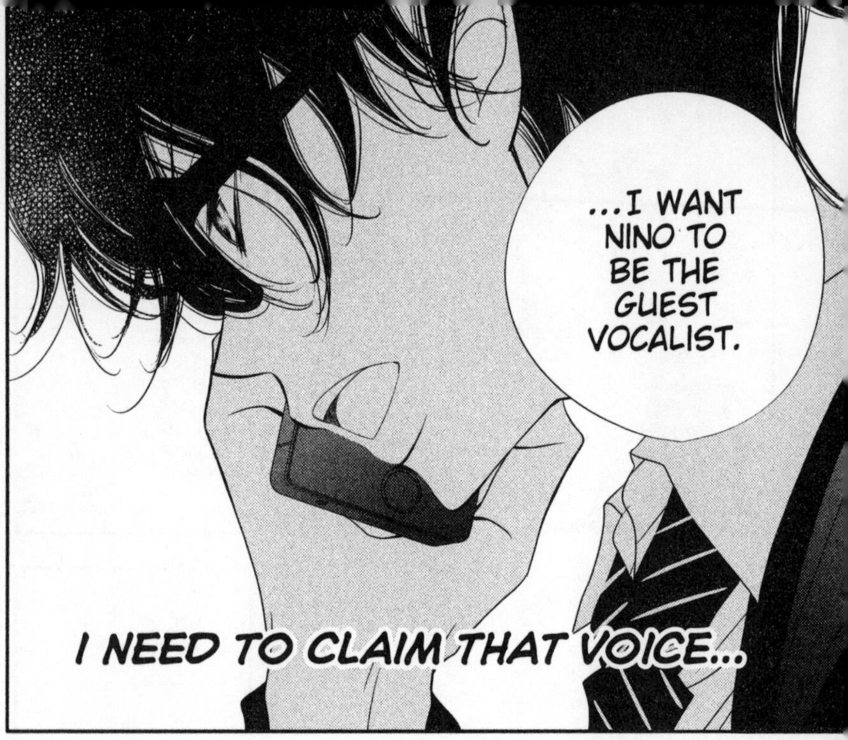
...I WANT NINO TO BE THE GUEST VOCALIST.
I NEED TO CLAIM THAT VOICE...

...BEFORE **HE** GETS BACK.

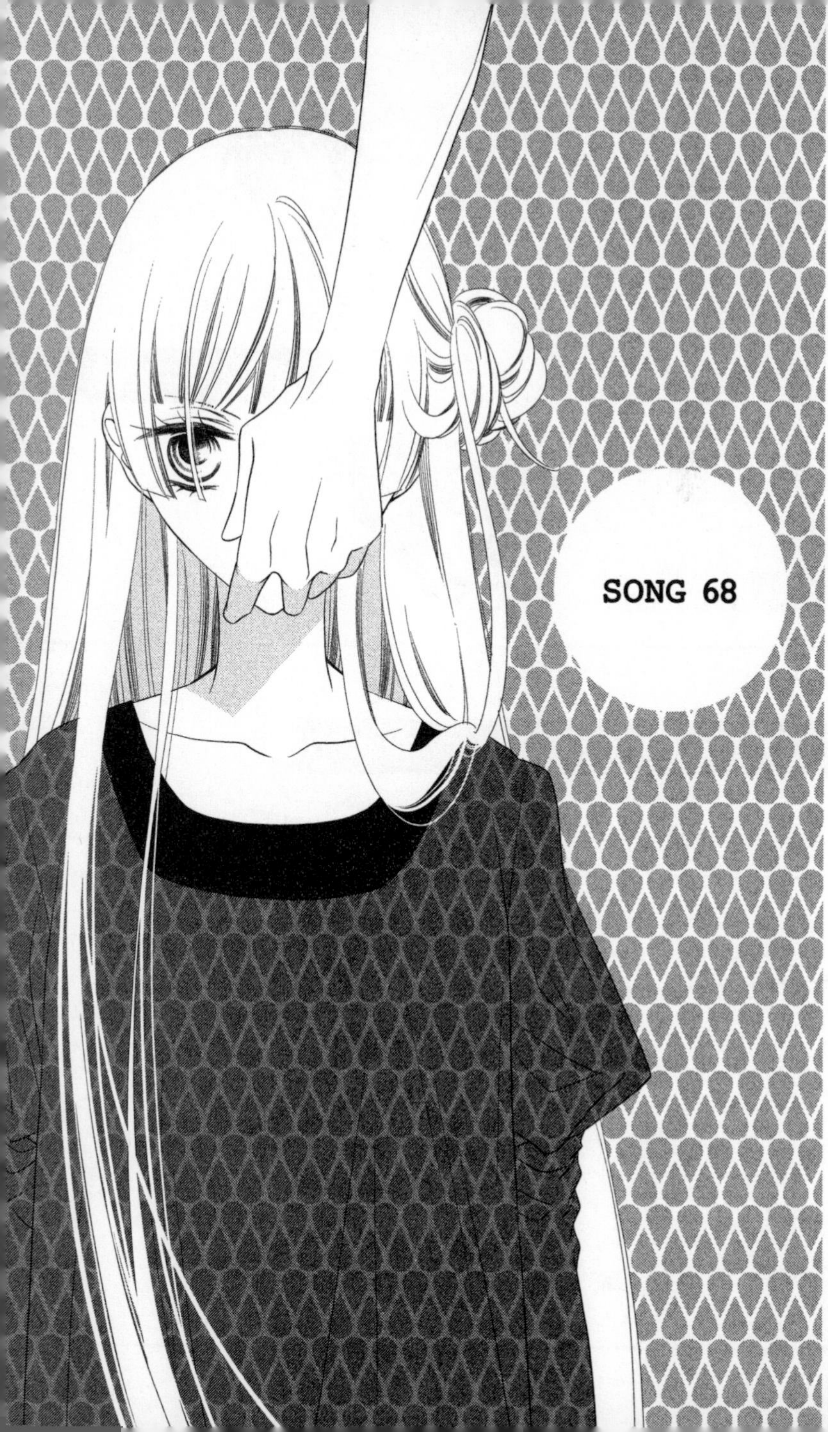
SONG 68

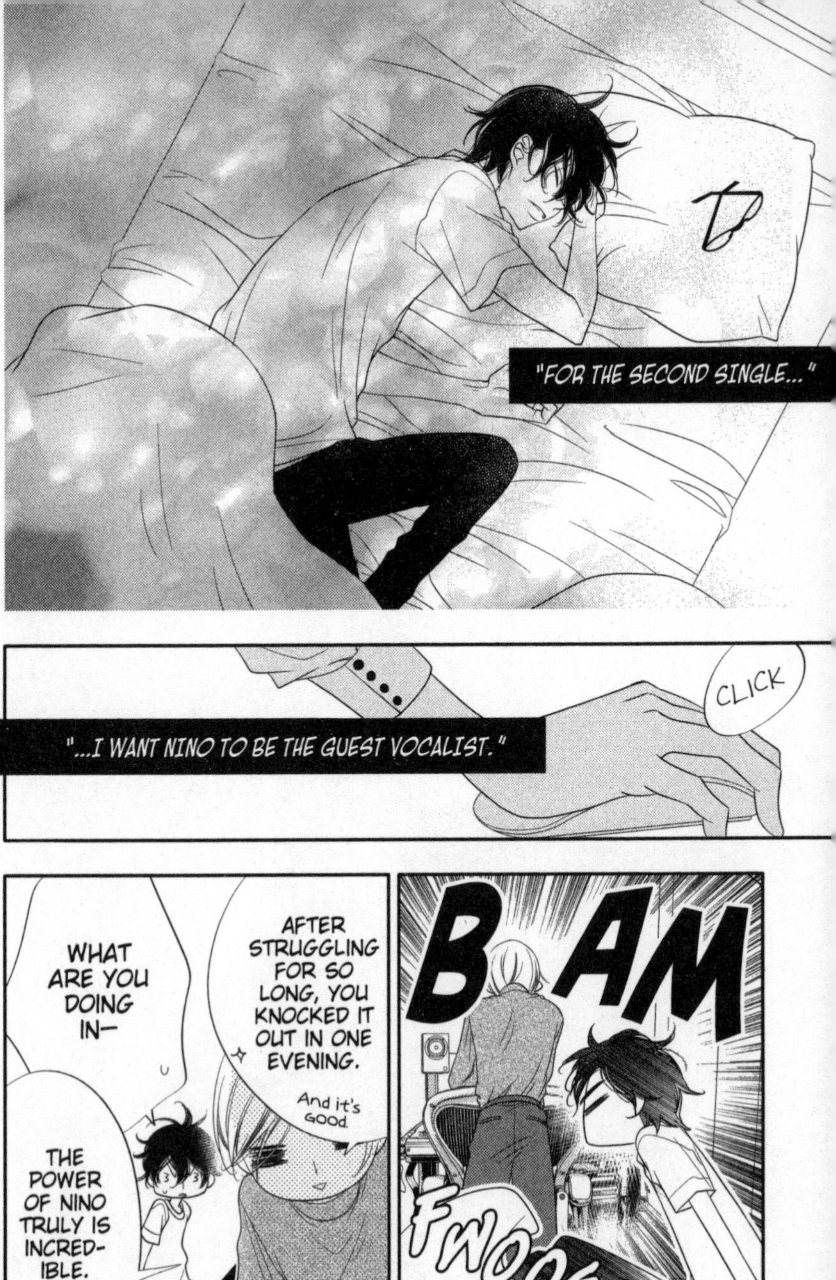
"FOR THE SECOND SINGLE..."
CLICK
"...I WANT NINO TO BE THE GUEST VOCALIST."
BAM
FWOOSH
AFTER STRUGGLING FOR SO LONG, YOU KNOCKED IT OUT IN ONE EVENING.
And it's good.
WHAT ARE YOU DOING IN—
THE POWER OF NINO TRULY IS INCRED-IBLE.

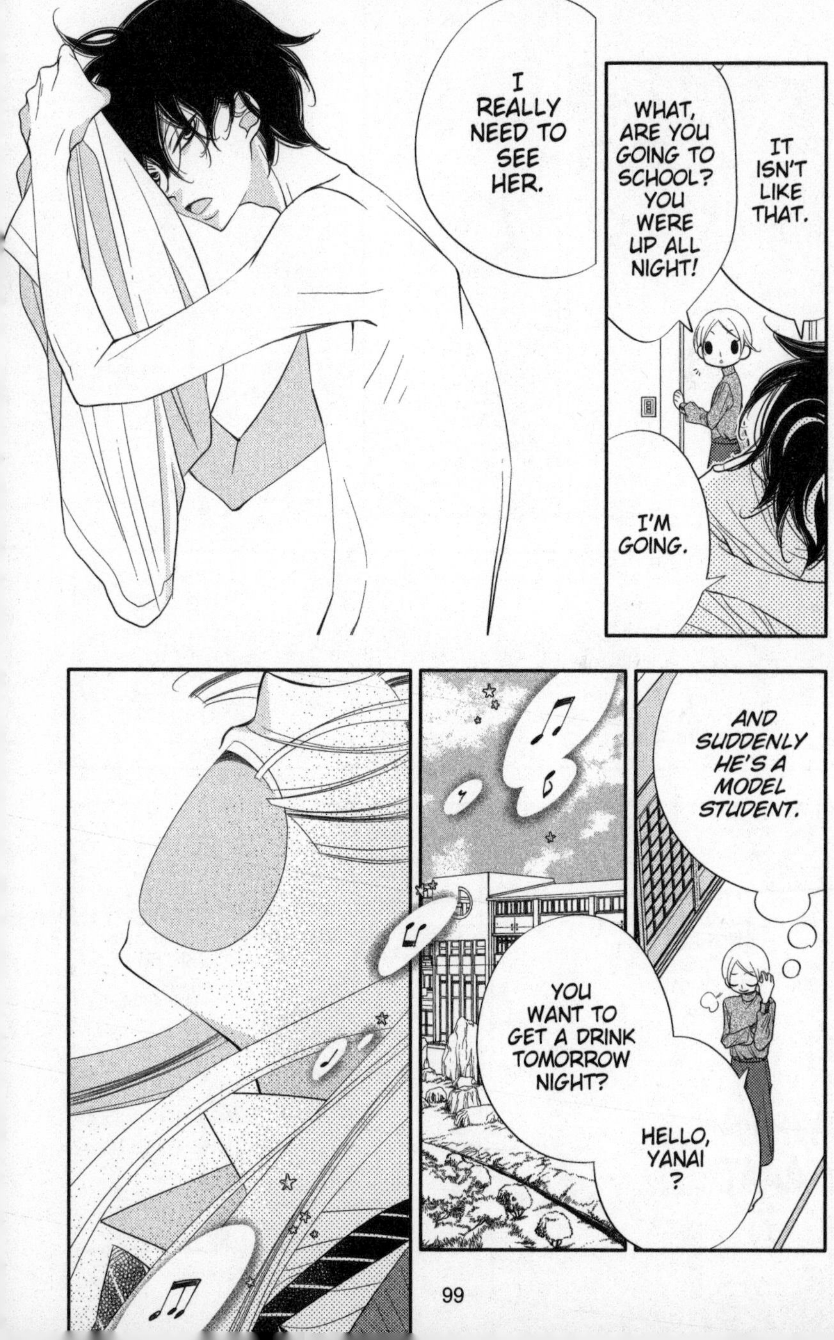
WHAT, ARE YOU GOING TO SCHOOL? YOU WERE UP ALL NIGHT!
IT ISN'T LIKE THAT.
I'M GOING.
I REALLY NEED TO SEE HER.
AND SUDDENLY HE'S A MODEL STUDENT.
HELLO, YANAI?
YOU WANT TO GET A DRINK TOMORROW NIGHT?

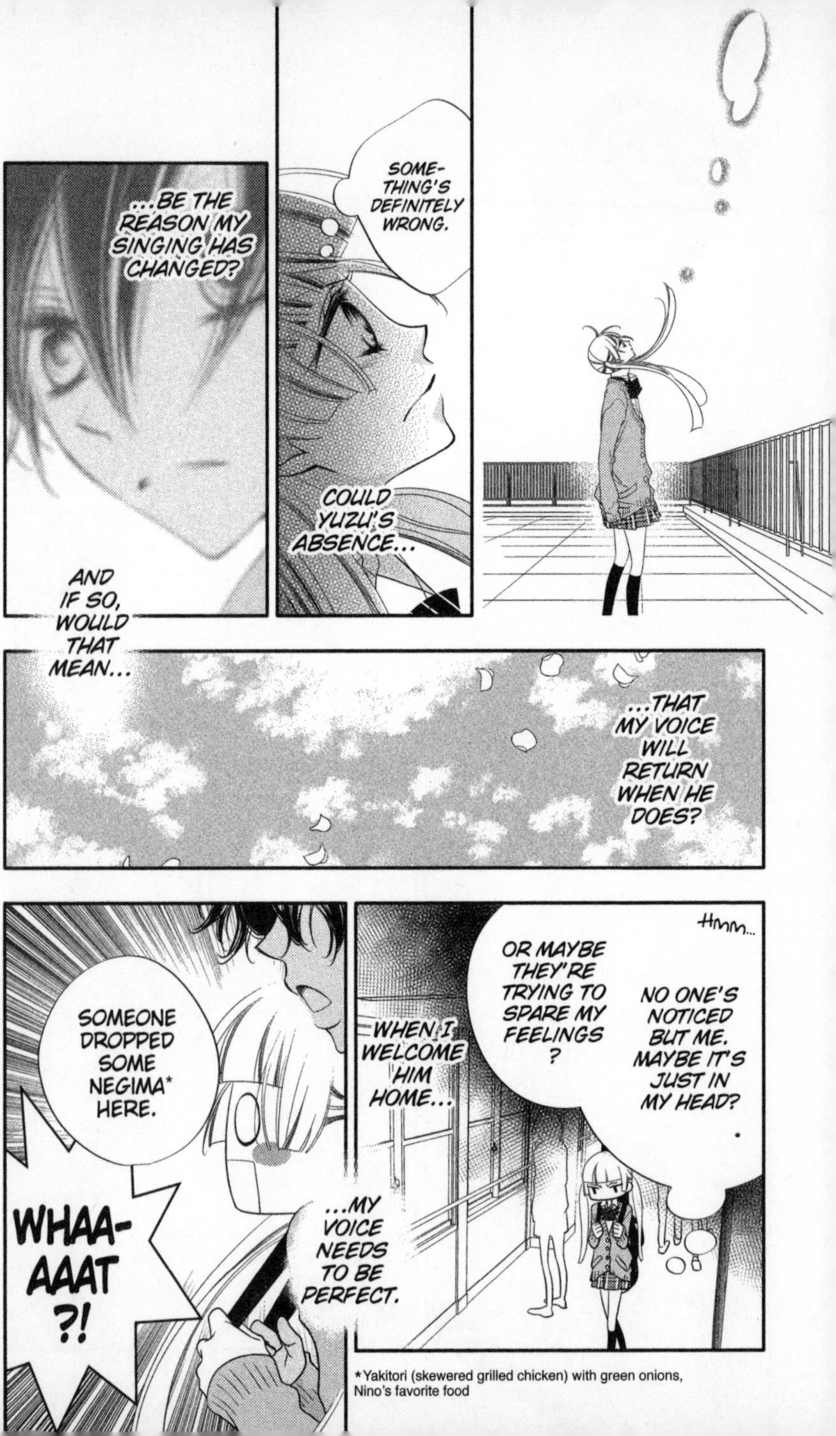
SOME-THING'S DEFINITELY WRONG.
COULD YUZU'S ABSENCE...
...BE THE REASON MY SINGING HAS CHANGED?
AND IF SO, WOULD THAT MEAN...
...THAT MY VOICE WILL RETURN WHEN HE DOES?
Hmm...
NO ONE'S NOTICED BUT ME. MAYBE IT'S JUST IN MY HEAD?
OR MAYBE THEY'RE TRYING TO SPARE MY FEELINGS?
WHEN I WELCOME HIM HOME...
...MY VOICE NEEDS TO BE PERFECT.
SOMEONE DROPPED SOME NEGIMA* HERE.
WHAA-AAAT?!

*Yakitori (skewered grilled chicken) with green onions, Nino's favorite food

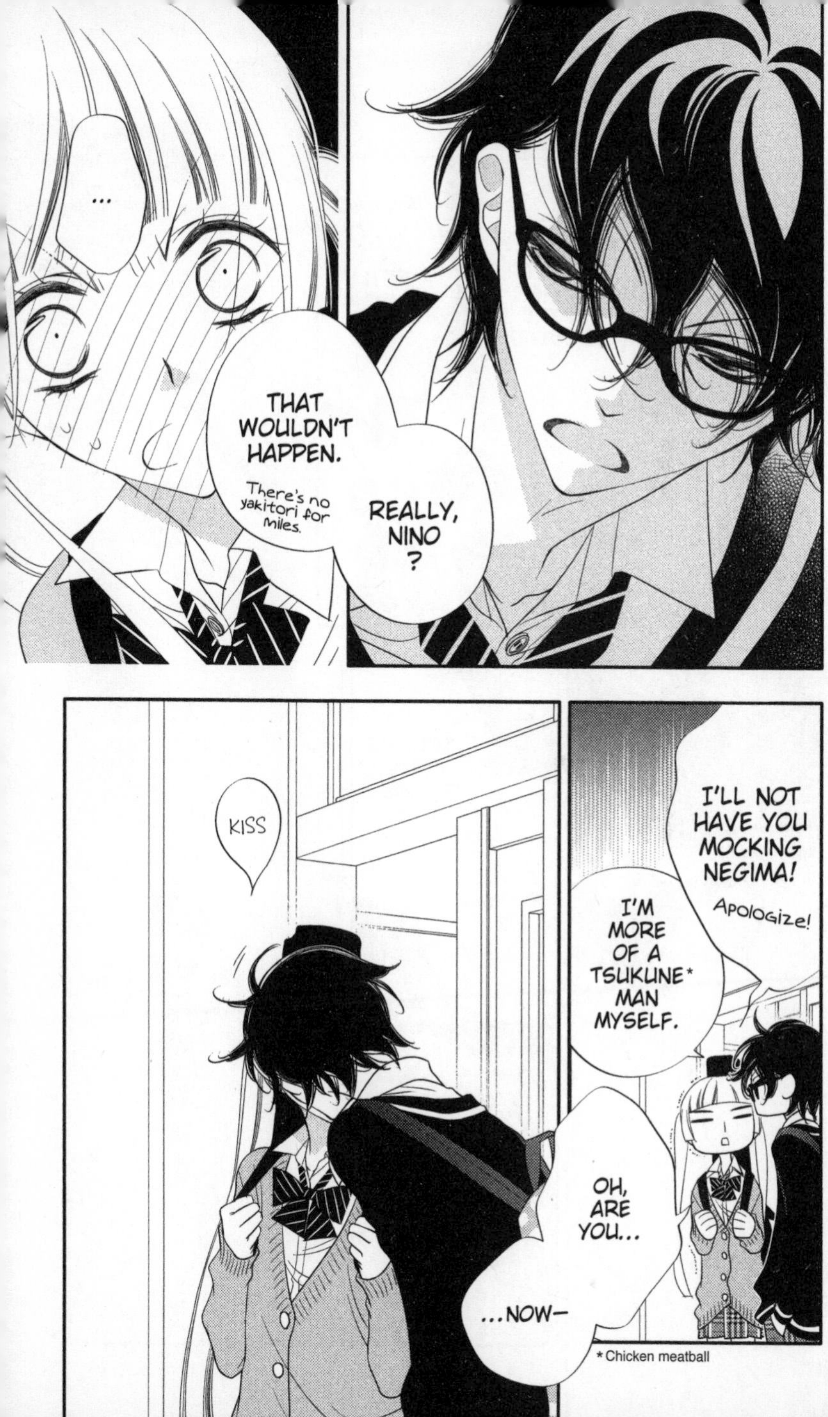
THAT WOULDN'T HAPPEN.
REALLY, NINO?
There's no yakitori for miles.
...
I'LL NOT HAVE YOU MOCKING NEGIMA!
Apologize!
I'M MORE OF A TSUKUNE* MAN MYSELF.
OH, ARE YOU...
...NOW—
KISS

*Chicken meatball

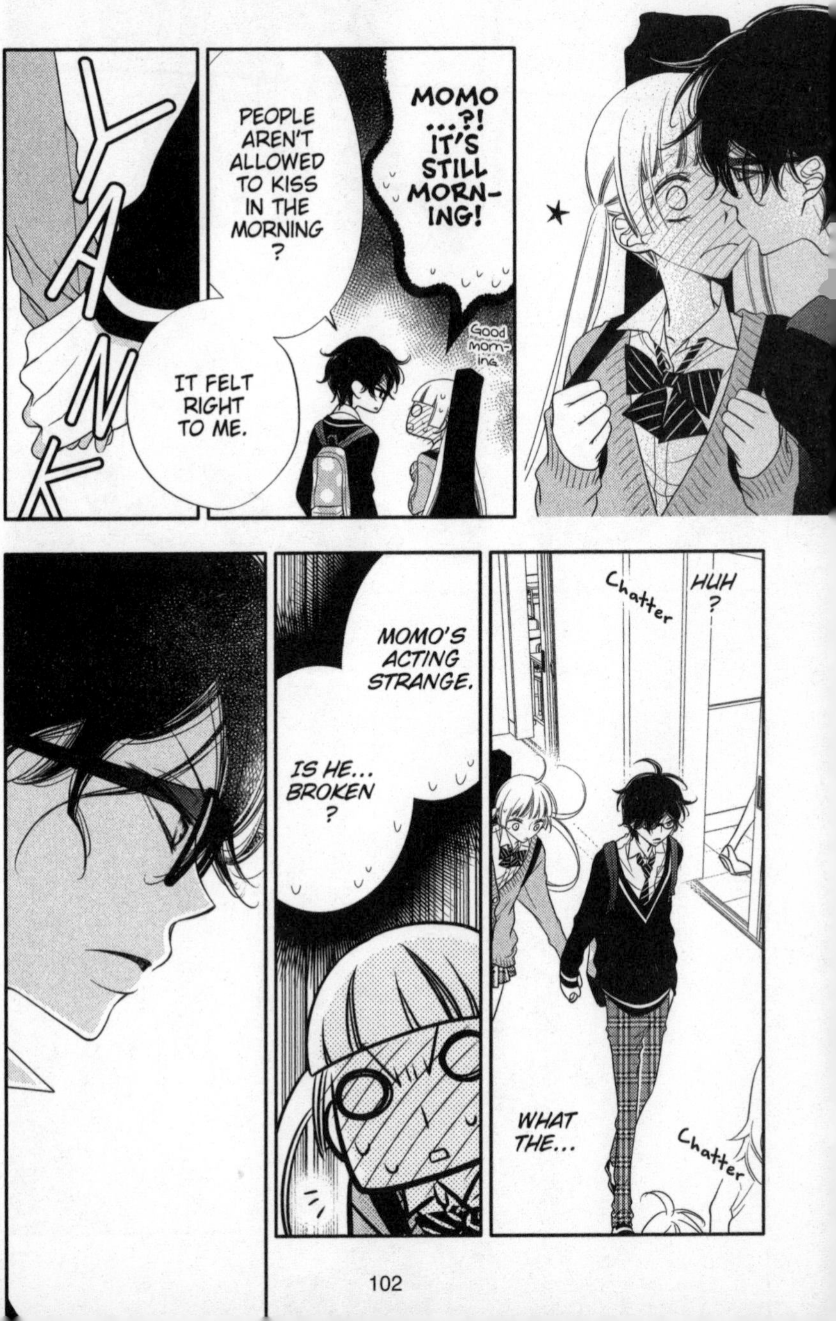
MOMO ...?! IT'S STILL MORN-ING!
Good morn-ing
PEOPLE AREN'T ALLOWED TO KISS IN THE MORNING?
IT FELT RIGHT TO ME.
YANK
HUH?
Chatter
WHAT THE...
Chatter
MOMO'S ACTING STRANGE.
IS HE... BROKEN?

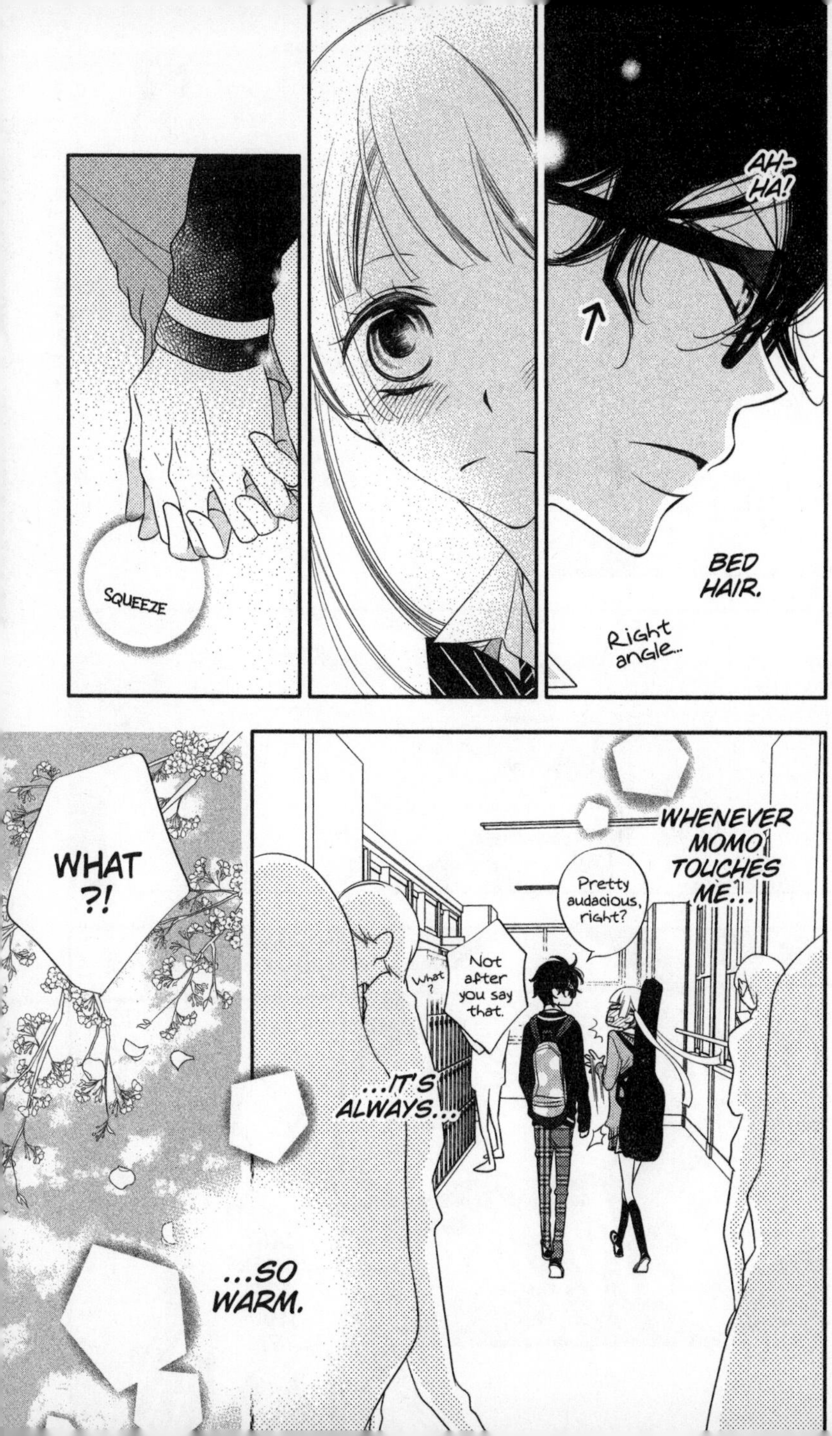
AH-HA!
BED HAIR.
Right angle...
SQUEEZE
WHENEVER MOMO TOUCHES ME...
Pretty audacious, right?
Not after you say that.
What?
...IT'S ALWAYS...
WHAT?!
...SO WARM.

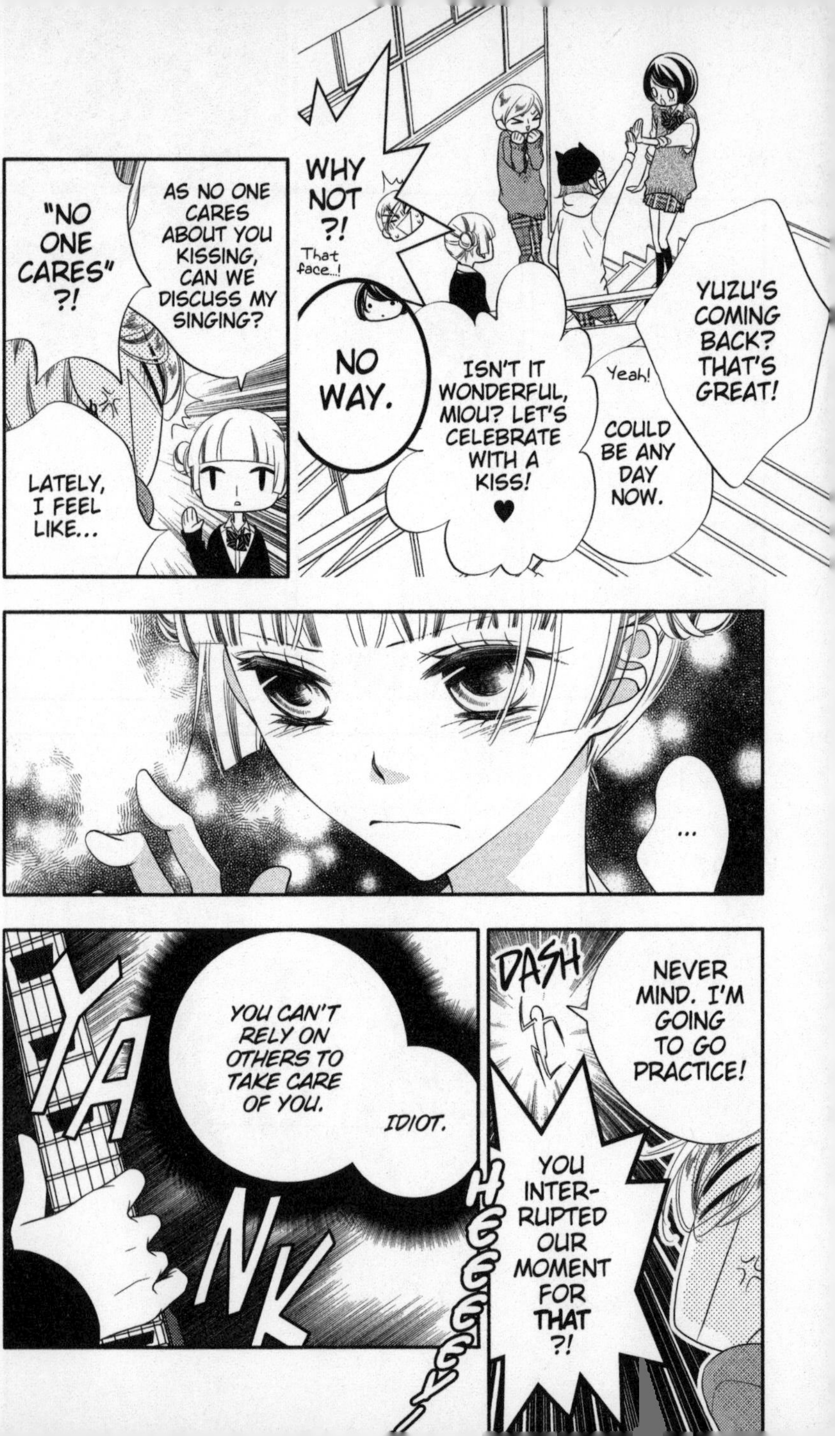
YUZU'S COMING BACK? THAT'S GREAT!
Yeah!
COULD BE ANY DAY NOW.
ISN'T IT WONDERFUL, MIOU? LET'S CELEBRATE WITH A KISS! ♥
NO WAY.
WHY NOT ?!
That face...!
AS NO ONE CARES ABOUT YOU KISSING, CAN WE DISCUSS MY SINGING?
"NO ONE CARES" ?!
LATELY, I FEEL LIKE...
...
NEVER MIND. I'M GOING TO GO PRACTICE!
DASH
YOU INTER-RUPTED OUR MOMENT FOR THAT ?!
YANK
YOU CAN'T RELY ON OTHERS TO TAKE CARE OF YOU.
IDIOT.

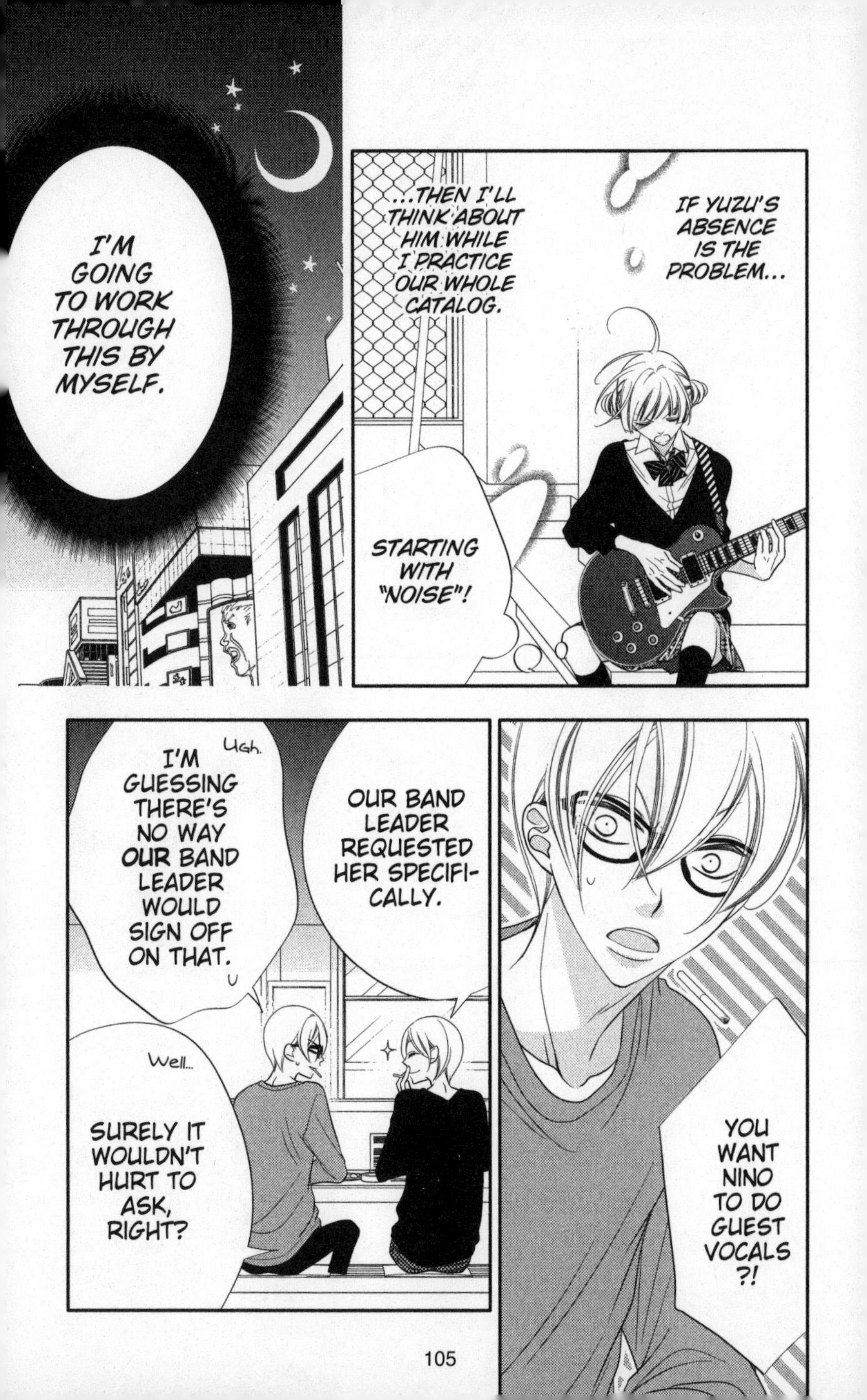
IF YUZU'S ABSENCE IS THE PROBLEM...
...THEN I'LL THINK ABOUT HIM WHILE I PRACTICE OUR WHOLE CATALOG.
STARTING WITH "NOISE"!
I'M GOING TO WORK THROUGH THIS BY MYSELF.
YOU WANT NINO TO DO GUEST VOCALS?!
OUR BAND LEADER REQUESTED HER SPECIFICALLY.
Ugh.
I'M GUESSING THERE'S NO WAY OUR BAND LEADER WOULD SIGN OFF ON THAT.
Well...
SURELY IT WOULDN'T HURT TO ASK, RIGHT?

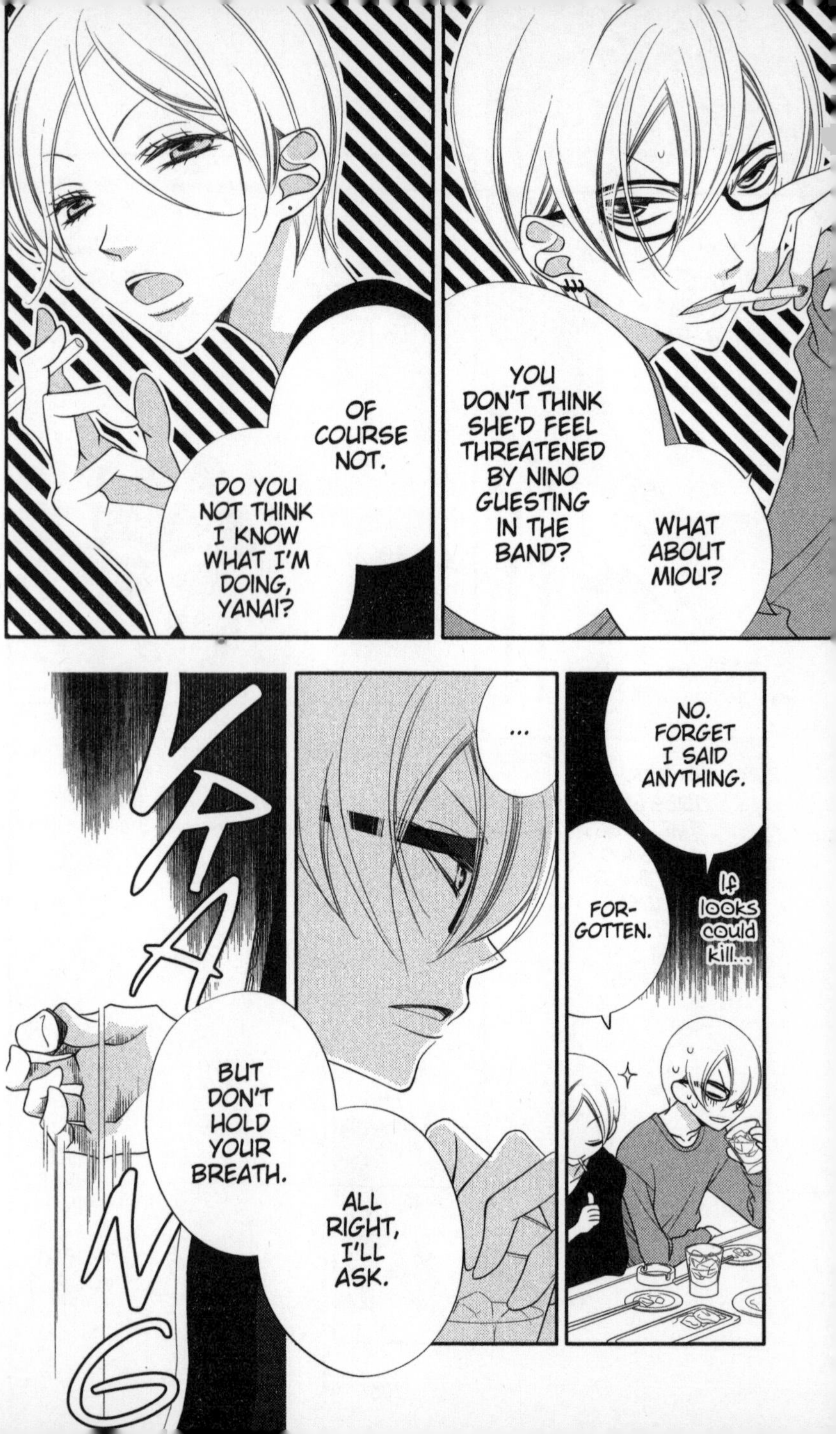
WHAT ABOUT MIOU?
YOU DON'T THINK SHE'D FEEL THREATENED BY NINO GUESTING IN THE BAND?
OF COURSE NOT.
DO YOU NOT THINK I KNOW WHAT I'M DOING, YANAI?
NO. FORGET I SAID ANYTHING.
If looks could kill...
FOR-GOTTEN.
...
ALL RIGHT, I'LL ASK.
BUT DON'T HOLD YOUR BREATH.
VRAANG

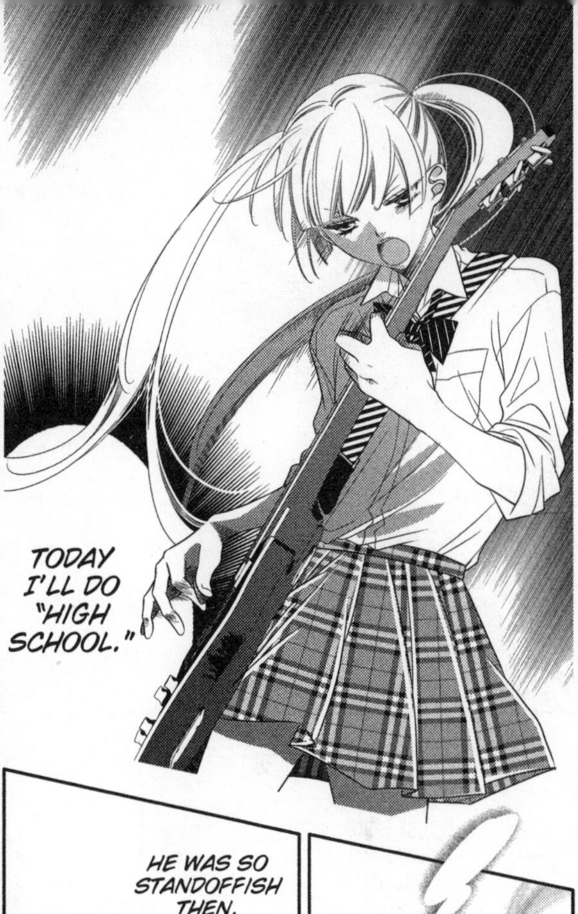
TODAY I'LL DO "HIGH SCHOOL."
IT WAS AROUND A YEAR AGO...
...WHEN YUZU AND I REUNITED OVER THIS SONG.
HE WAS SO STANDOFFISH THEN.
I REMEMBER WHAT A MESS HIS EYELASHES WERE...
DON'T TALK TO ME ANYMORE.
Ah, memories.

4

Volume 13 marks the beginning of the Tokyo Sailing arc, so I spent a lot of time around New Year's photographing various live music venues in Shibuya. They gave us permission to use their names, so who knows—your favorite haunt might just appear! I'm about to start drawing the chapters for serialization now, and I'm really looking forward to it! Drawing the interiors of clubs is really hard, so my assistants and I were so relieved to be allowed to take reference photos.
The experience of taking all those photos left me positively dying to go see some live shows! There's nothing quite like the passion and excitement of live music. Now I just need to cram that feeling into my manga...

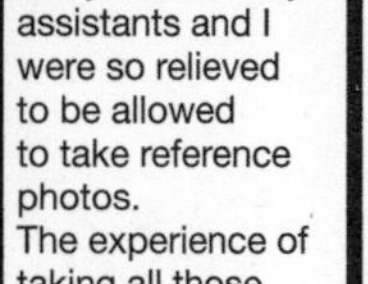
WHAM!

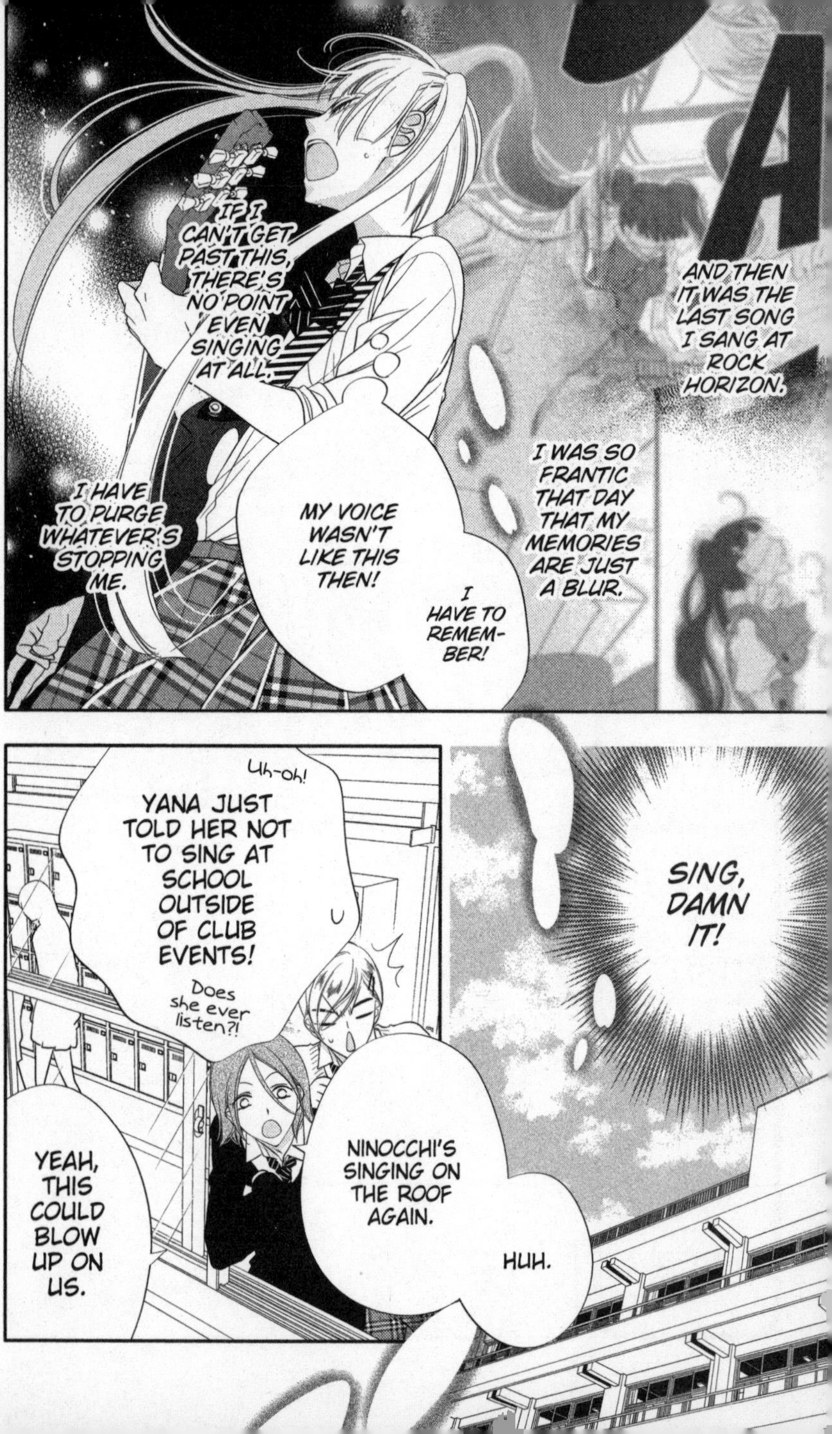
AND THEN IT WAS THE LAST SONG I SANG AT ROCK HORIZON.
I WAS SO FRANTIC THAT DAY THAT MY MEMORIES ARE JUST A BLUR.
I HAVE TO REMEMBER!
MY VOICE WASN'T LIKE THIS THEN!
IF I CAN'T GET PAST THIS, THERE'S NO POINT EVEN SINGING AT ALL.
I HAVE TO PURGE WHATEVER'S STOPPING ME.
SING, DAMN IT!
NINOCCHI'S SINGING ON THE ROOF AGAIN.
HUH.
Uh-oh!
YANA JUST TOLD HER NOT TO SING AT SCHOOL OUTSIDE OF CLUB EVENTS!
Does she ever listen?!
YEAH, THIS COULD BLOW UP ON US.

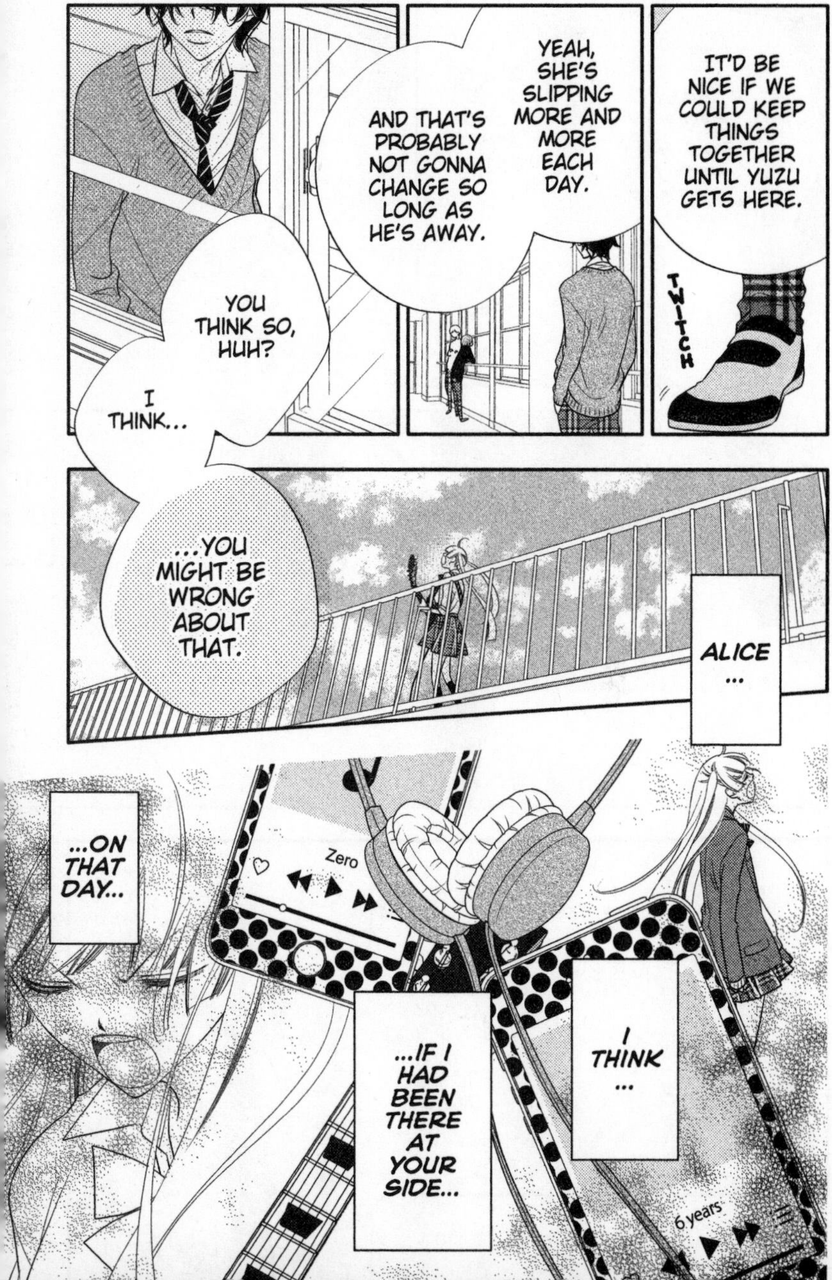
IT'D BE NICE IF WE COULD KEEP THINGS TOGETHER UNTIL YUZU GETS HERE.
TWITCH
YEAH, SHE'S SLIPPING MORE AND MORE EACH DAY.
AND THAT'S PROBABLY NOT GONNA CHANGE SO LONG AS HE'S AWAY.
YOU THINK SO, HUH?
I THINK...
...YOU MIGHT BE WRONG ABOUT THAT.
ALICE...
6 years
I THINK...
...IF I HAD BEEN THERE AT YOUR SIDE...
Zero
...ON THAT DAY...

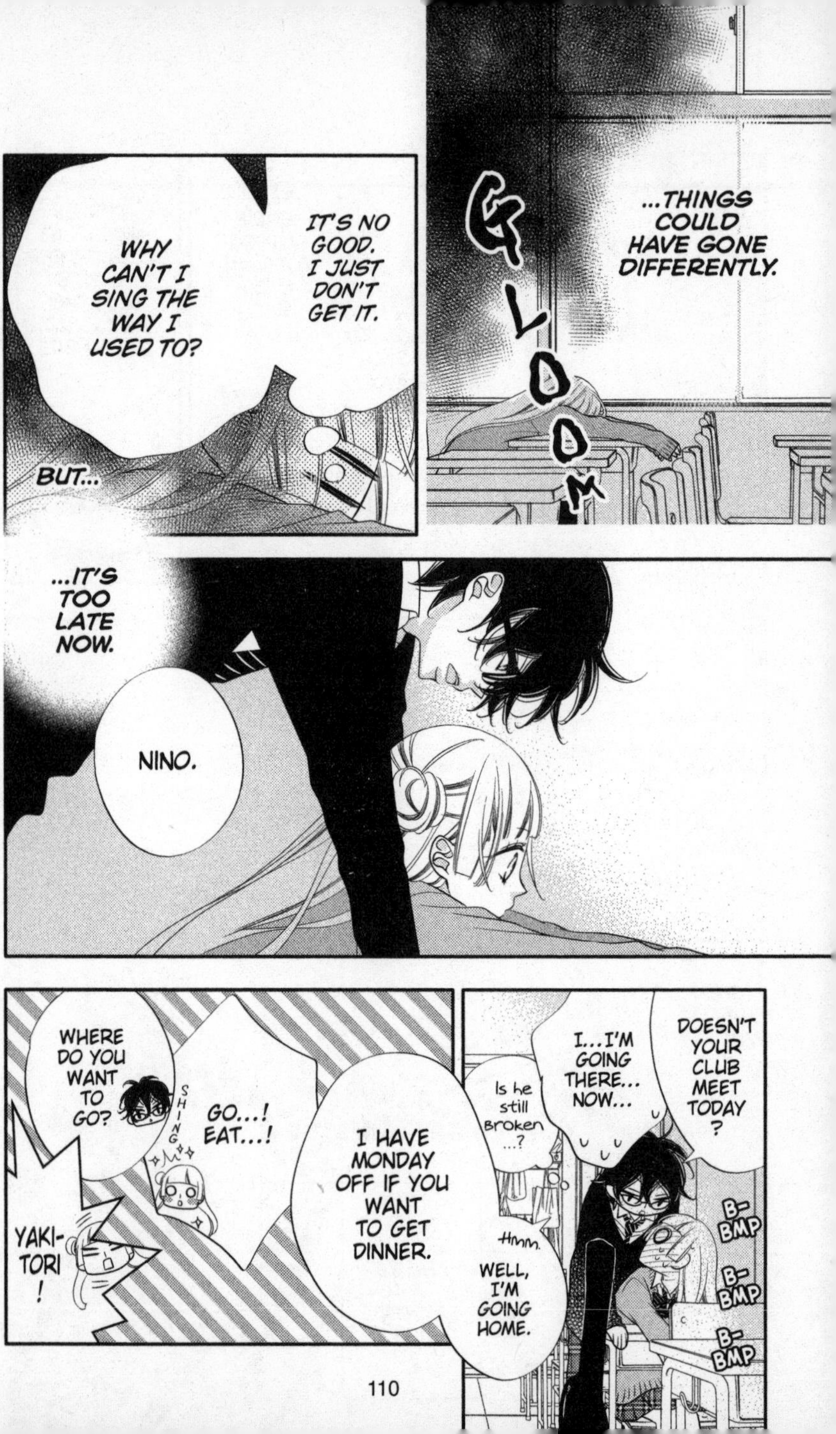
...THINGS COULD HAVE GONE DIFFERENTLY.
GLOOM
IT'S NO GOOD. I JUST DON'T GET IT.
WHY CAN'T I SING THE WAY I USED TO?
BUT...
...IT'S TOO LATE NOW.
NINO.
DOESN'T YOUR CLUB MEET TODAY?
B-BMP
B-BMP
B-BMP
I...I'M GOING THERE... NOW...
Is he still broken...?
Hmm.
WELL, I'M GOING HOME.
I HAVE MONDAY OFF IF YOU WANT TO GET DINNER.
GO...! EAT...!
SHING
WHERE DO YOU WANT TO GO?
YAKI-TORI!

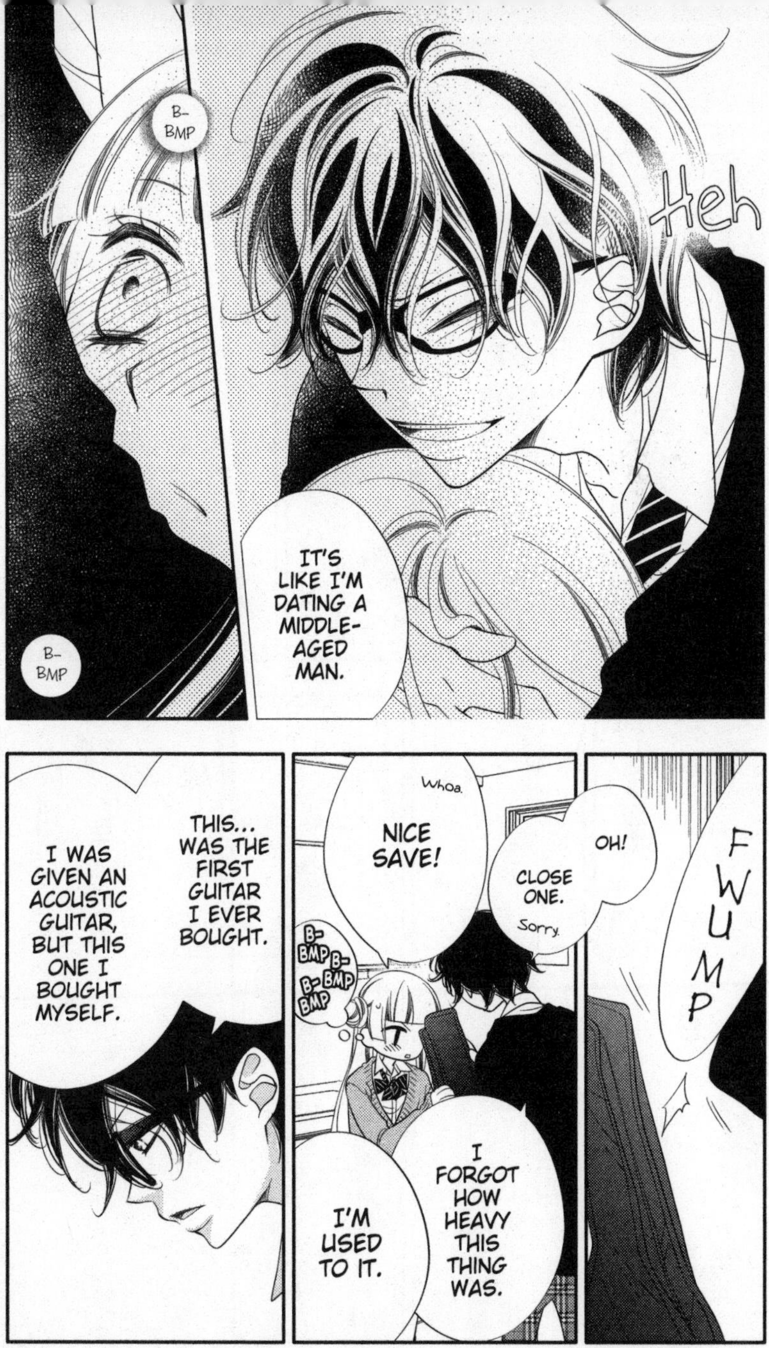
Heh
B-BMP
IT'S LIKE I'M DATING A MIDDLE-AGED MAN.
B-BMP
FWUMP
OH!
CLOSE ONE.
Sorry.
Whoa.
NICE SAVE!
B-BMP B-BMP B-BMP
I FORGOT HOW HEAVY THIS THING WAS.
I'M USED TO IT.
THIS... WAS THE FIRST GUITAR I EVER BOUGHT.
I WAS GIVEN AN ACOUSTIC GUITAR, BUT THIS ONE I BOUGHT MYSELF.

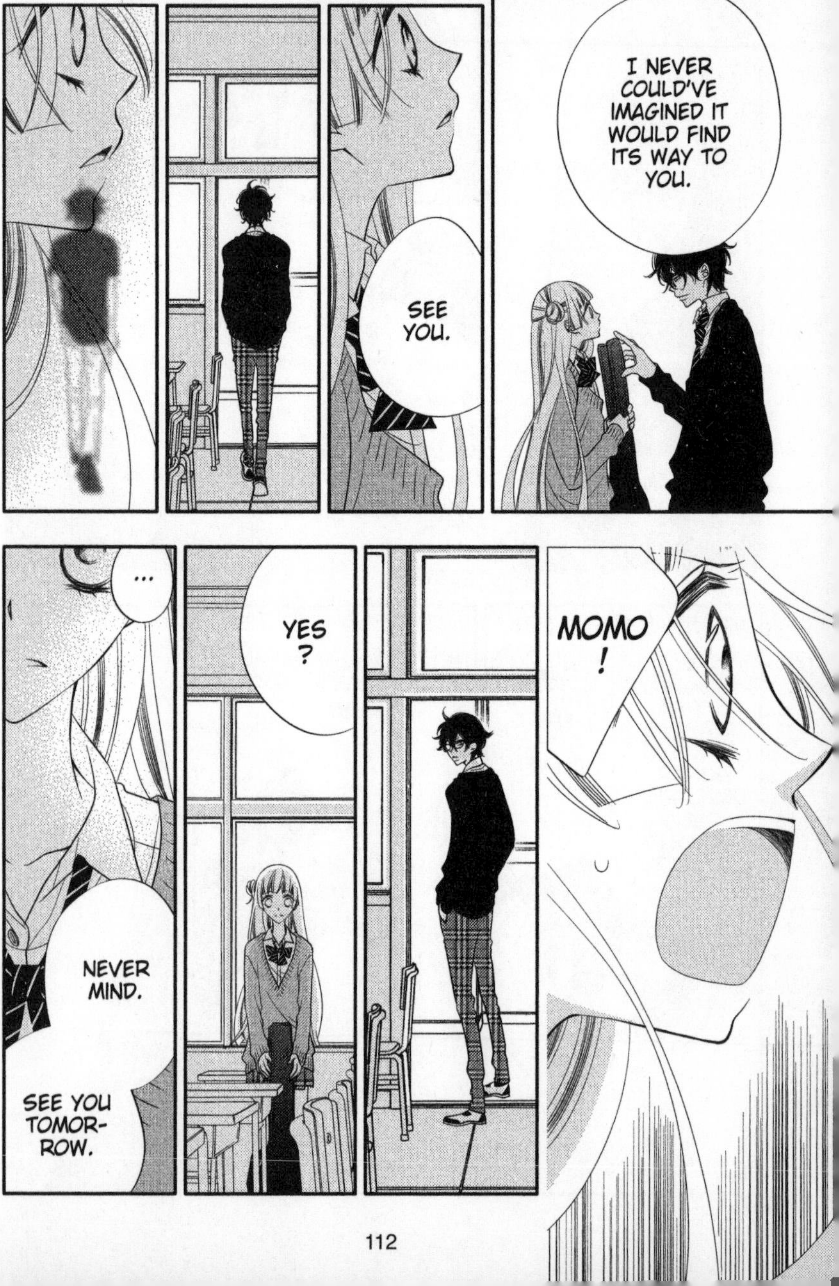
I NEVER COULD'VE IMAGINED IT WOULD FIND ITS WAY TO YOU.
SEE YOU.
MOMO!
YES?
...
NEVER MIND.
SEE YOU TOMORROW.

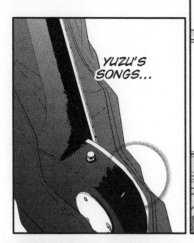

YUZU'S SONGS...
I'VE REVIEWED ALL OF THEM...
...EXCEPT FOR ONE.
"CANARY."
AFTER BEING REJECTED AT THE AUDITION...
...I SANG IT ON TV.
AND THAT WAS HOW...
...I GOT THIS GUITAR.

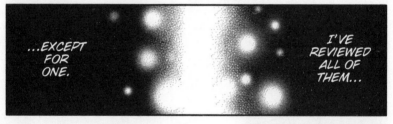

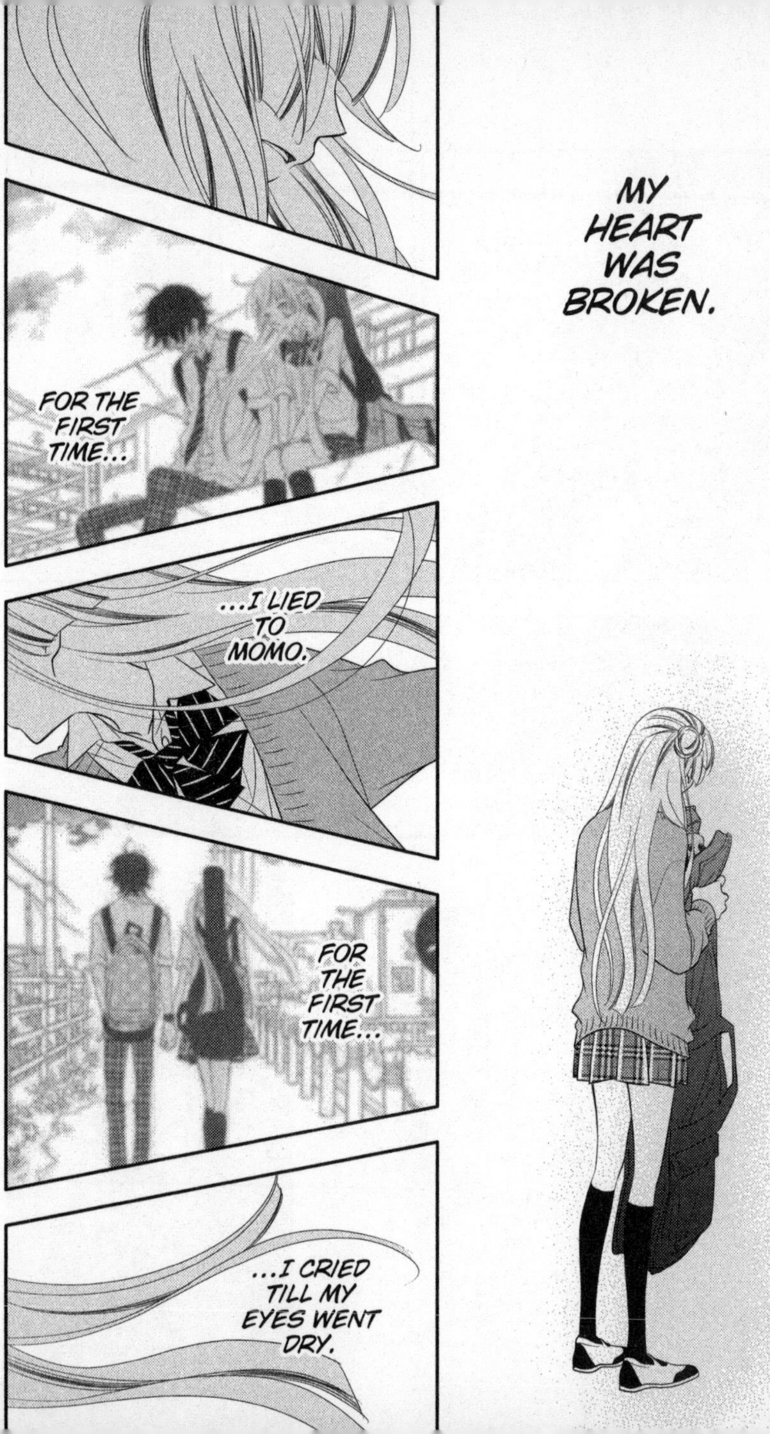
MY HEART WAS BROKEN.
FOR THE FIRST TIME...
...I LIED TO MOMO.
FOR THE FIRST TIME...
...I CRIED TILL MY EYES WENT DRY.

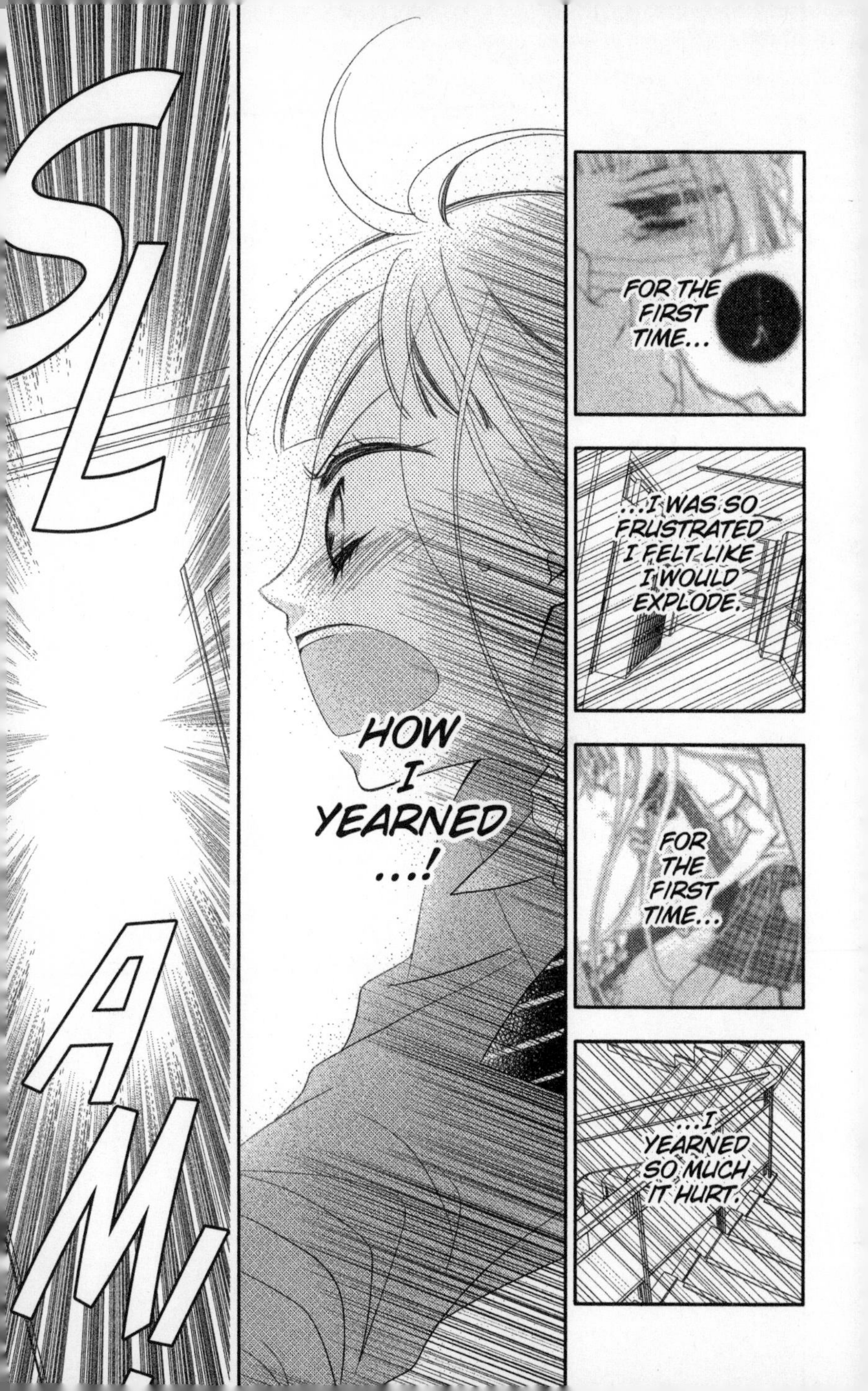
FOR THE FIRST TIME...
...I WAS SO FRUSTRATED I FELT LIKE I WOULD EXPLODE.
FOR THE FIRST TIME...
...I YEARNED SO MUCH IT HURT.
HOW I YEARNED ...!
SLAM!

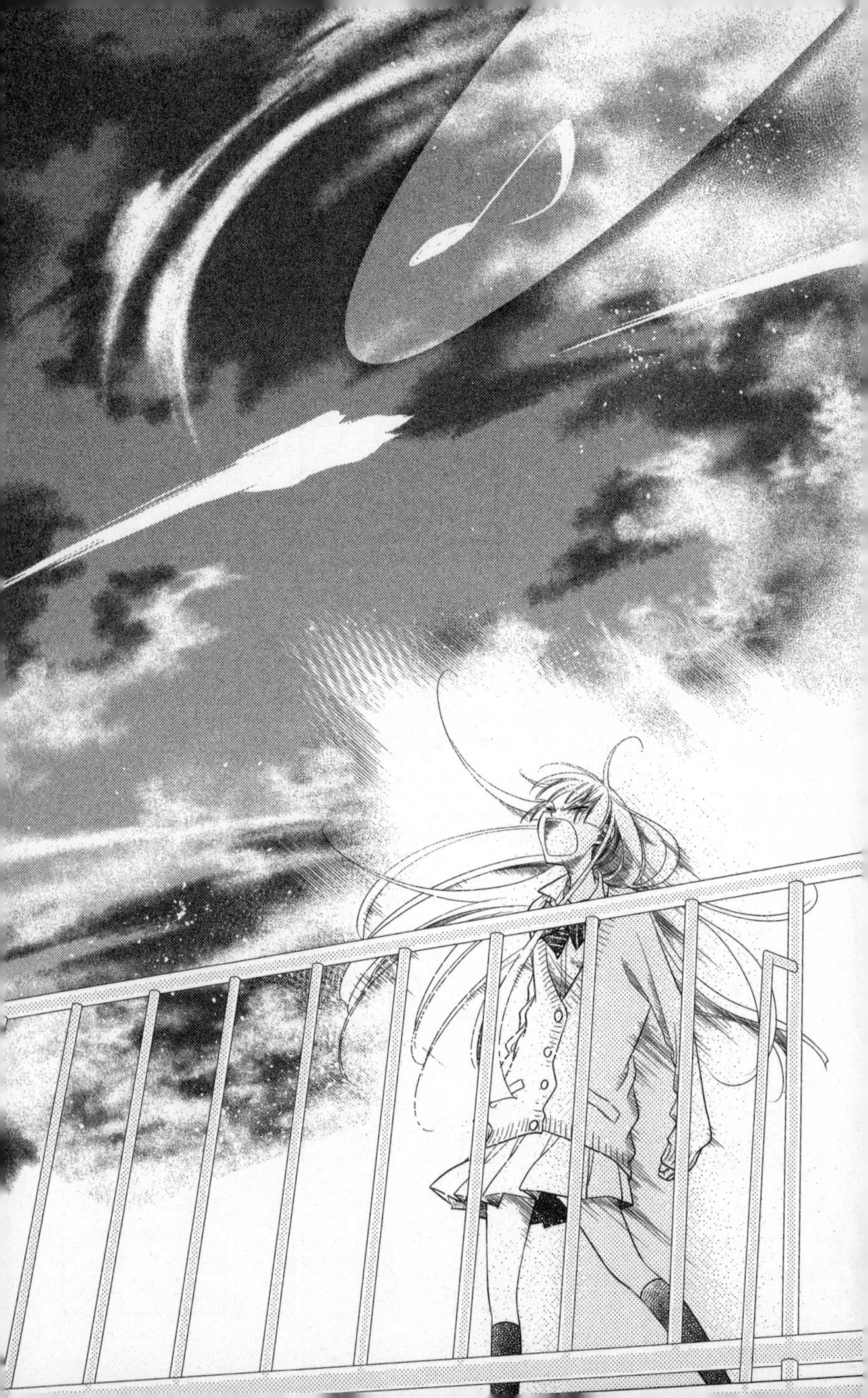

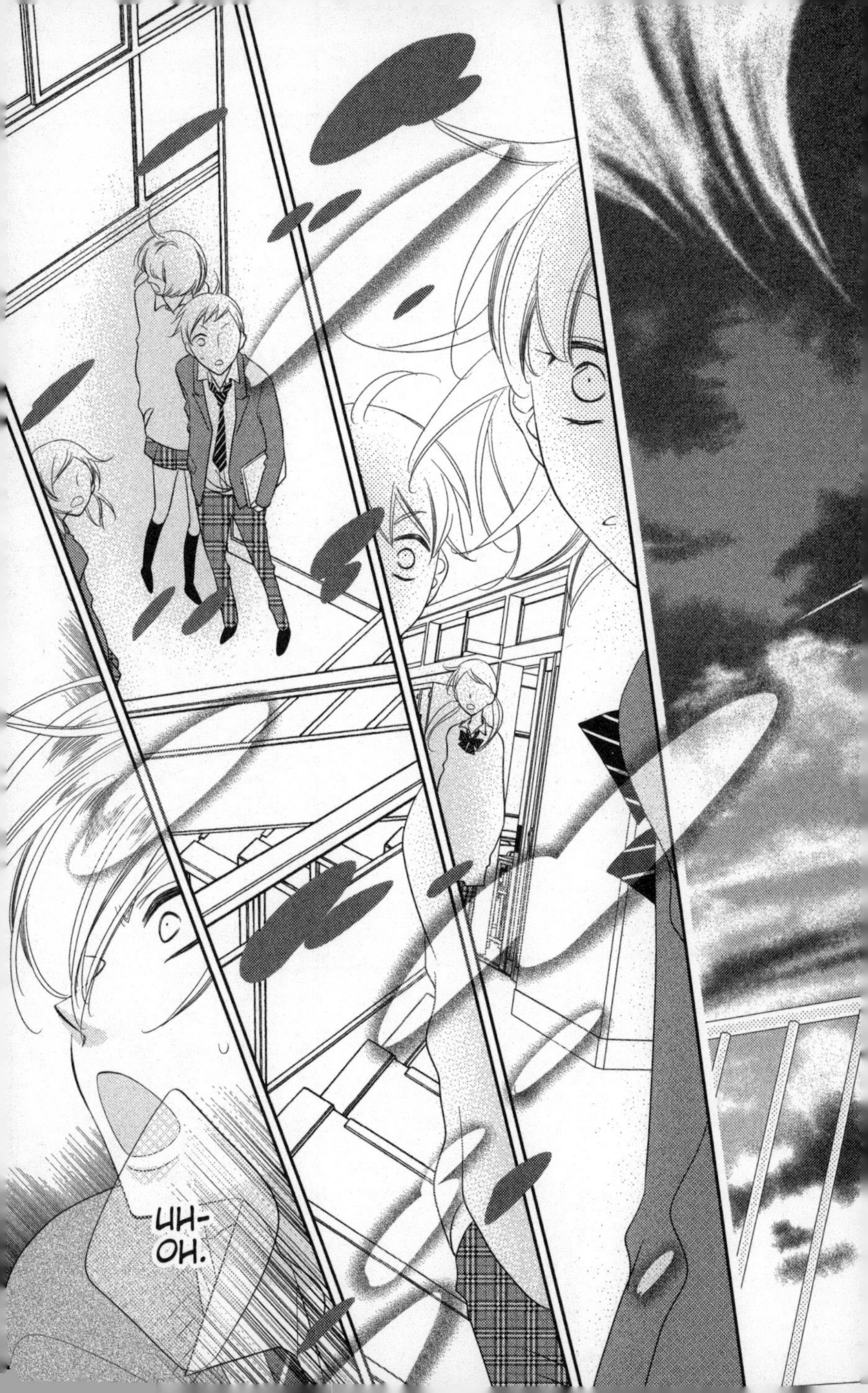
UH-OH.

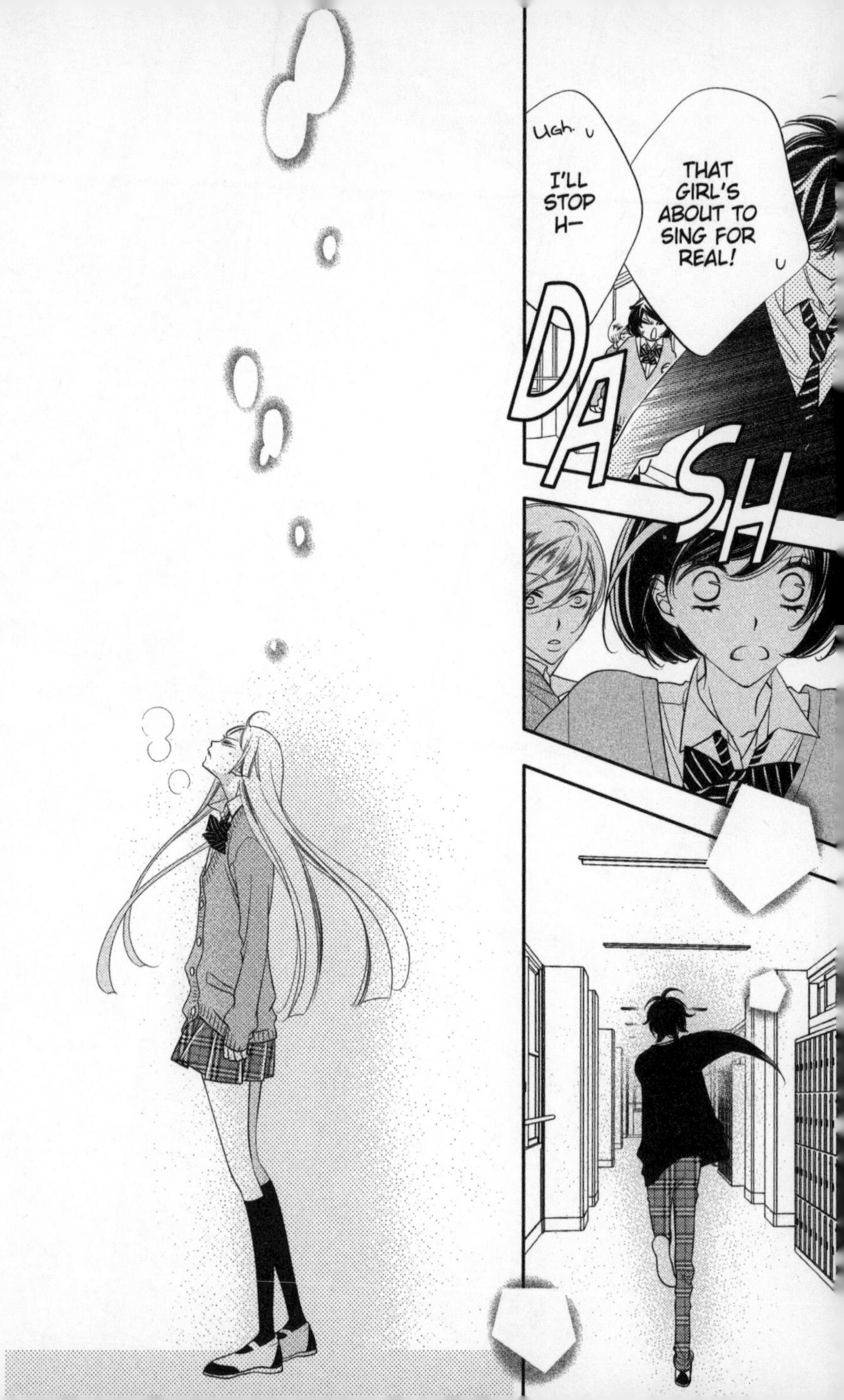
THAT GIRL'S ABOUT TO SING FOR REAL!
Ugh.
I'LL STOP H—
DASH

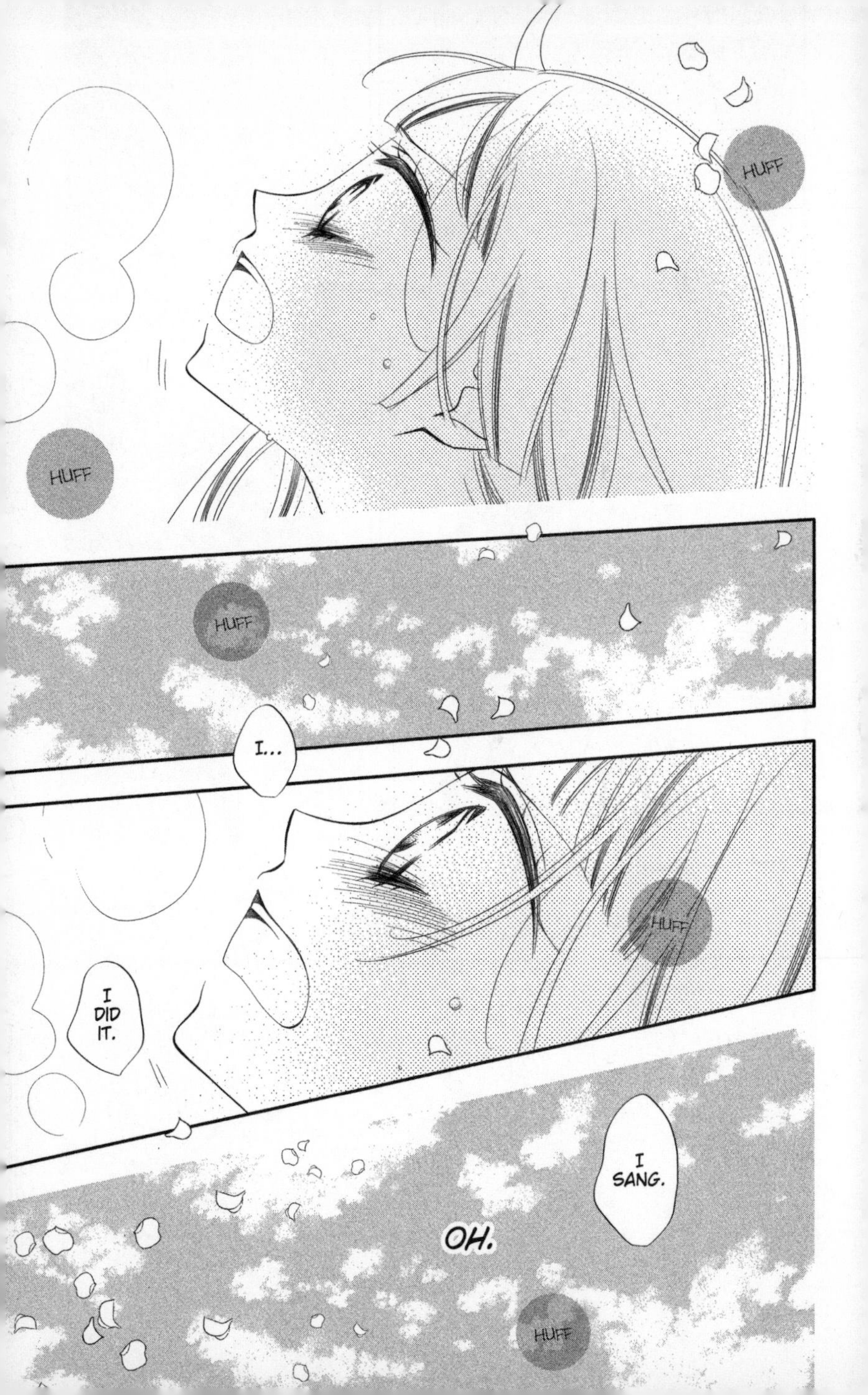
HUFF
HUFF
HUFF
I...
HUFF
I DID IT.
I SANG.
OH.
HUFF

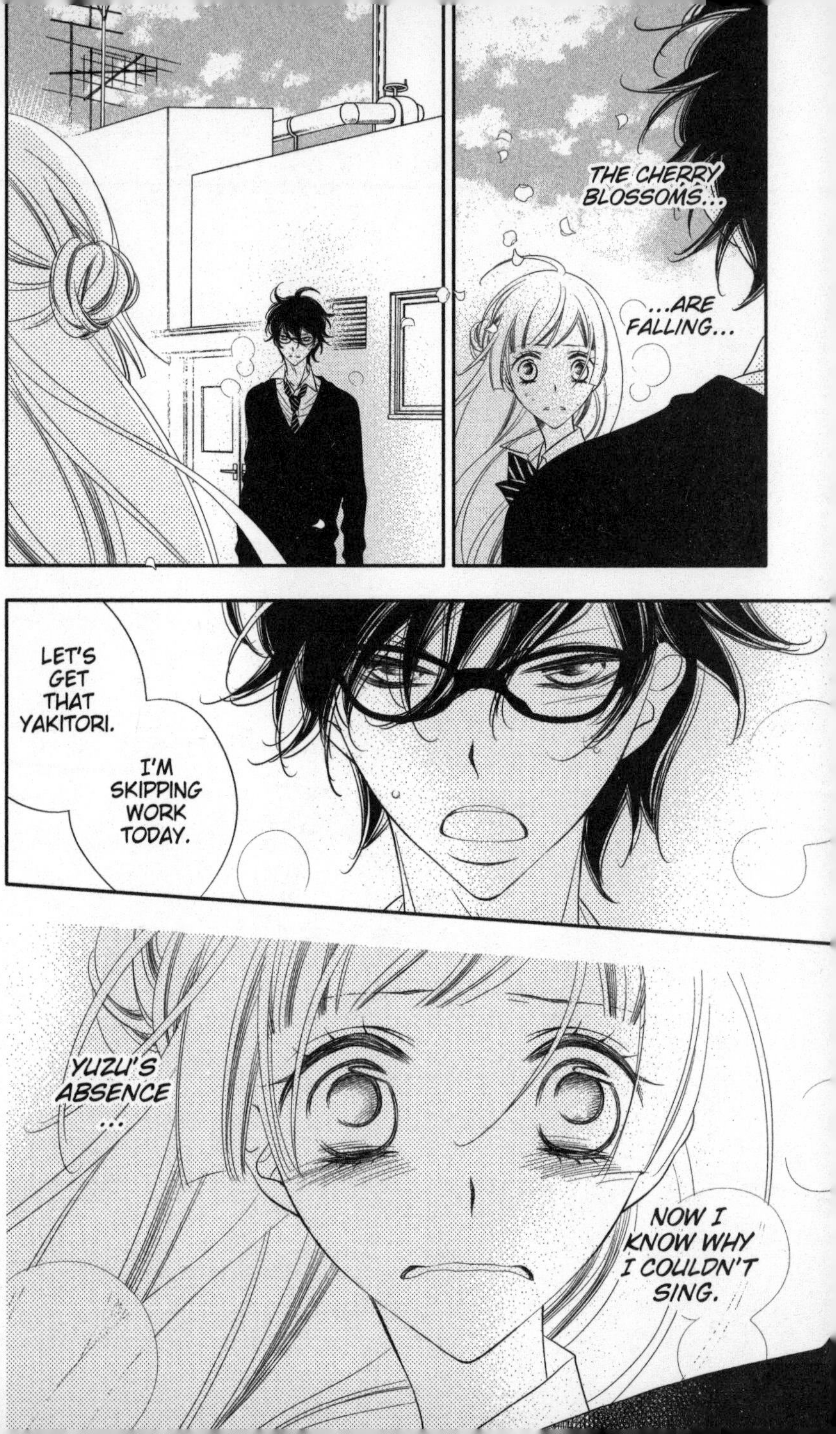
THE CHERRY BLOSSOMS...
...ARE FALLING...
LET'S GET THAT YAKITORI.
I'M SKIPPING WORK TODAY.
YUZU'S ABSENCE...
NOW I KNOW WHY I COULDN'T SING.

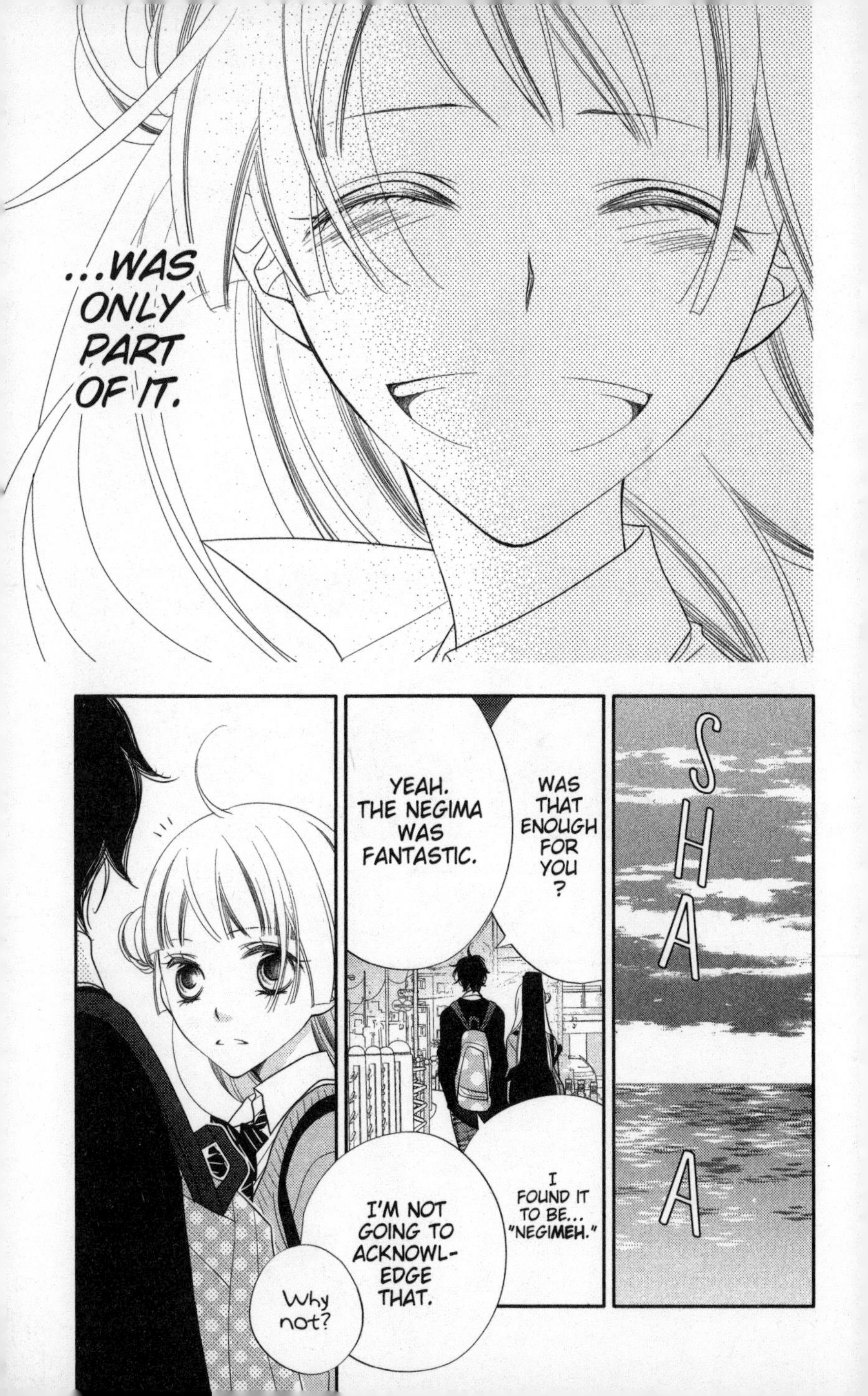

...WAS ONLY PART OF IT.
SHAA
WAS THAT ENOUGH FOR YOU?
YEAH. THE NEGIMA WAS FANTASTIC.
I FOUND IT TO BE... "NEGIMEH."
I'M NOT GOING TO ACKNOWL-EDGE THAT.
Why not?

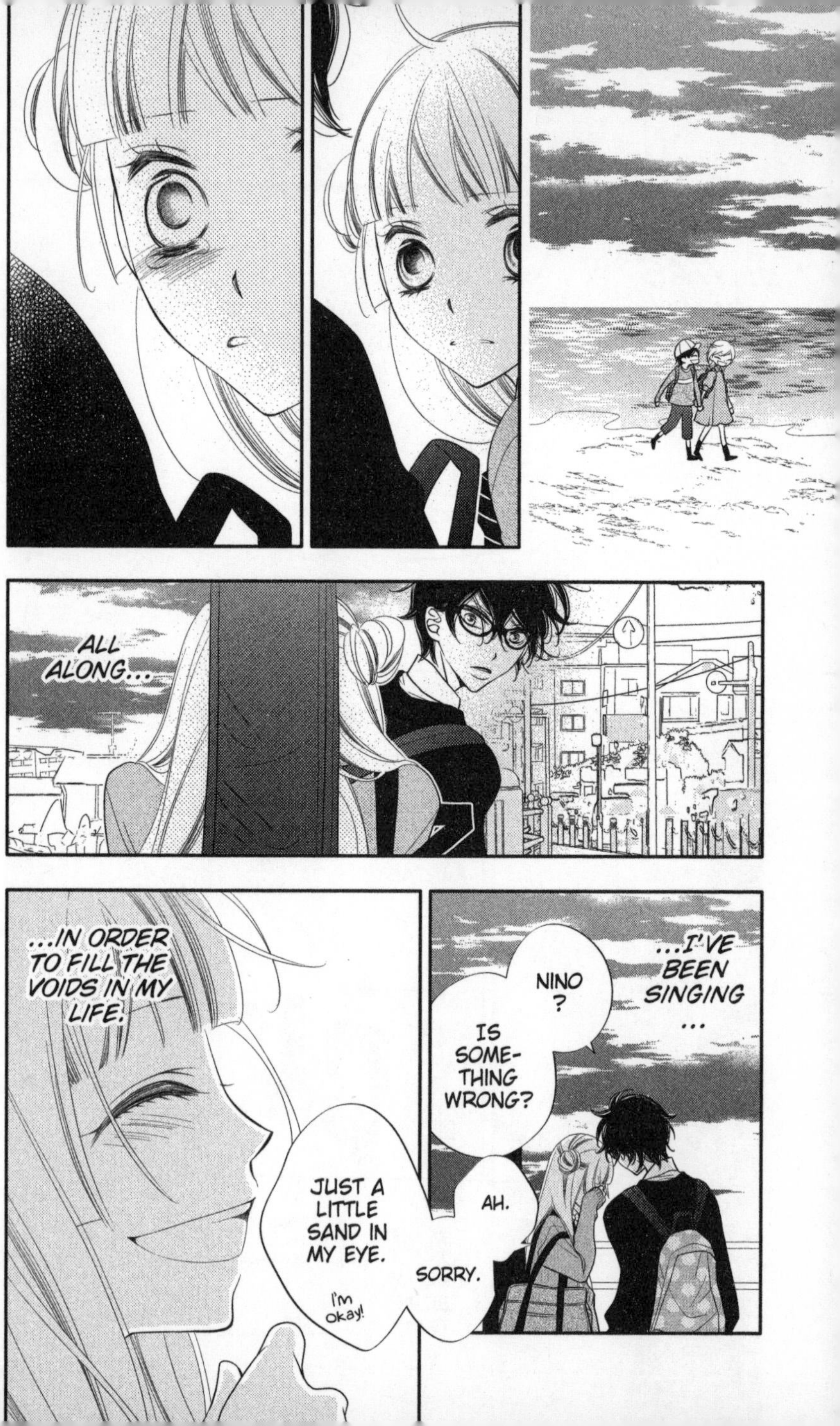
ALL ALONG...
...I'VE BEEN SINGING...
NINO?
IS SOMETHING WRONG?
AH.
SORRY.
...IN ORDER TO FILL THE VOIDS IN MY LIFE.
JUST A LITTLE SAND IN MY EYE.
I'm okay!

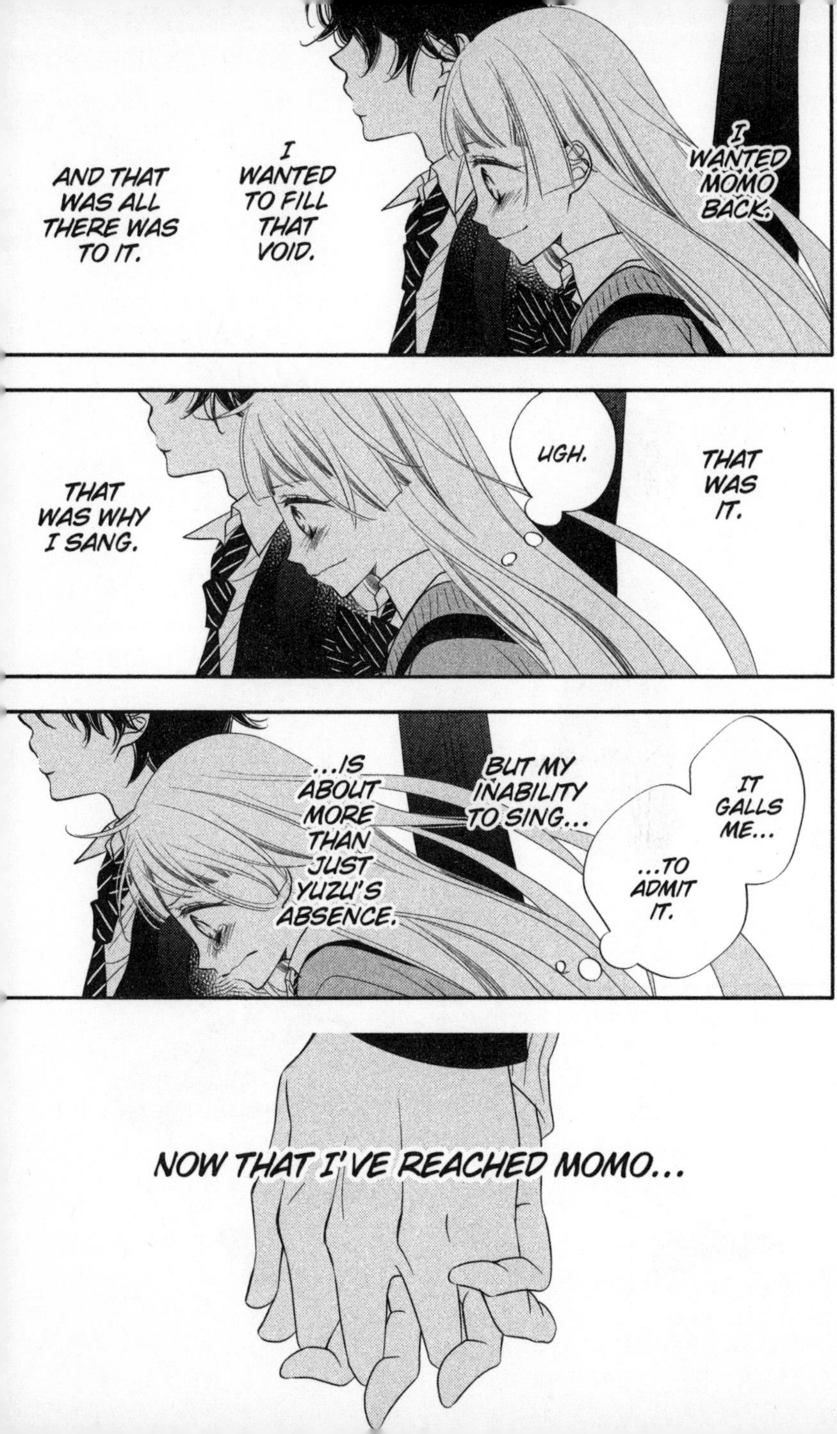
I WANTED MOMO BACK.
I WANTED TO FILL THAT VOID.
AND THAT WAS ALL THERE WAS TO IT.
THAT WAS IT.
UGH.
THAT WAS WHY I SANG.
IT GALLS ME...
...TO ADMIT IT.
BUT MY INABILITY TO SING...
...IS ABOUT MORE THAN JUST YUZU'S ABSENCE.
NOW THAT I'VE REACHED MOMO...

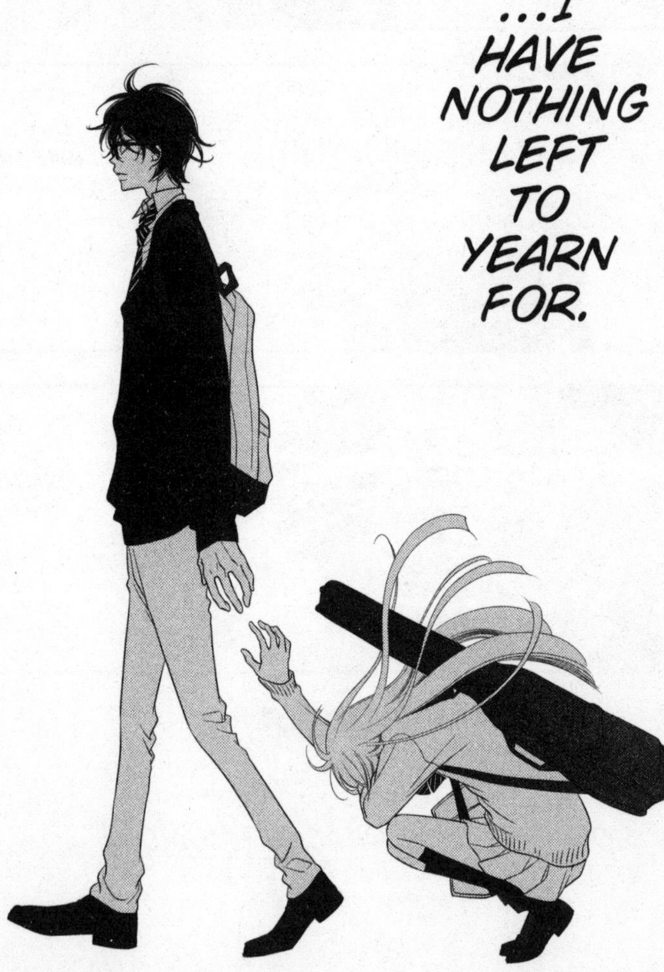
...I HAVE NOTHING LEFT TO YEARN FOR.

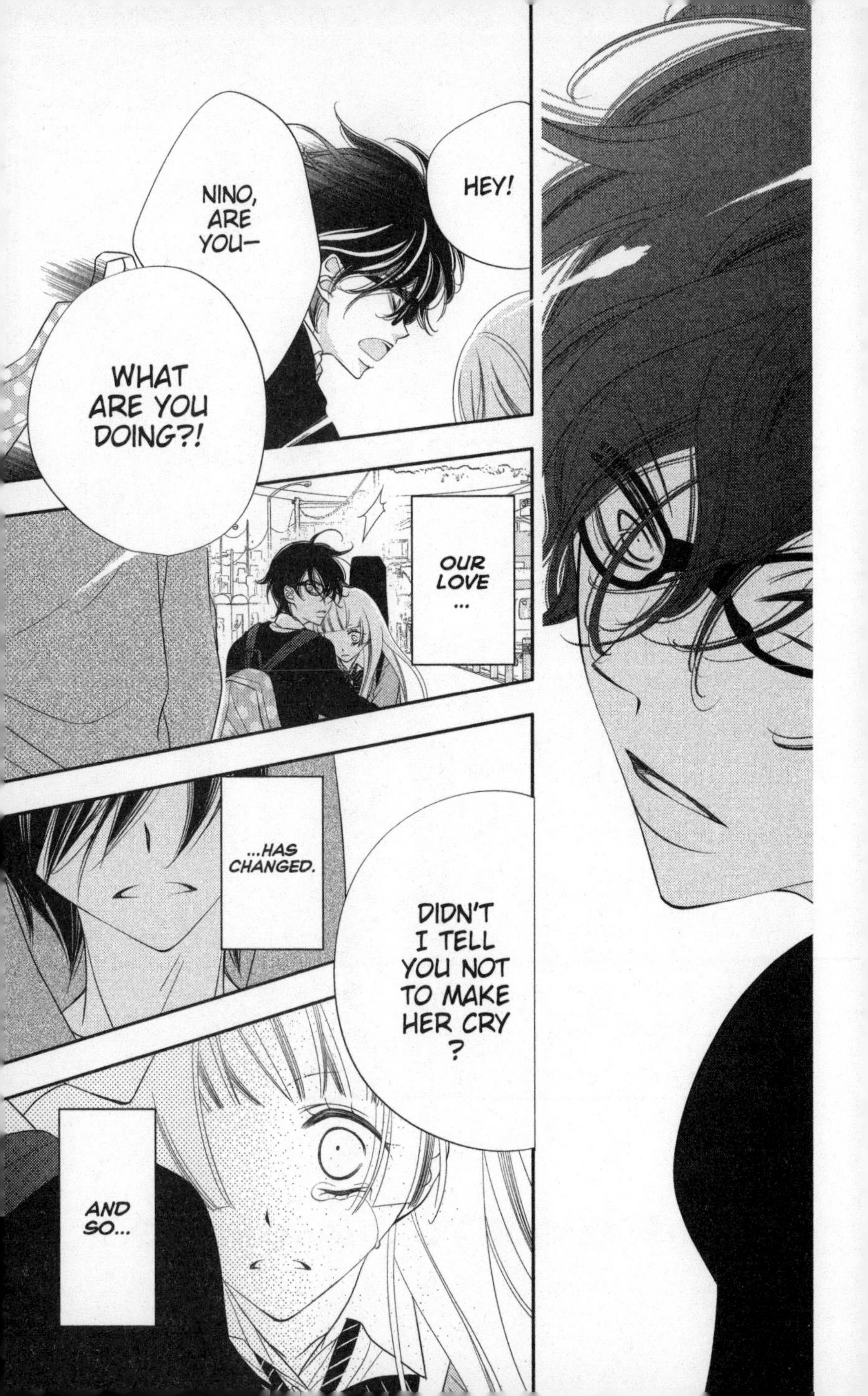
HEY!
NINO, ARE YOU—
WHAT ARE YOU DOING?!
OUR LOVE ...
DIDN'T I TELL YOU NOT TO MAKE HER CRY?
...HAS CHANGED.
AND SO...

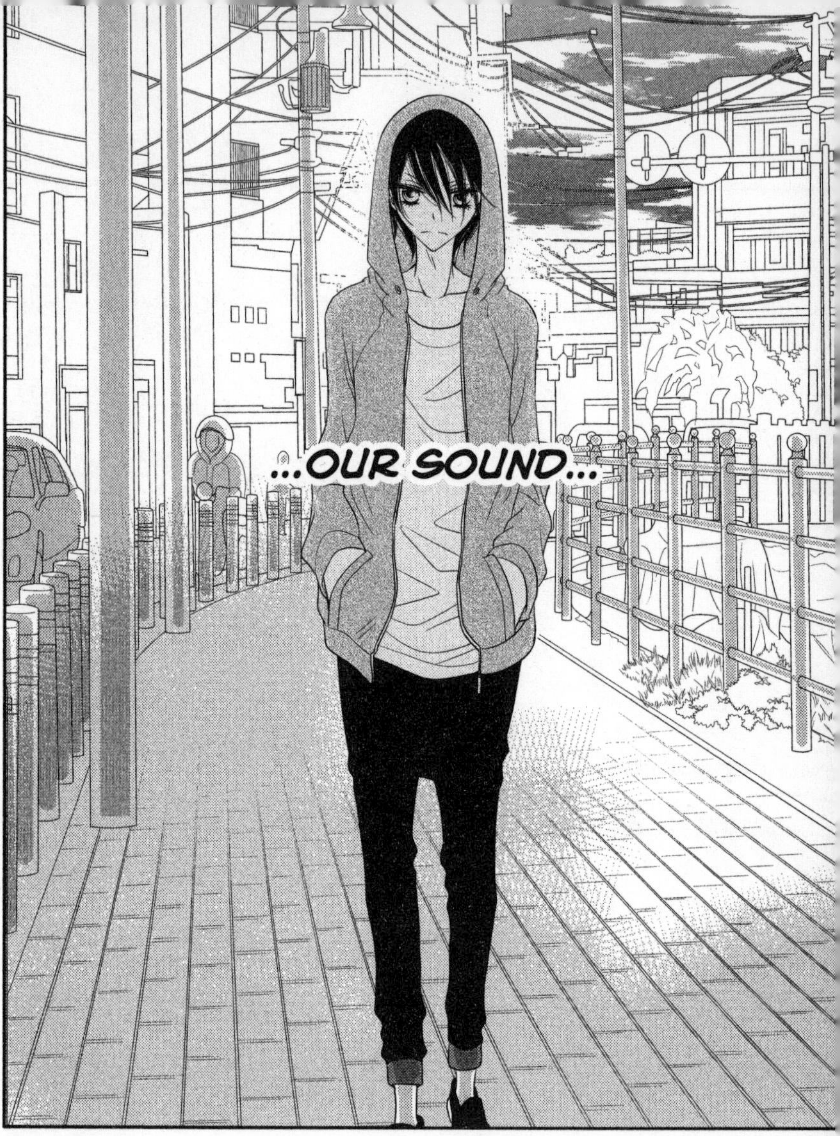
...OUR SOUND...

...IS ABOUT TO CHANGE TOO.

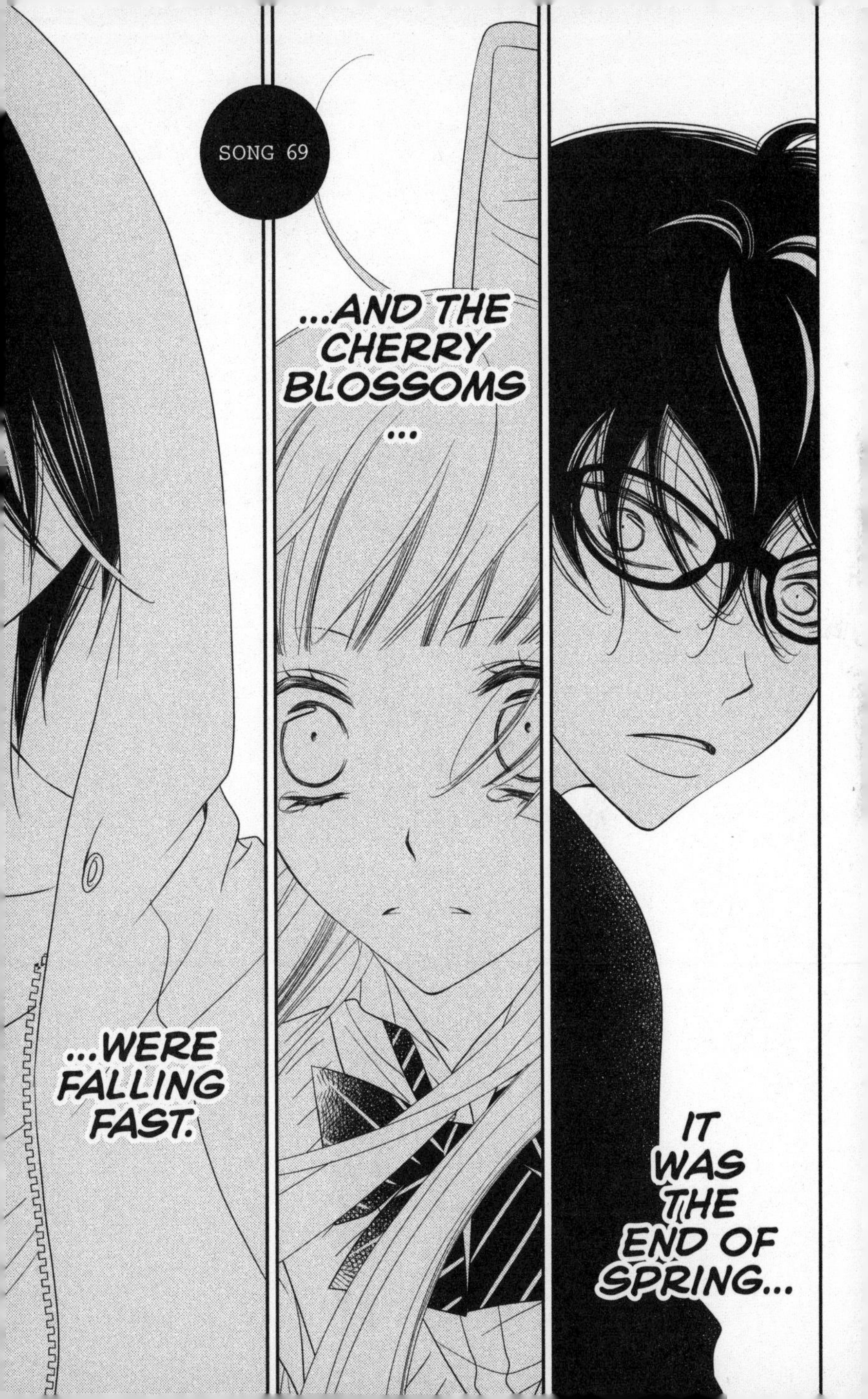
SONG 69
IT WAS THE END OF SPRING...
...AND THE CHERRY BLOSSOMS ...
...WERE FALLING FAST.

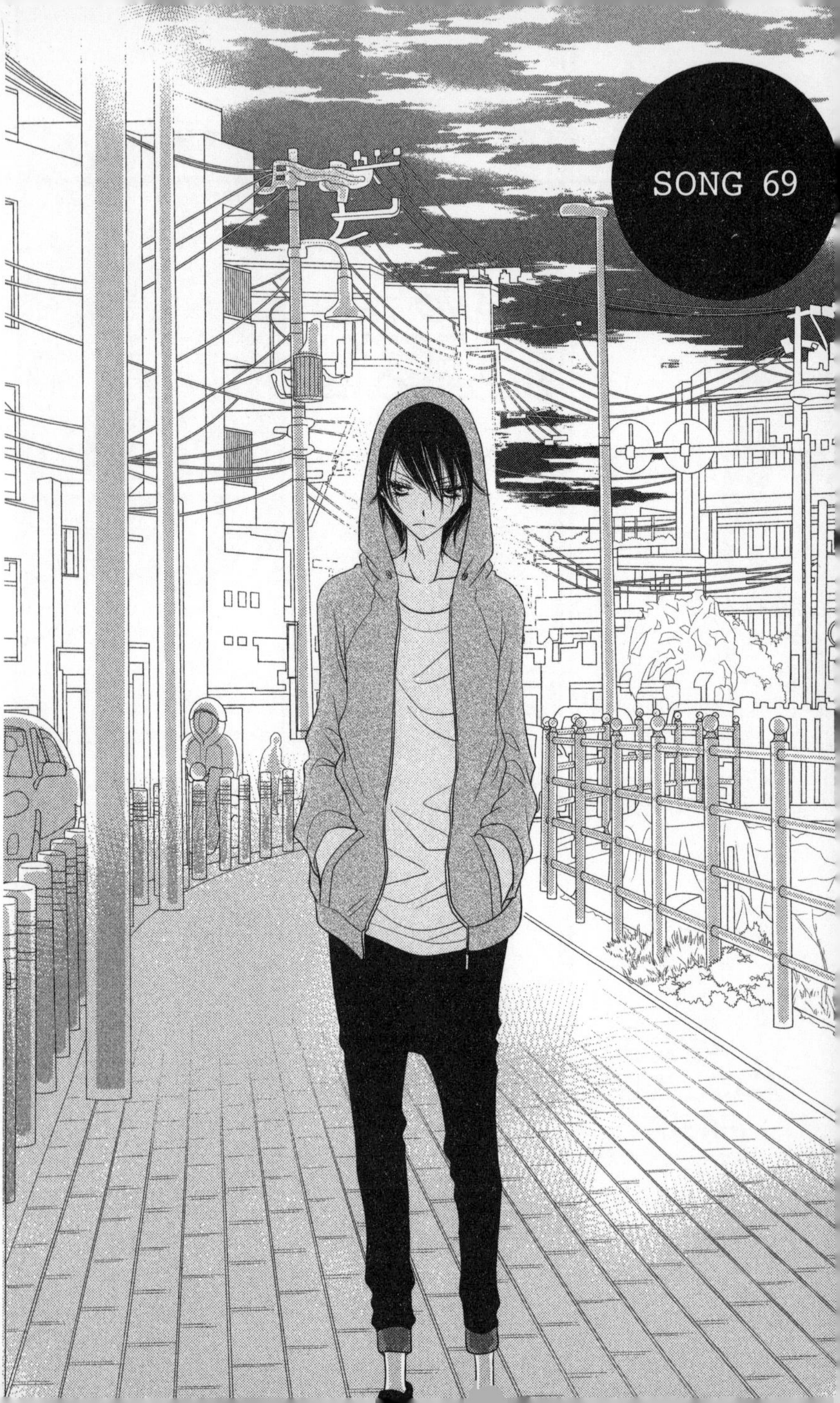
SONG 69

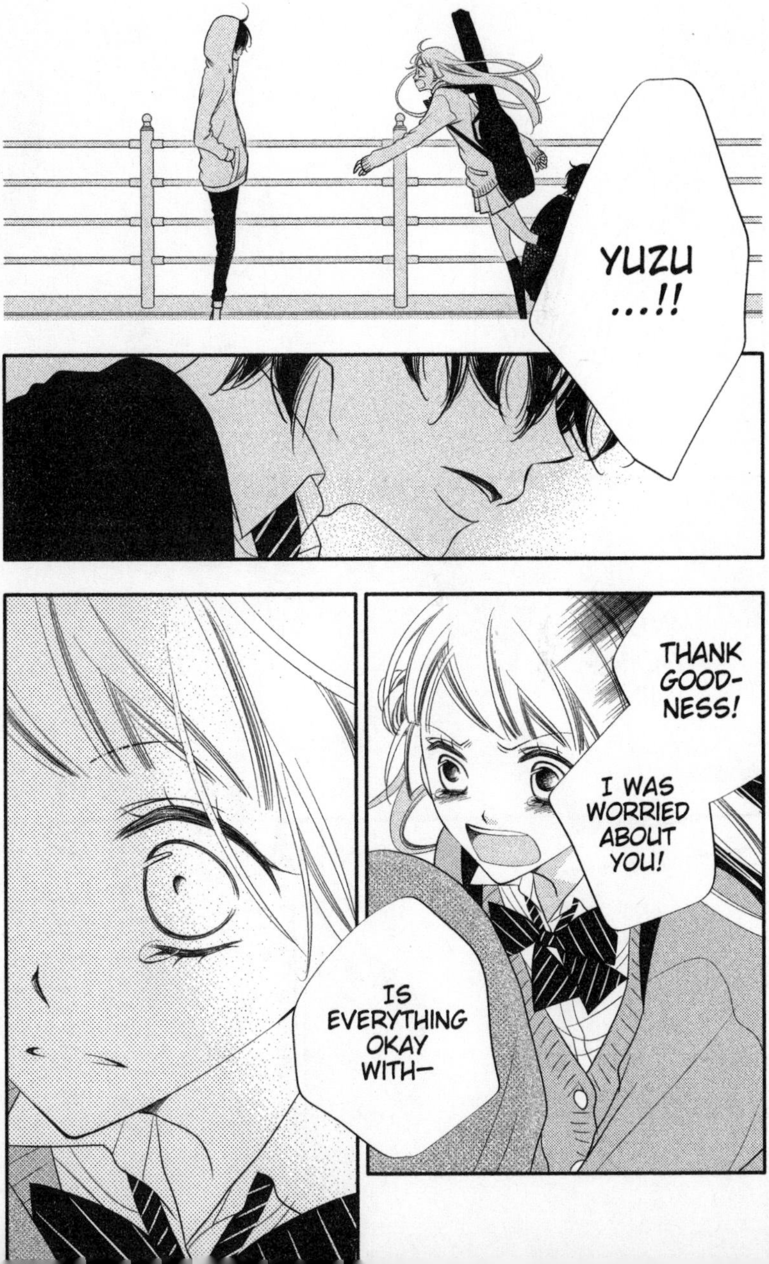
YUZU ...!!
THANK GOODNESS!
I WAS WORRIED ABOUT YOU!
IS EVERYTHING OKAY WITH—

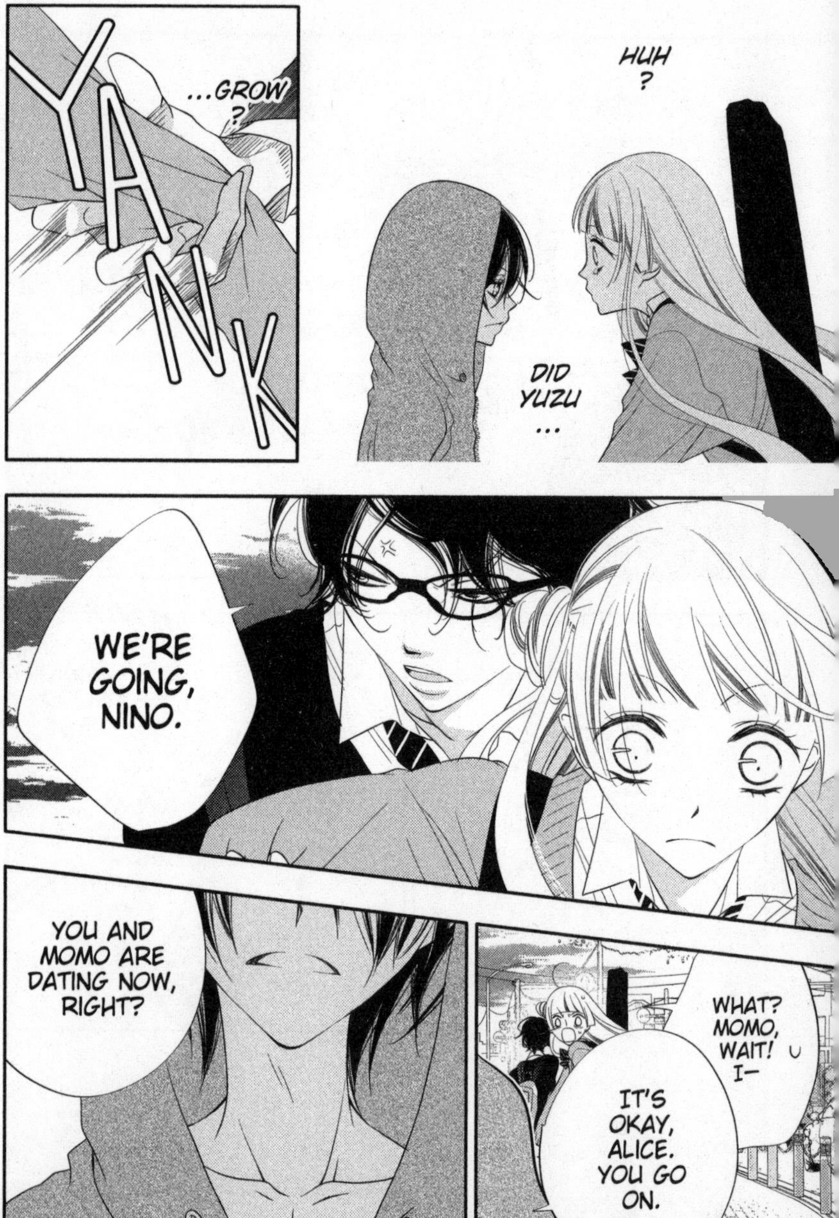
HUH?
DID YUZU...
...GROW?
YANK
WE'RE GOING, NINO.
WHAT? MOMO, WAIT! I—
IT'S OKAY, ALICE. YOU GO ON.
YOU AND MOMO ARE DATING NOW, RIGHT?

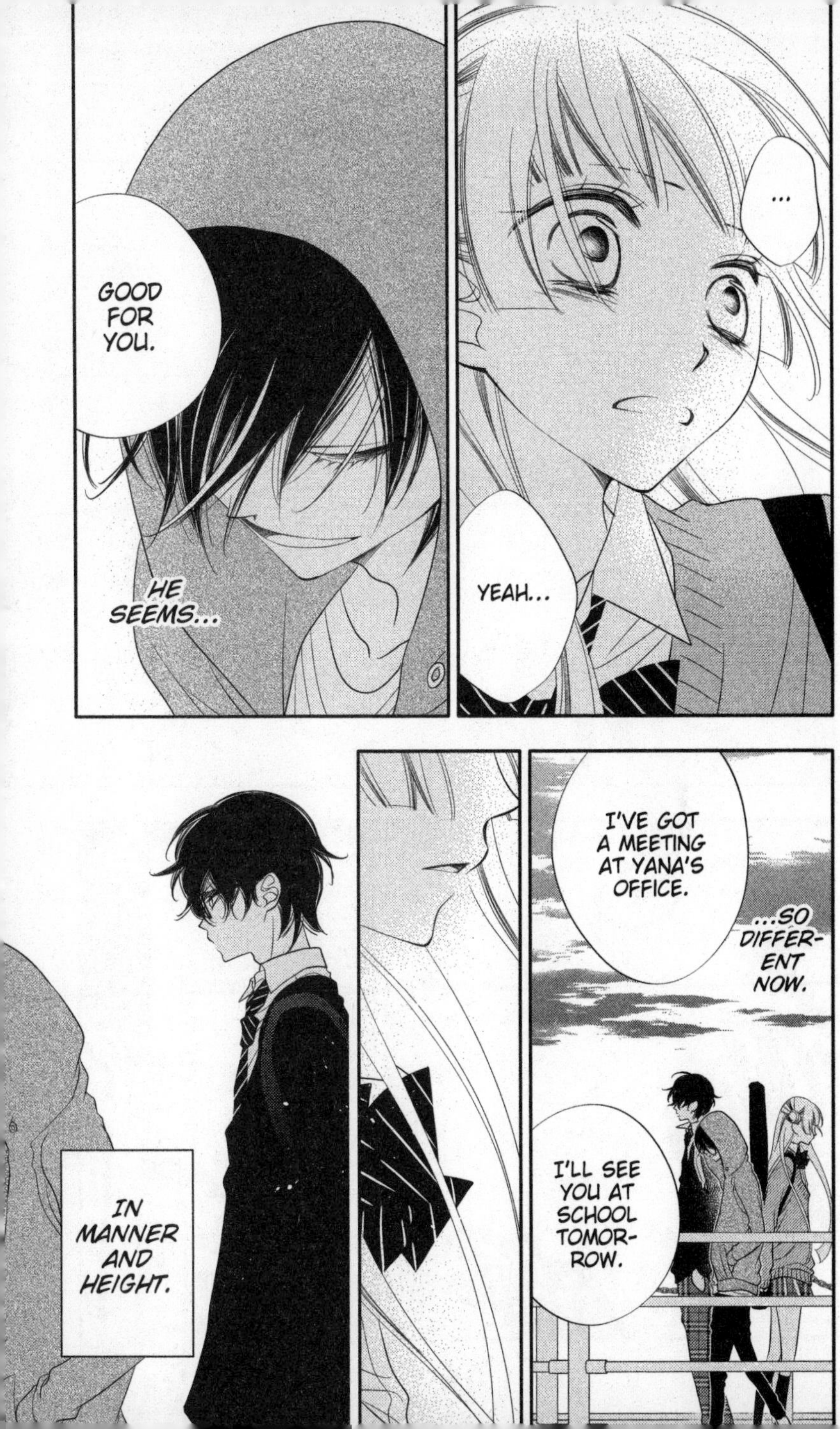
...
YEAH...
GOOD FOR YOU.
HE SEEMS...
I'VE GOT A MEETING AT YANA'S OFFICE.
...SO DIFFER-ENT NOW.
I'LL SEE YOU AT SCHOOL TOMOR-ROW.
IN MANNER AND HEIGHT.

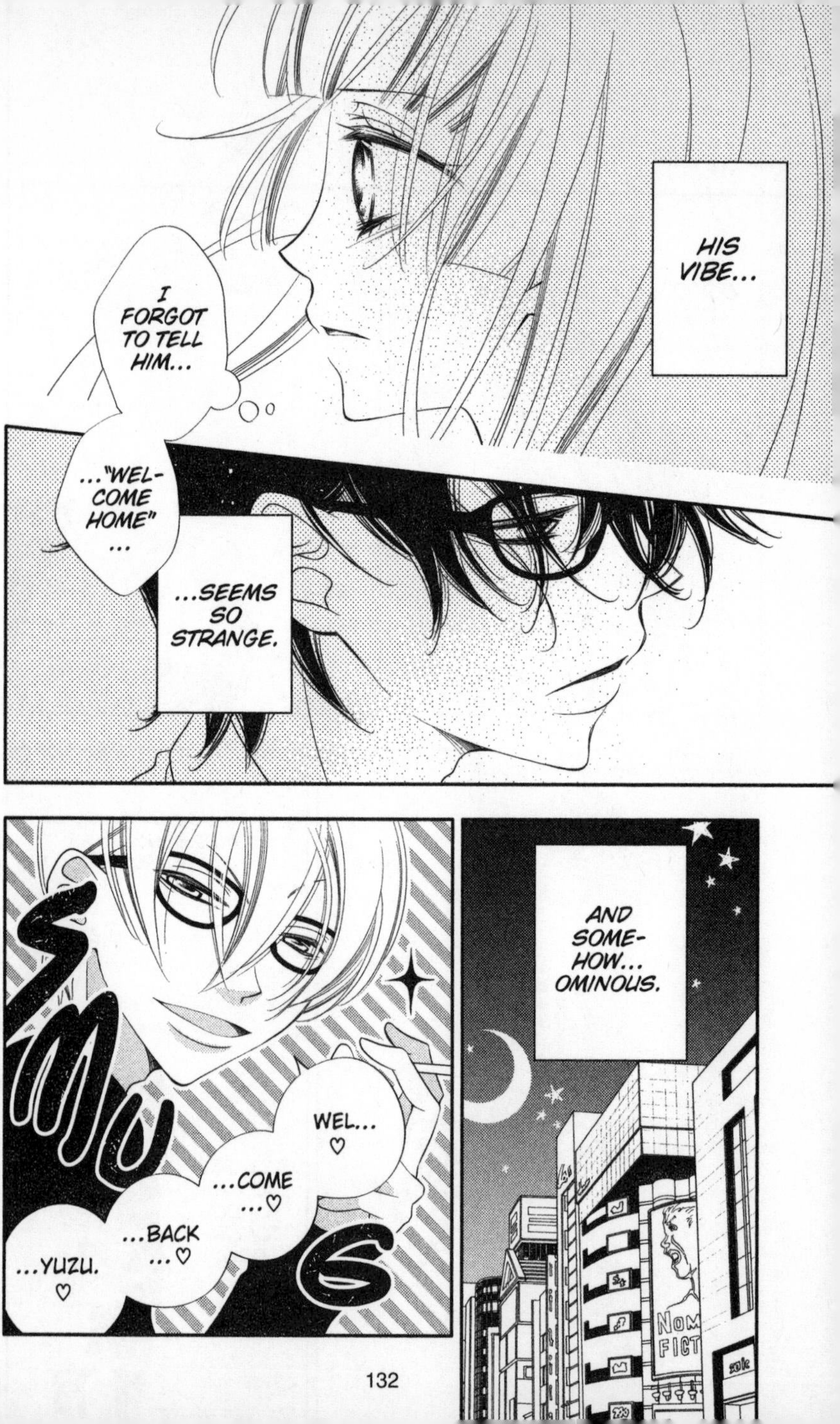
HIS VIBE...
I FORGOT TO TELL HIM...
..."WEL-COME HOME"...
...SEEMS SO STRANGE.
AND SOME-HOW... OMINOUS.
SMUG
WEL... ♡
...COME... ♡
...BACK... ♡
...YUZU. ♡

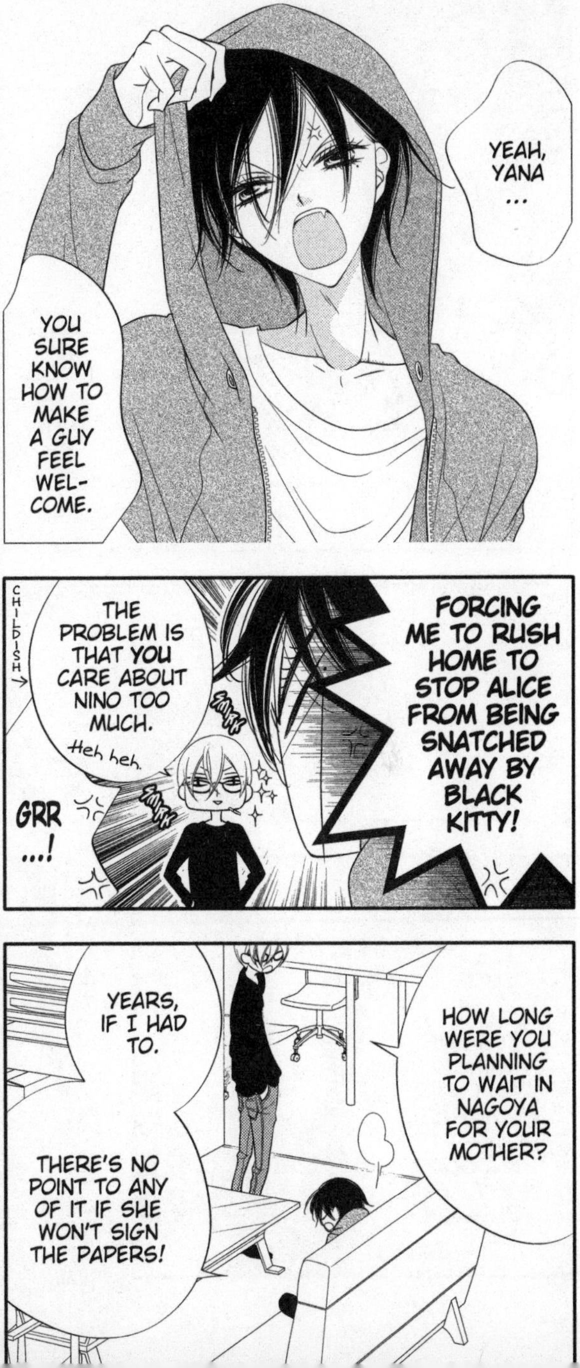
YEAH, YANA...
YOU SURE KNOW HOW TO MAKE A GUY FEEL WEL-COME.
FORCING ME TO RUSH HOME TO STOP ALICE FROM BEING SNATCHED AWAY BY BLACK KITTY!
THE PROBLEM IS THAT YOU CARE ABOUT NINO TOO MUCH.
Heh heh.
GRR...!
CHILDISH →
HOW LONG WERE YOU PLANNING TO WAIT IN NAGOYA FOR YOUR MOTHER?
YEARS, IF I HAD TO.
THERE'S NO POINT TO ANY OF IT IF SHE WON'T SIGN THE PAPERS!

5

Oh! I forgot to tell you! The *Anonymous Noise* bus is going to start running on the 20th!*

By the time you read this, maybe some of you will have already ridden on it? When I first heard about this marketing plan, I pictured an eerily empty bus and figured I'd need to buy all the tickets and beg my relatives to ride it around the clock. I wonder what's really going to happen...? I'm really worried! I did an original piece of art for the tickets, so I hope that a lot of people get to see it! If you have the chance, please take a ride. I'm begging you here!

* Only in Tokyo

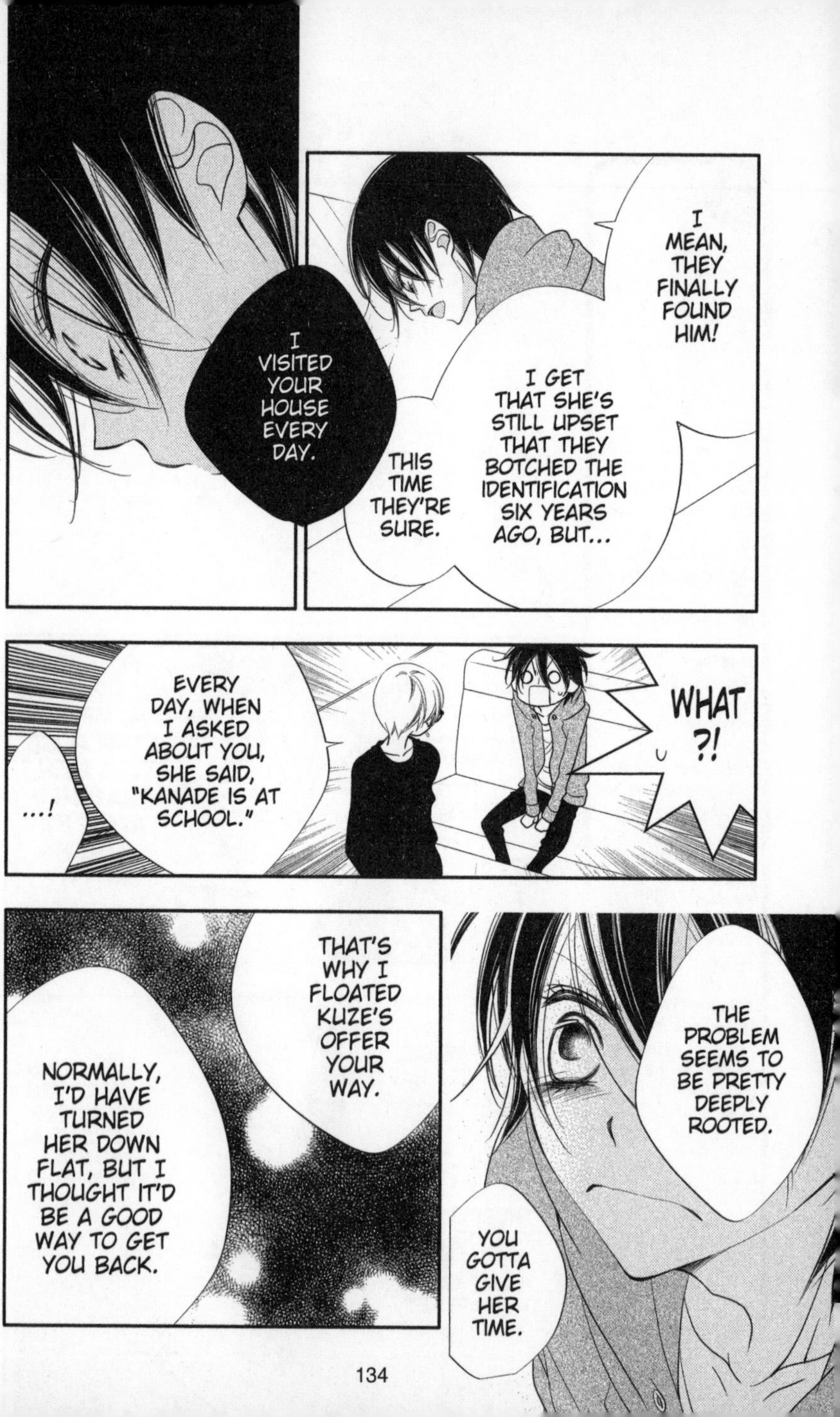
I MEAN, THEY FINALLY FOUND HIM!
I GET THAT SHE'S STILL UPSET THAT THEY BOTCHED THE IDENTIFICATION SIX YEARS AGO, BUT...
THIS TIME THEY'RE SURE.
I VISITED YOUR HOUSE EVERY DAY.
WHAT ?!
EVERY DAY, WHEN I ASKED ABOUT YOU, SHE SAID, "KANADE IS AT SCHOOL."
...!
THE PROBLEM SEEMS TO BE PRETTY DEEPLY ROOTED.
YOU GOTTA GIVE HER TIME.
THAT'S WHY I FLOATED KUZE'S OFFER YOUR WAY.
NORMALLY, I'D HAVE TURNED HER DOWN FLAT, BUT I THOUGHT IT'D BE A GOOD WAY TO GET YOU BACK.

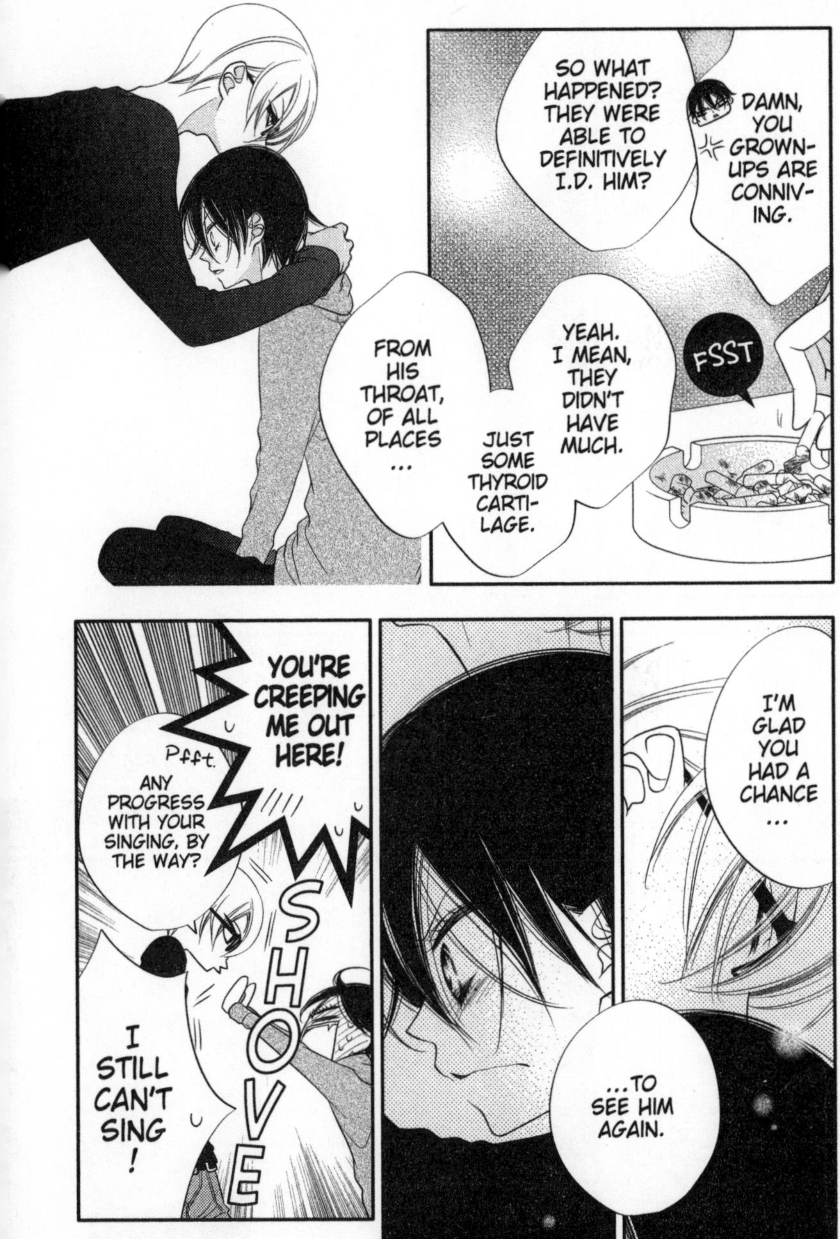
SO WHAT HAPPENED? THEY WERE ABLE TO DEFINITIVELY I.D. HIM?
DAMN, YOU GROWN-UPS ARE CONNIV-ING.
FSST
YEAH. I MEAN, THEY DIDN'T HAVE MUCH.
JUST SOME THYROID CARTI-LAGE.
FROM HIS THROAT, OF ALL PLACES ...
I'M GLAD YOU HAD A CHANCE ...
...TO SEE HIM AGAIN.
YOU'RE CREEPING ME OUT HERE!
SHOVE
Pfft.
ANY PROGRESS WITH YOUR SINGING, BY THE WAY?
I STILL CAN'T SING!

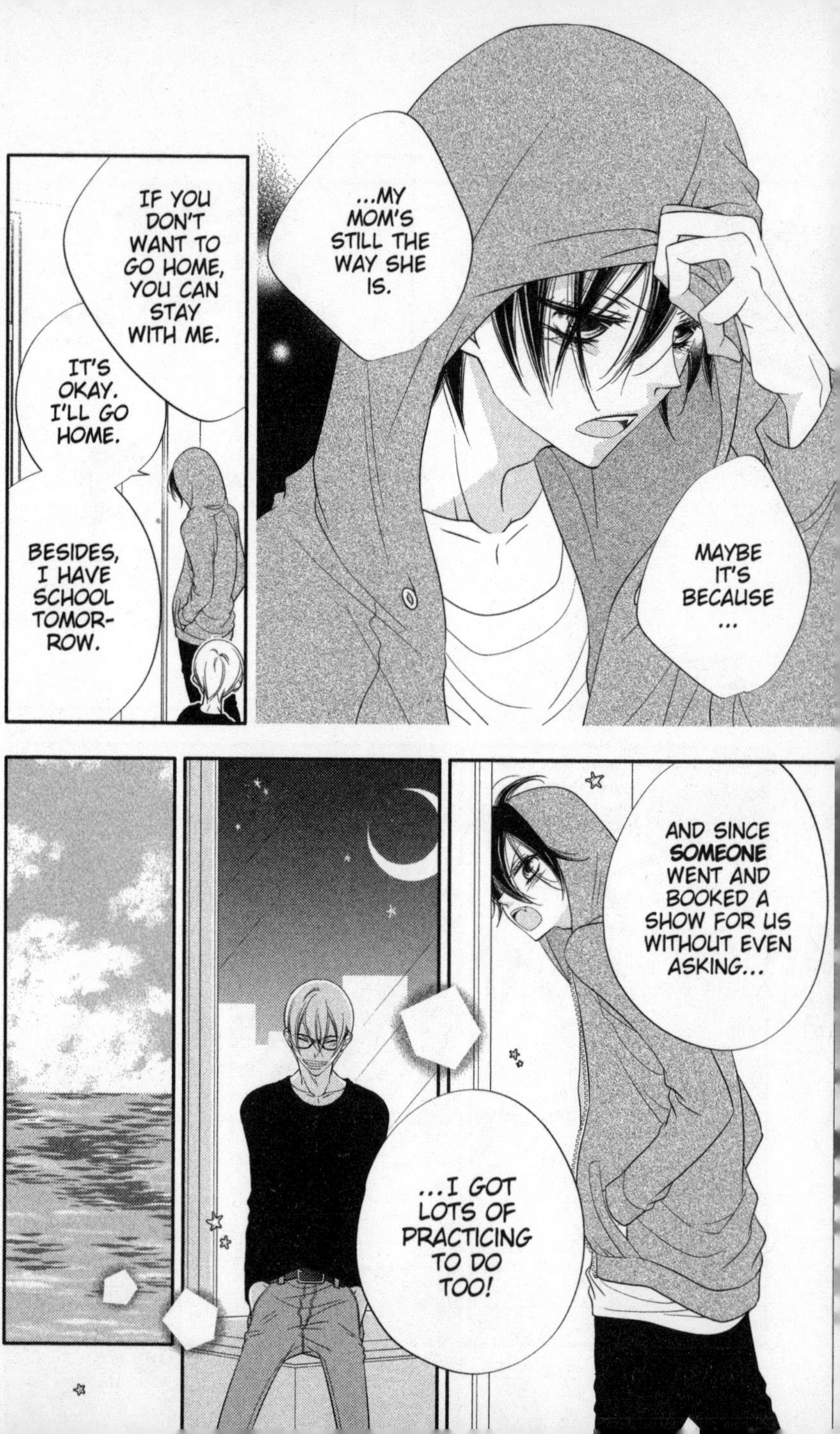
...MY MOM'S STILL THE WAY SHE IS.
MAYBE IT'S BECAUSE ...
IF YOU DON'T WANT TO GO HOME, YOU CAN STAY WITH ME.
IT'S OKAY. I'LL GO HOME.
BESIDES, I HAVE SCHOOL TOMOR-ROW.
AND SINCE **SOMEONE** WENT AND BOOKED A SHOW FOR US WITHOUT EVEN ASKING...
...I GOT LOTS OF PRACTICING TO DO TOO!

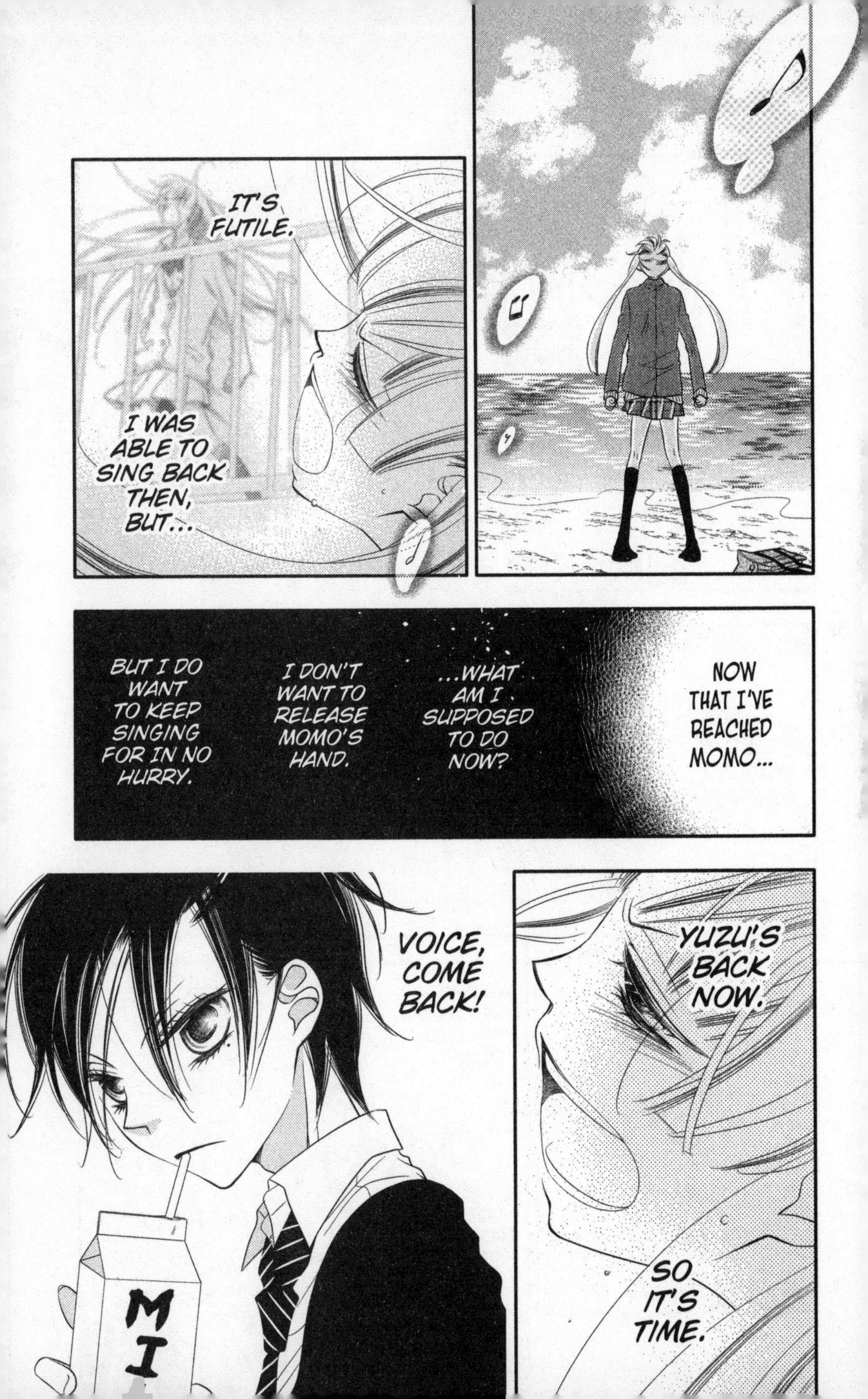
IT'S FUTILE.
I WAS ABLE TO SING BACK THEN, BUT...
NOW THAT I'VE REACHED MOMO...
...WHAT AM I SUPPOSED TO DO NOW?
I DON'T WANT TO RELEASE MOMO'S HAND.
BUT I DO WANT TO KEEP SINGING FOR IN NO HURRY.
YUZU'S BACK NOW.
SO IT'S TIME.
VOICE, COME BACK!
MI

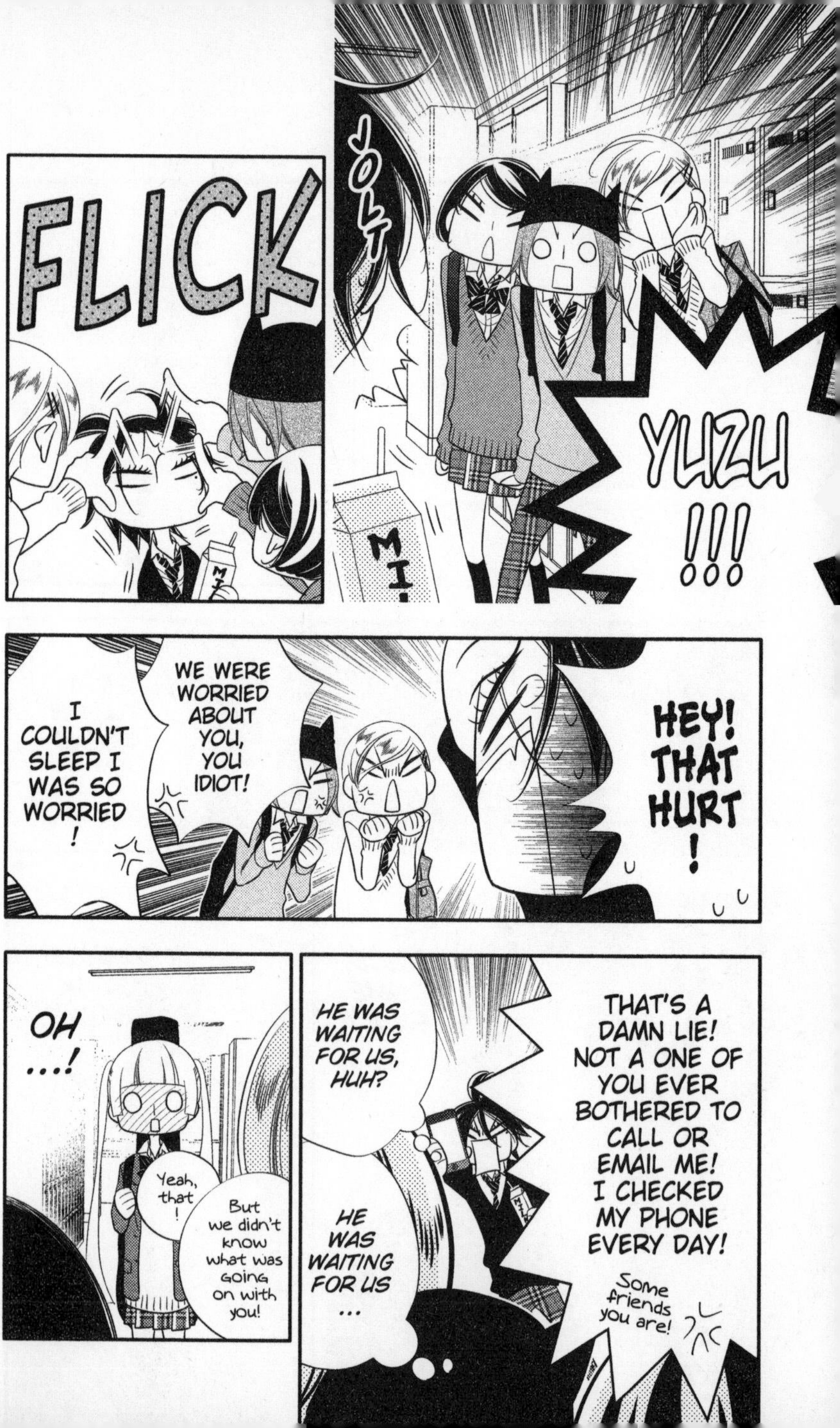
JOLT
YUZU!!!
FLICK
HEY! THAT HURT!
WE WERE WORRIED ABOUT YOU, YOU IDIOT!
I COULDN'T SLEEP I WAS SO WORRIED!
THAT'S A DAMN LIE! NOT A ONE OF YOU EVER BOTHERED TO CALL OR EMAIL ME! I CHECKED MY PHONE EVERY DAY!
HE WAS WAITING FOR US, HUH?
Some friends you are!
HE WAS WAITING FOR US...
OH...!
Yeah, that!
But we didn't know what was going on with you!

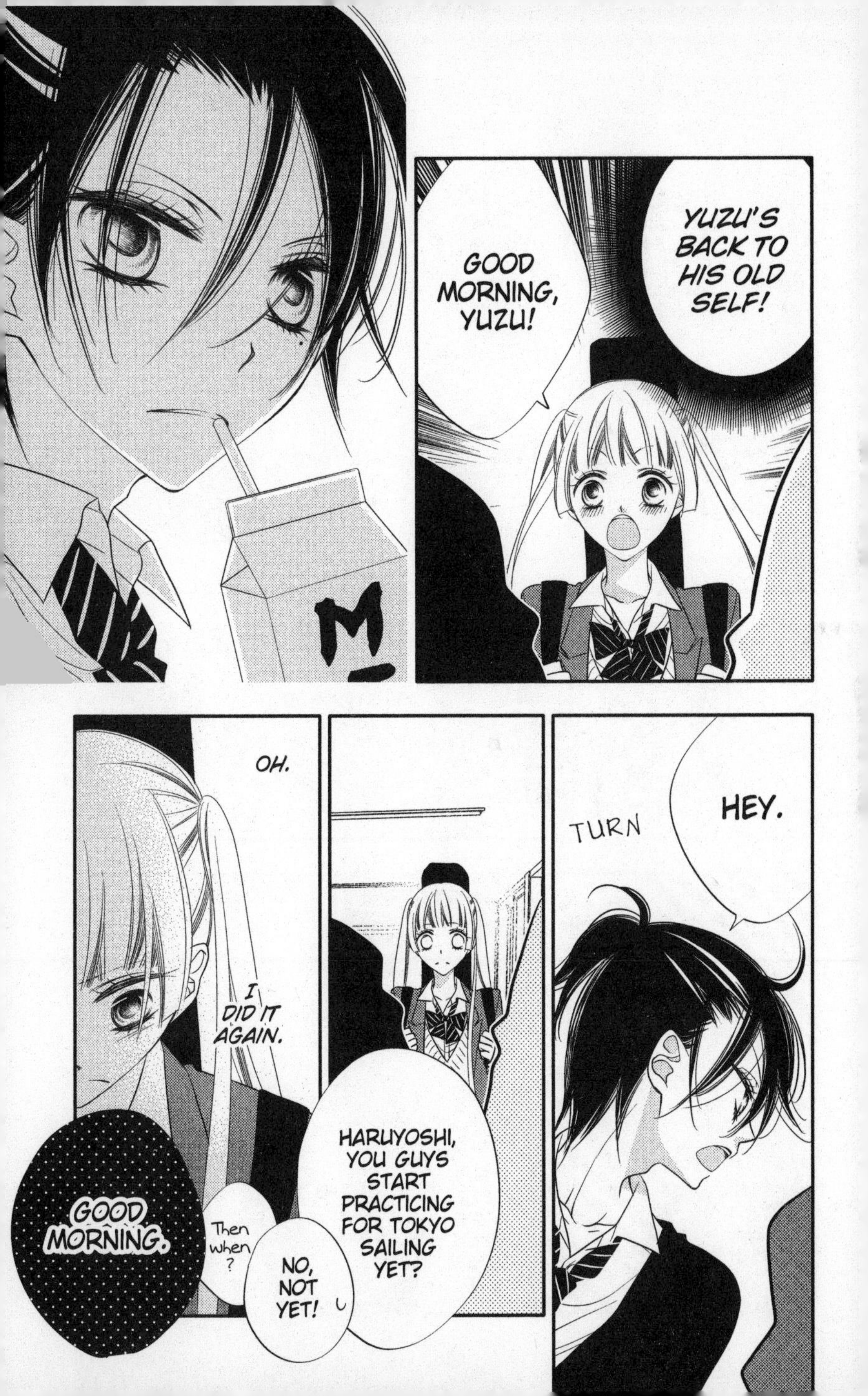
YUZU'S BACK TO HIS OLD SELF!
GOOD MORNING, YUZU!
HEY.
TURN
HARUYOSHI, YOU GUYS START PRACTICING FOR TOKYO SAILING YET?
NO, NOT YET!
Then when?
OH.
I DID IT AGAIN.
GOOD MORNING.

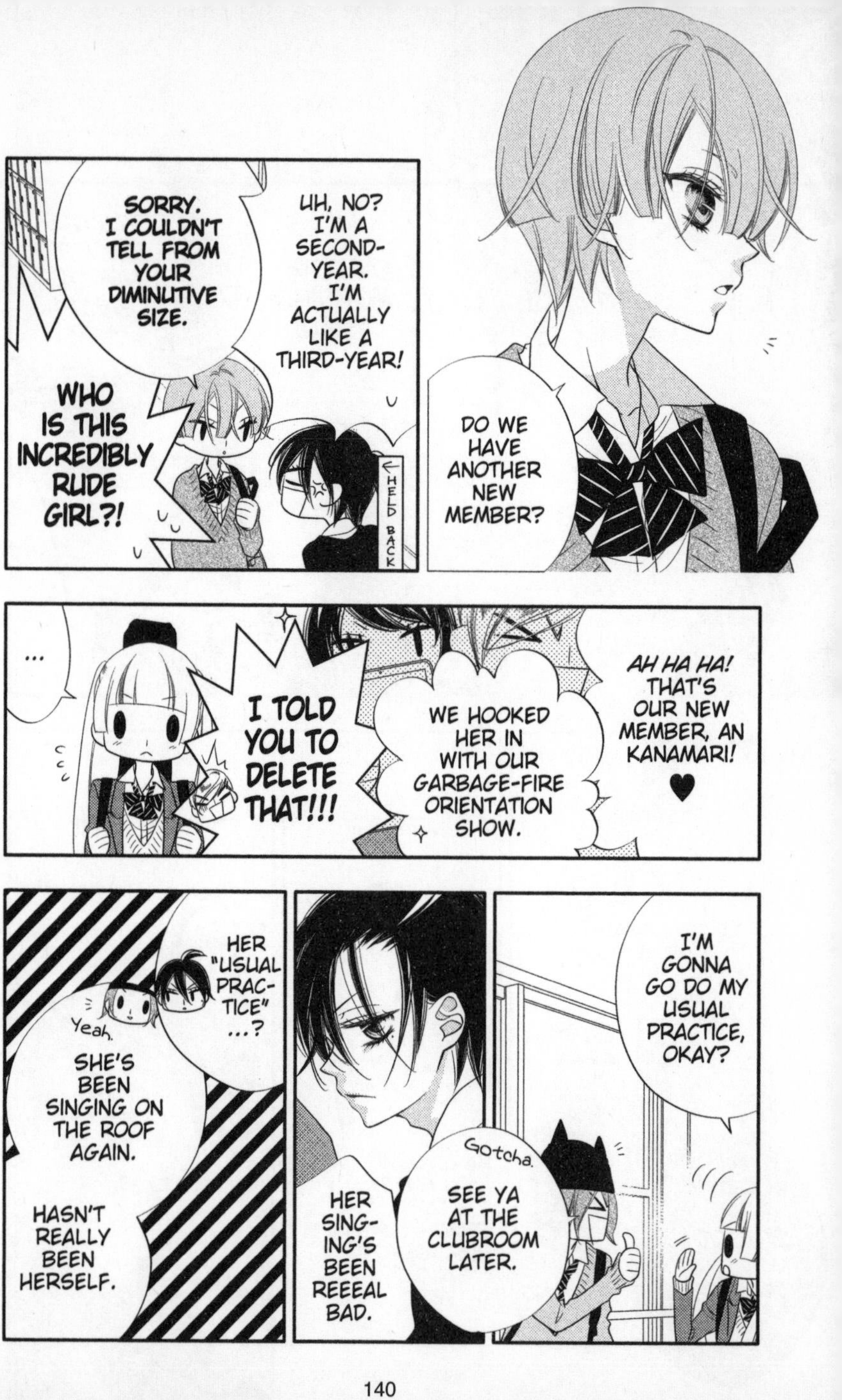
DO WE HAVE ANOTHER NEW MEMBER?
UH, NO? I'M A SECOND-YEAR. I'M ACTUALLY LIKE A THIRD-YEAR!
HELD BACK
SORRY. I COULDN'T TELL FROM YOUR DIMINUTIVE SIZE.
WHO IS THIS INCREDIBLY RUDE GIRL?!
AH HA HA! THAT'S OUR NEW MEMBER, AN KANAMARI! ♥
WE HOOKED HER IN WITH OUR GARBAGE-FIRE ORIENTATION SHOW.
I TOLD YOU TO DELETE THAT!!!
...
I'M GONNA GO DO MY USUAL PRACTICE, OKAY?
Gotcha.
SEE YA AT THE CLUBROOM LATER.
HER SING-ING'S BEEN REEEAL BAD.
HER "USUAL PRAC-TICE" ...?
Yeah.
SHE'S BEEN SINGING ON THE ROOF AGAIN.
HASN'T REALLY BEEN HERSELF.

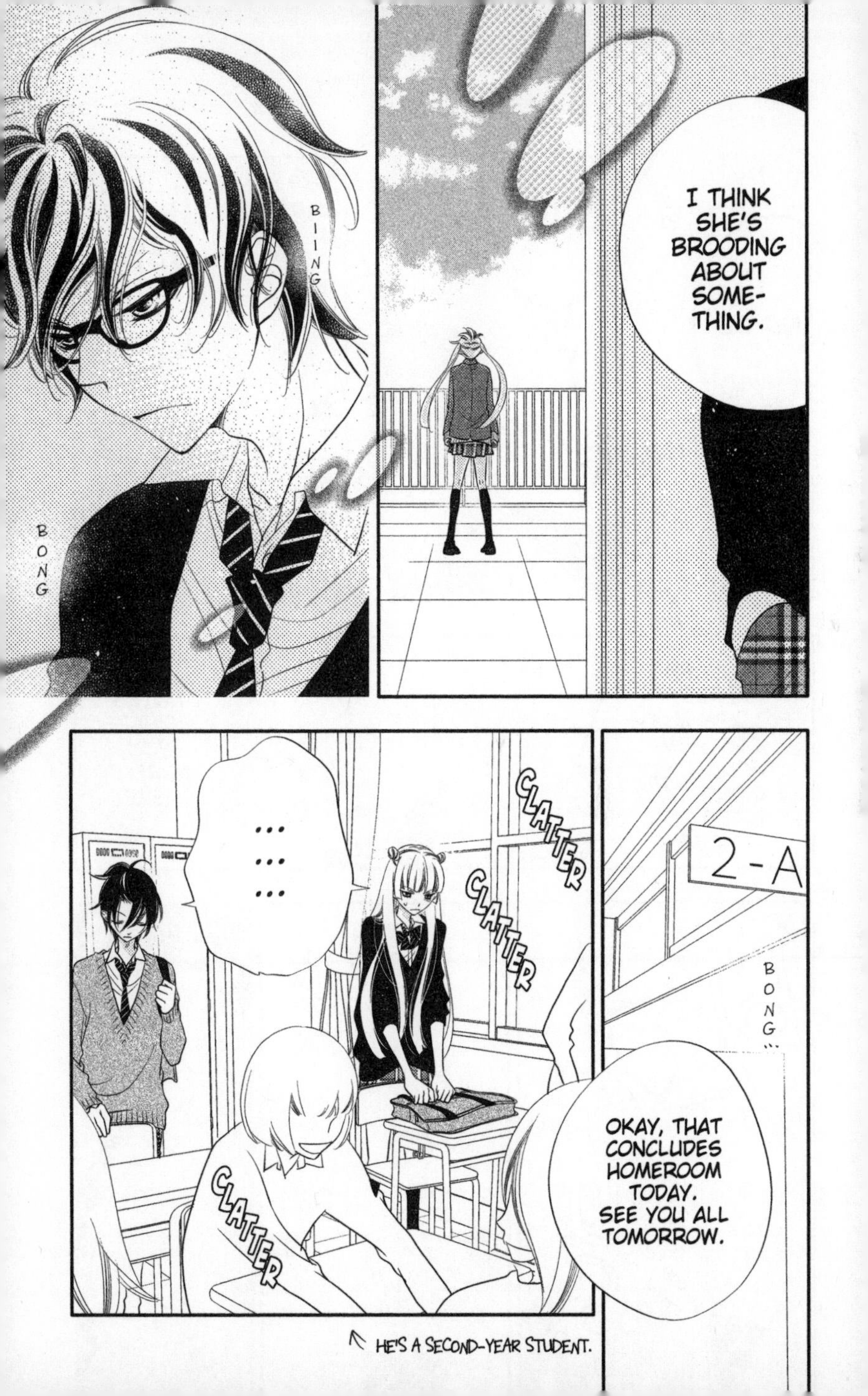
I THINK SHE'S BROODING ABOUT SOMETHING.
BIING
BONG
2-A
BONG
OKAY, THAT CONCLUDES HOMEROOM TODAY. SEE YOU ALL TOMORROW.
CLATTER
CLATTER
... ...
CLATTER

↖ HE'S A SECOND-YEAR STUDENT.

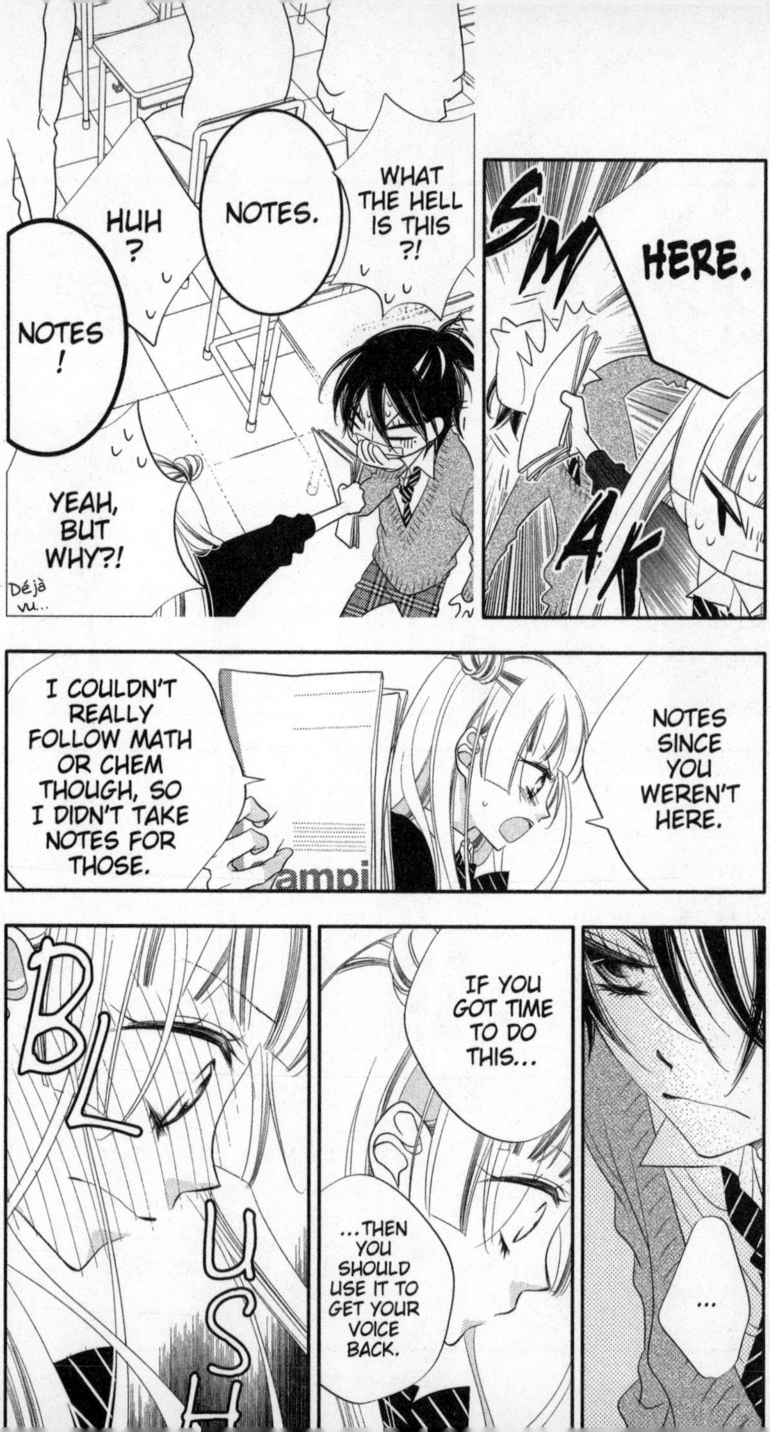
SMAK
HERE.
WHAT THE HELL IS THIS ?!
NOTES.
HUH ?
NOTES !
YEAH, BUT WHY?!
Déjà vu...
NOTES SINCE YOU WEREN'T HERE.
I COULDN'T REALLY FOLLOW MATH OR CHEM THOUGH, SO I DIDN'T TAKE NOTES FOR THOSE.
...
IF YOU GOT TIME TO DO THIS...
...THEN YOU SHOULD USE IT TO GET YOUR VOICE BACK.
BLUSH

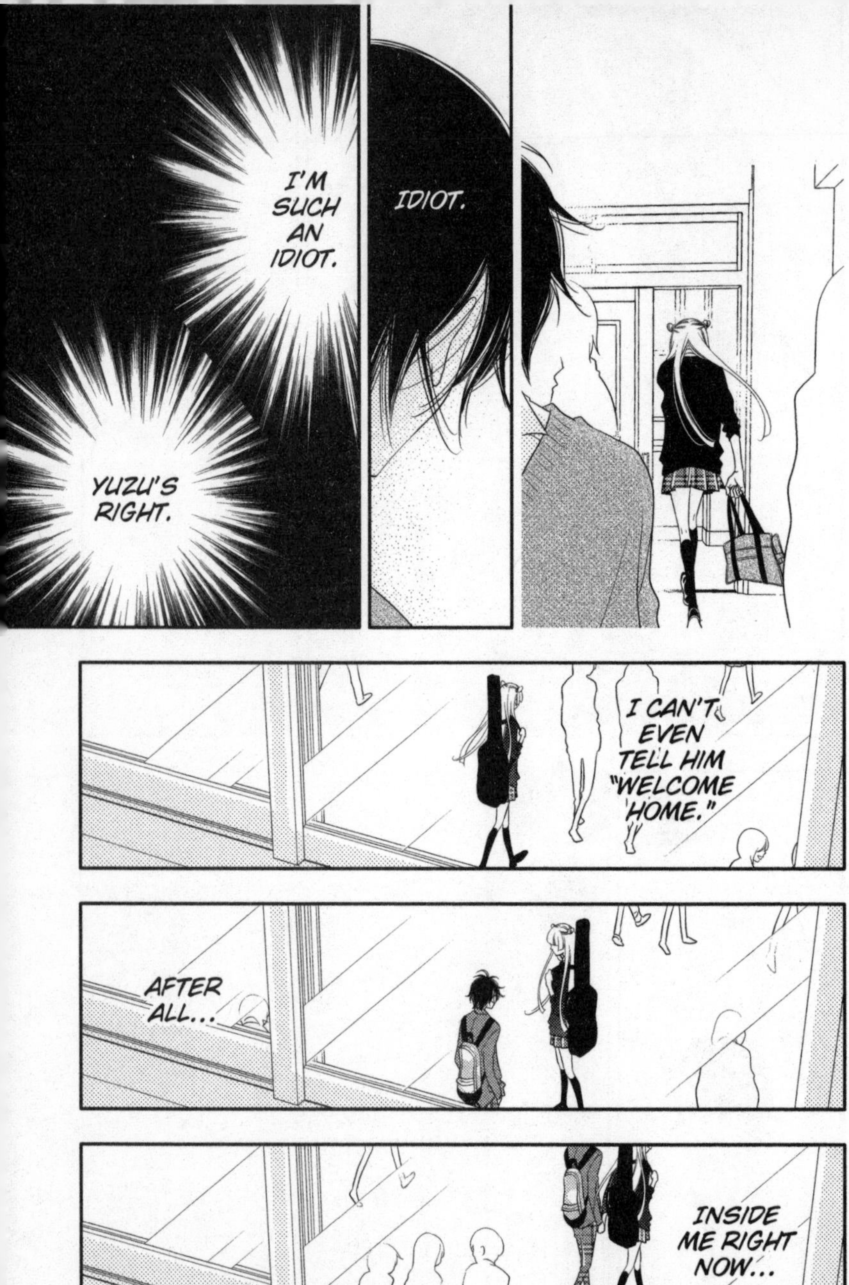
IDIOT.
I'M SUCH AN IDIOT.
YUZU'S RIGHT.
I CAN'T EVEN TELL HIM "WELCOME HOME."
AFTER ALL...
INSIDE ME RIGHT NOW...

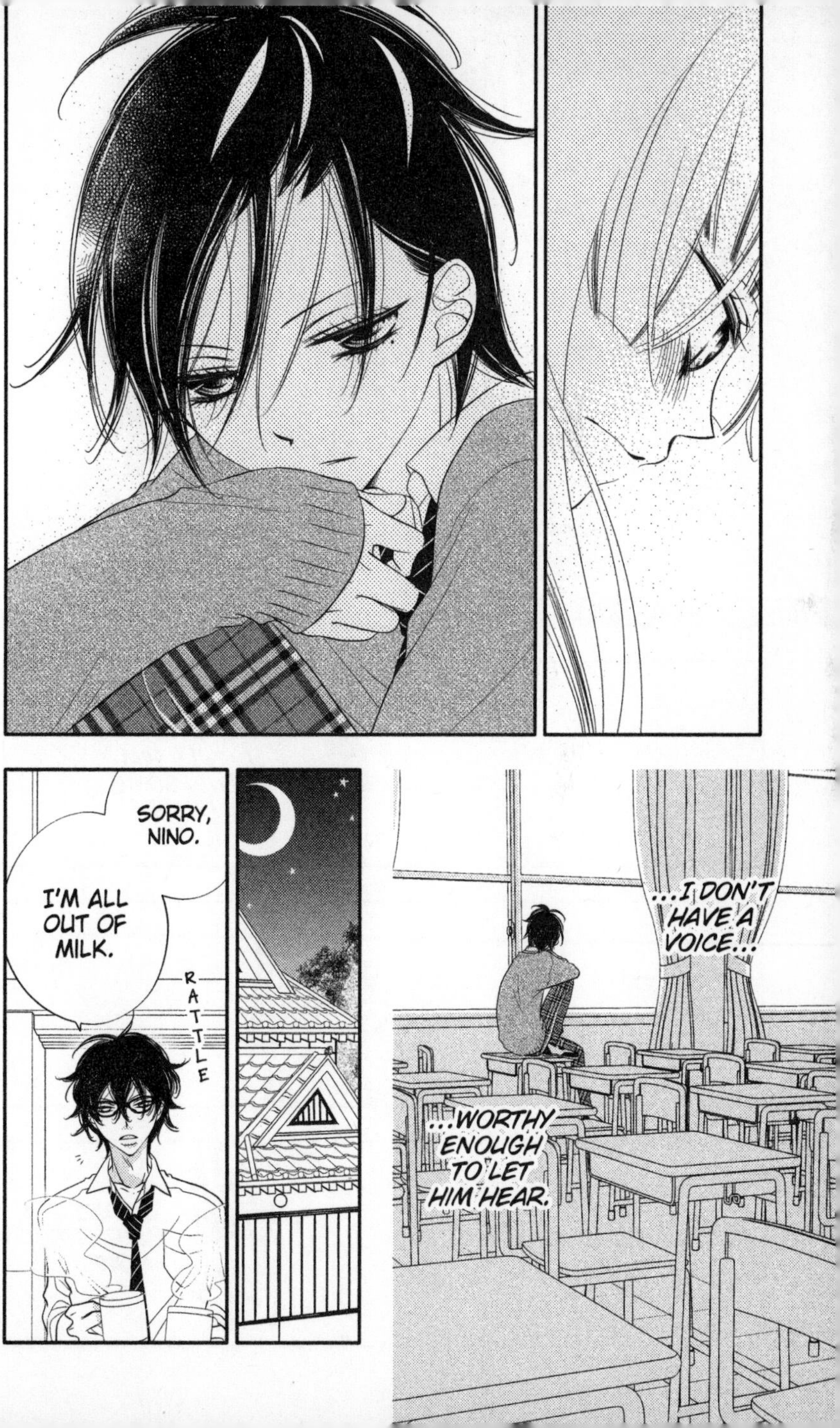
...I DON'T HAVE A VOICE...
...WORTHY ENOUGH TO LET HIM HEAR.
SORRY, NINO.
I'M ALL OUT OF MILK.
RATTLE

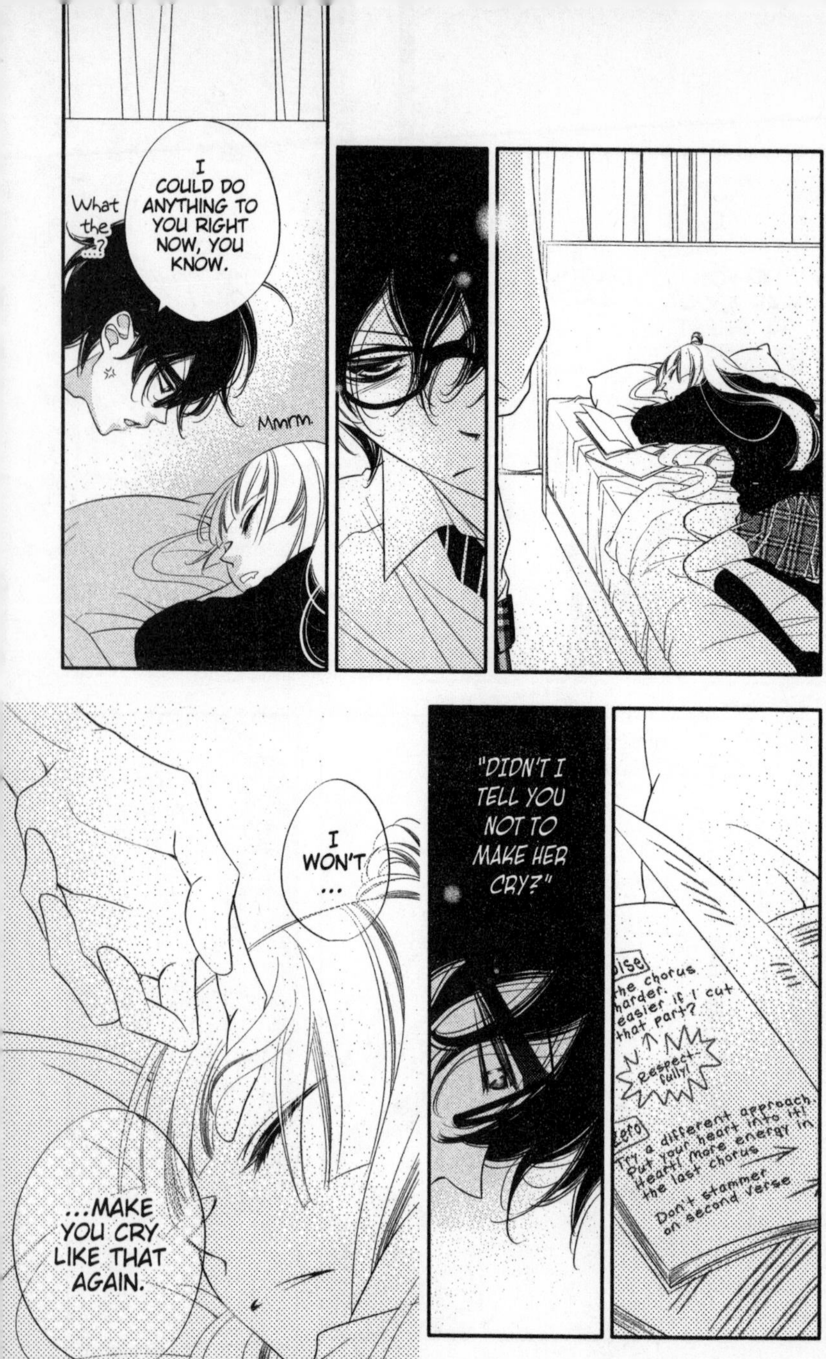
I COULD DO ANYTHING TO YOU RIGHT NOW, YOU KNOW.
What the ?
Mmrm.
ise
the chorus
harder.
easier if I cut that part?
Respect-fully!
eto
Try a different approach.
Put your heart into it!
Heart! More energy in the last chorus
Don't stammer on second verse
"DIDN'T I TELL YOU NOT TO MAKE HER CRY?"
I WON'T ...
...MAKE YOU CRY LIKE THAT AGAIN.

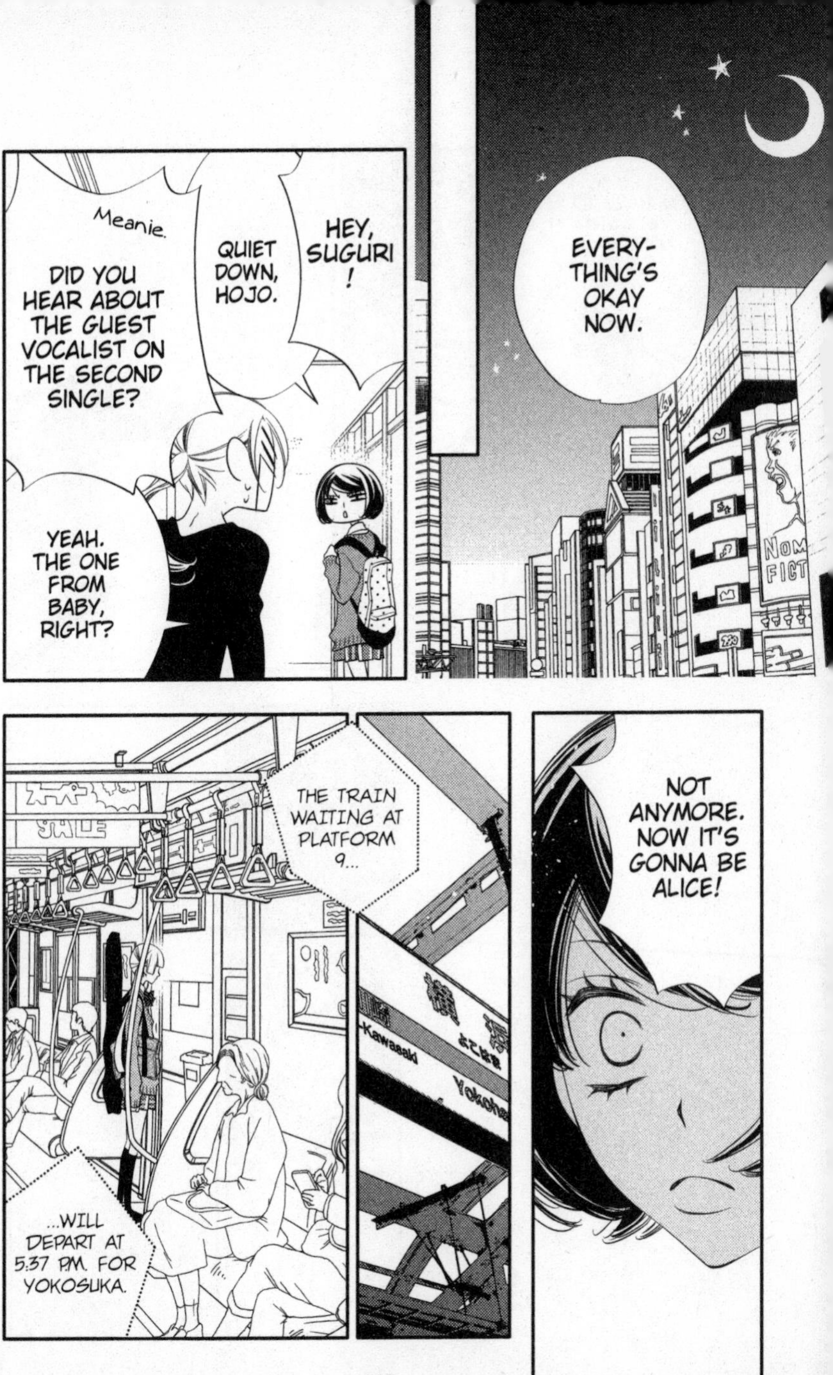
EVERY-THING'S OKAY NOW.
HEY, SUGURI!
QUIET DOWN, HOJO.
Meanie.
DID YOU HEAR ABOUT THE GUEST VOCALIST ON THE SECOND SINGLE?
YEAH. THE ONE FROM BABY, RIGHT?
NOT ANYMORE. NOW IT'S GONNA BE ALICE!
Kawasaki
THE TRAIN WAITING AT PLATFORM 9...
...WILL DEPART AT 5:37 P.M. FOR YOKOSUKA.

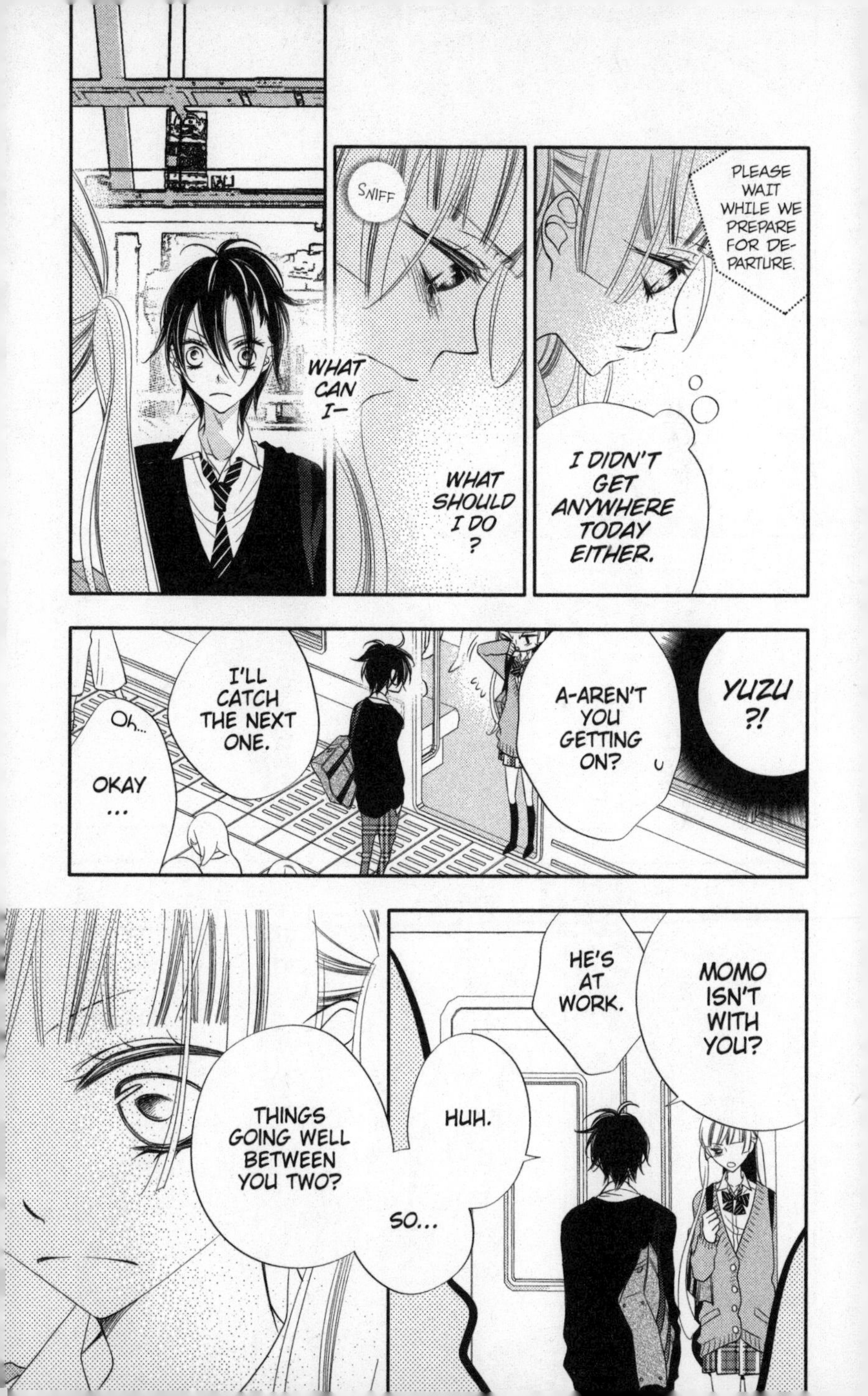
PLEASE WAIT WHILE WE PREPARE FOR DE-PARTURE.
I DIDN'T GET ANYWHERE TODAY EITHER.
SNIFF
WHAT CAN I—
WHAT SHOULD I DO ?
YUZU ?!
A-AREN'T YOU GETTING ON?
I'LL CATCH THE NEXT ONE.
Oh...
OKAY ...
MOMO ISN'T WITH YOU?
HE'S AT WORK.
HUH.
SO...
THINGS GOING WELL BETWEEN YOU TWO?

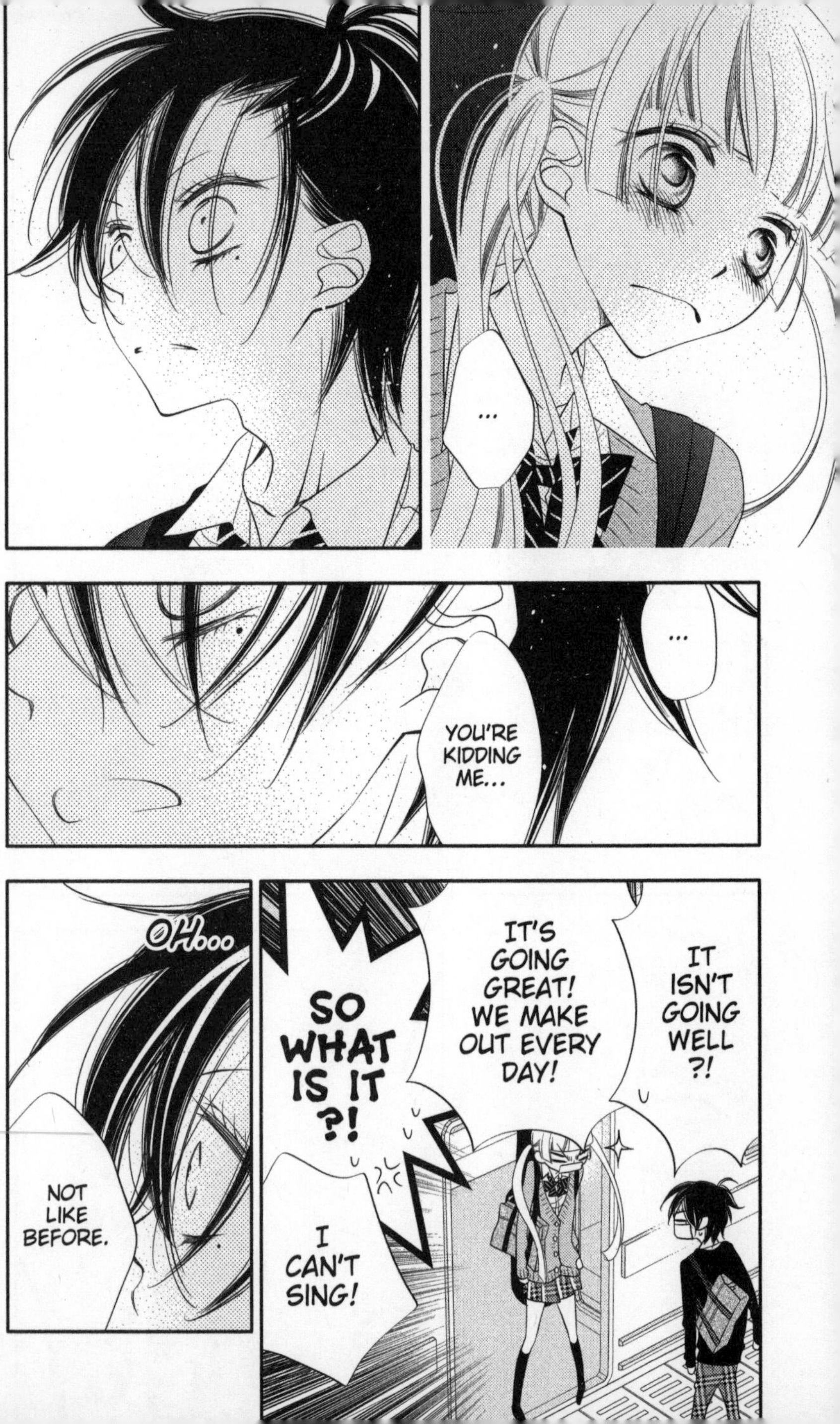
...
...
YOU'RE KIDDING ME...
IT ISN'T GOING WELL ?!
IT'S GOING GREAT! WE MAKE OUT EVERY DAY!
SO WHAT IS IT ?!
I CAN'T SING!
OHooo
NOT LIKE BEFORE.

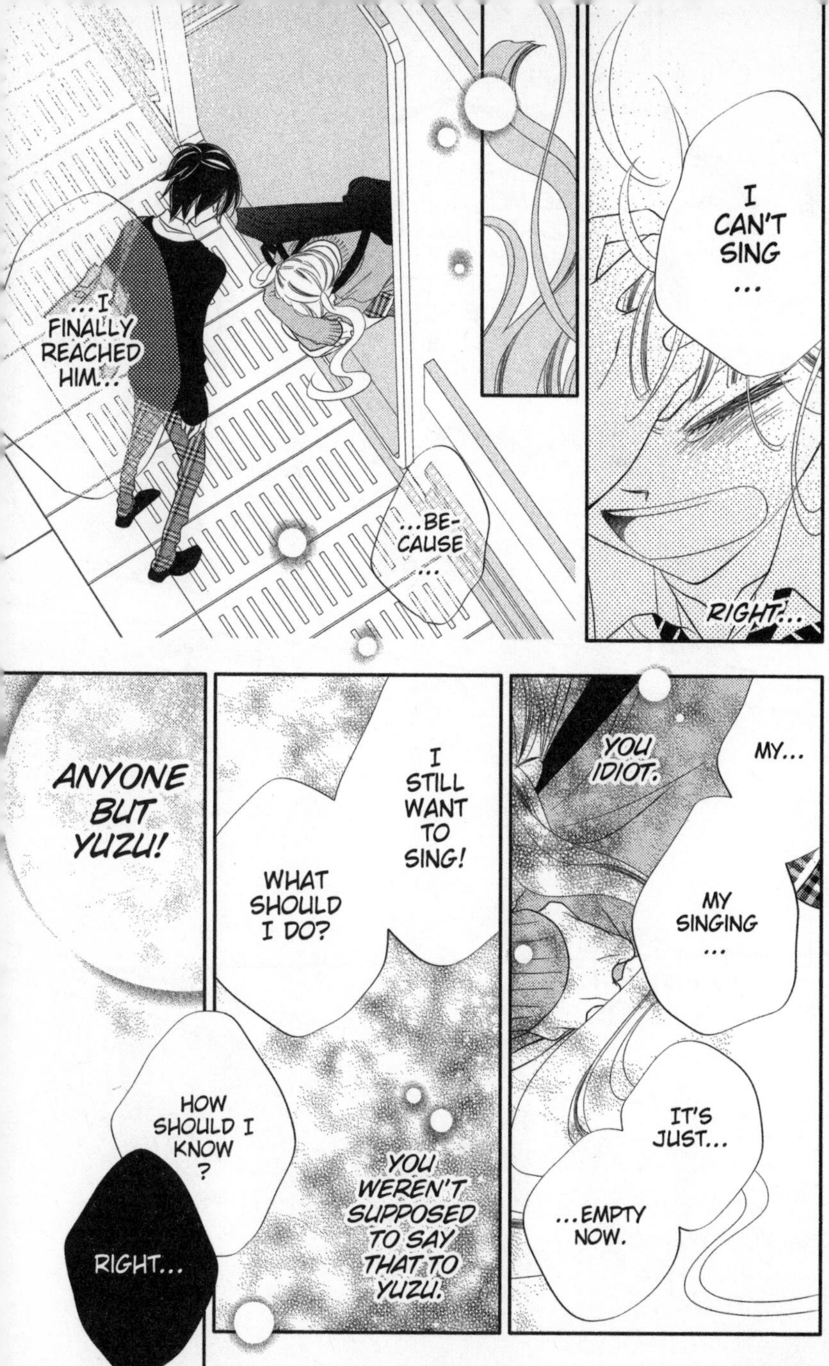
I CAN'T SING ...
RIGHT...
...BE-CAUSE ...
...I FINALLY REACHED HIM...
MY...
YOU IDIOT.
MY SINGING ...
IT'S JUST...
...EMPTY NOW.
I STILL WANT TO SING!
WHAT SHOULD I DO?
YOU WEREN'T SUPPOSED TO SAY THAT TO YUZU.
ANYONE BUT YUZU!
HOW SHOULD I KNOW ?
RIGHT...

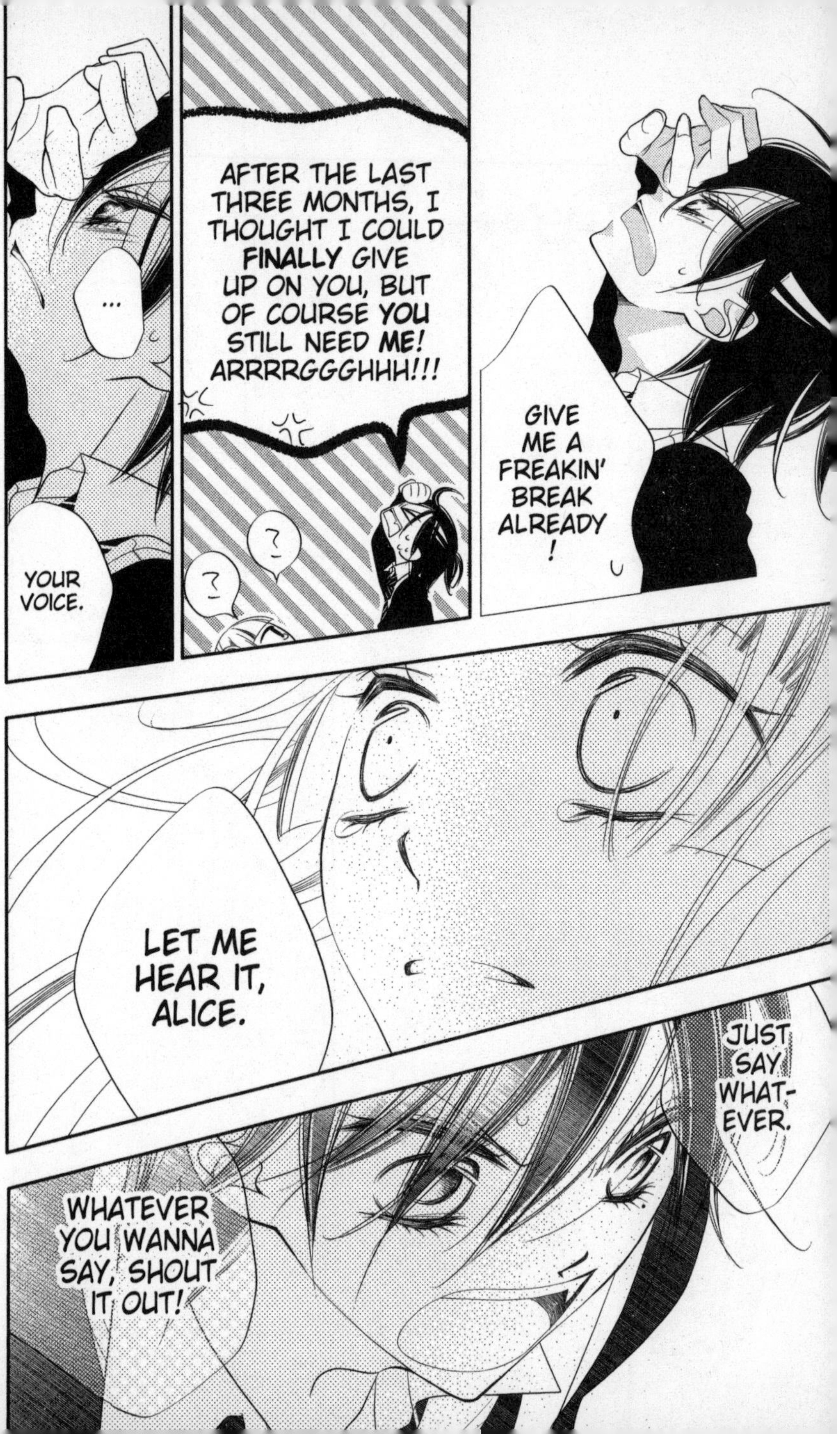
GIVE ME A FREAKIN' BREAK ALREADY!
AFTER THE LAST THREE MONTHS, I THOUGHT I COULD FINALLY GIVE UP ON YOU, BUT OF COURSE YOU STILL NEED ME! ARRRRGGGHHH!!!
?
?
...
YOUR VOICE.
LET ME HEAR IT, ALICE.
JUST SAY WHAT-EVER.
WHATEVER YOU WANNA SAY, SHOUT IT OUT!

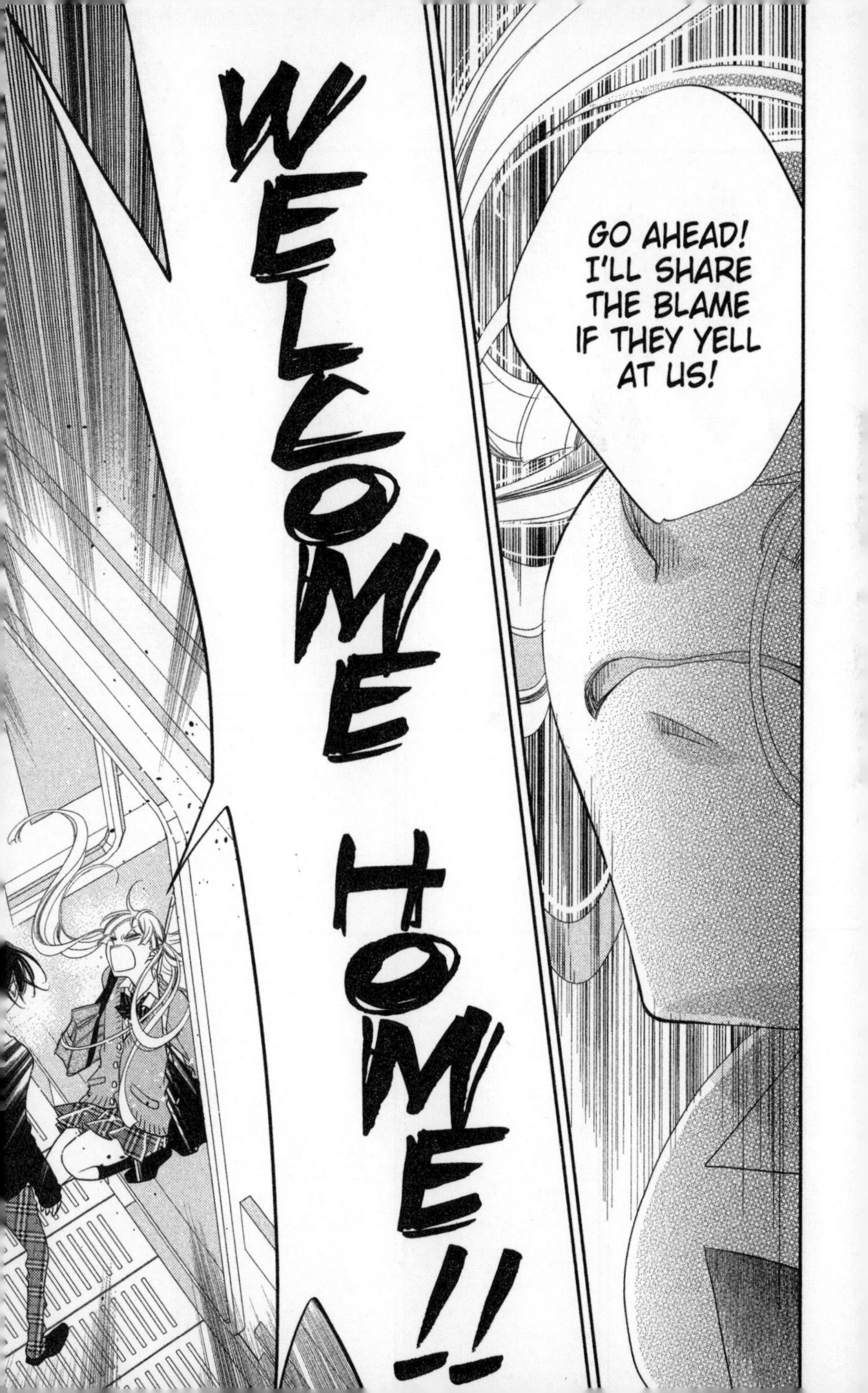
GO AHEAD! I'LL SHARE THE BLAME IF THEY YELL AT US!
WELCOME HOME!!

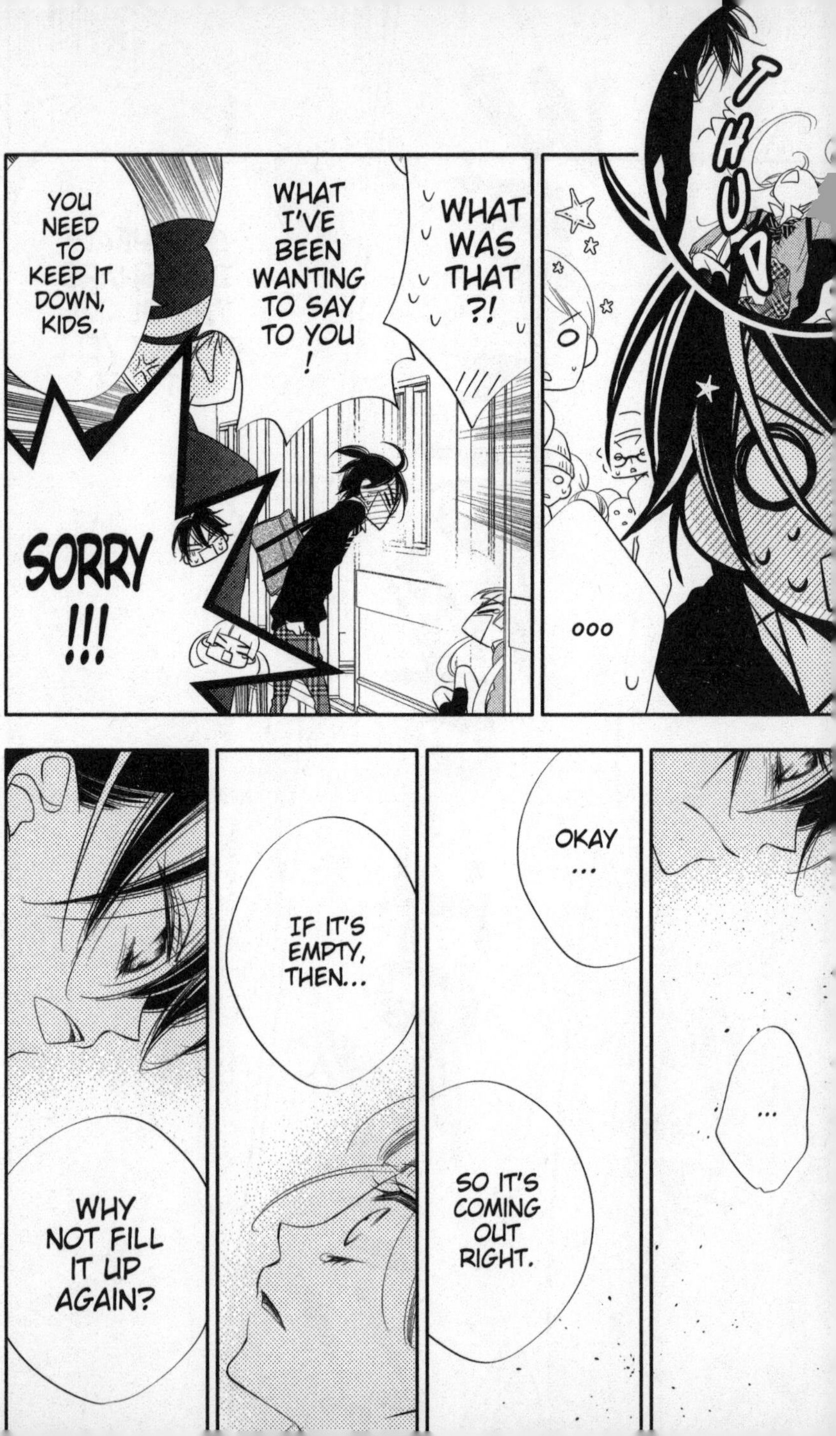
THUD
ooo
WHAT WAS THAT?!
WHAT I'VE BEEN WANTING TO SAY TO YOU!
YOU NEED TO KEEP IT DOWN, KIDS.
SORRY!!!
...
OKAY...
SO IT'S COMING OUT RIGHT.
IF IT'S EMPTY, THEN...
WHY NOT FILL IT UP AGAIN?

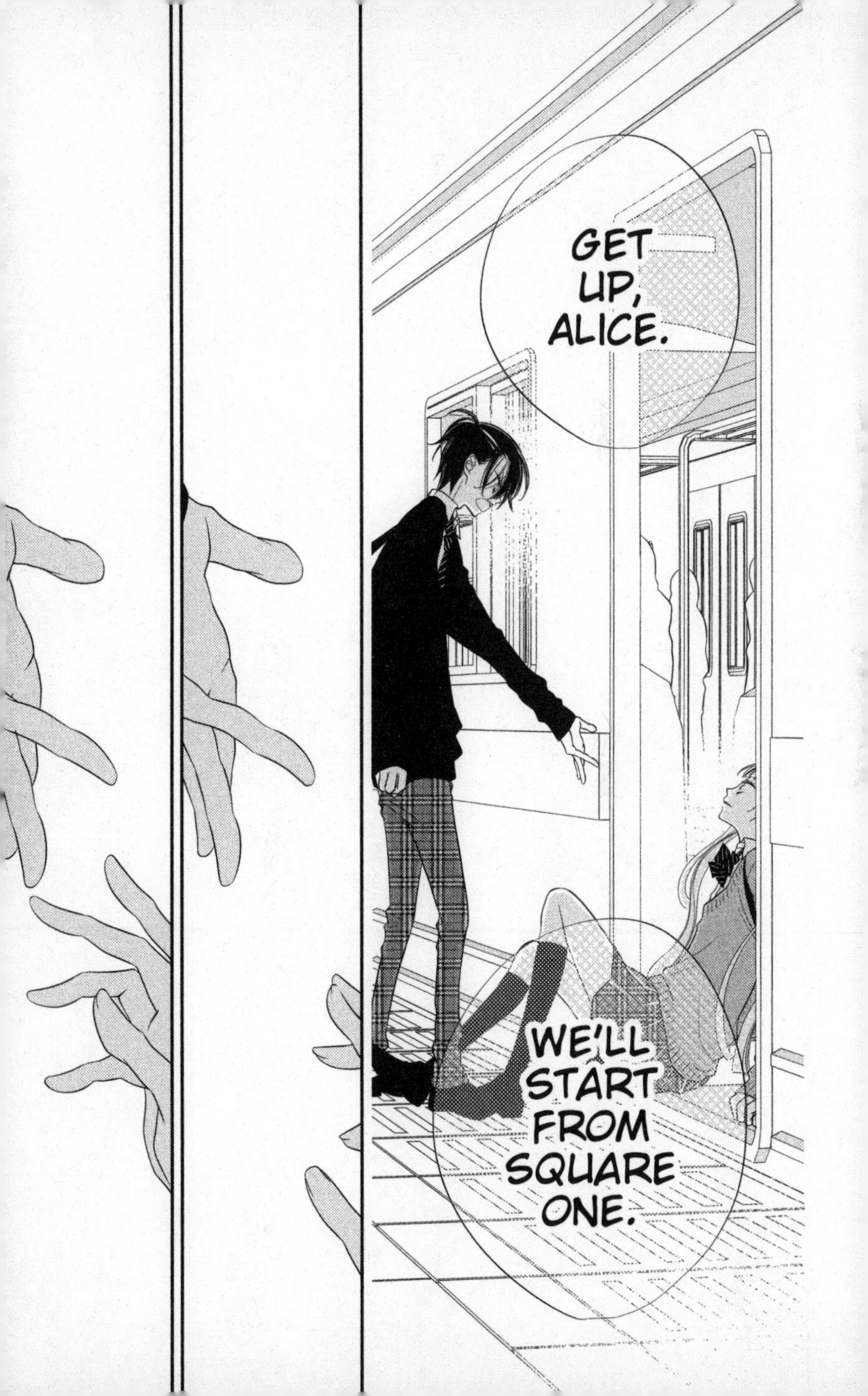
GET UP, ALICE.
WE'LL START FROM SQUARE ONE.

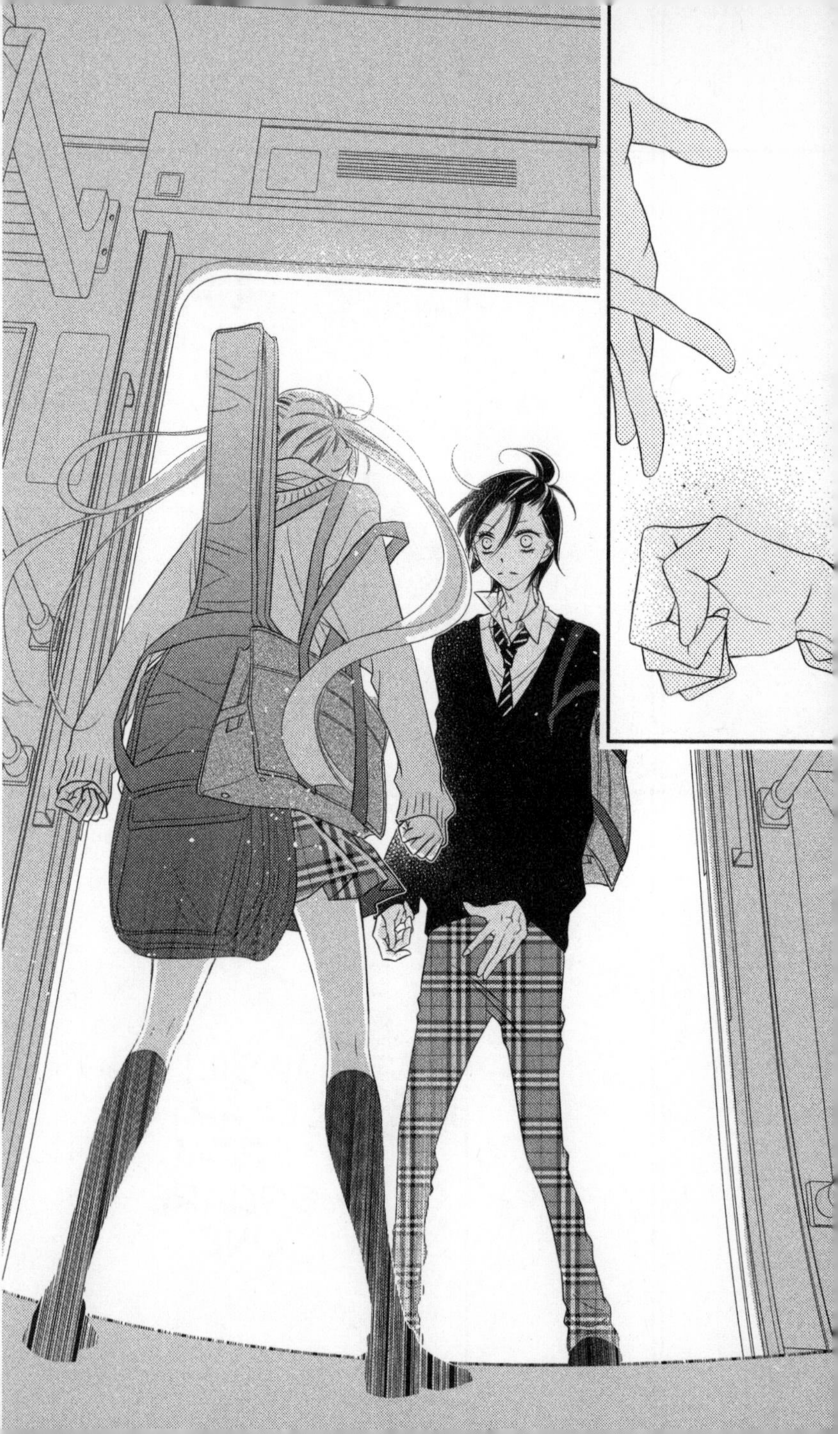

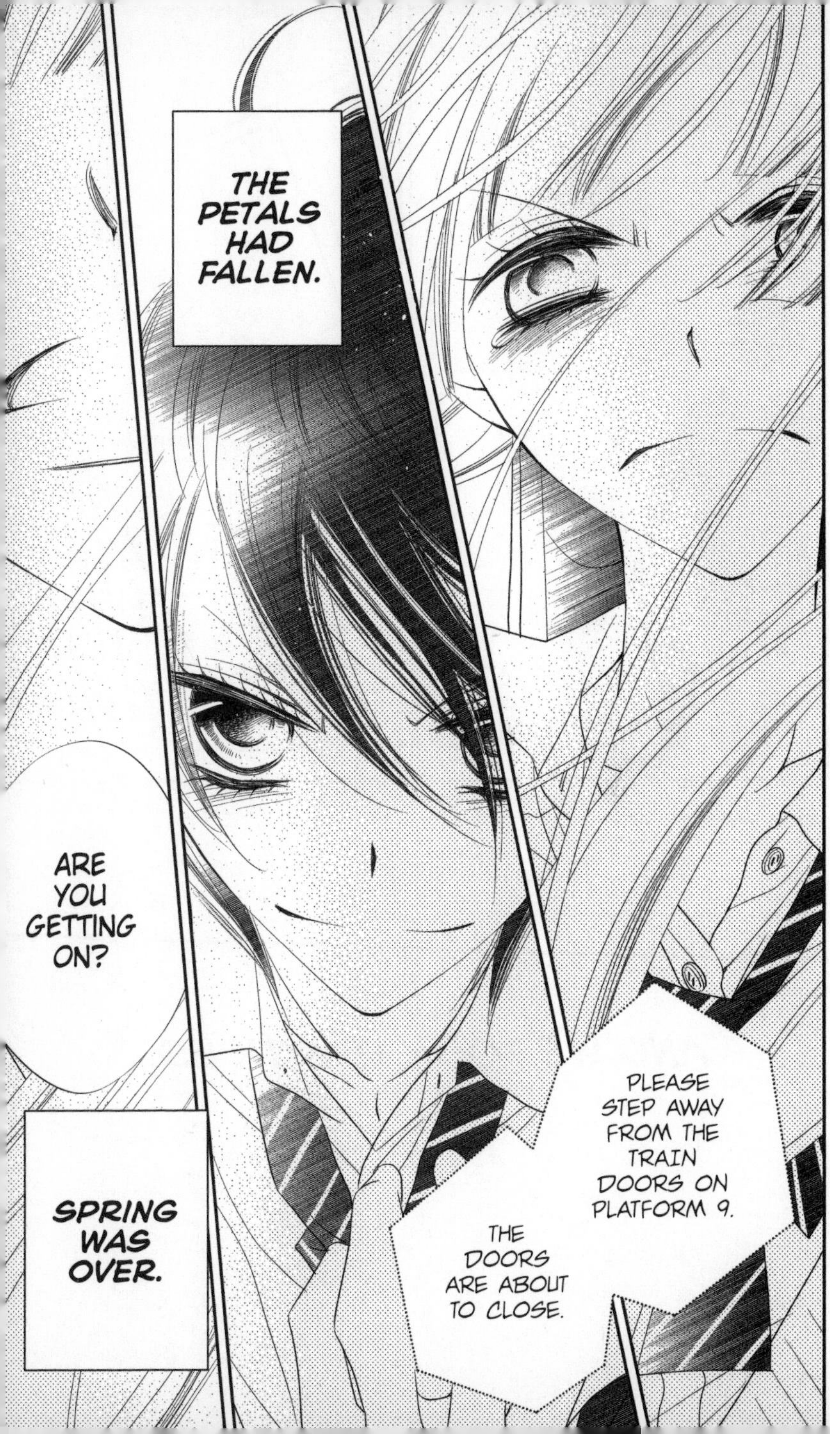
PLEASE STEP AWAY FROM THE TRAIN DOORS ON PLATFORM 9.
THE DOORS ARE ABOUT TO CLOSE.
THE PETALS HAD FALLEN.
ARE YOU GETTING ON?
SPRING WAS OVER.

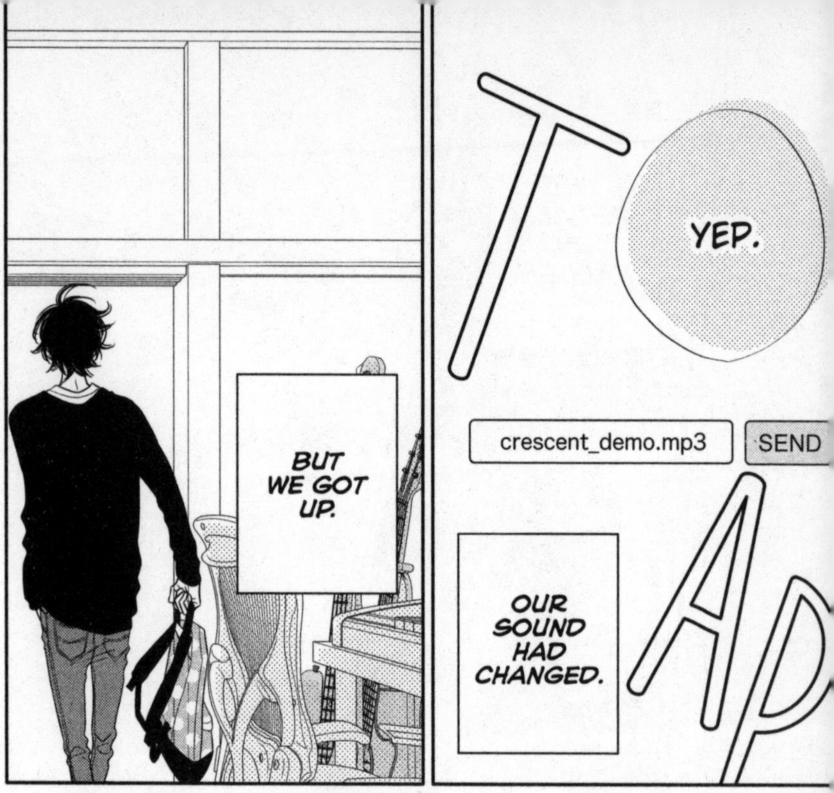
YEP.
TAP
crescent_demo.mp3
SEND
OUR SOUND HAD CHANGED.
BUT WE GOT UP.

AND WE TOOK IT WITH US.

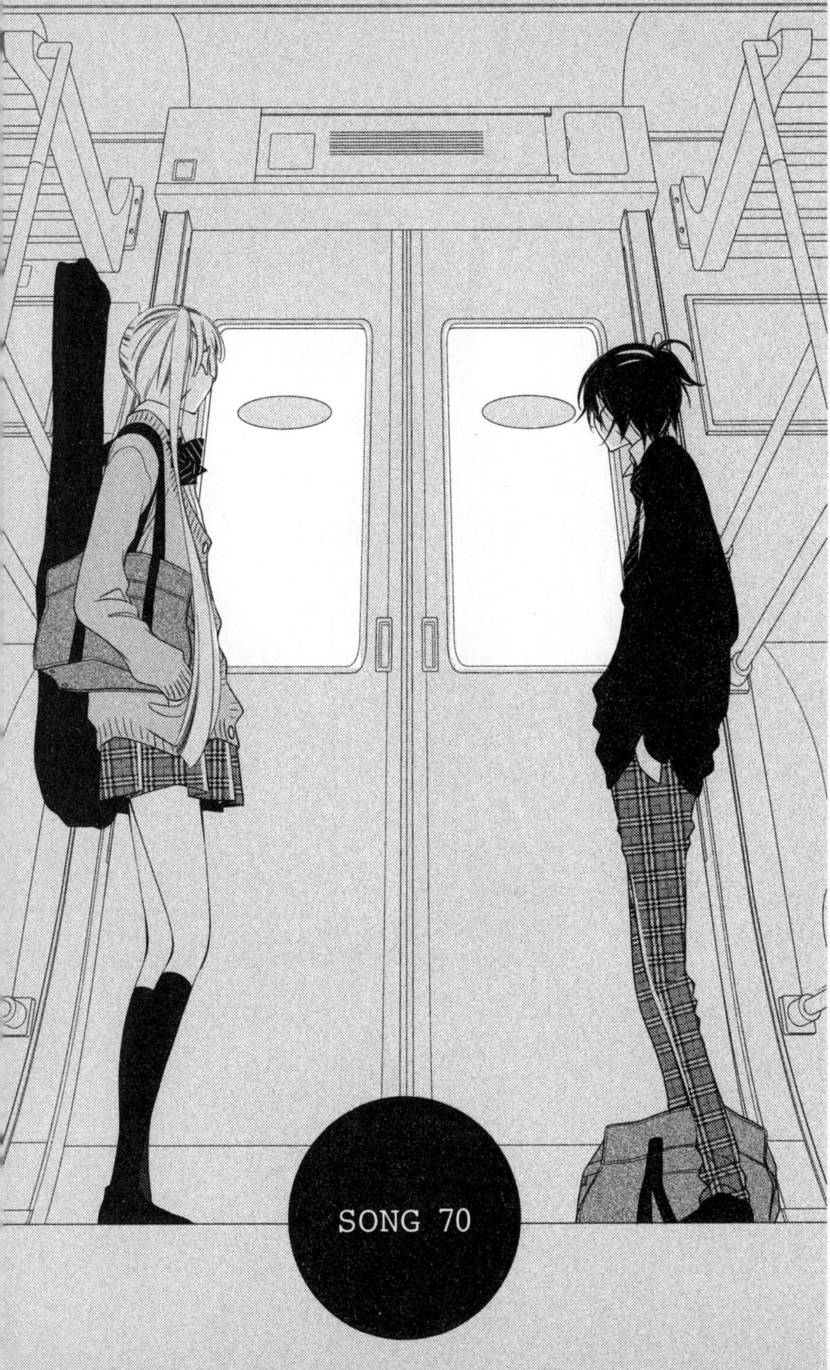
SONG 70

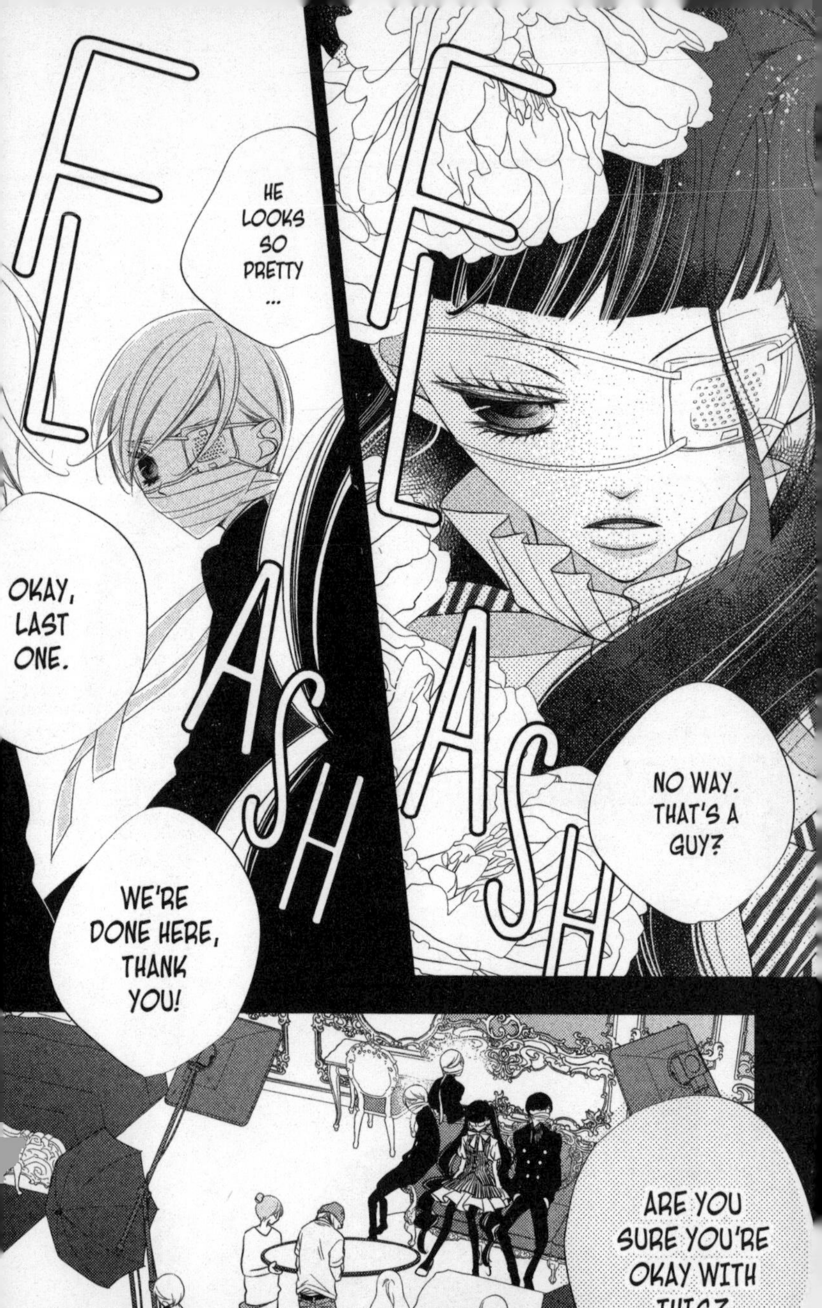
FLASH
NO WAY. THAT'S A GUY?
HE LOOKS SO PRETTY ...
OKAY, LAST ONE.
FLASH
WE'RE DONE HERE, THANK YOU!
ARE YOU SURE YOU'RE OKAY WITH THIS?

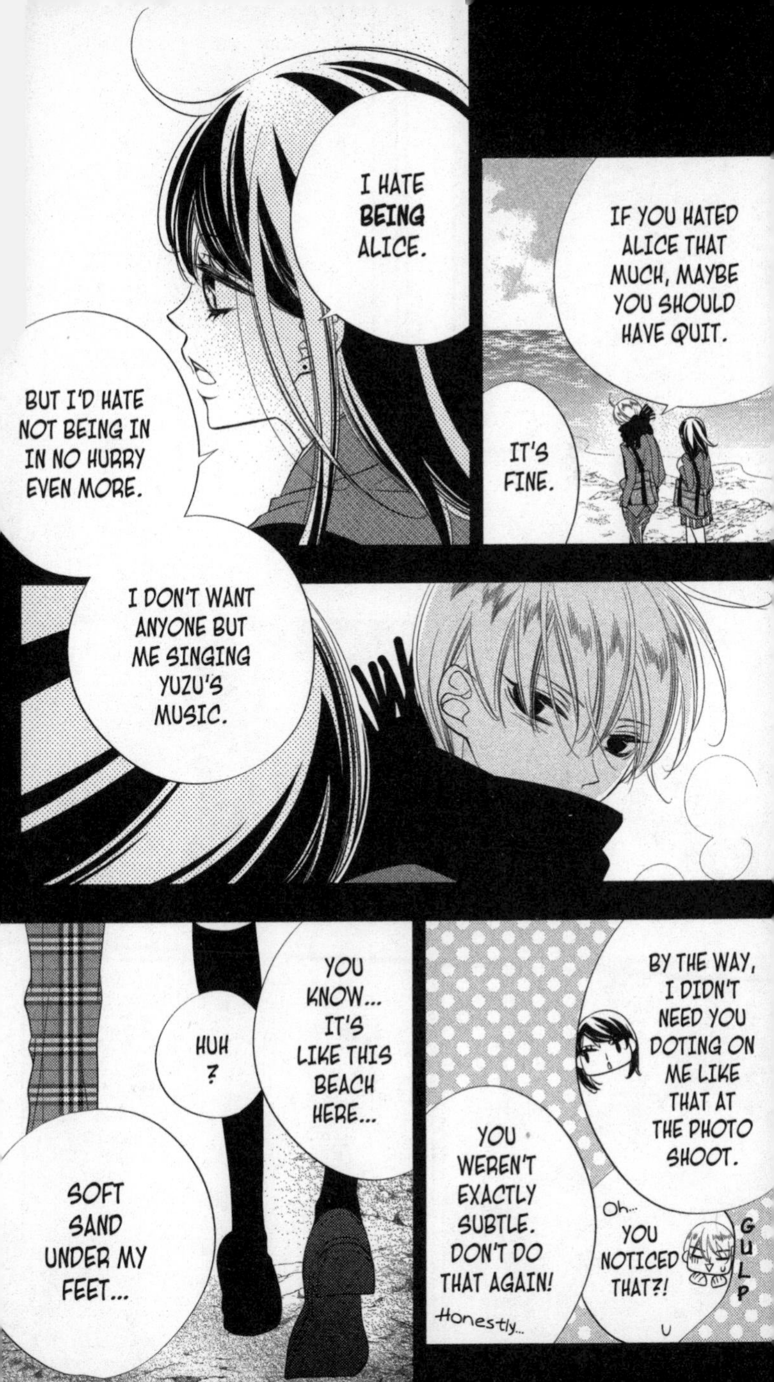
IF YOU HATED ALICE THAT MUCH, MAYBE YOU SHOULD HAVE QUIT.
IT'S FINE.
I HATE **BEING** ALICE.
BUT I'D HATE NOT BEING IN IN NO HURRY EVEN MORE.
I DON'T WANT ANYONE BUT ME SINGING YUZU'S MUSIC.
BY THE WAY, I DIDN'T NEED YOU DOTING ON ME LIKE THAT AT THE PHOTO SHOOT.
YOU WEREN'T EXACTLY SUBTLE. DON'T DO THAT AGAIN!
Honestly...
Oh... YOU NOTICED THAT?!
GULP
YOU KNOW... IT'S LIKE THIS BEACH HERE...
HUH?
SOFT SAND UNDER MY FEET...

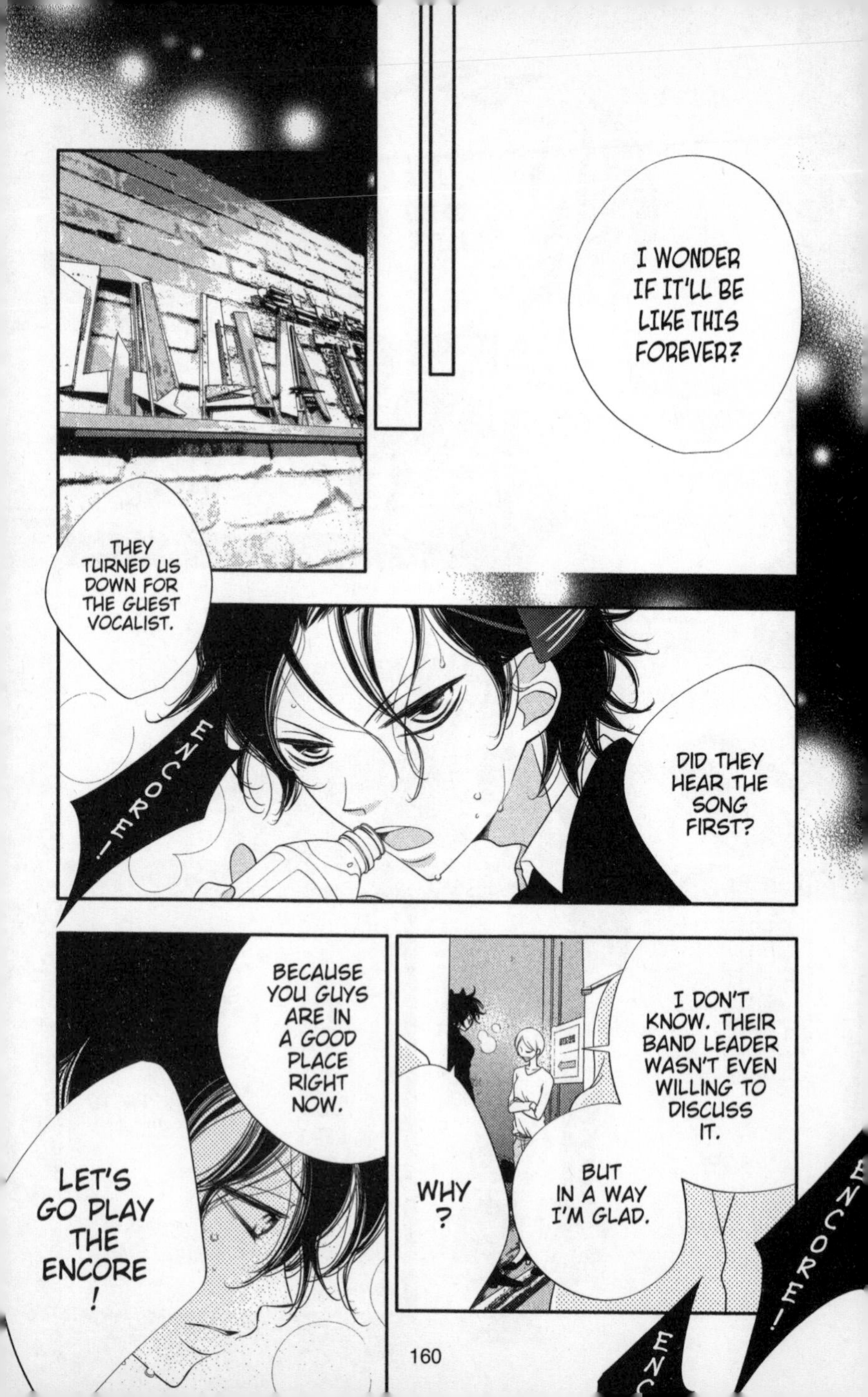
I WONDER IF IT'LL BE LIKE THIS FOREVER?
THEY TURNED US DOWN FOR THE GUEST VOCALIST.
DID THEY HEAR THE SONG FIRST?
ENCORE!
I DON'T KNOW. THEIR BAND LEADER WASN'T EVEN WILLING TO DISCUSS IT.
BUT IN A WAY I'M GLAD.
WHY?
ENCORE!
BECAUSE YOU GUYS ARE IN A GOOD PLACE RIGHT NOW.
LET'S GO PLAY THE ENCORE!

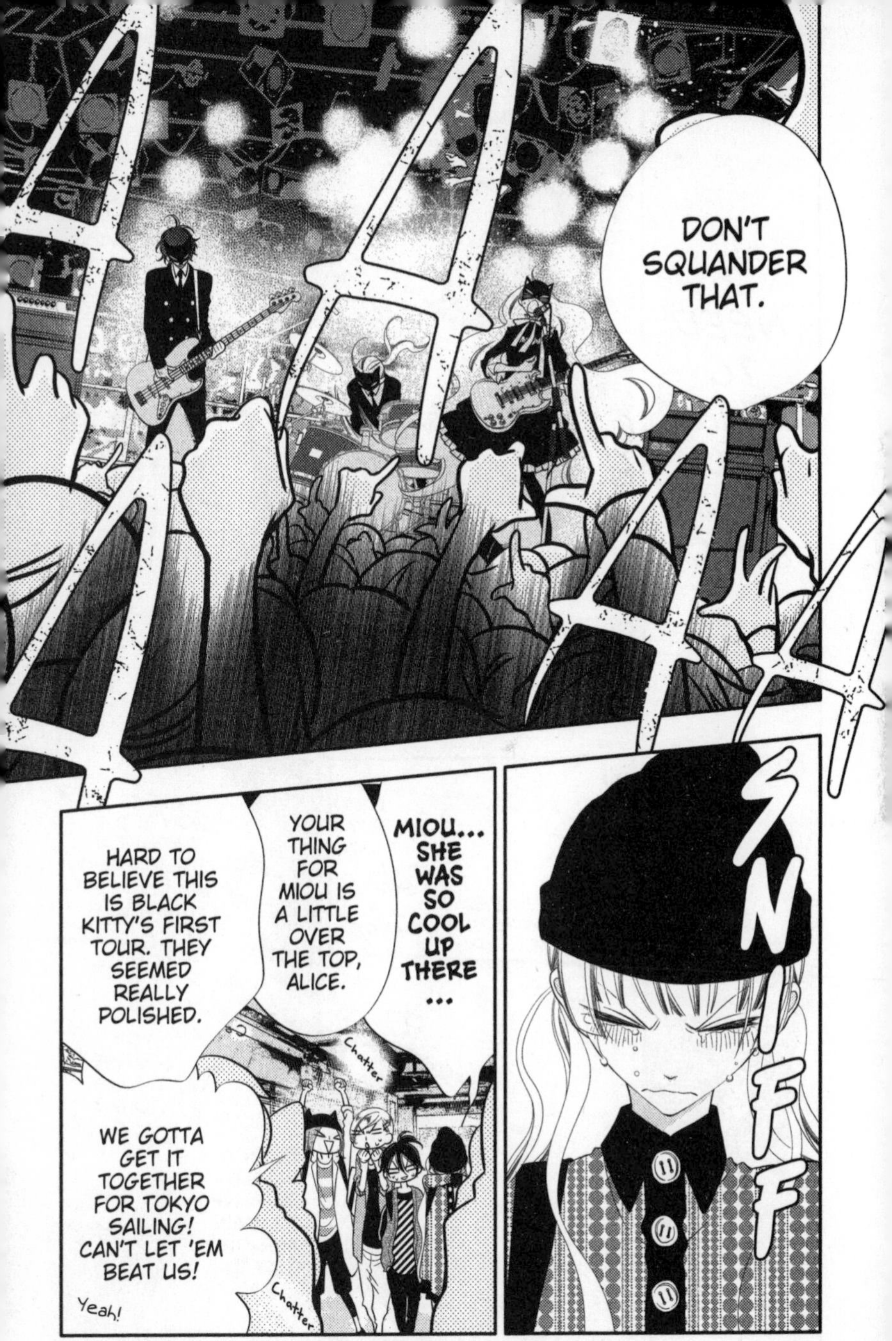
DON'T SQUANDER THAT.
SNIFF
MIOU... SHE WAS SO COOL UP THERE ...
YOUR THING FOR MIOU IS A LITTLE OVER THE TOP, ALICE.
HARD TO BELIEVE THIS IS BLACK KITTY'S FIRST TOUR. THEY SEEMED REALLY POLISHED.
Chatter
WE GOTTA GET IT TOGETHER FOR TOKYO SAILING! CAN'T LET 'EM BEAT US!
Chatter
Yeah!

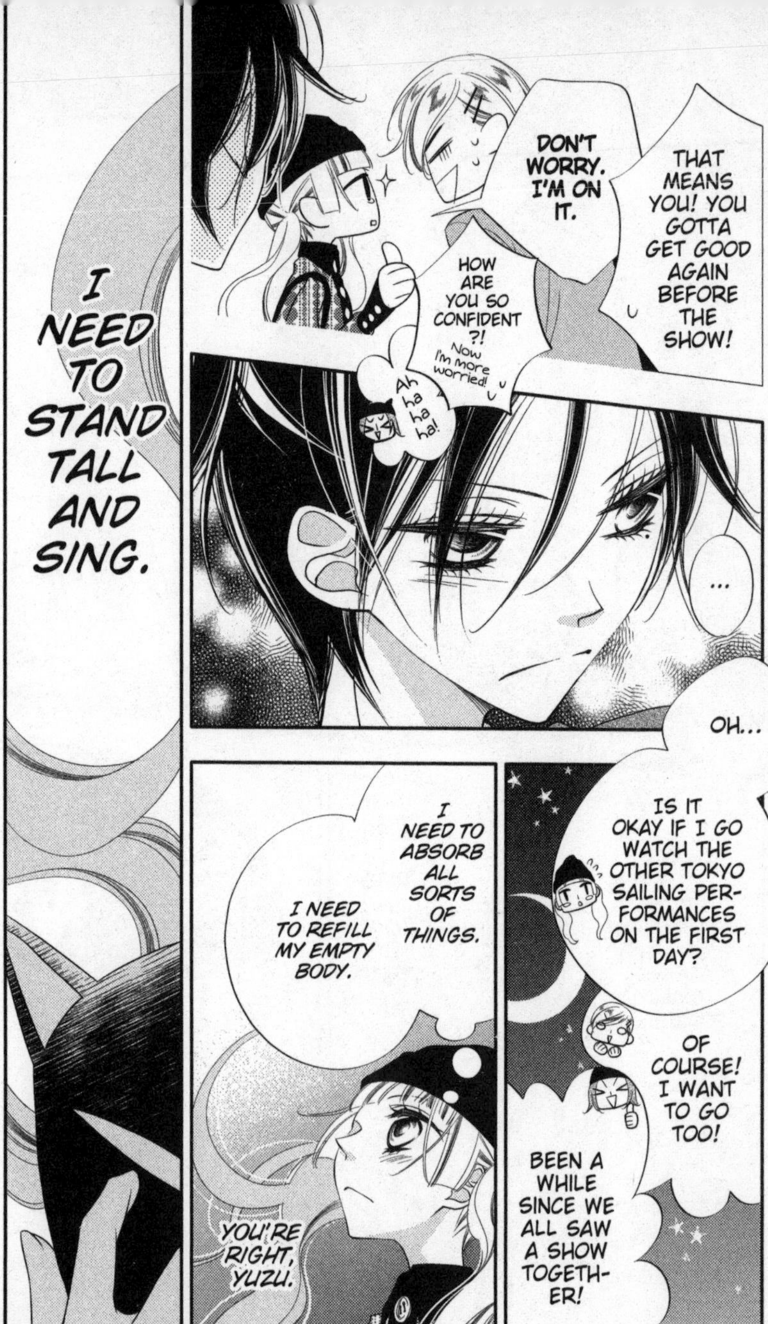
THAT MEANS YOU! YOU GOTTA GET GOOD AGAIN BEFORE THE SHOW!
DON'T WORRY. I'M ON IT.
HOW ARE YOU SO CONFIDENT?!
Now I'm more worried!
Ah ha ha ha!
...
OH...
IS IT OKAY IF I GO WATCH THE OTHER TOKYO SAILING PER-FORMANCES ON THE FIRST DAY?
OF COURSE! I WANT TO GO TOO!
BEEN A WHILE SINCE WE ALL SAW A SHOW TOGETH-ER!
I NEED TO ABSORB ALL SORTS OF THINGS.
I NEED TO REFILL MY EMPTY BODY.
YOU'RE RIGHT, YUZU.
I NEED TO STAND TALL AND SING.

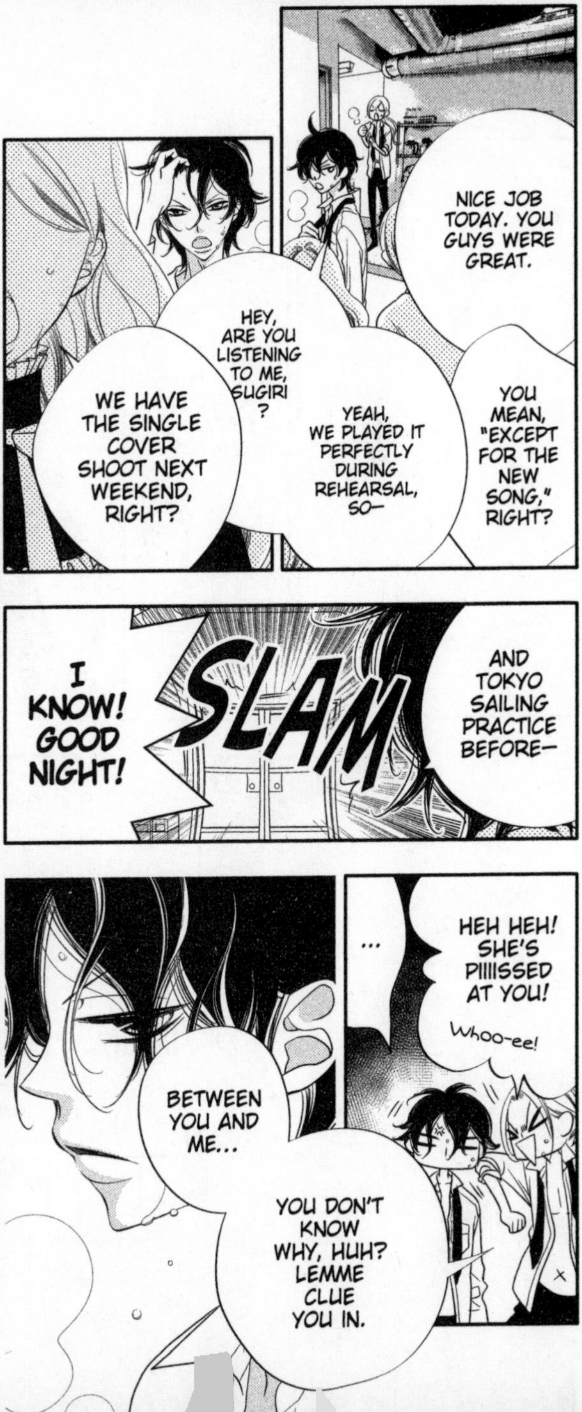
NICE JOB TODAY. YOU GUYS WERE GREAT.
YEAH, WE PLAYED IT PERFECTLY DURING REHEARSAL, SO—
YOU MEAN, "EXCEPT FOR THE NEW SONG," RIGHT?
HEY, ARE YOU LISTENING TO ME, SUGIRI?
WE HAVE THE SINGLE COVER SHOOT NEXT WEEKEND, RIGHT?
AND TOKYO SAILING PRACTICE BEFORE—
SLAM
I KNOW! GOOD NIGHT!
HEH HEH! SHE'S PIIIISSED AT YOU!
Whoo-ee!
...
BETWEEN YOU AND ME...
YOU DON'T KNOW WHY, HUH? LEMME CLUE YOU IN.

6

I hope you've enjoyed volume 12! I have a heaping ton of fun planned for volume 13—just the thing to invite another meltdown from Nino. I'd be so happy if you'd join me there. Also, please check out the anime, which is starting soon!

RYOKO FUKUYAMA
3/20/2017

[SPECIAL THANKS]
MOSAGE
TAKAYUKI NAGASHIMA
KENJU NORO
MY FAMILY
MY FRIENDS
AND YOU!!

Ryoko Fukuyama
c/o Anonymous Noise Editor
VIZ Media
P.O. Box 77010
San Francisco, CA 94107

HP http://ryoconet/
@ryocoryocoryoco
http://facebook.com/ryocoryocoryoco/

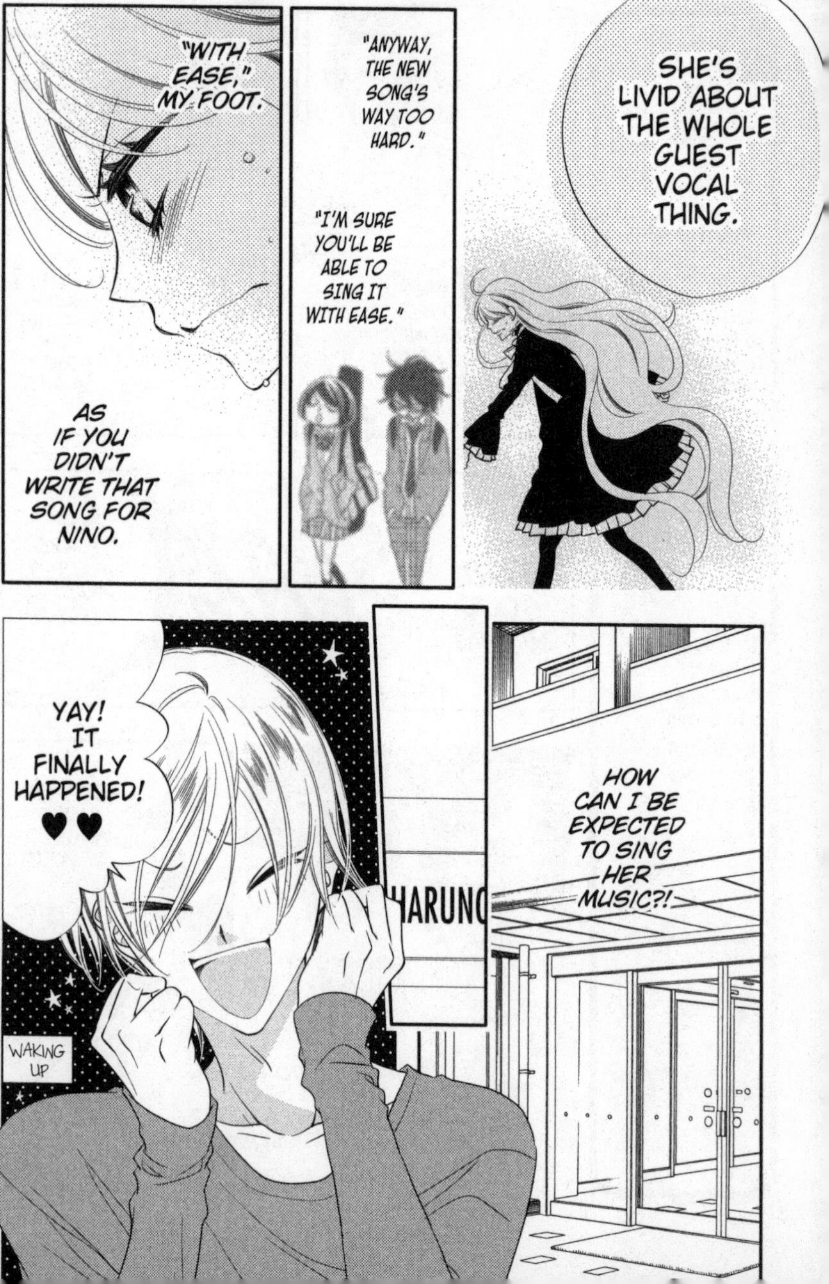
SHE'S LIVID ABOUT THE WHOLE GUEST VOCAL THING.
"ANYWAY, THE NEW SONG'S WAY TOO HARD."
"I'M SURE YOU'LL BE ABLE TO SING IT WITH EASE."
"WITH EASE," MY FOOT.
AS IF YOU DIDN'T WRITE THAT SONG FOR NINO.
HOW CAN I BE EXPECTED TO SING HER MUSIC?!
YAY! IT FINALLY HAPPENED! ♥♥
WAKING UP

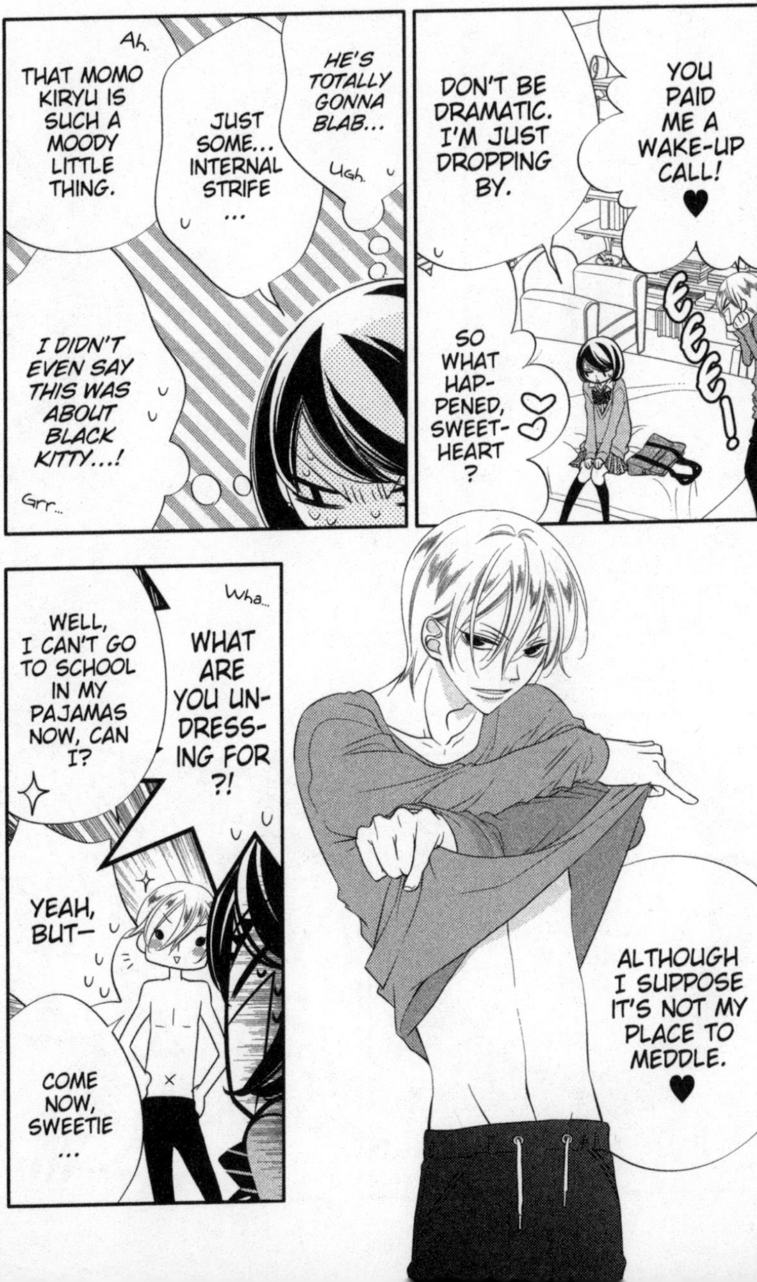
YOU PAID ME A WAKE-UP CALL! ♥
DON'T BE DRAMATIC. I'M JUST DROPPING BY.
EEEE!
SO WHAT HAP-PENED, SWEET-HEART?
HE'S TOTALLY GONNA BLAB...
Ugh.
JUST SOME... INTERNAL STRIFE...
Ah.
THAT MOMO KIRYU IS SUCH A MOODY LITTLE THING.
I DIDN'T EVEN SAY THIS WAS ABOUT BLACK KITTY...!
Grr...
ALTHOUGH I SUPPOSE IT'S NOT MY PLACE TO MEDDLE. ♥
Wha...
WHAT ARE YOU UN-DRESS-ING FOR?!
WELL, I CAN'T GO TO SCHOOL IN MY PAJAMAS NOW, CAN I?
YEAH, BUT—
COME NOW, SWEETIE...

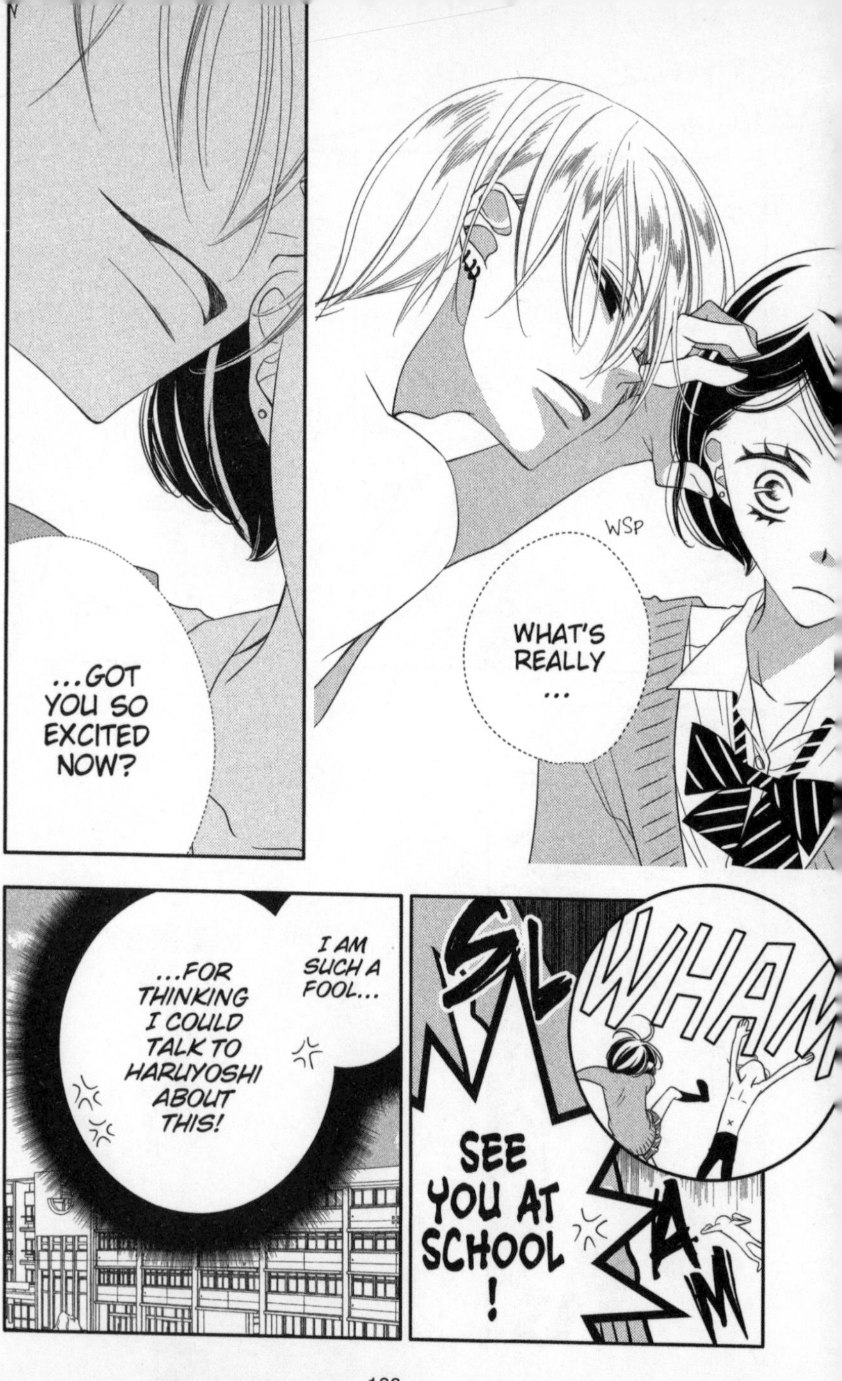
WSP
WHAT'S REALLY ...
...GOT YOU SO EXCITED NOW?
SLAM
WHAM
SEE YOU AT SCHOOL!
I AM SUCH A FOOL...
...FOR THINKING I COULD TALK TO HARUYOSHI ABOUT THIS!

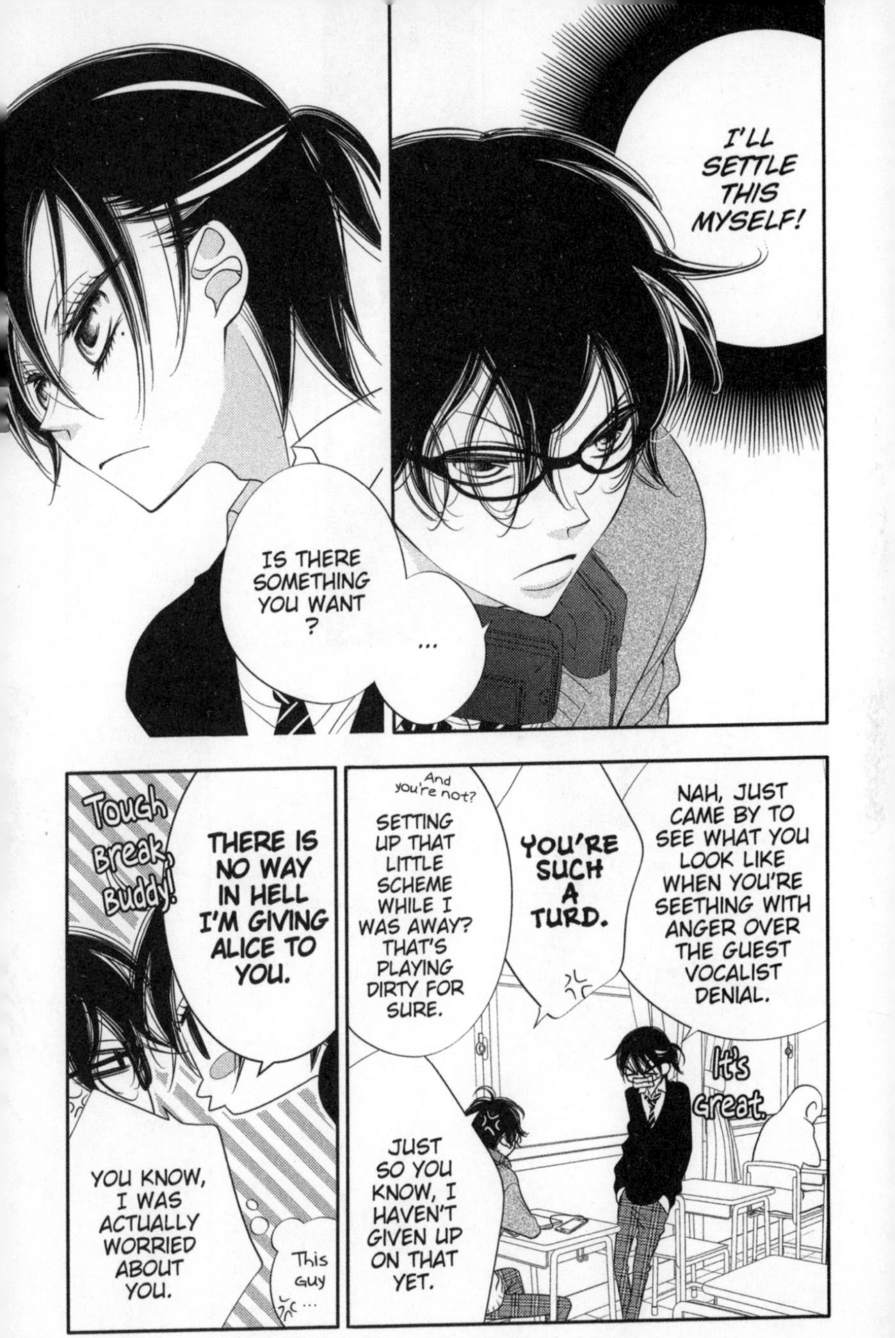
I'LL SETTLE THIS MYSELF!
IS THERE SOMETHING YOU WANT?
...
NAH, JUST CAME BY TO SEE WHAT YOU LOOK LIKE WHEN YOU'RE SEETHING WITH ANGER OVER THE GUEST VOCALIST DENIAL.
It's great.
YOU'RE SUCH A TURD.
And you're not?
SETTING UP THAT LITTLE SCHEME WHILE I WAS AWAY? THAT'S PLAYING DIRTY FOR SURE.
JUST SO YOU KNOW, I HAVEN'T GIVEN UP ON THAT YET.
Touch break, Buddy!
THERE IS NO WAY IN HELL I'M GIVING ALICE TO YOU.
YOU KNOW, I WAS ACTUALLY WORRIED ABOUT YOU.
This guy ...

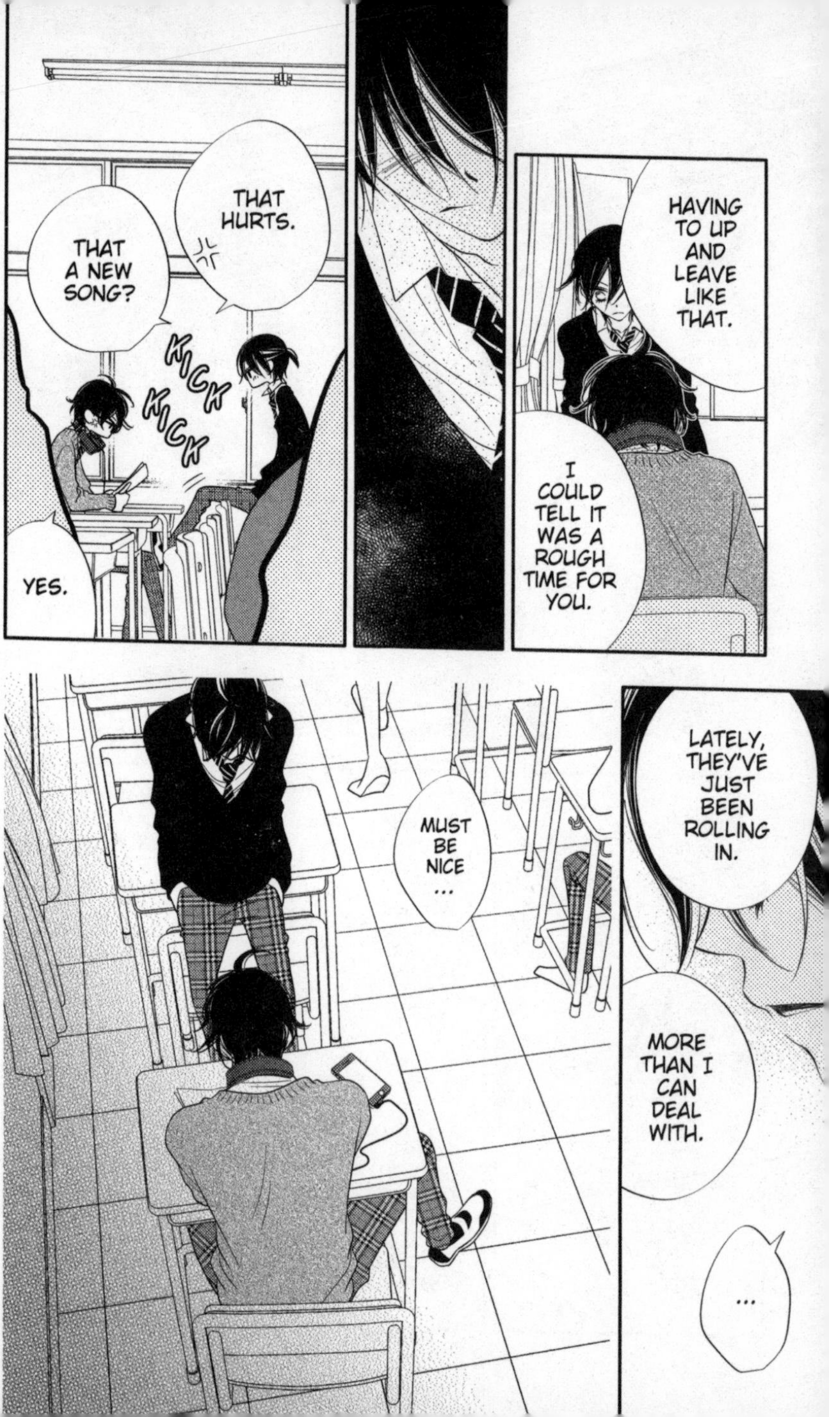
HAVING TO UP AND LEAVE LIKE THAT.
I COULD TELL IT WAS A ROUGH TIME FOR YOU.
THAT HURTS.
THAT A NEW SONG?
KICK KICK
YES.
LATELY, THEY'VE JUST BEEN ROLLING IN.
MORE THAN I CAN DEAL WITH.
...
MUST BE NICE ...

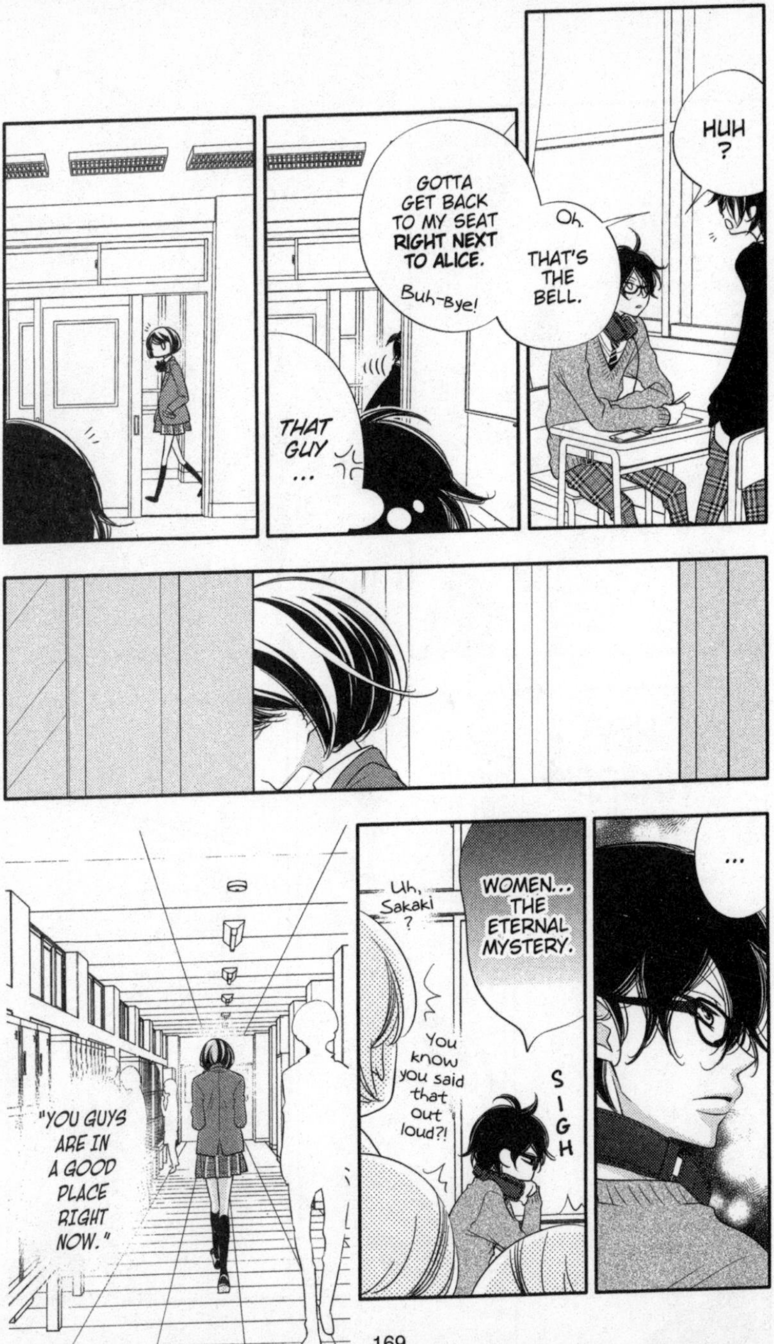
HUH?
Oh. THAT'S THE BELL.
GOTTA GET BACK TO MY SEAT **RIGHT NEXT TO ALICE.**
Buh-Bye!
THAT GUY...
...
WOMEN... THE ETERNAL MYSTERY.
SIGH
Uh, Sakaki?
You know you said that out loud?!
"YOU GUYS ARE IN A GOOD PLACE RIGHT NOW."

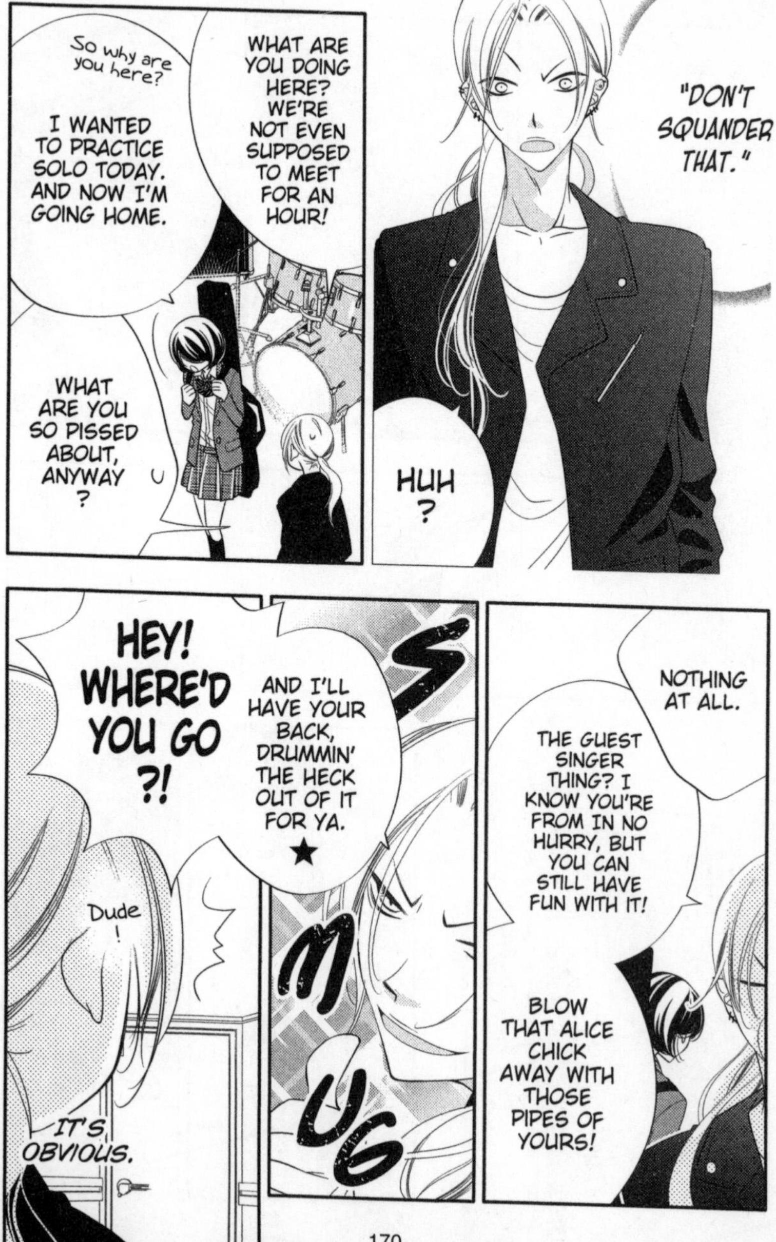
"DON'T SQUANDER THAT."
HUH?
WHAT ARE YOU DOING HERE? WE'RE NOT EVEN SUPPOSED TO MEET FOR AN HOUR!
So why are you here?
I WANTED TO PRACTICE SOLO TODAY. AND NOW I'M GOING HOME.
WHAT ARE YOU SO PISSED ABOUT, ANYWAY?
NOTHING AT ALL.
THE GUEST SINGER THING? I KNOW YOU'RE FROM IN NO HURRY, BUT YOU CAN STILL HAVE FUN WITH IT!
BLOW THAT ALICE CHICK AWAY WITH THOSE PIPES OF YOURS!
AND I'LL HAVE YOUR BACK, DRUMMIN' THE HECK OUT OF IT FOR YA. ★
SMUG
HEY! WHERE'D YOU GO?!
Dude!
IT'S OBVIOUS.

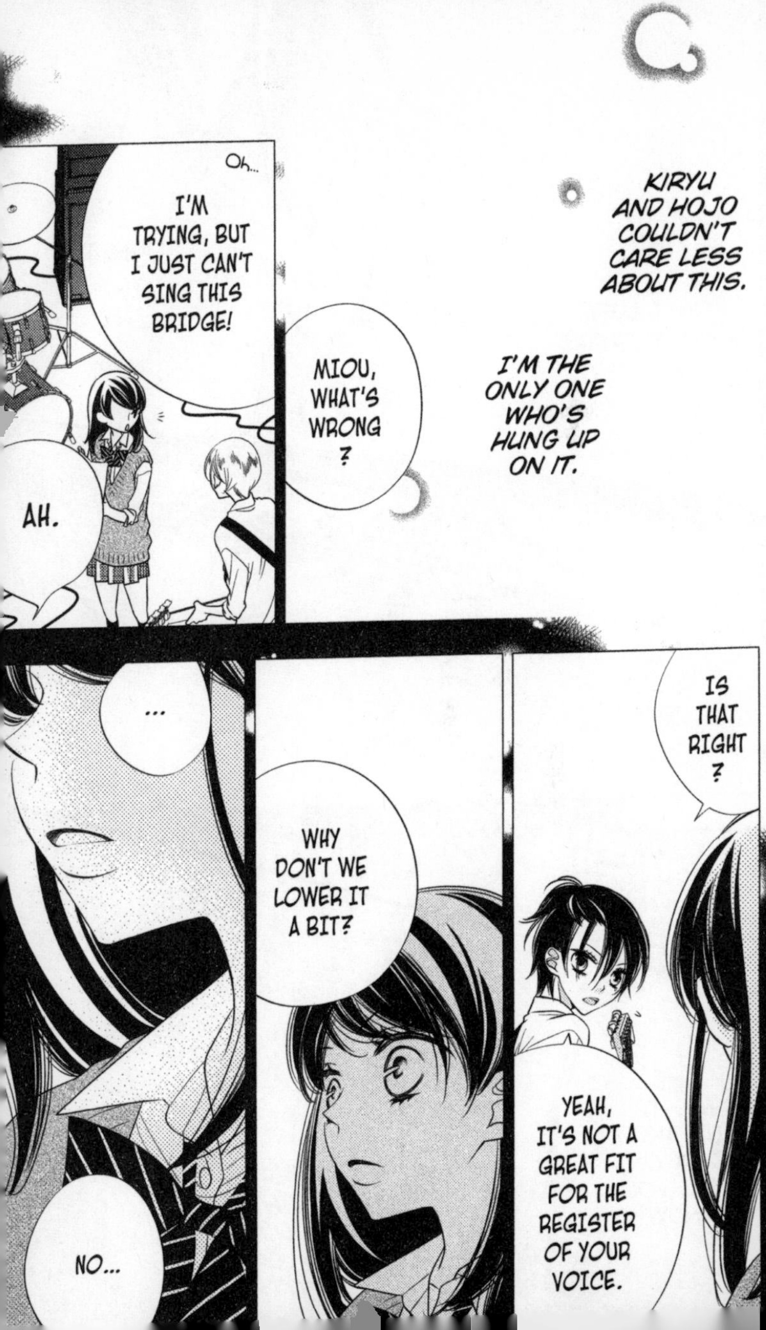
KIRYU AND HOJO COULDN'T CARE LESS ABOUT THIS.
I'M THE ONLY ONE WHO'S HUNG UP ON IT.
MIOU, WHAT'S WRONG?
Oh...
I'M TRYING, BUT I JUST CAN'T SING THIS BRIDGE!
AH.
IS THAT RIGHT?
YEAH, IT'S NOT A GREAT FIT FOR THE REGISTER OF YOUR VOICE.
WHY DON'T WE LOWER IT A BIT?
...
NO...

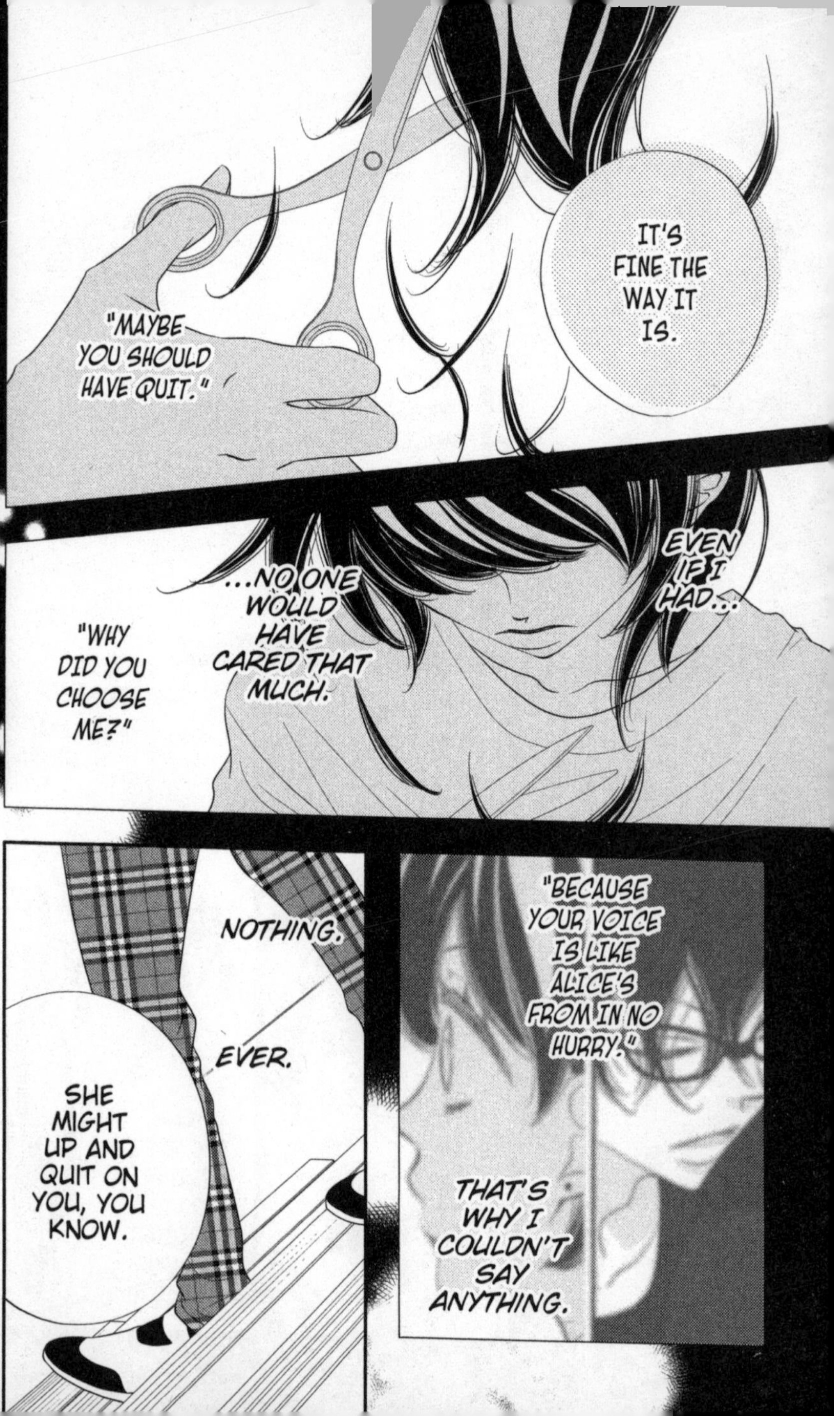
IT'S FINE THE WAY IT IS.
"MAYBE YOU SHOULD HAVE QUIT."
EVEN IF I HAD...
...NO ONE WOULD HAVE CARED THAT MUCH.
"WHY DID YOU CHOOSE ME?"
"BECAUSE YOUR VOICE IS LIKE ALICE'S FROM IN NO HURRY."
THAT'S WHY I COULDN'T SAY ANYTHING.
NOTHING.
EVER.
SHE MIGHT UP AND QUIT ON YOU, YOU KNOW.

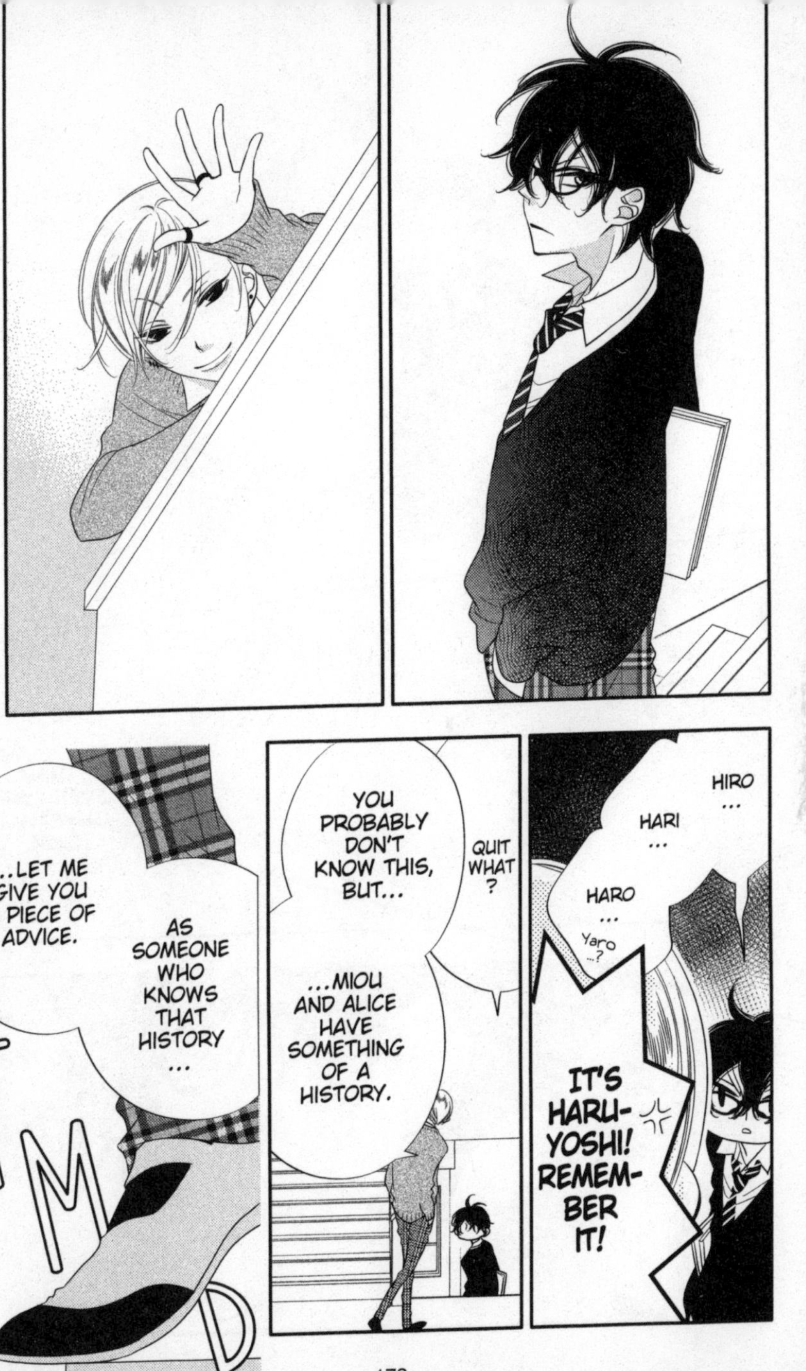
HIRO …
HARI …
HARO …
Yaro …?
IT'S HARUYOSHI! REMEMBER IT!
QUIT WHAT?
YOU PROBABLY DON'T KNOW THIS, BUT…
…MIOU AND ALICE HAVE SOMETHING OF A HISTORY.
AS SOMEONE WHO KNOWS THAT HISTORY …
…LET ME GIVE YOU A PIECE OF ADVICE.
TMP

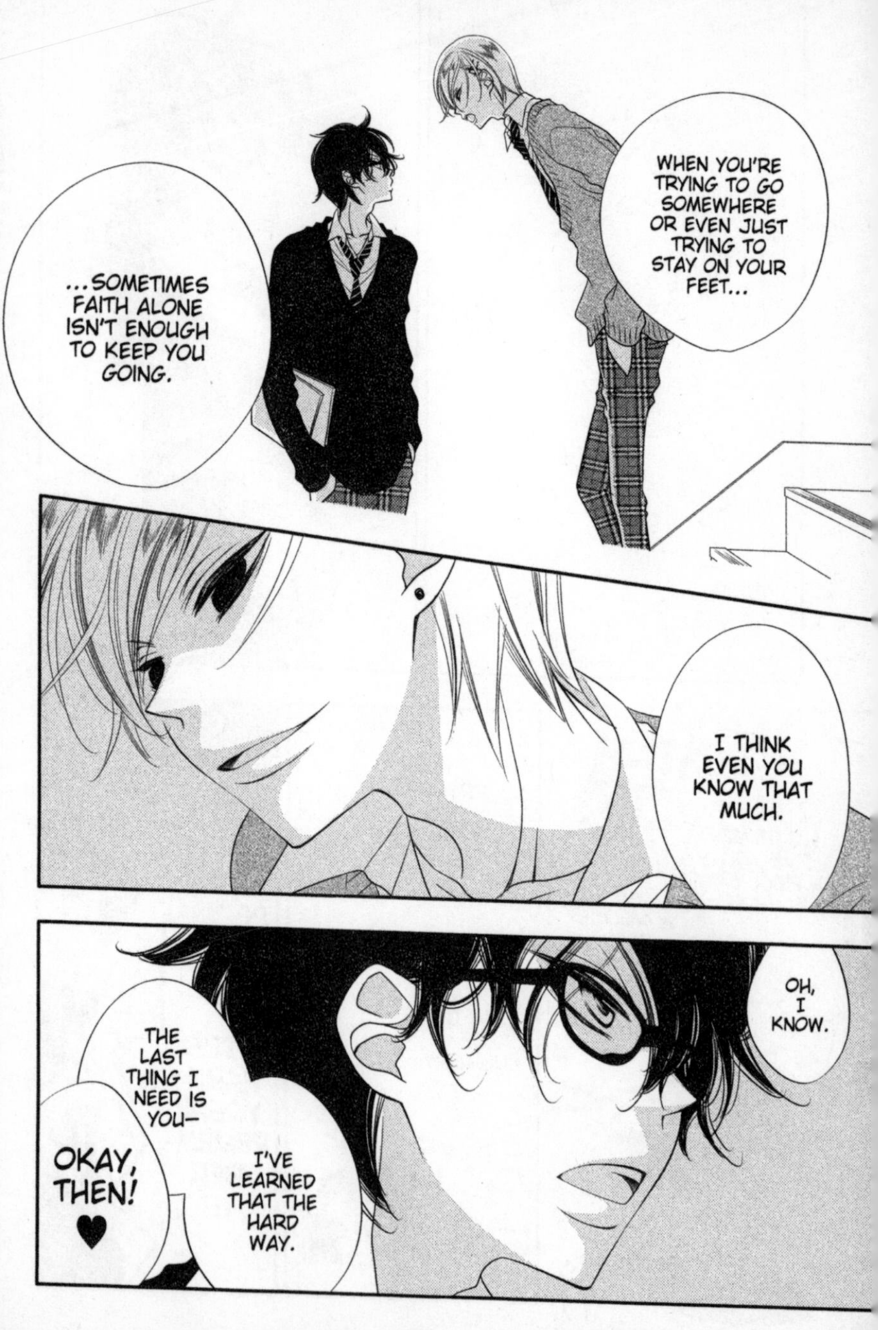
WHEN YOU'RE TRYING TO GO SOMEWHERE OR EVEN JUST TRYING TO STAY ON YOUR FEET...
...SOMETIMES FAITH ALONE ISN'T ENOUGH TO KEEP YOU GOING.
I THINK EVEN YOU KNOW THAT MUCH.
OH, I KNOW.
I'VE LEARNED THAT THE HARD WAY.
THE LAST THING I NEED IS YOU—
OKAY, THEN! ♥

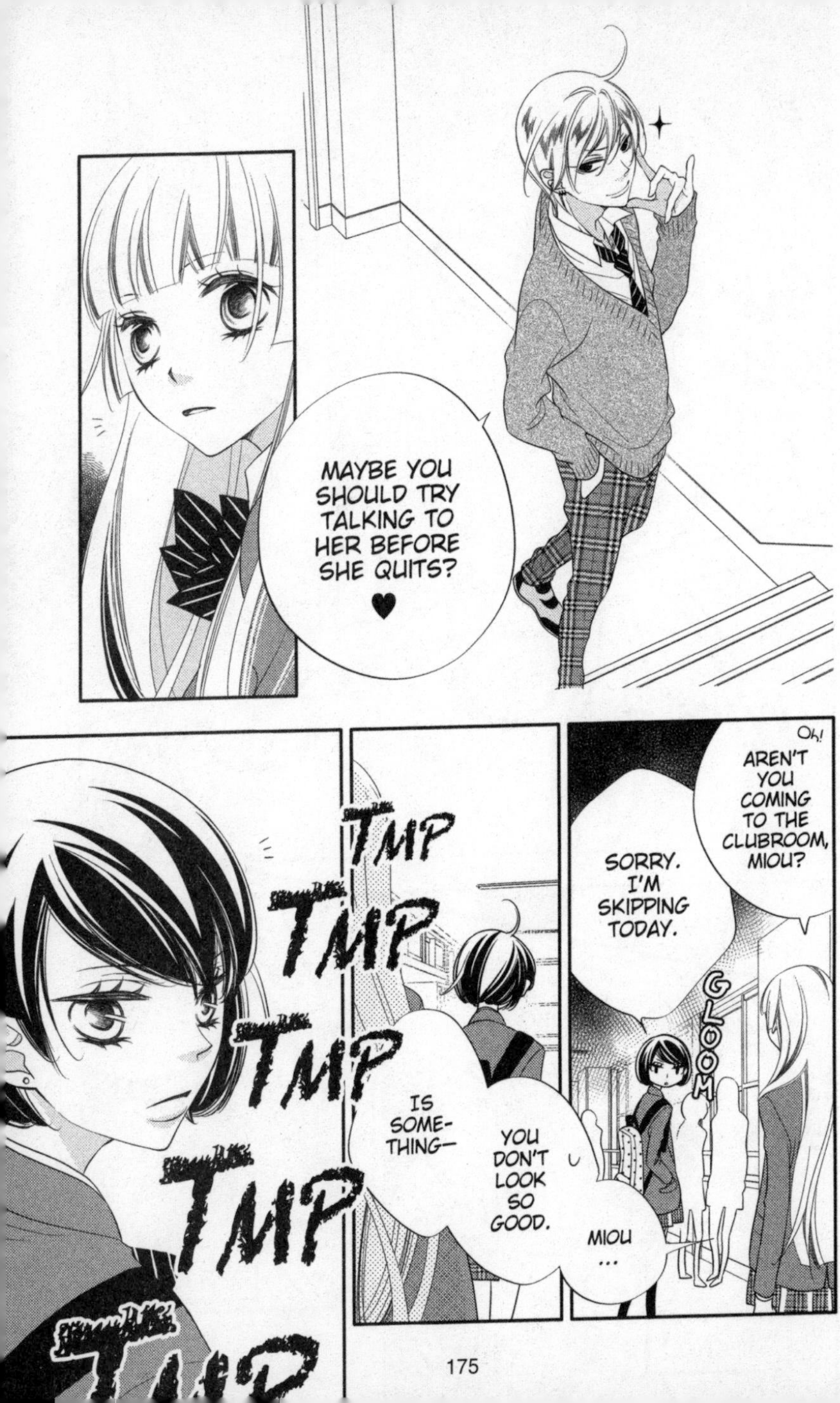
MAYBE YOU SHOULD TRY TALKING TO HER BEFORE SHE QUITS? ♥
Oh!
AREN'T YOU COMING TO THE CLUBROOM, MIOU?
SORRY. I'M SKIPPING TODAY.
GLOOM
MIOU ...
YOU DON'T LOOK SO GOOD.
IS SOME-THING—
TMP
TMP
TMP
TMP

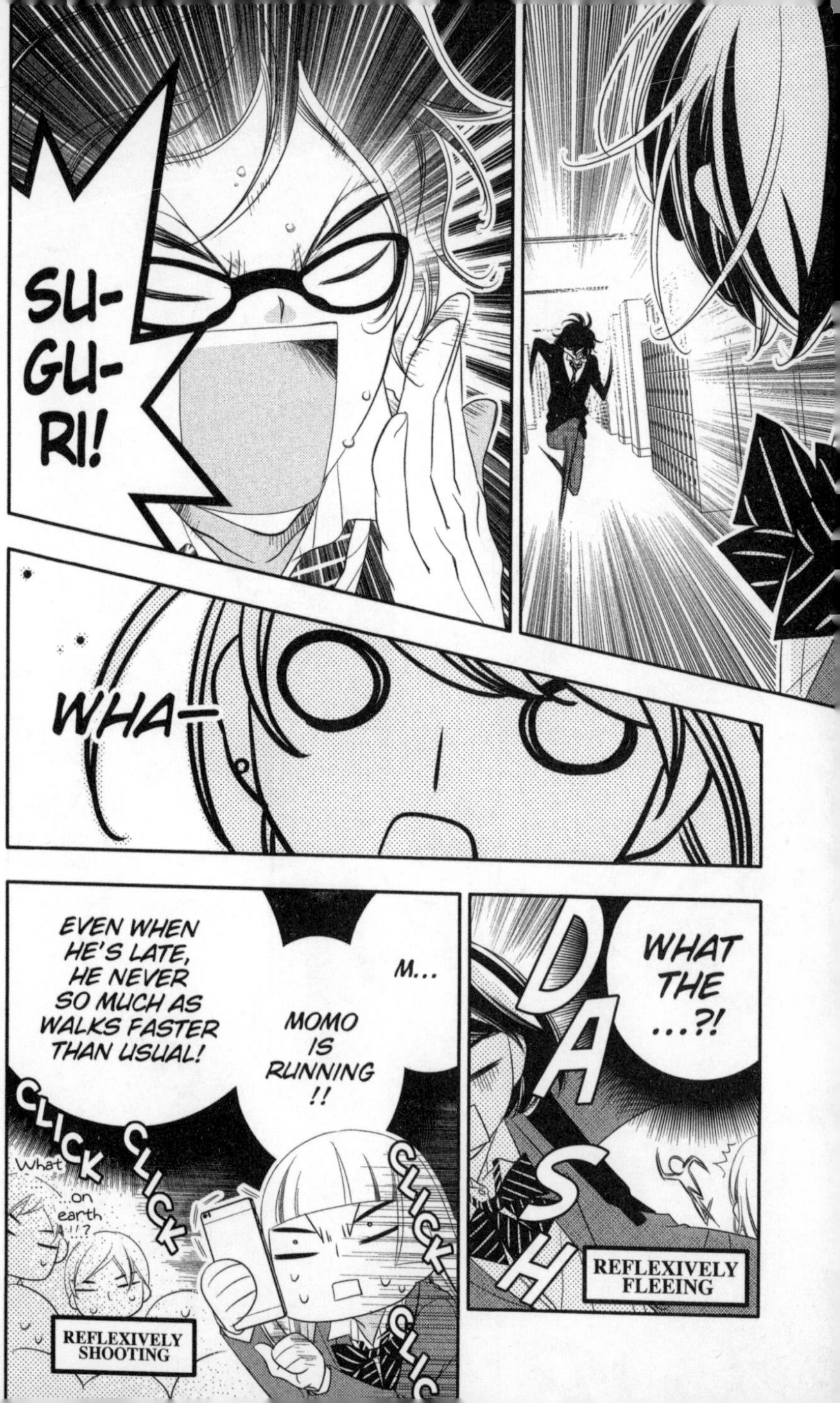
SU-GU-RI!
WHA—
WHAT THE ...?!
DASH
REFLEXIVELY FLEEING
M...
MOMO IS RUNNING !!
EVEN WHEN HE'S LATE, HE NEVER SO MUCH AS WALKS FASTER THAN USUAL!
CLICK CLICK CLICK
What ...on earth ...!?
REFLEXIVELY SHOOTING

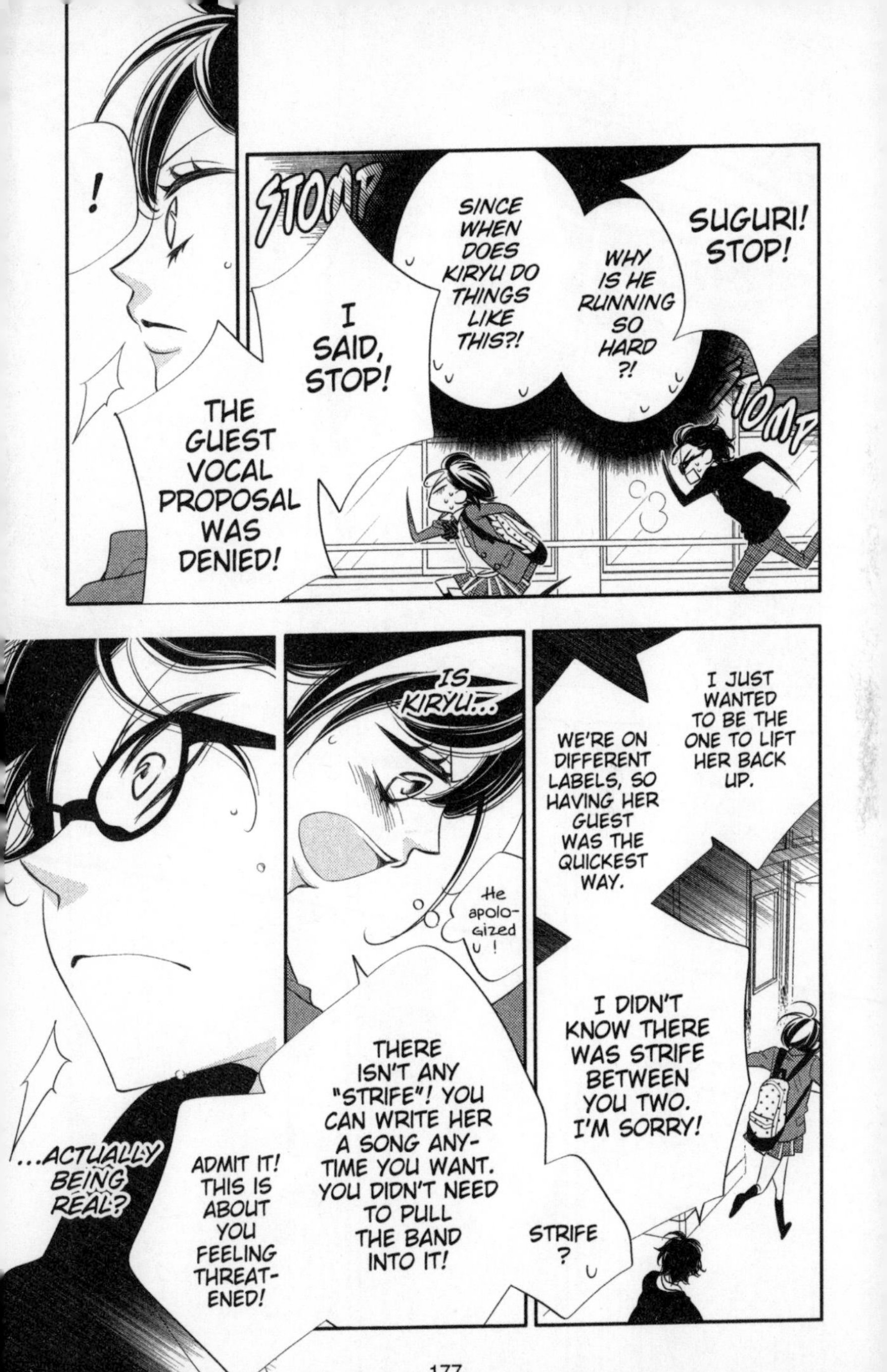
SUGURI! STOP!
WHY IS HE RUNNING SO HARD ?!
SINCE WHEN DOES KIRYU DO THINGS LIKE THIS?!
STOMP
STOMP
I SAID, STOP!
THE GUEST VOCAL PROPOSAL WAS DENIED!
!
I JUST WANTED TO BE THE ONE TO LIFT HER BACK UP.
WE'RE ON DIFFERENT LABELS, SO HAVING HER GUEST WAS THE QUICKEST WAY.
I DIDN'T KNOW THERE WAS STRIFE BETWEEN YOU TWO. I'M SORRY!
STRIFE ?
IS KIRYU...
He apologized!
THERE ISN'T ANY "STRIFE"! YOU CAN WRITE HER A SONG ANY-TIME YOU WANT. YOU DIDN'T NEED TO PULL THE BAND INTO IT!
ADMIT IT! THIS IS ABOUT YOU FEELING THREAT-ENED!
...ACTUALLY BEING REAL?

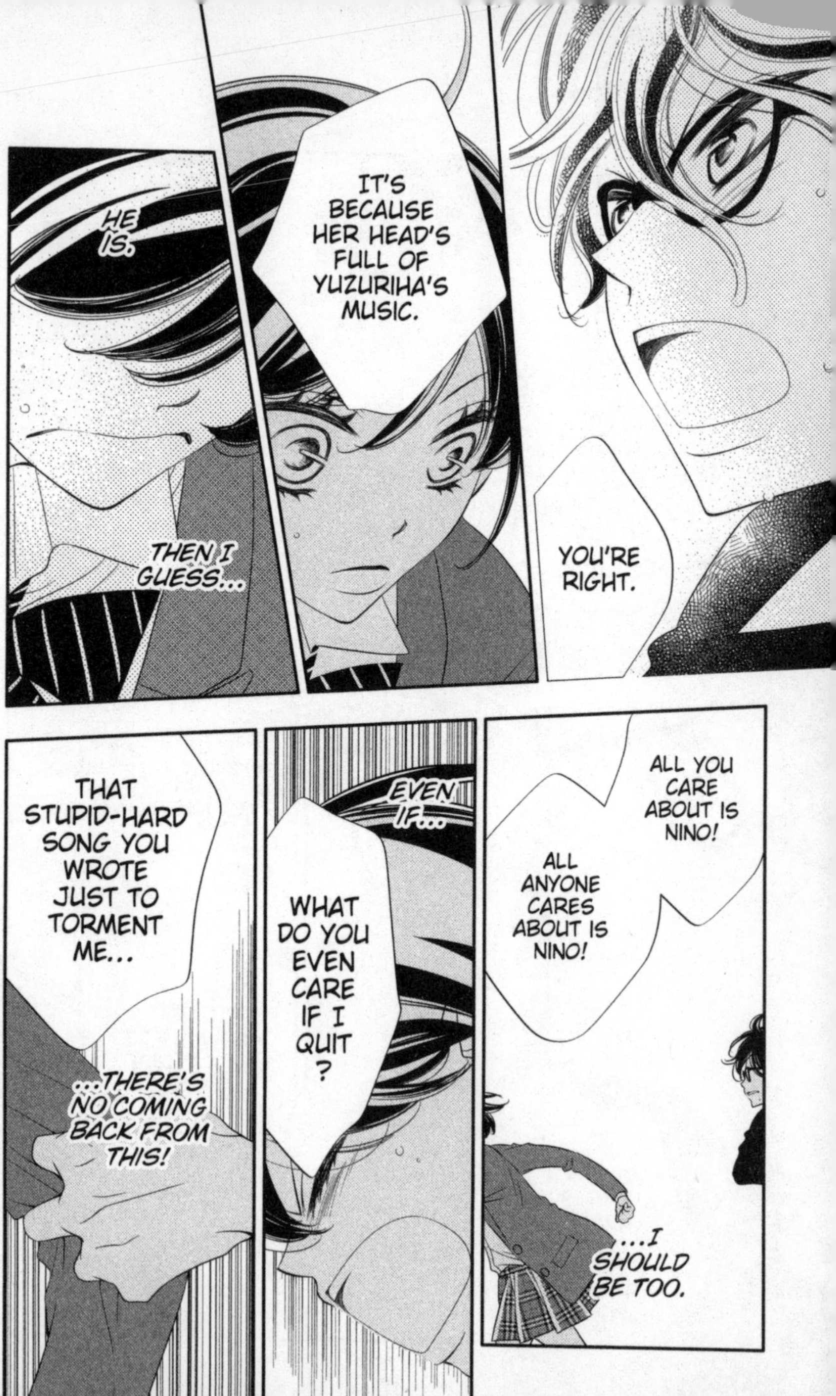
YOU'RE RIGHT.
IT'S BECAUSE HER HEAD'S FULL OF YUZURIHA'S MUSIC.
HE IS.
THEN I GUESS...
ALL YOU CARE ABOUT IS NINO!
ALL ANYONE CARES ABOUT IS NINO!
...I SHOULD BE TOO.
EVEN IF...
WHAT DO YOU EVEN CARE IF I QUIT?
THAT STUPID-HARD SONG YOU WROTE JUST TO TORMENT ME...
...THERE'S NO COMING BACK FROM THIS!

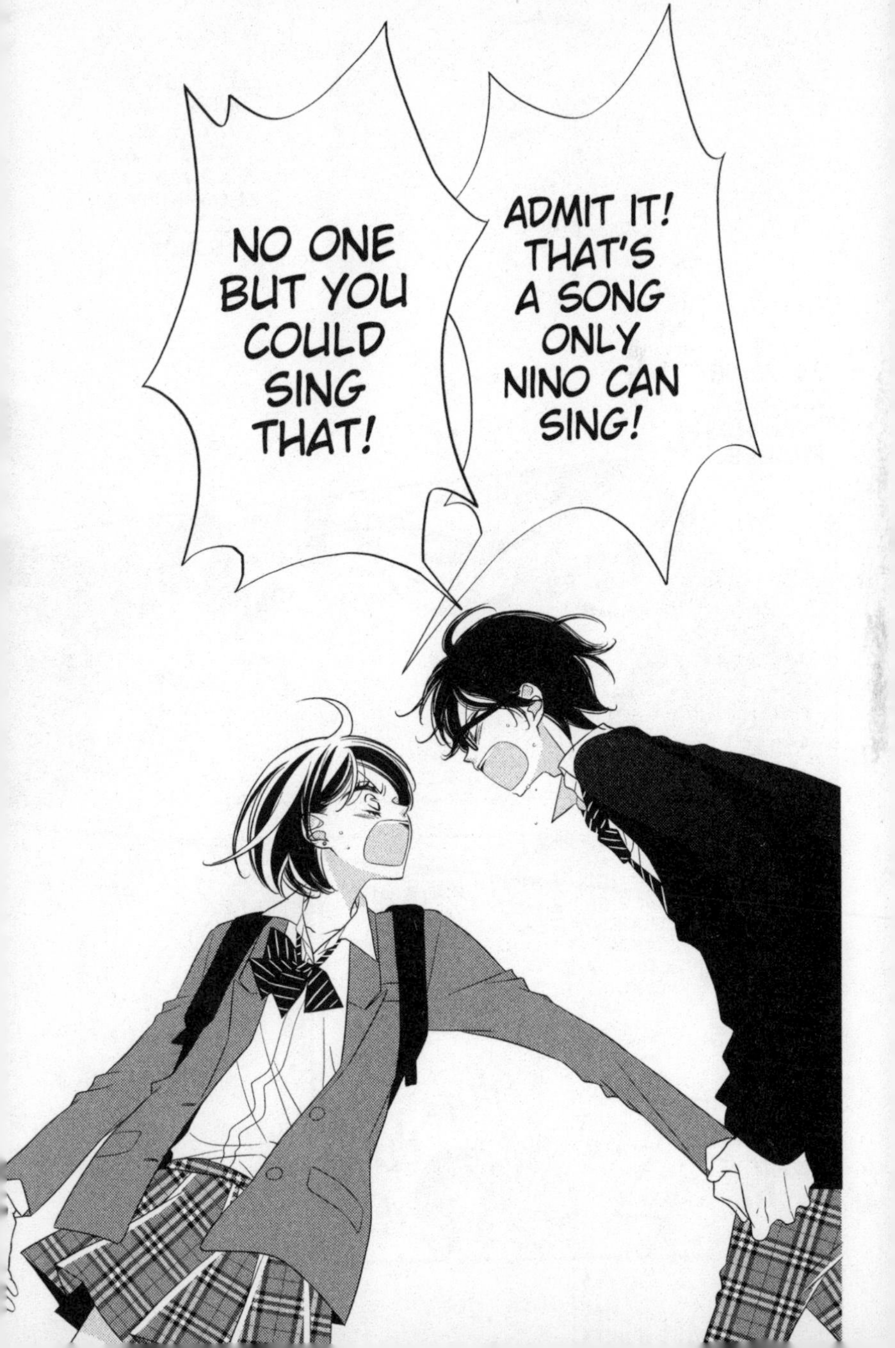
ADMIT IT! THAT'S A SONG ONLY NINO CAN SING!
NO ONE BUT YOU COULD SING THAT!

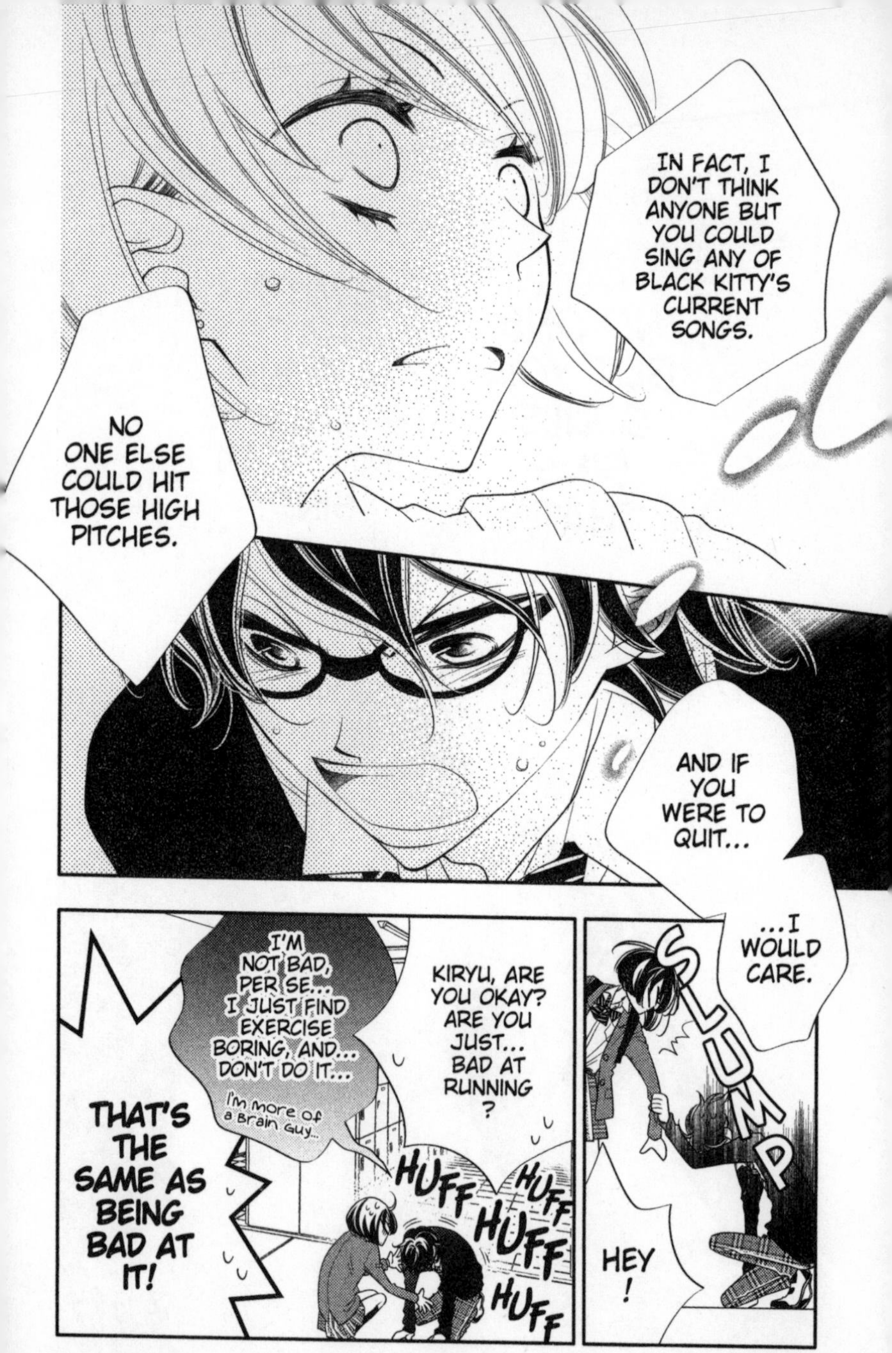
IN FACT, I DON'T THINK ANYONE BUT YOU COULD SING ANY OF BLACK KITTY'S CURRENT SONGS.
NO ONE ELSE COULD HIT THOSE HIGH PITCHES.
AND IF YOU WERE TO QUIT...
...I WOULD CARE.
SLUMP
HEY!
KIRYU, ARE YOU OKAY? ARE YOU JUST... BAD AT RUNNING?
I'M NOT BAD, PER SE... I JUST FIND EXERCISE BORING, AND... DON'T DO IT...
I'm more of a Brain Guy...
HUFF
HUFF
HUFF
HUFF
THAT'S THE SAME AS BEING BAD AT IT!

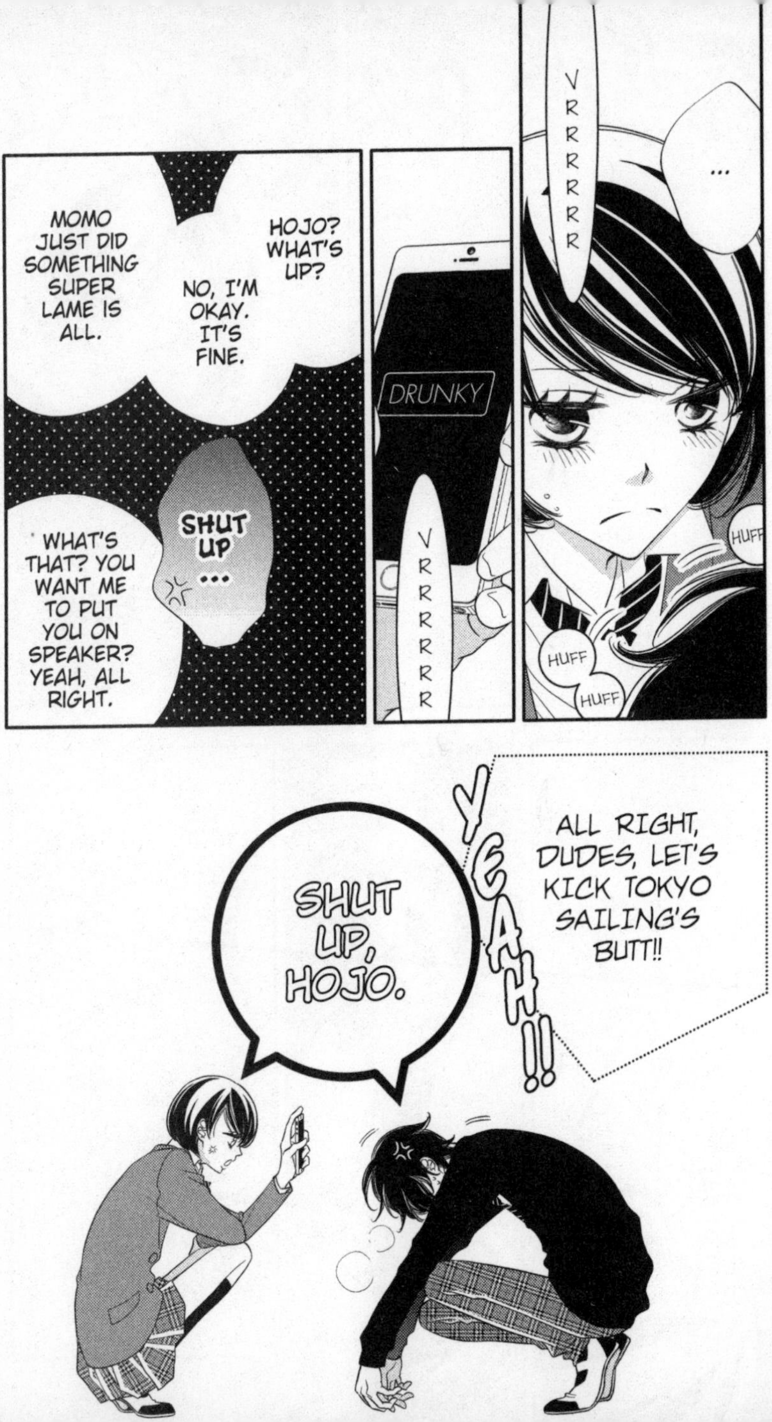
VRRRRRR
...
HUFF
HUFF
HUFF
DRUNKY
VRRRRRRR
HOJO? WHAT'S UP?
NO, I'M OKAY. IT'S FINE.
MOMO JUST DID SOMETHING SUPER LAME IS ALL.
SHUT UP...
WHAT'S THAT? YOU WANT ME TO PUT YOU ON SPEAKER? YEAH, ALL RIGHT.
ALL RIGHT, DUDES, LET'S KICK TOKYO SAILING'S BUTT!!
YEAH!!
SHUT UP, HOJO.

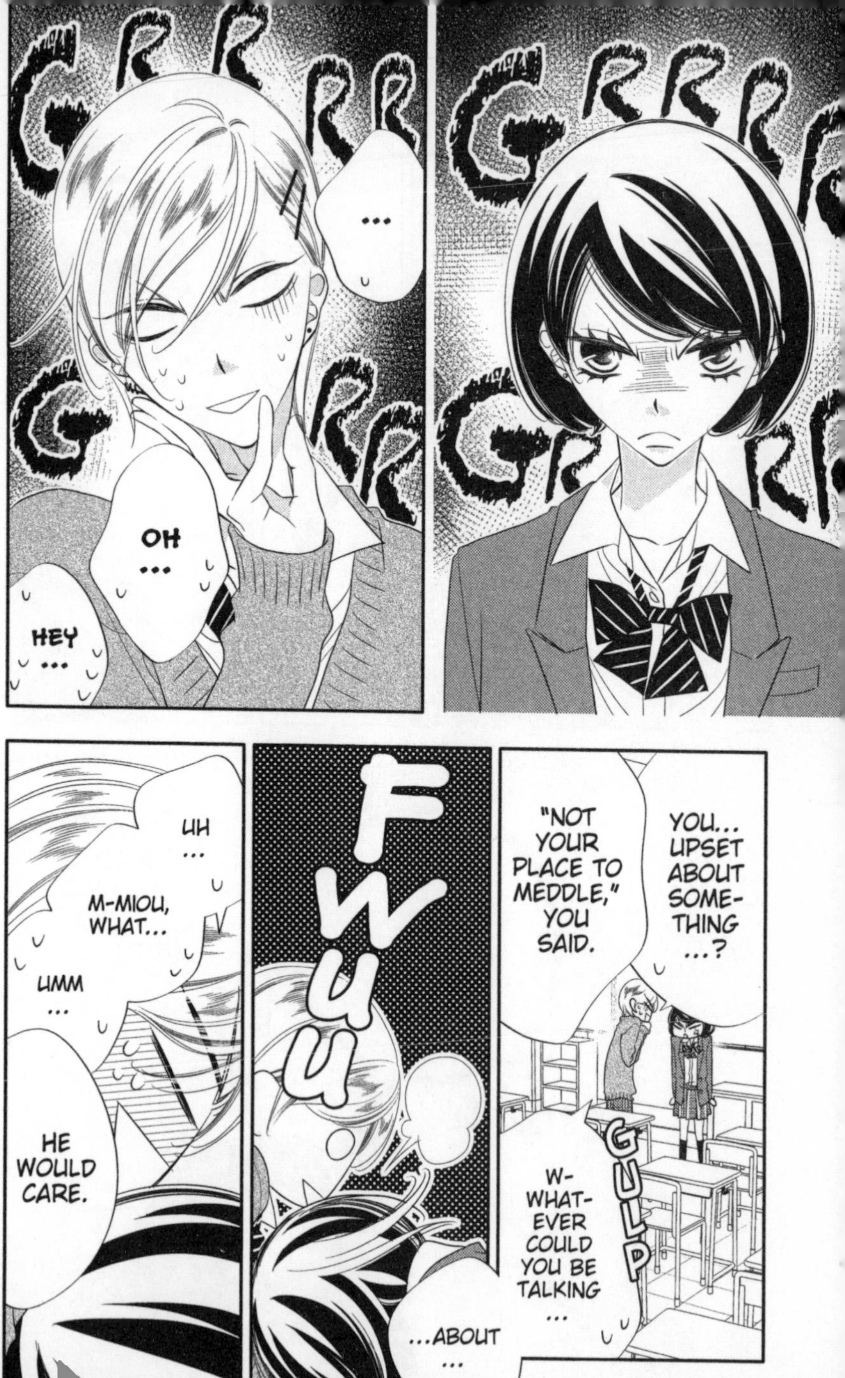
GRRRRR
GRRR
GRRRR
GRRR
...
OH...
HEY...
YOU... UPSET ABOUT SOME-THING...?
"NOT YOUR PLACE TO MEDDLE," YOU SAID.
GULP
W-WHAT-EVER COULD YOU BE TALKING...
...ABOUT...
FWUU
UH...
M-MIOU, WHAT...
UMM...
HE WOULD CARE.

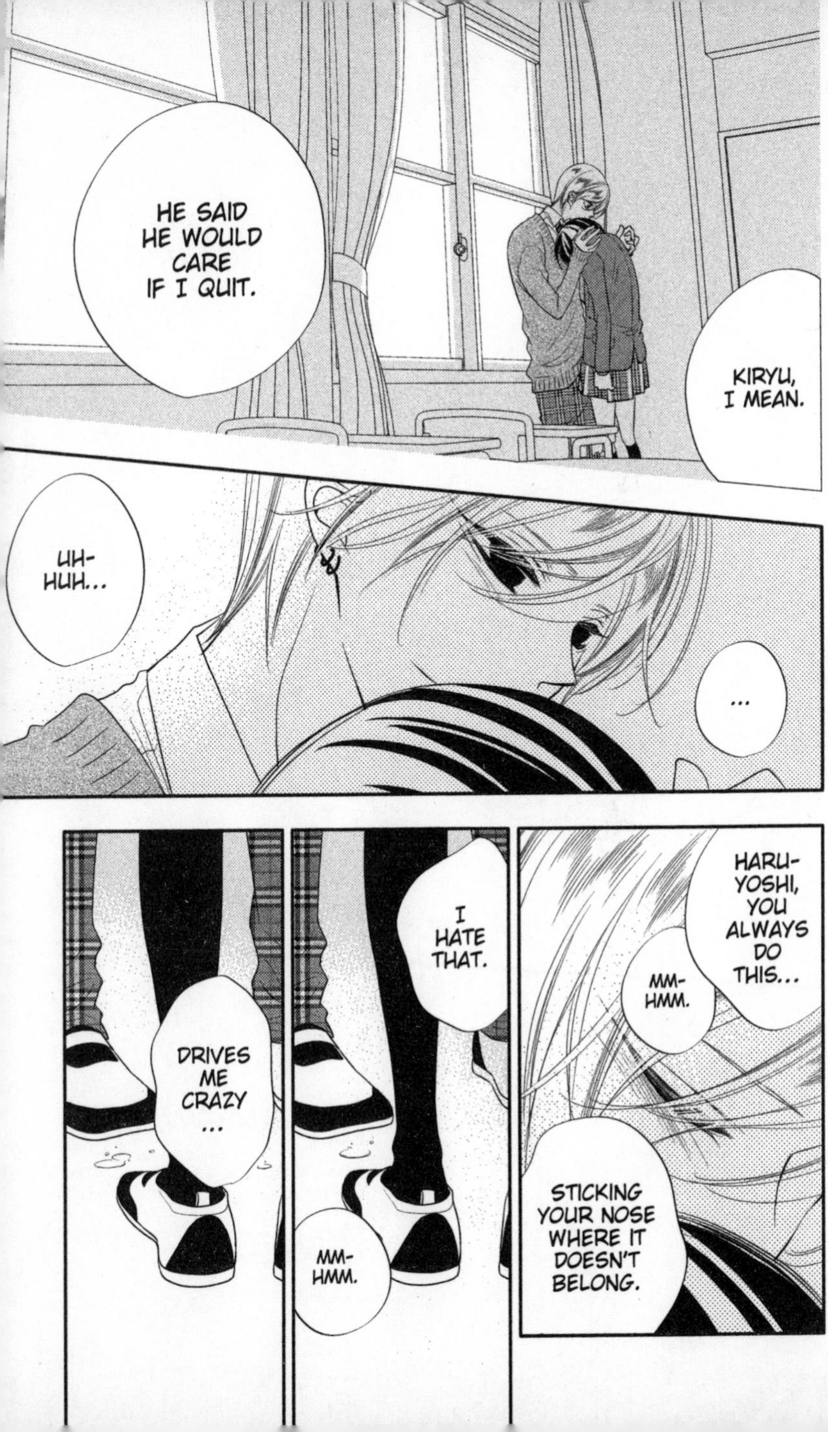
HE SAID HE WOULD CARE IF I QUIT.
KIRYU, I MEAN.
...
UH-HUH...
HARU-YOSHI, YOU ALWAYS DO THIS...
MM-HMM.
STICKING YOUR NOSE WHERE IT DOESN'T BELONG.
I HATE THAT.
MM-HMM.
DRIVES ME CRAZY ...

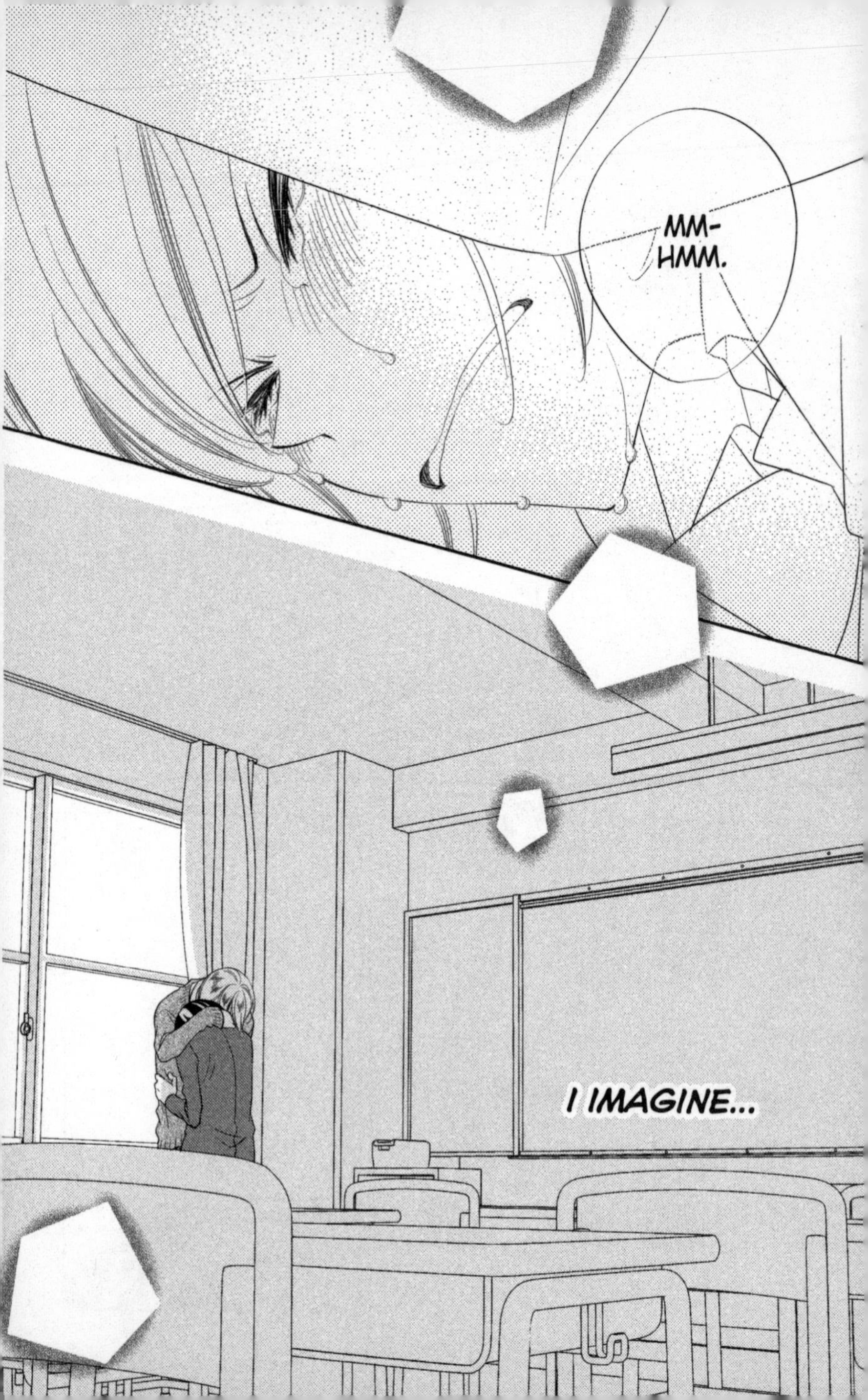
MM-
HMM.
I IMAGINE...

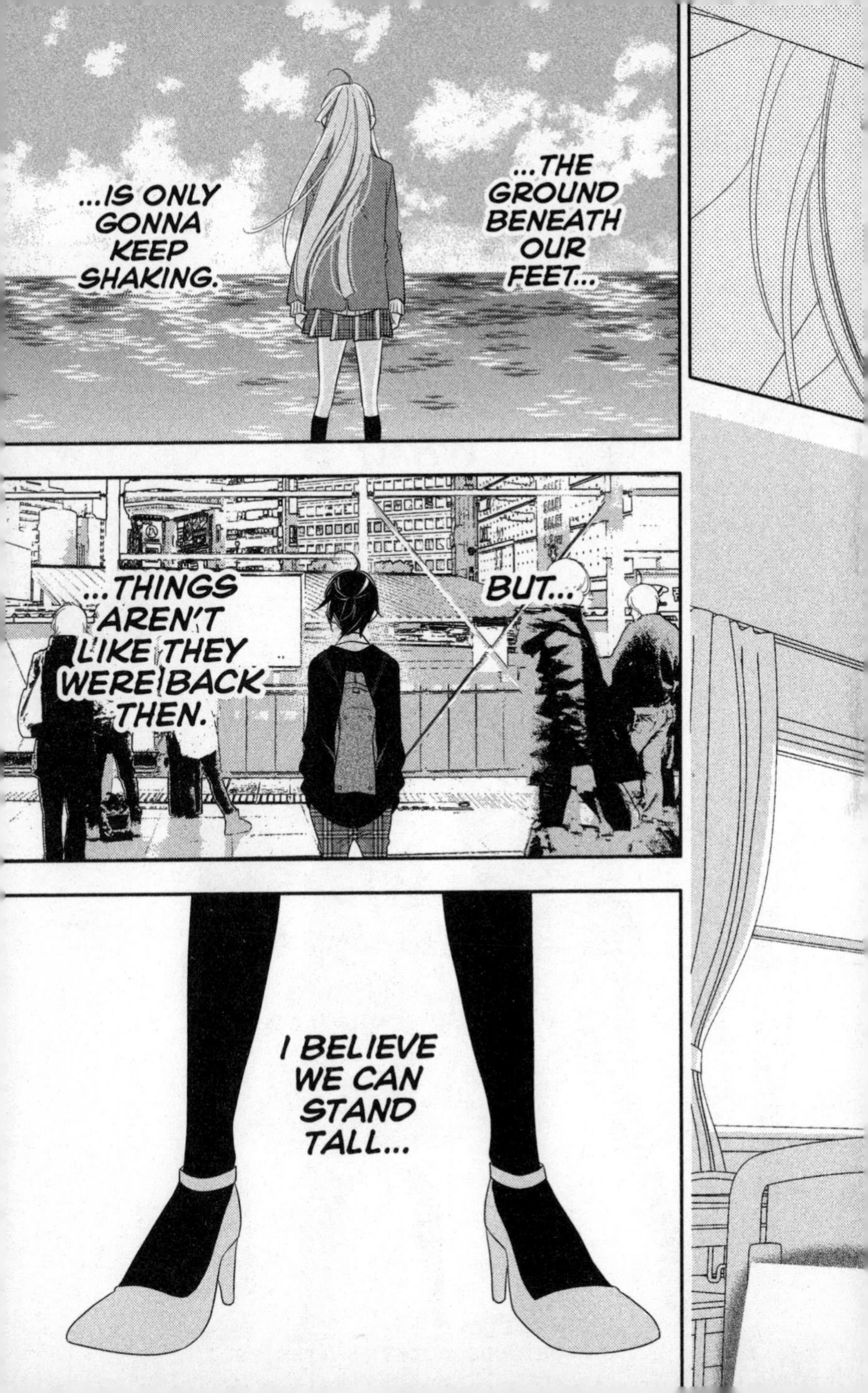
...THE GROUND BENEATH OUR FEET...
...IS ONLY GONNA KEEP SHAKING.
BUT...
...THINGS AREN'T LIKE THEY WERE BACK THEN.
I BELIEVE WE CAN STAND TALL...

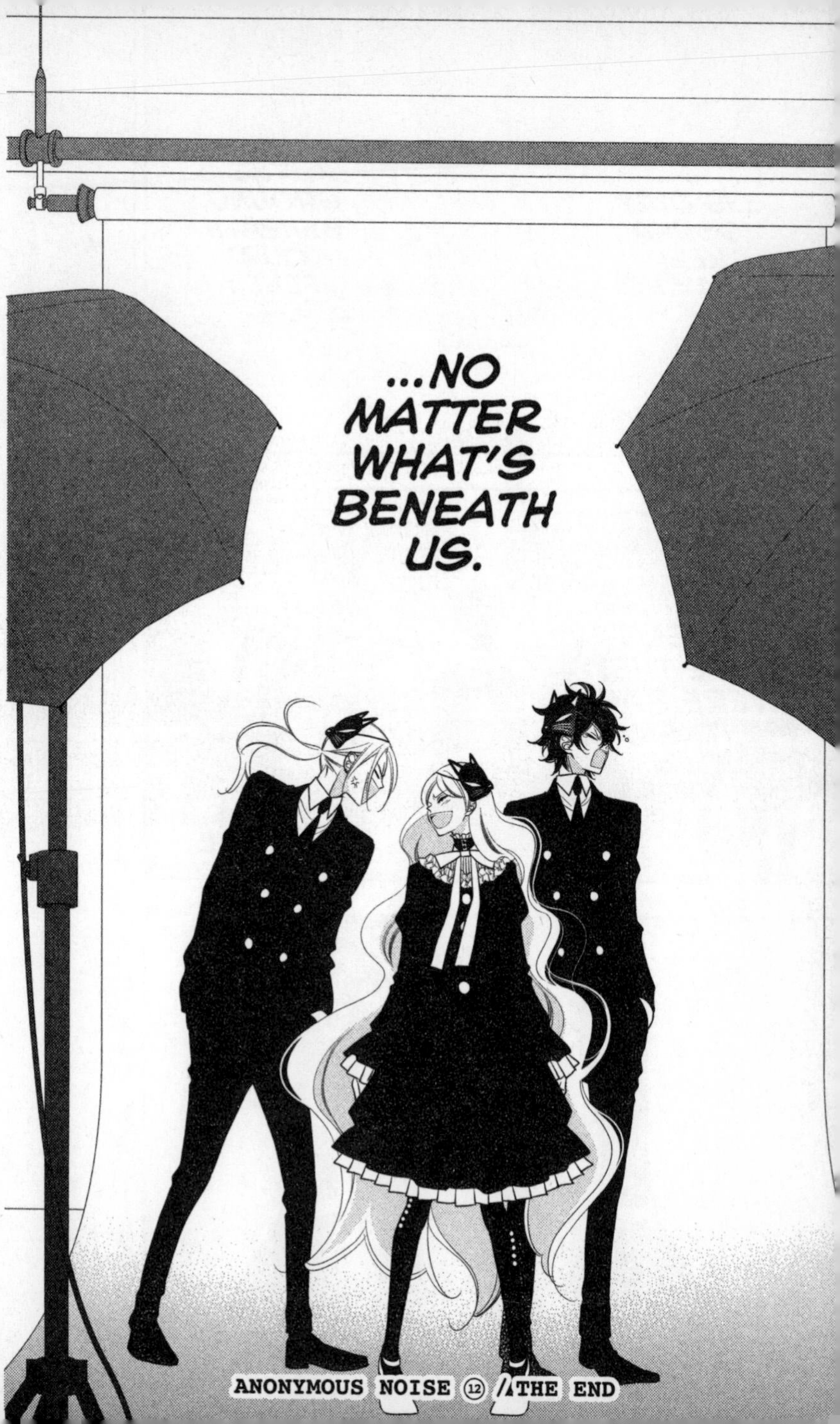
...NO MATTER WHAT'S BENEATH US.
ANONYMOUS NOISE ⑫ / THE END

TO BE CONTINUED IN ANONYMOUS NOISE 13

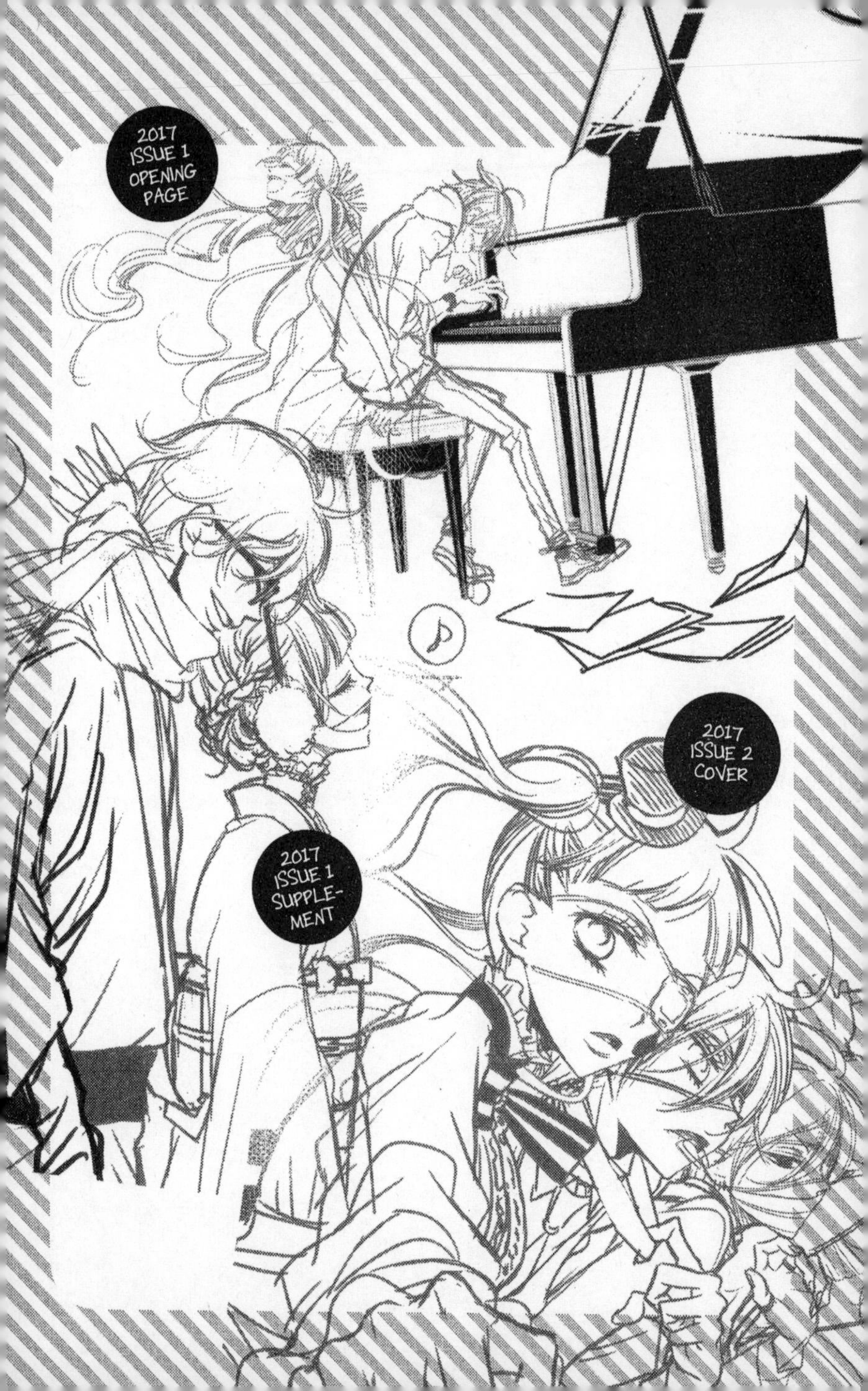
2017 ISSUE 1 OPENING PAGE
2017 ISSUE 2 COVER
2017 ISSUE 1 SUPPLEMENT

Surprise!

You may be reading the wrong way!

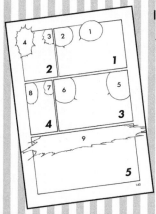

It's true: In keeping with the original Japanese comic format, this book reads from right to left—so action, sound effects and word balloons are completely reversed. This preserves the orientation of the original artwork—plus, it's fun! Check out the diagram shown here to get the hang of things, and then turn to the other side of the book to get started!

ANONYMOUS NOISE
Vol. 12
Shojo Beat Edition

STORY AND ART BY
RYOKO FUKUYAMA

English Translation & Adaptation/Casey Loe
Touch-Up Art & Lettering/Joanna Estep
Design/Yukiko Whitley
Editor/Amy Yu

Fukumenkei Noise by Ryoko Fukuyama
© Ryoko Fukuyama 2017
All rights reserved.
First published in Japan in 2017 by HAKUSENSHA, Inc., Tokyo.
English language translation rights arranged with HAKUSENSHA, Inc., Tokyo.

Printed in the U.S.A.

Published by VIZ Media, LLC
P.O. Box 77010
San Francisco, CA 94107

10 9 8 7 6 5 4 3 2 1
First printing, January 2019

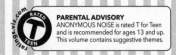

viz.com

shojobeat.com

The Anonymous Noise anime is scheduled to begin airing shortly after this volume's release (in Japan). It's finally here! I hope everyone will be willing to give it a chance!

- Ryoko Fukuyama

Born on January 5 in Wakayama Prefecture in Japan, Ryoko Fukuyama debuted as a manga artist after winning the Hakusensha Athena Shinjin Taisho Prize from Hakusensha's *Hana to Yume* magazine. She is also the author of *Nosatsu Junkie*. *Anonymous Noise* was adapted into an anime in 2017.

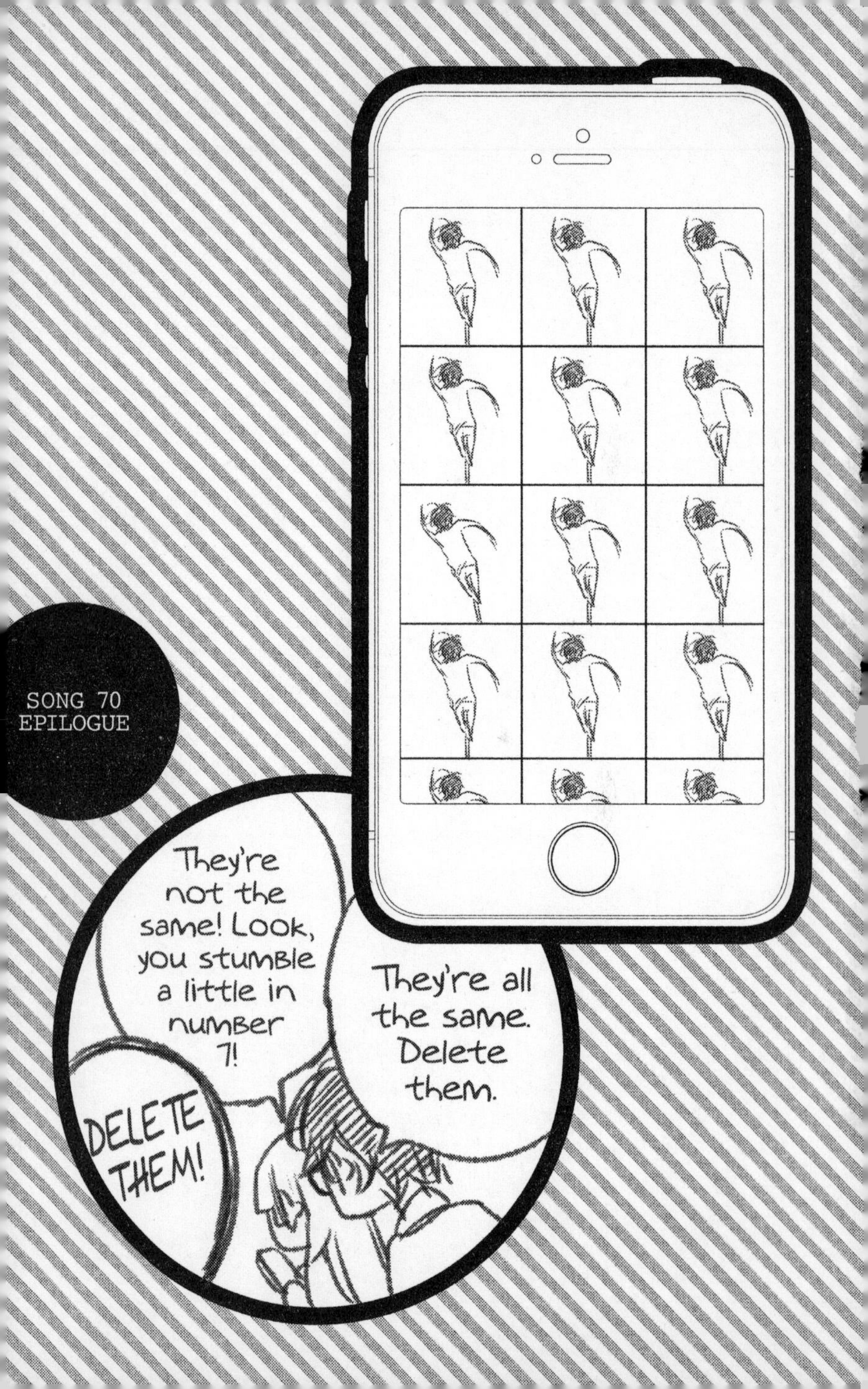
SONG 70
EPILOGUE
They're all the same. Delete them.
They're not the same! Look, you stumble a little in number 7!
DELETE THEM!